Alexander Viets Griswold Allen

The Continuity of Christian Thought

A Study of modern Theology in the Light of its History

Alexander Viets Griswold Allen

The Continuity of Christian Thought
A Study of modern Theology in the Light of its History

ISBN/EAN: 9783337167264

Printed in Europe, USA, Canada, Australia, Japan

Cover: Foto ©Lupo / pixelio.de

More available books at **www.hansebooks.com**

THE CONTINUITY OF CHRISTIAN THOUGHT: A STUDY OF MODERN THEOLOGY IN THE LIGHT OF ITS HISTORY

BY

ALEXANDER V. G. ALLEN

PROFESSOR IN THE EPISCOPAL THEOLOGICAL SCHOOL,
IN CAMBRIDGE

BOSTON AND NEW YORK:
HOUGHTON, MIFFLIN AND COMPANY
The Riverside Press, Cambridge
1897

To

THE SACRED MEMORY OF

PHILLIPS BROOKS

BISHOP OF MASSACHUSETTS

† JANUARY 23, 1893

𝕿𝖍𝖎𝖘 𝖁𝖔𝖑𝖚𝖒𝖊 𝖎𝖘 𝕯𝖊𝖉𝖎𝖈𝖆𝖙𝖊𝖉

BY

THE AUTHOR

THE JOHN BOHLEN LECTURESHIP.

JOHN BOHLEN, who died in this city on the twenty-sixth day of April, 1874, bequeathed to trustees a fund of One Hundred Thousand Dollars, to be distributed to religious and charitable objects in accordance with the well-known wishes of the testator.

By a deed of trust, executed June 2, 1875, the trustees, under the will of MR. BOHLEN, transferred and paid over to "The Rector, Church Wardens, and Vestrymen of the Church of the Holy Trinity, Philadelphia," in trust, a sum of money for certain designated purposes, out of which fund the sum of Ten Thousand Dollars was set apart for the endowment of THE JOHN BOHLEN LECTURESHIP, upon the following terms and conditions : —

"The money shall be invested in good, substantial, and safe securities, and held in trust for a fund to be called The John Bohlen Lectureship; and the income shall be applied annually to the payment of a qualified person, whether clergyman or layman, for the delivery and publication of at least one hundred copies of two or more lecture sermons. These lectures shall be delivered at such time and place, in the city of Philadelphia, as the persons nominated to appoint the lecturer shall from time to time determine, giving at least six months' notice to the person appointed to deliver the same, when the same may conveniently be done, and in no case selecting the same person as lecturer a second time within a period of five years. The payment shall be made to said lecturer, after the lectures have been printed, and received by the trustees, of all the income for the year derived from said fund, after defraying the expense of printing the lectures, and the other incidental expenses attending the same.

"The subject of such lectures shall be such as is within the terms set forth in the will of the Rev. John Bampton, for the delivery of what are known as the 'Bampton Lectures,' at Oxford, or any other subject distinctively connected with or relating to the Christian Religion.

"The lecturer shall be appointed annually in the month of May, or as soon thereafter as can conveniently be done, by the persons who for the time being shall hold the offices of Bishop of the Protestant Episcopal Church of the Diocese in which is the Church of the Holy Trinity; the Rector of said Church; the Professor of Biblical Learning, the Professor of Systematic Divinity, and the Professor of Ecclesiastical History, in the Divinity School of the Protestant Episcopal Church in Philadelphia.

"In case either of said offices are vacant, the others may nominate the lecturer."

Under this trust the Reverend A. V. G. ALLEN, D. D., Professor in the Episcopal Theological School in Cambridge, was appointed to deliver the lectures for the year 1883.

PHILADELPHIA, EASTER, 1883.

Æterna Sapientia, sese in omnibus rebus, maximè in humana mente, omnium maximè in Christu Jesu manifestavit.

PREFACE TO FIRST EDITION.

THIS treatise owes its shape to the circumstance of its having been written as a course of lectures which were delivered in Philadelphia on the foundation of the late John Bohlen. The lectures being six in number required what may seem a somewhat artificial division of the subject-matter. But the grouping of topics, which I was in consequence constrained to make, will not, I think, be found an unnatural one. The lectures have been as carefully revised as my engagements would allow; they are published substantially as they were spoken, with the exception of several portions omitted in the delivery for the sake of brevity.

It is too much to hope that, in a treatise like this which criticises so freely the various phases of religious belief in their historical development, I may not be regarded as having written for a controversial end against opinions as they are still held to-day. I should like, however, to disclaim such an intention. I have tried to deal with the subject after the historical method. My main endeavor has been to show that a purpose runs through the whole history of Christian thought, despite the apparent confusion which is to many its predominant characteristic. I have not written as if the history of theology were a panorama of dissolving views. It is the record of a development moving onward, in accordance with a divine law, to some remoter consummation. It is because such a law is being divinely revealed to us that we are able to recognize the place which we occupy in history.

I am afraid it may seem to some as if I had undertaken too large a task for the compass of one small volume. It would have been much easier to have expanded than it has been to condense. I regret that time has not allowed me to condense more than I have done. A history of religious thought, it must be remembered, deals only with a few fundamental principles easily traced, to which all our differences in opinion can be referred.

I have sought to confine myself to the immediate task which I proposed to pursue; namely, to follow the course of Christian thought. It has not been possible, however, to avoid the contiguous departments of Christian life, or the history of the church as an institution. They are often so closely connected with Christian thought, that to separate them is as impossible as it is undesirable. Some may feel that sufficient prominence has not been given to names which have long been held in honor by the church. I confess it has not been always easy to decide upon the relative degree of importance to be assigned to individuals, so far as their influence upon Christian thought is concerned. But as it has not been my object to merely chronicle the opinions of every one entitled to a place in the history of theology, I have dwelt only upon those names that mark changes or transitions in its progress, and have been content to pass over others, however great their prominence or usefulness in the institutional life of the church or as saintly examples of Christian character. I should like to say, however, that if I were revising my book I should try to enforce more than I have done the importance of the work of Origen. He was a true specimen of a great theologian, the study of whose life is of special value to-day, as a corrective against that tendency to underrate dogma in our reaction from outgrown dogmas, or the disposition to treat the feelings and instincts of our nature as if they were a final refuge from the reason, instead of a means to a larger use of the reason, — a process which, it is to be feared, in many is closely allied in its spirit with the temper which leads men to seek shelter in an infallible church.

Because I believe that the history of theology is of the most absorbing interest as well as of the highest importance, that it concerns those called the laity as well as the clergy, I have sought to divest the subject, as far as I could, from the unnecessary technicalities of theological language, whose use often serves only to conceal thought or to deaden its activity. I wish that I might have devoted more attention to the course of philosophical speculation in its relations to theology. But while the connection is a close and important one, it also involves issues which have not been yet determined. I have therefore alluded to philosophy when its connection with Christian thought could not be avoided, and for the rest have passed it reluctantly by.

I have not felt it necessary to fortify every statement by the quotation of authorities in foot-notes, or even by references to them, since, for the most part, I have been traveling over ground which has been rendered familiar to the students of theology by the labors of many eminent historical scholars. In those cases where I have done so, it has been in order to assist the general reader, who may not be acquainted with theological literature. Much has passed from the minds of others into my own thought which it would be no longer possible to trace. Those who are acquainted with the work of a teacher will know how easy it is to appropriate and use ideas till, by force of repetition, they become inseparable from one's own. In this way I have used Neander and Baur, Maurice and Dorner, till it has almost seemed unnecessary to render them the tribute of indebtedness. To my colleague, Professor Steenstra, I wish to acknowledge my obligation for criticisms and suggestions while the work has been going through the press; but he is not in any way responsible for the opinions it expresses.

CAMBRIDGE, *August* 24, 1884.

PREFACE TO NEW EDITION.

In sending forth a new edition of this book, I have found no occasion for changes affecting its substance of doctrine. That it should have roused opposition in some quarters is an illustration of the far-seeing conviction of the late Baron Bunsen, that "a severe trial awaits any one who looks primitive Christianity in the face," an illustration also of an apothegm of Bishop Wilson, that "Truth provokes those whom it does not convert." To any objections springing from zeal without knowledge, where critical preparation does not keep pace with devotion, it is not necessary to make reply. But objections have been raised to my manner of treating the subject, as well as to my conclusions, to which, at least, a reference should be made. The word "Continuity" has been called a misnomer, inasmuch as discontinuity appears to characterize the outline of Christian thought as I have traced it. Let it be said, then, that what we know as development is not an unbroken monotonous advance, but involves conflict and readjustment, — the never-ending struggle between the truth and the contradiction which invariably rises to challenge the truth; in this constant course of conflict and reconciliation is preserved for us the continuity of our life, whether national or ecclesiastical.

It has been felt as a difficulty that I have treated St. Clement of Alexandria, as well as others, with a degree of freedom which makes it hard to disentangle my own interpretation from his real thought. But in such a case, quotations, however full, would contribute little to our understanding of the man. The only way by which we can get to know these ancient writers, who lived in an atmosphere in many respects so different from our own, is through the mirror of one's own self-consciousness. There is, indeed, always the danger that the interpreter may mingle his own thought with that of the writer whom he seeks to interpret. If any one suspects the verity of the reproduction, he must go for himself to the original source; and when he in turn seeks to expound for others, he will be driven to this same method of reproduction. My confidence in my own interpretation is sustained by its agreement with the work of others, as Neander or Gieseler, Bunsen and Pressensé.

That I have exaggerated the differences between the Greek and Latin theologies is a similar charge. But the method which seeks to bring out divergencies is still a true and important one, even though it may have its attendant dangers. Before we are prepared to trace resemblances we must have seen distinction and difference. The old method of studying the history of religious thought, the method still followed in the so-called Catholic school of the English Church, has been to minimize differences, to overlook or explain away the divergence, in the interest of the supposed unity or harmony of Catholic tradition. Protestant scholars, also, may have been a little premature in producing their Harmonies of the Gospels before they had sounded the discrepancies. When the difference is clearly perceived, then it can be estimated and the way be opened for the discernment of hidden and deeper relationships.

As to St. Augustine, I am not surprised that my estimate has appeared to some inadequate, if not unjust. The personality of the man was so weighty, his sensitive spirit reflected so many of the contradictory moods of his age, that it is difficult at times to pronounce upon the real Augustine. The attitude of his later years contradicted and superseded the principles which moulded his earlier thought. If he is held in reverence alike by Romanist and by Protestant, yet that for which the one admires, the other apologizes or condemns. Indeed, Protestant tradition has dwelt so exclusively upon certain aspects of his teaching as to be oblivious of other aspects just as real and genuine, until, as a result, Protestants are sometimes inclined to deny, with indignation, that there ever was such an Augustine as Roman tradition venerates. Nevertheless it was he who first fairly set the Latin Church upon its feet; who gave also the inspiration and the method for its peculiar work. Nor was there any one before him, as Harnack has remarked, " who, in so determined and open a manner, has rested Christendom upon the authority of the church, and has confounded the living authority of a holy person which generates a homogeneous life with the authority of the institution."[1] If for this reason he is dear to the Latin Church or to minds of a Latinizing tendency, he commends himself none the less to the heart of evangelical Protestantism as having undergone what they regard as the typical process of conversion from sin to holiness; he has created the language of evangelical piety; he has asserted the divine sovereignty with its inevitable correlative, the doctrine of predestination. One may admit that both estimates are true, while still holding that the defect of his system, to quote the words of Maurice, "lies in throwing us back upon a time when the Gospel of God's reconciliation had not been actually established, when the Covenant, 'I will be to them a Father, and they shall be my sons and daughters, and their sins and iniquities will I remember no more,' had not been actually established."

The charge of pantheism which those who still feel the influence of Calvin are inclined to allege against the truth of the divine immanence, I must dismiss with the remark that, if it be pantheism, it is the duty of the church to overcome by assimilating it. It must be remembered that in the ancient church the same suspicion attached to the doctrine of the Trinity, that the tenet of the co-equality of the Son with the Father was so obnoxious to the majority of the

[1] *Augustin's Confessionen*, p. 30.

bishops, because of its supposed pantheistic tendency, that for more than fifty years they resisted the confirmation of the Nicene Creed. Between these poles of thought the mind of man forever moves, in the attempt to conceive of Deity, — on the one hand, deism of the Jewish or Mohammedan type, which sharply divides and separates between God and the world, and on the other, pantheism, which either identifies God with the world or the world with God. It is one of the reasons commending the doctrine of the Trinity to the confidence of Catholic Christendom that it was an attempt to mediate between these attitudes; and difficult as that doctrine may be to interpret or explain, it is still almost the only common article in the creeds of the churches, whether Protestant or Anglican, or Greek or Roman. The immanence of God does not imply the rejection of the divine transcendence; it is transcendent Deity who indwells in his creation. In the exposition of these mysterious truths, it becomes us to be modest and to refrain from attempts to transgress the limits of thought or experience. How we are to distinguish between the divine and the human, or where the line is to be drawn, is a task beyond the scope of human faculties. On this question, which once so profoundly agitated the ancient church, it may be wisest to acquiesce in the formula of the great Council of Chalcedon as expressing at once our knowledge and our ignorance, — the seemingly impossible formula which declares concerning the divine and the human, that they are not to be separated or divided, and not to be mixed or confounded.

In recent years the method by which God reveals himself to the world has become a subject of renewed and earnest inquiry. To trace the process of the divine revelation or manifestation is the purpose of what has become known as the "Higher Criticism." To this end it seeks a more intimate acquaintance with the authors of the books of Scripture and of the age in which they lived; it collates more carefully the ancient manuscripts; it cultivates a mood sensitive to the slightest change or emphasis in language or style; it is quick to detect differences of outlook, contradictions or possible errors, — things to which a former age was more indifferent. But just as the natural sciences met with suspicion and opposition when it was first proposed to inquire into the ways of God in the world of external nature, so the higher biblical criticism encounters opposition as it pursues its divinely appointed mission. It is so much easier, it seems, too, so much more religious, to accept the revelation without inquiring into the process by which it came; and it seems also to some so much more important to certify the record of the revelation as true, — for reasons such as these, the attempt to study the ways in which God has spoken to the human soul appears as full of danger or as inspired by the spirit of an impious recklessness. But in this path of inquiry lies a fresh and even stronger guarantee of the reality of the Divine Word which our own age sorely needs and demands. If the declaration of papal infallibility was an act of apostasy from the reason which is the light of Christ in the soul, no less so is the declaration of the Presbyterian General Assembly in America, that the original text of Scripture, if it had been preserved in its integrity, would be found without error. Of both these recent dogmas, which alike defy historical scholarship and learning, it may be said that they are not representative utterances of the Christian mind in the past or in the present. They proceed rather from the two most extreme as well as antagonistic tendencies in Christendom, — the Jesuit, and the Calvinist; the final confession, too, on the part of both, of a gulf of ignorance and uncertainty which they fain would bridge. If such dogmas have a sad significance for these closing years of the nineteenth century, it is also a comfort to know that, because they have no root in the truth, they must wither away. Even already it has become evident that papal infallibility is an empty sound; no Pope is admitted to have yet spoken *ex cathedra*, — it is safe to prophesy that no Pope will be allowed to do so; while the declaration of American Presbyterians reduces itself to the melancholy confession that we no longer have, or, for that matter, can ever hope to have, an unerring text of Scripture.

If I may now call attention to the principle of studying the church's history which I have followed, I should like to reaffirm my conviction that the spirit of Christianity possesses a living commentary,' not only in the New Testament, but in the life and thought of the church from age to age. In this varied record of Christian experience, the spirit of Christ appears as sanctioning all truth wherever found, whatever may be its origin; as recognizing all human ideals which further the higher welfare of humanity, while lending itself to purify and inspire and strengthen them. In turn, also, it borrows from them whatever will facilitate the progress of the kingdom of God. The human forms or usages of diverse origin, in which the spirit of Christ has found or still finds its embodiment, must therefore be judged on their own merits, nor is the protest sufficient to dismiss them that they have had their source in pagan religion, or find no recognition in the New Testament. Any such canon of criticism, if offered as a practical solution for existing difficulties, will be found, I believe, impossible and vain. Christ the perfect man forever makes his appeal to our lower but common humanity in the various stages of its advance, and the force of this divine appeal is to be seen in the manifold forms which the development of humanity assumes or may require. The return to Christ which is now urged as the only mode of securing Christian unity surely cannot mean that we are to be shut up henceforth to the New Testament or to certain parts of it, as if the only valid records of his teaching. If he be, indeed, the light of the world and of every man that cometh into the world, his light shone in the darkness of heathen philosophy or heathen ethics, or found expression, it may be, however faint, in heathen worship. If among the early fathers of the church there were those who dared to rank Socrates as a Christian, or thought of Plato as writing under divine inspiration, if even the worship of sun and moon seemed to them a preparatory stage for a higher worship, would they not also, if they had known of other and more remote religions, have held that Buddha or Confucius, so far as they taught the truth, were not independent and rival teachers, but they too had been taught by Christ, though they knew him not. While we are discussing the possible terms of Christian unity, the world is thinking of another and larger unity, the formula of which shall include the whole race of man. Must not then the return to Christ be so construed as to become the basis of this larger unity? The centripetal force in Christian thinking or experience which looks to the personality of Christ as alone the way, the truth, and the life may have an exclusive tendency needing to be counterbalanced by a centrifugal force whose aim is the widest possible inclusion of all the scattered rays of life and truth.

While adding these words of preface to my book, I must take occasion to acknowledge with deep gratitude the kind reception which has been accorded to it. It is, indeed, cause for thankfulness, if to any it has brought respect for historic Christianity, or has indicated a way out of the confusion of theories which tended to destroy belief; if it has emancipated any from the thralldom of some exclusive interpretation of the religion of Christ, which they supposed to be true and yet could not accept. What we call the final word in the interpretation of human history may lie beyond the power of human insight or utterance; for the mystery in the life of man participates in the mystery of the Divine existence. None the less is the obligation upon us to interpret our human records. Nor can any sincere effort in this direction be in vain, if it reveal to us ground for hope, or if it bring strength and consolation amid the sorrows and perplexities of life and of death. Whatever has been beautiful to us, reflecting for us, as it were, the light and the beauty of God, cannot perish, but remains always with us and always our own. The greatest of our teachers, also, may speak to us with even greater force when withdrawn from our bodily vision. It is not, therefore, in sadness unmingled with diviner hope, that I dedicate to the sacred and everlasting remembrance of Phillips Brooks a book which was formerly inscribed to the man living among us.

CAMBRIDGE, *October* 14, 1894.

TABLE OF CONTENTS.

I.

THE GREEK THEOLOGY.

THE secrecy which attends the transition from the age of the apostles to the age of the early Christian fathers. — Suggestiveness of the fragments of the post-apostolic age when viewed in the light of later history. — Clement of Rome, the Pastor of Hermas, Papias, the "Epistle to Diognetus," the recently discovered "Teaching of the Twelve Apostles." — Ignatius. — The Epistle to Diognetus serves as an introduction to Greek theology. — The Christian principle according to the mind of its unknown author. — The evidence of the incarnation. — Revelation as commending itself to the spiritual consciousness of man. — Importance assigned to knowledge. — The nature of Christian worship. — Ridicule of Jewish superstitions and usages. — Idea of the catholicity of the church. — The church emerges into the clear light of history by the time of Justin (A. D. 166). — In the account of his conversion we have a picture of the world in his age. — Phases of his intellectual career. — His residence in Rome and its influence upon his thought. — How he differed from other teachers of Christianity in the Latin Church by the importance he attached to philosophy. — In this respect he represents the first great intellectual issue that divided the ancient church. — He maintains the continuity between the higher forms of paganism and Christianity. — Christ the divine reason which is universally diffused. — Influence of the Stoic philosophy traced in his conception of Christ. — But he was also influenced by Platonism. — Explanation of the return to Plato in the second century. — Traces in Justin of the conflict of thought which finally ripened into the trinitarian controversy. — His opinions on other points betray a legal tendency of Latin or Jewish origin. — Christian theology the fruit of the Greek genius. — Its birth in Alexandria. — Intellectual freedom of the age. — Resemblance of the second century to the nineteenth. — Confusion of thought and the search after a principle of unity. — The complexity of the problem which Greek theology was called upon to solve. — Value to it of its close contact with heathen thought. — The heresies arose in Alexandria, but it was there also that they were met. — Greek theology resisted successfully the oriental tendency. — Clement of Alexandria. — What is known of his life. — He vindicated the alliance between Greek philosophy and Christianity. — Tendency in the age to divorce God from the world. — The cause which underlay this tendency. — Affinities between Plato's thought and Buddhism. — The course of Greek philosophy after Plato. — Influence of Stoicism. — Why it failed to satisfy. — Clement is mainly concerned in enforcing the immanence of God. — He does not indulge in speculations about the mode of the divine existence. — Christ is God indwelling in the world. — Evidence of the connection between the man Jesus and the Deity incarnate in Him. — Organic relation of the incarnation to the course of human history. — Revelation takes place through the reason. — The image of God in man, the fundamental point in Clement's anthropology. — He knows nothing of the doctrine of the fall of man in Adam. — Ignorance the source of sin. — Revelation as light, the remedy of sin. — The education of the human race under the tuition of indwelling Deity. — What the idea of such an education implies as to the nature of man. — The function of fear in religion. — The methods of the Divine Instructor. — The nature of the judgment. — The object of punishment. — How Clement met the heresies of the age. — Marcion, the Ebionites, other forms of Gnosticism, the oriental principle. — The doctrine of sacrificial expiation for sin finds no place in his system. — The nature of redemption. — The incarnation in itself the true atonement with God. — The nature of faith. — Its relation to reason. — Clement's use of Scripture. — Idea of inspiration. — Relation toward the principle of heresy in general. — Definition of the church. — The sacraments and rites of worship. — The nature of sacrifice. — Opposition to asceticism. — The principle on which it was resisted. — The future life and the "last things." — The ideas of a second personal coming of Christ in the flesh and the millennium irrational. — Rejection of the material notions about the resurrection. — Life in the future world a progressive development. — The love of God must eventually vindicate its power in a universal triumph over sin. — Why the theology of Clement has been presented at length. — His relation to those that came after him. — His influence upon his age. — His name stricken from the calendar of Saints in the Roman Catholic church about the beginning of the seventeenth century. — Clement succeeded by Origen. — Why he should have been identified more prominently than Clement with Greek theology. — His divergence from Clement. — Influence upon him of Neo-Platonism. — His primary aim as a Christian philosopher. — Significance of his doctrine of the "Eternal Generation of the Son." — How his thought needed to be supplemented. — Divergent directions of thought after his death. — Athanasius. — Estimate of his greatness. — His Greek culture. — His treatises "Against the Greeks," and "The Incarnation of the Word." — Method of argument against polytheism. — The divine immanence makes a multiplicity of lower gods unnecessary. — God indwells in the world through the Logos. — God to be known by looking within the soul. — Revelation a disclosure of man's true nature. — Freedom of the will an inalienable heritage. — Solidarity of the human race in Christ. — Defense of the incarnation on the principles of Stoic philosophy. — Identification of the historical Christ with the "Word made flesh." — The church's life the best evidence of the resurrection of Christ. — Appearance of Arius. — His precursors. — His training at Antioch, where the tendency was to separate the human from the divine. — Impossibility of the incarnation from such a point of view. — The times favorable to Arius. — His conception of God as transcendent Deity apart from the world. — His idea of Christ and of the nature of revelation. — The gulf between God and the world. — Arianism a reversion to Jewish deism. — Inferiority to Mohammedanism. — Excitement attending the teaching of Arius. — Athanasius' defense of the incarnation and the Christian doctrine of the trinity. — Reason for the hesitation of the church in accepting it. — The doctrine of the trinity the fulfillment of what was true in Greek philosophy. — The doctrine of the Holy Spirit in Greek theology . . . . Pages 23-94

II.

THE LATIN THEOLOGY.

The relationship between Christian and Pagan Rome. — The revival of Roman heathenism. — The Roman genius for government and law manifested its influence in the conception of the church. — First sketches of ecclesiastical polity. — The Clementine Recognitions. — The ideal of Ignatius. — The Roman Christians see no incongruity in having a head for the church at large. — The Latin church and not the Greek cultivated the study of ecclesiastical government. — The character of this development inferred from the Montanist reaction. — Relation of the Montanist doctrine of the Holy Spirit to the ecclesiastical ambition of Roman Christians. — Cyprian, about the middle of the third century, first enunciates the theory of "Apostolical Succession." — Criticism of the theory. — The motives which inspired the growth of the Latin church. — Resistance to heresy. — Gnosticism the typical heresy. — The "Apostles' Creed" a protest against Gnosticism. — Why the Greeks were not alarmed by heresy as were the Latins. — Irenæus asserts the tradition of the Roman church as the best safeguard against heresy. — The same line of reasoning adopted by Tertullian in his "Prescription of Heretics." — Bishops the guardians of the faith. — Salvation interpreted by the Latin church as escape from endless punishment. — How Tertullian presented this motive to the heathens. — Cyprian's "Address to Demetrian." — First emphatic announcement by him of this life as the only probation. — Superstitious elements creeping into the *cultus* of the church. — The relation of the controversies about the baptism of heretics, and the restoration of apostates, to the Latin idea of the church. — Influence of Constantine's policy upon the church as an institution. — Why the Latins upheld so strenuously the doctrinal decision of Nicæa. — Rapid growth of the church in the fourth and fifth centuries not accompanied by a corresponding moral improvement. — Relation of this fact to Christian theology. — The decline of the old civilization as affecting intellectual activity. — Rise of a new school in theology at Antioch. — Significance of the long controversy about the relations of the human and divine natures in Christ. — Decisions of general councils. — The historical and the spiritual Christ. — How the sentiment of the church decided the great issue, and its bearings upon later history. — The conversion of Augustine. — His early life, in its connection with this event. — He submits his reason to external authority. — His earlier theology reveals the influence of Greek thought. — The transition to Latin Christianity. — The authority of the church to teach the world asserted against the Manichæans. — The authority of the church to rule the world maintained against the Donatists. — The inner dogmatic principle which justifies the church's existence and its necessity to human salvation maintained against Pelagius. — The doctrine of original sin in its ecclesiastical bearings. — Its effect upon the view of baptism. — Opposition to Augustine from the East, from Rome, and by Vincent of Lerins. — Augustine's doctrine of "grace," a substitute for the personal Christ. — The doctrine of endless punishment in the writings of Augustine, for the first time dogmatically affirmed. — The idea of purgatory a necessary inference from Augustine's attitude. — Its relation to the belief in an intermediate state. — The influence of Augustine upon the church of his own and later ages. — Why the Latin church was able to resist Mohammedanism . . . . Pages 97–172

III.

THEOLOGY IN THE MIDDLE AGES.

Summary of the differences between the Greek and Latin theologies. — They stand to each other in the relation of the higher to the lower. — Later history of Greek theology. — The pseudo-Dionysius. — Position of the Greek church in the present day. — Its possible future. — Mission of the Latin church to the new races. — Increasing reverence for the Bishop of Rome. — Gregory the Great. — The papacy not a usurpation. — Further development of the Latin idea of the church. — Characteristics of the early Middle Ages. — Analogy to Judaism. — Traces of Greek influence among the Irish-Scotch clergy, and in John Scotus Erigena. — Theological controversies in the ninth century. — Why the Latins preferred the *filioque*. — Relation of the adoptionist controversy to the humanity of Christ. — Discussion of transubstantiation. — Modification of the Augustinian doctrine of election. — The Gottschalk controversy shows that the decrees of the church have been substituted for the decrees of God. — The change which came over the church and the age in consequence of the calamities of the ninth century. — How it affected the relation of the people to the church. — The cathedral as an expression of mediæval religion. — Anselm. — Statement of his doctrine of atonement. — Why it represents an advance in theological thought. — The notion of a ransom paid to Satan is superseded by it. — Meaning of the clause in the Creed, "He descended into hell."— Anselm's idea of atonement reflects the local influences of the Middle Ages as well as the legal attitude of the Latin mind. — It falls short of the full teaching of Christ. — Its connection with the doctrine of indulgences. — The object of Scholasticism to show that the traditional dogmas of the Latin church were in harmony with the reason. — Why such an effort could not be successful. — The fact that the church was not meeting the demands of the people in the twelfth century showed the deficiency in its theology. — Common characteristics of the heretical movements. — Explanation of the intellectual freedom of the twelfth century. — The revolt of Abelard against Latin theology. — Comparison with Anselm. — Anomaly of the intellectual situation. — The significance of his work. — Signs of the approaching ecclesiastical reaction. — Condemnation of Abelard. — The church endeavors to subjugate the reason. — The means adopted for this end. — Value to the church of Peter the Lombard's "Book of Sentences." — The work of Thomas Aquinas in reconciling reason with the dogmas of the Latin church. — Transition in Scholasticism from Plato to Aristotle. — Reasons why Platonism had fallen into discredit with the School-men. — Comparison between Plato and Aristotle. — The latter interpreted as standing for conservatism. — Under the influence of Aquinas he became the standard for the reason. — Dangers from the devotion to Aristotle. — It predisposed to the study of nature. — How nature had been regarded in the history of Latin thought. — Unconscious purpose which in this respect the Latin church had served. — Relation of the study of nature to asceticism. — Rise of the Mendicant orders coincides with the adoption of Aristotle. — Theology of Aquinas. — Distinction between the kingdoms of nature and grace, and its application. — Aquinas first distinguishes between natural and revealed religion. — He does not change the basis of Latin theology, but represents the church in the fullness of its splendor. — Criticism of Duns Scotus upon Aquinas. — He limits still further the range of the reason, but asserts the importance of the will. — Contradictions in his thought. — His work tends to magnify the importance of the church. — How Aquinas and Duns Scotus differ in their ideas regarding God. — The distinction a fundamental one and closely connected with the experience of life. — Duns Scotus more in harmony with the spirit of Latin Christianity. — Why the Jesuits have preferred Duns Scotus. — Significance of the modern attempt to revive the study of Aquinas . . . . Pages 175-237

IV.

THEOLOGY IN THE AGE OF THE REFORMATION.

Latin theology begins to decline after the thirteenth century. — Monasticism loses its vigor. — Scholasticism becomes skeptical. — The work of the papacy for Christendom had been accomplished. — Review of the mediæval *cultus* in its positive aspects as contributing to the progress of humanity. — Relic and saint worship. — Ecclesiastical art. — Beneficial influences of the papacy. — Monasticism represented the principle of individualism. — Value of nominalism in philosophy. — The growth of the national spirit and not Luther, the power that dismembered Christendom. — Development of the vernacular. — What the evangelical reformers and the mystics held in common. — The rise of preaching as a means of religious culture. — Rejection of the principle of church authority. — The Bible as the charter of the church. — Wycliffe's translation of the Scriptures. — Revelation as contained in the Bible. — Historical source of mysticism. — Relation of the pseudo-Dionysius to Latin Christianity. — How the aim of Latin Christianity subordinated the mystic principle. — French mysticism in the twelfth century. — Superiority of the German mysticism of the fourteenth century. — Eckart and the doctrine of the divine immanence. — Comparison of mysticism with the aim of the evangelical reformers. — German mysticism had a practical spirit. — Why it could not accomplish a reform. — Point at which Luther diverged from it. — The issue which the evangelical reformers had made clear to the world before Luther appeared. — Luther declares the supremacy of the conscience. — The Reformation no break in history. — Its object not merely to correct abuses. — The principle from which abuses sprang. — Luther's "Address to the German Nobility" the answer to Tertullian, Irenæus, Cyprian, and Augustine. — The church not identical with the hierarchy. — No difference in principle between priest and layman, or between religious and secular things. — Meaning of private judgment. — The doctrine of justification by faith. — Process involved in Luther's conversion. — Change in his conception of God. — The assurance of faith. — Criticism of the phrase " justification by faith." —Why the reformers would not add the word "works" to faith. — Luther not a scientific theologian. — His opinions on other subjects. — Melancthon's desire to regain the episcopate. — Confession and absolution. — Specimens of Luther's biblical criticisms. — Higher significance of the denial of human liberty by the reformers. — Difference between Luther and Zwingle. — God, with Zwingle, the indwelling life of the universe. — His view of the miraculous. — In what sense the Bible is the word of God. — Revelation in the heathen world. — Denial of the doctrine of original sin. — Salvability of the heathen. — Discussion with Luther on the eucharist. — The larger truth implied in Zwingle's denial of a special presence of Christ in the Lord's Supper. — His views of church and state. — His system not understood in his own age. — The French nationality of Calvin. — Change in the situation when he began his work. — Melancthon represents the desire for compromise. — Increasing confusion and disorder. — Calvin represents the demand for order and discipline. — His conception of the church in some of its aspects not essentially different from the Latin. — His view of the Bible and of revelation. — He rejects the idea of the divine immanence. — Doctrine of the fall and election. — Modification of Anselm's theory of atonement. — The present humiliation of Christ and His future glory. — Calvin's theology, an emphatic reassertion of the principles of Latin Christianity. — His idea of God as absolute and arbitrary will. — Separation between God and humanity. — Points in which his system differs from Latin theology. — The spirit of modern skepticism lurked beneath his assumptions . . . . . Pages 241–304

V.

CONFLICT OF THE TRADITIONAL THEOLOGY WITH RATIONALISM.

Characteristics of the theology generally received in the seventeenth century. — Its better aspects as seen in Milton's "Paradise Lost," Bunyan's "Pilgrim's Progress," the career of Cromwell. — Its latent skepticism revealed in Pascal. — Contrast of Pascal with George Herbert. — The life of the world apart from the church. — Roman church as compared with Protestantism. — Reappearance of mysticism, Arndt, Böhme, the Quietists, the Quakers, Molinos, the Pietists. — The struggle for civil and religious freedom. — Organizations of the Protestant churches. — The Reformation in the Church of England essentially a lay movement. — Retention in the English church of the old ecclesiastical order. — Theory of the church which underlay the English Reformation. — Theology of the Church of England. — Character and influence of the Liturgy. — How the ecclesiastical order was essentially changed by the emancipation of the presbyter from unqualified subjection to the bishop. — Remark of Bishop Hampden. — Rise of Puritanism. — Significance of the controversy about church authority. — Original attitude of the Church of England against the Puritans. — Its change of attitude in the seventeenth century. — Revival of Latin theology under Archbishop Laud. — How it may be interpreted. — Independents, Baptists, and Quakers. — Relation of these movements to civil and religious liberty. — Importance of the eighteenth century in the history of Christian thought. — Why the clew to the history is apt to be lost at this point. — The apparent retrogression in theology connected with the Catholic reaction led by the Jesuits. — Merit of Calvinism in resisting the reaction. — The authority of Scripture as the bulwark against Rome. — The Protestant position a strong one. — Preparation for the deistic movement. — Why the authority of reason was substituted for that of Scripture. — The Cambridge school of Platonists. — Significance of the importance attached to nature in the last century. — History of the transition from the study of revealed theology to natural theology. — Meaning of the love for the miraculous. — Hindrance to the study of nature. — How nature was regarded by the mystics. — Influence of scientific discoveries upon the idea of God. — Definition of the religion of nature. — Disposition to subordinate to it revealed religion. — Toland opens the deistic controversy. — How the apologists thought natural religion needed to be supplemented. — Reply of Tindal in "Christianity as Old as the Creation." — Objections to natural religions, optimism, and pessimism. — Weakness of deism as a proposed substitute for Christianity. — The apologists maintained that revelation is evidenced by miracles. — This position attacked by Collins, Woolston, and Middleton. — The larger question raised as to the nature of historical evidence. — How the deists regarded the subject. — Why the apologists won an easy victory. — Influence of deism in France and America. — German illuminism. — Vulgar rationalism. — The cause which explains the prevailing indifference or hostility to theology. — The Latin theology succumbed to the opposition of the reason ; the idea of God, the trinity, the atonement, endless punishment. — Criticism of the deistic movement. — The issue which it bequeathed to the nineteenth century . . . . Pages 307–369

VI.

RENAISSANCE OF THEOLOGY IN THE NINETEENTH CENTURY.

Principles of speculative thought anticipated in great popular movements. — The transition from the last century to our own age traced in the evangelical movement. — The idea of conversion. — Its influence upon modern Christianity. — Social or churchly character of the evangelical movement. — The principle which divided Wesley and Whitefield, and its manifestation in practical religious experience. — Defect of the evangelical movement. — Schleiermacher the regenerator of theology. — His conception of religion. — Antecedent influences that moulded his thought; Moravianism, Spinoza, Greek philosophy, German illuminism, the philosophy of Schelling, the French Revolution. — His doctrine of the divine immanence. — The Person of Christ in the experience of the religious life. — Christ the manifestation of the glory of God. — Modification in the ideas of election and probation. — Revival of the truth that life is an education. — Definition of the supernatural, and its relation to the natural. — The application of this principle to Scripture. — Creates the modern method of Biblical criticism. — Progress in the history of revelation as seen in the Old Testament. — Effect of this principle when applied to the New Testament. — The religious consciousness and the Christian consciousness. — Revelation in the history of the church. — Importance of the idea of the church. — The extent of Schleiermacher's influence. — He legitimates mysticism in the church. — Mysticism the Latin name for the Greek theology. — The negations of Schleiermacher those of Greek theology. — The modification in the idea of God as seen in Goethe, Coleridge, Wordsworth, Shelley, in modern art and modern science. — The ecclesiastical reaction. — Inability to apprehend the larger idea of revelation. — Revival of a belief in the church's sanctity as distinct from the state. — Distrust of the democratic tendencies of the French Revolution. — John Henry Newman leads the reaction in England. — The principles which he avowed. — Return to the Latin basis in theology. — Comparison of Pusey with Maurice. — The idea of the spiritual life as held by the Tractarians. — The theory of the church. — Their misapprehension of historical continuity. — The working of their principles modified by the tendencies of the age. — Weakness of the Tractarian movement. — The principle of agnosticism avowed by Mansel. — The ecclesiastical reaction has not succeeded in checking the activity of the reason. — Its beneficial effects. — Definition of a reaction. — The intellectual confusion of the age. — Weakness in the modern attitude toward theology. — The deficiency in Schleiermacher. — Relation of the feelings to the reason. — Comparison of Schleiermacher with Clement of Alexandria. — In what respects the resemblance consists between the modern age and the Nicene period of the ancient church. — Relation of Origen and Athanasius to Clement of Alexandria. — Hegel the successor of Schleiermacher. — The principle for which he stands. — Coleridge and Maurice agree with Hegel in this respect, and not with Schleiermacher. — Significance of the attack of Strauss upon historical Christianity. — Why such a tendency as he represented was to have been expected. — The conditions of the problem which he has raised. — How the antagonism is to be reconciled. — Conclusion . . . . Pages 373–438

INDEX . . . . Pages 439–445

CONTINUITY OF CHRISTIAN THOUGHT.

INTRODUCTION.

THE traditional conception of God which has come down to us from the Middle Ages through the Latin church is undergoing a profound transformation. The idea that God is transcendent, not only exalted above the world by His moral perfection, but separated from it by the infinite reaches of space, is yielding to the idea of Deity as immanent in His creation. A change so fundamental involves other changes of momentous importance in every department of human thought, and more especially in Christian theology. The epithets applied to God, such as absolute and infinite, have a different significance when applied to Deity indwelling within the universe. When we no longer localize Him as a physical essence in the infinite remoteness, it is easier to regard Him as ethical in His inmost being; righteousness becomes more readily the primary element in our conception of His essential nature. There is no theological doctrine which does not undergo a change in consequence of the change in our thought about God. Creation and revelation, the relation between God and humanity, the incarnation and the things which concern our final destiny, are lifted into a higher sphere and receive a deeper, a more comprehensive and more spiritual meaning.

'The object of the following treatise is to present the outlines of that early Christian theology which was formulated by thinkers in whose minds the divine immanence was the underlying thought in their consciousness of God. The Greek fathers, from the second to the fifth centuries, could not escape, even had they been inclined to do so, from the influence of a philosophy like the Stoic, so entirely in accordance with the well-known tendencies of Hellenic life and culture, and which existed for five hundred years, as the genuine expression of the Greek mind before it was overcome by other forms of theosophical speculation. Although from the second century a retrogressive movement toward Platonism was gaining strength, as seen in Justin and more especially in Origen, yet it was impossible for Christian thinkers, even so late as the age of Constantine, to emancipate their minds from the subtle spell of that philosophy whose distinguishing feature was the belief that God indwelt in the universe and in the life of man. Such an influence was as inevitable as that of scholasticism upon the reformers of the sixteenth century, or of Calvin upon some modern thinkers, who congratulate themselves on having abandoned his system while still adhering to what was fundamental in his method. But the Greek theologians did not stand in an attitude of revolt or alienation from Hellenic philosophy and culture. They knew its value in their own experience, and held it to be a divine gift to the Greek people,—a divinely ordered course of preparation for the "fullness of time." From the alliance of Greek philosophy with Christian thought arose the Greek theology, whose characteristics are a genuine catholicity, spiritual depth and freedom, a marked rationality, and a lofty ethical tone by which it is pervaded throughout. For a time its influence was felt and acknowledged in the West, as is seen in the writings of Irenæus, Hippolytus, Minucius Felix, and to a limited extent even in Tertullian. But the East and West began to grow apart after the time of Constantine, and the first foundations of the later schism between the Greek and Latin churches were already laid, when there arose in the West, under the influence of Augustine, a peculiar theology with which the Greek mind could have no sympathy, whose fundamental tenets it regarded with aversion.

The Augustinian theology rests upon the transcendence of Deity as its controlling principle, and at every point appears as an inferior rendering of the earlier interpretation of the Christian faith. Augustine is the most illustrious representative in history of a process very familiar to our own age, by which men of considerable intellectual activity, wearied with the questionings and skepticisms which they cannot resolve, fall back upon external authority as the only mode of silencing the reason and satisfying the conscience. After the modern fashion, he had swung round the circle of theories and systems in which his age abounded, without finding relief; like Newman, he was painfully impressed with the moral skepticism concealed beneath the superficial appearance of ordinary life; also, like Newman, he possessed an unrivaled skill in dialectic, which he employed in defense of the system which he had chosen to identify with the Christian faith. His conversion took place at Milan, where he was struck by the external power and splendor of the church under its majestic administration by Ambrose; he received, on assent, the Christianity of the time, and included in it the popular notions and tendencies which were current in the church, as part of the divine revelation. After he became Bishop of Hippo, and especially after his entanglement in the Donatist and Pelagian controversies, he stood forth as the type of the ecclesiastic in all later ages: like Newman after his perversion, there was nothing so obnoxious or irrational that he could not make it plausible to the reason; that which seemed to be useful or desirable for maintaining the control and ascendency of the church was stamped to his mind with the signet of the truth. The needs of ecclesiastical policy became the standard by which to test the validity of Christian belief.

The Augustinian theology made possible the rise of the papacy.[1] Leo the Great, in the generation after Augustine, put forth the claim for the authority of the Roman see which was never afterward relaxed, and which saw its realization in the imperial authority over Christendom of Hildebrand and Innocent III. Augustinianism and the papacy owe their appearance to an age when free inquiry and intellectual activity were struck with decline, when the reign of barbarism was

[1] How the work of Augustine contributed to the development of the papacy is clearly shown by Geffcken, *Staat und Kirche, in ihrem Verhältniss geschichtlich entwickelt*, pp. 95-98. The "City of God" is a prophetic anticipation of the church of the Middle Ages. In Geffcken's words: "Er stellt Natur, Individualität, Familie, Nationalität, Staat als etwas verhältnissmässig Gleichgultiges hin und ordnet alles der sichtbaren, allgemeinen Kirche unter ausserhalb deren es kein Heil giebt, er stellt die Autorität ihrer Tradition neben die der Schrift, behauptet den sacramentalen Character der Ordination und des Priesterstandes. Und wenn er die Vertretung der Kirche noch in die Aristokratie der Bischöfe setzt, so war es, nachdem einmal ein gesonderter Stand der Leviten hingestellt war, nur ein Schritt, diesen auch einen Hohepriester als einheitlichen Mittelpunkt der Kirche zu geben."

about to begin. Under such circumstances we may see in both alike a providential adaptation of Christianity to a lower environment. They did not grow out of the Christian idea as its necessary development, but were rather retrograde forms under which the Christian principle might still be operative, though in greatly diminished degree. One need not speak of the papacy as a usurpation: it was a dispensation divinely appointed for the races of Europe; a schoolmaster, like the Jewish theocracy which it so closely resembled, to bring them to Christ. But the same divine hand which is revealed in its rise and its fortunes is revealed also in the process which led to its overthrow and rejection. The Augustinian theology had subserved a temporary purpose, and began to wane with the papacy when the human mind once more regained its freedom. So far as both yet linger in the modern world, it is an evidence that there are those who still need, or think they need, a religion based upon external authority, or a morality whose sanction is fear of the consequences of sin in the future world.

The motive which lends interest and value to a study of the history of Latin theology in the Middle Ages, or in its later Protestant modifications, is to seek in its varied fortunes for that tendency to revert again to the true interpretation of the Christian faith, from which it was originally a falling away. The transitions of modern thought in regard to the nature of God and His relation to the world are in nowise abrupt or sudden, or the result of a preparation to be found exclusively in our own time. It is of the highest importance to show, if it can be shown, that the preparation for the higher and fuller truth may be traced in the progress of thought during the Middle Ages as well as in the later Protestantism. For all our thought concerning God has its foundation in the consciousness of man, — or rather, it is in and through the consciousness that the divine revelation is made, — and therefore, among those in every age who have set themselves seriously to find out God, we should expect some testimony, however feeble or overborne by contradictions, to the later and fuller utterance of the consciousness as it speaks in ourselves. There is scarcely a thinker in the whole range of Latin or Protestant theology who has not at moments given expression to a higher thought of Deity than that which underlies the formal theology, the ecclesiastical institutions, or the current modes of belief which command his adherence and approval. It is Augustine who, at a certain stage in his career, could write: —

"For God is diffused through all things. He saith Himself by the Prophet, 'I fill heaven and earth,' and it is said unto Him in a certain psalm, 'Whither shall I go from Thy Spirit, or whither shall I flee from Thy presence? If I ascend up to heaven, Thou art there; if I make my bed in hell, behold Thou art there;' because God is substantially diffused everywhere. God is not thus diffused through all things as though by diffusion of mass, so as to be half in one half of the world's body and half in the other, and thus entire in the whole; but entire in heaven alone, and entire in earth alone, and entire in both heaven and earth, and comprehended in no place, but everywhere entire in Himself. He is nowhere and everywhere."

And again, speaking of the incarnation, it is Augustine who says: —

"And though He is everywhere present to the inner eye when it is sound and clear, He condescended to make Himself manifest to the outward eye of those whose inward sight is weak and dim. *Not then in the sense of traversing space, but because he appeared to mortal men in the form of mortal flesh, He is said to have come to us.* For He came to a place where He had always been, seeing that He was in the world and the world was made by Him." [1]

Even Thomas Aquinas, when the exigencies of reason required it, could write:—

"There have been some, as the Manichees, who said that spiritual and incorporeal things are subject to divine power, but visible and corporeal things are subject to the power of a contrary principle. Against these we must say that God is in all things by His power. There have been others again who, though they believed all things subject to divine power, still did not extend divine Providence down to the lower parts, concerning which it is said in Job, 'He walketh upon the hinges of heaven and considereth not our concerns.' And against these it is necessary to say, that God is in all things by His presence. There have been again others, who, though they said all things belonged to the Providence of God, still laid it down that all things are not created immediately by God, but that He immediately created the first, and these created others. And against them it is necessary to say that He is in all things by His essence." [2]

Passages like these are gleams of a higher thought, flashing forth at exceptional moments, when the religious heart speaks out or the reason forgets its trammels. But the formal theology, the ecclesiastical institutions, which Augustine sanctioned for the ages that followed him, which Calvin renewed for the Protestant churches, are built upon the ruling principle that God is outside the world and not within; that

[1] *De Doc. Christ,* i. c. 13.
[2] *Sum. Theol. Prima Pars,* qu. viii. art. 3, quoted in Hampden's *Bampton Lectures,* p. 184.

He is absolute Deity in the sense that His being would be complete without the creation or humanity or the Eternal Son.

What is sometimes called "modern infidelity" is mainly, I had almost said exclusively, a protest against the theology based upon such a conception of God. It is not Christianity in itself which is to-day obnoxious to serious men, but a Latinized Christianity which the thought of the world has outgrown while it is still perpetuated in the formal attitude of the churches. The traditional doctrines concerning the nature and method of the divine revelation, the atonement, and the final destiny of man, are called in question, not because they are irrational in themselves, but because they no longer spring by an inward necessity from that changed conception of God which is consciously or unconsciously postulated by the mind. We often hear of a Catholic faith which is an older reality than any of the theologies which command the popular assent, but those who profess to hold it are too apt to identify the ancient creeds with their Latin interpretation. It is not till we get back into an earlier age, before Christianity was translated into its Latin idioms, that we can discern another interpretation of the Christian faith, — the religion of Christ as it appeared to men who were living and thinking under intellectual conditions more similar to our own than any intervening age has since exhibited. The ancient Greek theology, as it was developed from the second to the fourth century under the hand of great masters like Clement and Athanasius, differs at every point from Latin theology as it received its final impress from Augustine in the fifth century.

I have attempted in the following pages to contrast

the two theologies, and to trace the genesis of each to its ruling principle. In so doing, I am not presenting any novel view of the history of Christian thought. The distinction between the Greek and Latin theologies has been made by every recent writer of any importance in the field of church history, among whom may be mentioned, as best known, Gieseler, Neander, Dorner, Ritschl, Baur, Pressensé, Renan, Bunsen, Maurice, and Milman. Gieseler attached the highest importance to Greek theology, and saw in the theology of the Latin church, as it originated with Tertullian, a debased rendering of the spiritual truths of Christianity. The distinction also runs through the great work of Dorner on the "Person of Christ;" it is significant that he finds neither in Augustine nor in Thomas Aquinas, the two most celebrated theologians of the Latin church, an adequate conception of the incarnation. Neander appreciated clearly the differences between the two theologies, but was so averse to all that bore upon ecclesiastical organization that he has not traced the western theology to its genuine root; nor does he see as clearly as Dorner, that the Augustinian doctrines of sin and grace implied a fundamental departure from what was highest and most real in the earlier theology.

Ritschl has devoted an elaborate treatise to the "Christian Doctrine of Justification and Reconciliation," and begins his treatment of the subject with Anselm's theory of the atonement, as if the early church had been utterly silent upon so momentous a theme. While he admits that Greek theology stands upon a different *niveau* from Latin, and that to this cause, and not to political complications alone, was owing the schism between the Greek and Latin churches, he gives no intimation that the Greek theologians looked at redemption and reconciliation from a point of view distinctly their own, and would have been as averse to Anselm's doctrine of atonement as they were to Augustine's doctrine of original sin.[1] The value of Ritschl's discussion of the subject lies in his exhibition of the progress of thought among the thinkers who followed Anselm, till they approximate the leading principle of Greek theology, that the incarnation does not differ from the atonement as the means from the end, but that in the incarnation itself is manifested the reconciliation of man with God, and the actual redemption of humanity from its lost estate. But this conclusion Ritschl fails to draw. The mind of Baur was so preoccupied with the antithesis between the Petrine and Pauline types of Christianity and their reconciliation in the Catholic church, that he has failed to read another and deeper antithesis in the history of ancient theology for whose reconciliation the world is still waiting. It is because he sees

[1] The late Rev. J. M. Neale, in the preface to his translation of the Eastern Liturgies, remarks that he finds no trace in them of the modern theory of the atonement, as it has been held in the Latin or Protestant churches, according to which the sufferings of Christ were an *equivalent* for human punishment. " For nearly twenty years," he says, "these and the other early liturgies have been my daily study; there are very few passages in them which I could not repeat by heart; and scarcely any important works on the subject which I have not read. I may therefore claim some little right to be heard with respect to them. And I say most unhesitatingly, that while I conceive that some passages in them might be tortured into a Calvinistic sense were sufficient ingenuity employed, no ingenuity can make any single clause even *patient* of the theory of equivalence. If that theory be true, the eucharistic teaching of every eastern liturgy is absolutely false."

in the Fourth Gospel only a product of Alexandrian thought in the second century, and not an original independent tradition of the teaching of Christ, of equal antiquity and authority with the tradition given in the synoptical gospels, that he is inclined to disparage also the work of the earlier Alexandrian writers like Clement and Origen, as if with the Fourth Gospel it was but a variation of the Gnostic heresy.[1] Apart from this defect, no one has thrown a keener light upon the condition of religious thought in the ancient church, or seen more clearly how great a departure from primitive Christianity was involved in the Augustinian dogma of original sin.[2]

A formidable obstacle to the intelligent study of the Greek theology is the lingering hold of Augustine upon the modern mind. The tenets of the Bishop of Hippo have been for so many ages identified with divine revelation, that it requires an intellectual revolution in order to attain the freedom to interpret correctly, not only the early Fathers of the church, but Scripture itself. As there has been a traditional interpretation of Scripture, so there has been a traditional reading of the theologians before Augustine's

[1] And yet Baur and others who deny the genuineness of the Fourth Gospel, recognize a finer and more elevated spiritual touch in its portraiture of Christ than in what they hold to be the only genuine tradition. "Le doux et profond langage du Christ gnostique, a désarmé, conquis les plus sévères critiques modernes. Ils nient hautement l'historicité des récits du quatrième Évangile, et plus encore celle des discours, mais ils en prennent si bien l'esprit, qu'ils l'opposent aux données les plus certaines des Évangiles judéo-chrétiens, absolument comme s'ils avaient un Jean authentique." *La Révolution Religieuse au Dix-neuvième Siècle*, par F. Huet, p 194.

[2] Baur, *Die Christliche Kirche*, ii. 163–181.

time, by which they were all made to say about one and the same thing. The idea of a Catholic faith, supported by the unanimous consent of the Fathers, continues to perpetuate the error. A false conception of development has done much to confuse the study of ancient theology, by taking it for granted that because Augustine lived at a later time, he therefore built upon the same foundation with his predecessors and carried their work to a higher stage.

Whatever the source from which it springs, there is one charge so often alleged against the Greek theology that it deserves a moment's notice. It is said that it was deficient in the doctrines of sin and grace.

It is true that the Greek fathers did not accept the doctrine of original sin as propounded by Augustine,[1] with its correlated tenets of total depravity, the loss of the freedom of the will, the guilt of infants, predestination or reprobation by a divine decree, or the endlessness of future punishment. But it does not follow that their conception of sin was on this account wanting in depth or adequacy. If the attitude of Augustine is to be taken as the standard of Christian teaching upon the nature of sin, its origin and its consequences, then other religions, such as Mohammedanism or Buddhism, would seem in these respects to have excelled Christianity. Compared with the few allusions to the future consequences of sin, and these of a somewhat general character, to be found in the New Testament, the Koran invokes on almost every page the horrors of an endless torment in definite language not to be misunderstood. If the nature of man is wholly corrupted by sin, as Augustine taught,

---

[1] A summary of the Greek and Latin anthropologies is given in Shedd's *History of Christian Doctrine*, ii. pp. 42, 91.

Buddhism rises to a clearer declaration of the same principle, when, running counter to life itself, it makes sin exist in all desire. If views like these constitute what some are pleased to call the backbone of theology, then the ancient Greek theology was indeed deficient, for it assigned the chief importance to the belief that man was made in God's image, and relied upon indwelling Deity to lead mankind from sin to righteousness.

In the spirit of this earlier theology sin is regarded as a transgression of the law, not the law which is conceived as an arbitrary appointment of a will external to man, but the law written in his constitution, — the life and the truth of God imprinted on the human nature in order that it may become partaker of the divine nature. To this end the incarnation takes place, that man may be delivered from the power of sin, and brought into harmony with that law which constitutes the life of God, in the obedience of which consists the real life of the creature. As obedience is life, so in disobedience is death. The design of God, as revealed in the ages that preceded the coming of Christ, was to teach mankind how sin brought forth death, in order that, in the light of the incarnation, might be discerned the meaning and the value of life.[1] It is said of the late Mr. Maurice, that being asked for the best treatise on the nature of sin, he replied, St. Paul's Epistle to the Ephesians; or, in other words, that method which most clearly presents Christ

---

[1] This qualitative or ethical use of the words "life" and "death" is common to Clement, Origen, and Athanasius, and is in harmony with their use in the Fourth Gospel. It was, however, objected to Mr. Maurice, by a distinguished controversialist, that this use was non-natural. Cf. Mozley's *Essays*, vol. i., on Maurice's theology.

in his spiritual exaltation is best fitted to reveal the nature, the extent, the enormity of sin. Such might have been the reply of Clement of Alexandria or of Athanasius, such surely was the method of Greek theology in the days of its vigor; and even in its decline, it still remained true, in a formal way, to that which had been its ruling principle. The Greek church, it has been often remarked, had but one dogma, that of the incarnation, — a dogma, it should be remembered, resting primarily, not on the authority of a council, but on the reason or the Christian consciousness, — and with the evolution of this truth in its relation to God and to humanity, Greek thought and speculation were occupied for over four hundred years. In this truth lay involved all the issues of the Christian faith; in its presence, other questions paled in importance; by its light were to be interpreted all tenets and opinions concerning man and his destiny. Hence the early fathers did not base their theology upon speculations regarding the origin of evil; it was enough to know that the redemption of mankind was an accomplished fact, that humanity had been endowed through Christ in its own right with a recuperative power, which would enable it to struggle successfully against all that was contrary to its true nature. The sense of sin was not regarded as an experience generated in the soul apart from God, for there was a divine presence in the world and in human hearts whose mission it was to convince of sin and righteousness. There was no artificial division in human experience, according to which the sense of sin must first prevail and dominate in the consciousness before a man could receive the Saviour; but the knowledge of Christ, and his reception in the heart, became the power by which sin was increasingly revealed, and by which also it was overcome.

It is unnecessary to add that all this was reversed in the Augustinian theology. Another conception of sin and of its remedy dates its rise in the church from his influence, and was maintained by the Latin church through the Middle Ages. The system of the confessional, with its penitential books, its penances, its priestly absolutions, and conveyancing of grace; the distinction between mortal and venial sins, the morbid introspection, may seem to some minds to attach a deeper or more adequate significance to sin, but it is gained by a great sacrifice, — for it necessarily involves an inadequate conception of Christ and his redemption.

The objection to the Greek theology, that its view of sin is superficial or defective, is an old and familiar one, and it is suggestive to note how often it turns up in history when any teaching arises which contradicts the traditional methods of dealing with the problem of human evil. To the enemies of Christ, it appeared as though the Saviour himself was relaxing the bonds of moral order when He sat down to eat with publicans and sinners, or when He dismissed the woman who had sinned with no reproof, but with the gentle injunction, "Go and sin no more." It seemed to the hostile Judaism tracking the footsteps of St. Paul, as if his doctrine of justification by faith were not only deficient in its estimate of sin, but as if it put a premium upon sin, — "Shall we continue in sin that grace may abound?" It seemed to the heathen mind, judging from Celsus' attack upon Christianity, that the doctrine of forgiveness was shallow and immoral; that in order to overcome evil it must be held that forgiveness was impossible, and that every sin must reap its penalty according to irrevocable law. It seemed to the excited mind of Latin Christendom in the sixteenth century, as if the methods of Luther and Calvin, in dealing with sin, were of a nature to undo the sanctions of morality and to promote unbridled libertinism. It is not strange, therefore, that so time-honored an objection, the embodiment of so conservative an instinct, should be alleged against the theology of the Greek fathers.

When it is said that the Greek theology failed, not only in its conception of sin, but in its doctrine of grace, the remark implies a misapprehension of its spirit. The doctrine of grace, as a *specific influence* passing from God to the individual spirit through external channels or in some arbitrary way, a grace applied to the soul from without to recreate or strengthen the will apart from the natural action of the human faculties, a grace which might be forfeited and regained, which on occasions might be and was withdrawn, — of such a doctrine, which has played so large a part in the sacramental and Calvinistic theologies, it must be admitted the early Greek theology knew nothing.[1] The place occupied by *grace* in Latin the-

---

[1] Cf. Wilson's Bampton Lectures (1851), *The Communion of Saints*, p. 302, for an analysis of the passages in the New Testament in which the word *grace* occurs. Very few of them, the author infers, can be thought to have any bearing on what are popularly known as the "doctrines of grace," or would give any support to such doctrines. "There is not one text in which the word occurs in any connection with either of the sacraments." It is a remark of Joubert's, *Pensées*, 35 : — "Les jansénistes font la *grâce* une espèce de quatrième personne de la sainte Trinité. Saint Paul et Saint Augustin, trop étudiés ou étudiés uniquement, ont tout perdu si on ose le dire. Au lieu de *grâce*, dites aide, se-

ology is filled by the presence of a divine teacher, whose own eternal life, by contact with human souls, becomes the source of life, of all strength and growth; the infinite indwelling Spirit, whose action is not arbitrary, but uniform as the laws of nature. The doctrine of *grace*, as taught by Augustine, or as it has been held in mediæval and Protestant theology, was the Latin substitute for that belief in the immanence of God in humanity, which had constituted the principle of Greek theology, and was giving way in the fifth century to another and lower conception of the relations of God to man.

It may be said, that to revert to the theology of a distant age would be a retrogressive movement in religious thought; that we are to seek for some reconstruction in theology by the light of our own reason rather than under the guidance of the Nicene fathers. But such an attitude toward the past carries with it its own condemnation. The ground of hope and progress in this recognition of a theology in the ancient church, higher than that which has hitherto prevailed in Christendom, is the attestation thus gained for the human consciousness as the ultimate source of author-

cours, influence divine, celeste rosée: on s'entend alors. Ce mot est comme un talisman dont on peut briser le prestige et le maléfice en le traduisant: on en dissout le danger par l'analyse. Personnifier les mots est un mal funeste en théologie."

In Tyndale's translation of the New Testament, the attempt was made to break the mediæval prestige of the word *grace* by rendering it "*favor.*" Cf. St. Luke i. 28, where "*Ave, gratia plena*" of the Vulgate becomes, "Hail, thou that art highly favored," etc. King James's translators retained in some places the old rendering, and in others followed Tyndale. The revised version follows the same usage.

ity in religious truth. Were the present movement in theological thought emphatically new, had it never found substantial utterance in all these ages of Christian history, one might well be inclined to suspect that it had no foundation in the nature of man. That which is new in theology cannot be true; a proposition of which the converse holds equally good, that what is true cannot be new. A return to the theology of the ancient church does not mean the abandonment of the reason, or the shutting our eyes to the light which God especially vouchsafes to the later ages of the church. Our task to-day is not a mechanical reproduction of past thought, or a literal adherence to the forms in which it was cast. There were elements in the methods of Greek theology which we cannot accept; there was much which the early fathers saw imperfectly, or not at all. And yet, in spite of their defects, and the disadvantages under which they labored, the Greek theologians may be to us, what Plato and Aristotle have been to modern philosophical thought, — our emancipators from false conceptions, our guides to a more spiritual, more intellectual, more comprehensive interpretation of the Christian faith, than the church has known since the German races passed under the tutelage of the Roman bishops, and accepted a Latinized Christianity in place of the original divine revelation. In the words of a recent writer,[1] —

"We have lost much of that rich splendor, that large-hearted fullness of power, which characterizes the great Greek masters of theology. We have suffered our faith for so long to accept the pinched and narrow limits of a most unapostolic divinity, that we can hardly persuade peo-

[1] Rev. H. S. Holland, M. A., *Logic and Life, with other Sermons*, page vii.

ple to recall how wide was the sweep of Christian thought in the first centuries, how largely it dealt with these deep problems of spiritual existence and development, which now once more impress upon us the seriousness of the issues amid which our souls are traveling. We have let people forget all that our creed has to say about the unity of all creation, or about the evolution of history, or about the universality of the divine action through the Word. We have lost the power of wielding the mighty language with which Athanasius expands the significance of creation and regeneration, of incarnation and sacrifice, and redemption and salvation and glory."

After all, however, the question is not whether we shall return or ought to return to what is called the Nicene theology; the fact is, that the return has already begun. The tendencies of what we call modern religious thought have been reproducing the outlines of an elder theology, while we have been unconscious even of its existence. There is hardly a point on which there is to-day a disposition to diverge from the traditional theology, which has not been anticipated by the Greek fathers. None of the individual doctrines or tenets, which have so long been the objects of dislike and animadversion to the modern theological mind, formed any constituent part of Greek theology. The tenets of original sin and total depravity, as expounded by Augustine, and received by the Protestant churches from the Latin church; the guilt of infants, the absolute necessity of baptism in order to salvation, the denial of the freedom of the will, the doctrine of election, the idea of a schism in the divine nature which required a satisfaction to retributive justice before love could grant forgiveness, the atonement as a principle of equivalence by which the sufferings of Christ were weighed in a balance against the endless sufferings of the race, the notion that revelation is confined within the book, guaranteed by the inspiration of the letter or by a line of priestly curators in apostolic descent, the necessity of miracles as the strongest evidences of the truth of a revealed religion, the doctrine of sacramental grace and priestly mediation, the idea of the church as identical with some particular form of ecclesiastical organization, — these and other tenets which have formed the gist of modern religious controversy find no place in the Greek theology, and are irreconcilable with its spirit. And, on the other hand, the doctrine of the incarnation, in the fullness and sublimity of its real import, — the essence of the Christian faith, from which other beliefs and convictions must spring, and with which they must correspond, — this truth is finding in modern times a recognition and appreciation akin to that which it held in the theology of Athanasius.

THE GREEK THEOLOGY.

Deus erat in Christo mundum reconcilians sibi. — 2 Cor. v. 19.

Erat lux vera, quæ illuminat omnem hominem venientem in hunc mundum. — St. John i. 9.

CHRONOLOGICAL TABLE.

B. C.
800. [c.] The great age of Hebrew prophecy begins.
600. [c.] The rise of Buddhism.
584. (?) Birth of Pythagoras.
469-400. Socrates.
430-348. Plato.
384-322. Aristotle.
340-264. Zeno, founder of the Stoic school.

A. D.
65. Seneca died.
70. Fall of Jerusalem.
89. Epictetus flourished.
115. (?) Martyrdom of Ignatius.
120. (?) Plutarch died.
150. [c.] Celsus, Montanus, Marcion.
160-170. Pseudo-Clementine writings.
161-180. Marcus Aurelius, Emperor.
166. (?) Justin became a martyr.
185-254. Origen.
202. Irenæus died, Pantænus died.
204-270. Plotinus.
220 Clement of Alexandria died.
243. Ammonius Saccas died.
250. [c.] Sabellius.
260. Paul of Samosata.
274. Manichæism.
296-373. Athanasius.
318. Rise of Arianism.
325. Council of Nicæa.
326-379. Basil of Cæsarea.
330-389. Gregory of Nazianzus.
400. [c.] Gregory of Nyssa died.

THE GREEK THEOLOGY.

THE transition from the age of the apostles to the age of the early Christian fathers is involved in the darkness and secrecy which seems to attend, as by a universal law, the beginning of all great movements in history. At the very moment when we are most anxious to follow the fortunes of the Christian church, we are thrown back upon conjecture and hypothesis. The period extending from the fall of Jerusalem (A. D. 70) to the middle of the second century, a period covering the lifetime of more than two generations, is almost a blank so far as any positive knowledge can be drawn from the writers who have been designated the Apostolic Fathers. But we turn to them still with a curious interest, — these writers who might have told us so much, but who have told us so little. We can feel as we read them that we are watching in the early dawn of a great day, by whose cool, dim light are faintly outlined the characteristics of the church that is to be. In the Roman Clement's exhortations to humility, so significant as proceeding from the home of the later papacy, or in the military aspects which in his pages the ecclesiastical administration is assuming; in Ignatius's reflection that the confession made by martyrdom would bring him into a more intimate relation to the Lord; in the sombre mood of the Pastor of Hermas, where the tower which represents the destinies of the church is seen rapidly nearing its completion; in the fragments of Papias, who was storing up in his memory the oral traditions of an earlier age, under the feeling that "what was to be got from books was not so profitable to him as what came from the living and abiding voice;" in the speculations of the unknown author of the "Epistle to Diognetus," as to the reason of Christ's late appearance in the world, — in hints like these are seen the germs of the larger movements, whether of sentiment, thought, or action, which mark the church when it emerges into the clearer light of history.

While the fragments of this obscure period shed little or no light on the points about which ecclesiastical controversy has turned, — such, for example, as the nature of the church's government,[1] and her ritual usages, or the origin of the gospels and the authorship and purpose of the disputed books of the New Testament, — we may still be thankful that they reveal as much as they do, that in them we may discern the tendencies operating from the beginning which are to color the history of the church in all coming time. Especially do they disclose to us how races were still preserving their national characteristics under the shelter of the common faith, how the peculiarities of

[1] The recently discovered *Teaching of the Twelve Apostles*, which probably belongs to the same age, adds more definite information regarding Christian antiquities, as they are called, than any other of the writings attributed to the apostolic fathers. But into what confusion it plunges long established traditions respecting the ministry and the sacraments! If anything could excite suspicion as to its genuineness, it would be the abundant confirmation it yields to the conclusions of historical scholarship as to the origin of the church's order and the nature and administration of the sacraments.

inherited cultures were to modify the interpretation of the Christian principle. Clement of Rome writes as a genuine Roman, concerned with matters of administration and of subordination to authority. Ignatius, who may be taken as representing the Christian communities of Asia Minor, displays the traditional conservative spirit, — the timidity and anxiety in the presence of innovations, which continue to this day such prominent features of oriental Christendom. The writer of the beautiful epistle to Diognetus betrays by his style and thought the influence of Hellenic culture, and gives, as it were in epitome, the theology which was to be developed under the great masters of a later age, a Clement of Alexandria, an Origen, and an Athanasius.

A brief survey of this epistle may serve as an introduction to the Greek theology. The date of its composition cannot be definitely determined, but it is generally admitted that its author lived very near to the time of the apostles.

I.

In the mind of this unknown author, the Christian principle is identical with what Plato had taught to be the highest aspiration of man, — the "free imitation of God." To love God is to be an imitator of his character, an imitation which is possible to man because he is made in the divine image. He who assumes his neighbor's burdens, who is ready to communicate to those who are deficient the blessings he has received, becomes in his turn, as it were, a God to those who receive his benefits, and truly follows that which is most characteristic of the nature of Deity. To such an one it is given to see God and to enter into

the mysteries of the divine nature. When God would
redeem the world from wickedness to the obedience of
the faith, he does not send any servant or angel, or
any ruler in the celestial hierarchies, however exalted
his rank, but He comes who is the creator and fash-
ioner of all things. The evidence of the incarnation
of the eternal Wisdom in humanity is not sought for
in miracles, but in the moral transformation exhibited
in Christian lives, in the heroic endurance of persecution, in the growth of the church, which no earthly
power can hinder.

Such a revelation commends itself to the spiritual
consciousness of man. No allusion is made by the
writer of this epistle to Jewish prophecies foretelling
the advent of Christ; he does not attempt to reproduce the apostolic teaching, but he is occupied with
grounding what he conceives to be the Christian idea
in the inmost instincts of man; he speaks of Christ in
His spiritual being as established firmly by God in
human hearts. In the importance assigned to knowledge he shows still further the influence of his Hellenic culture. It was not the tree of knowledge in the
ancient paradise that proved destructive. The tree of
life was planted close to the tree of knowledge, to indicate that there can be no life without knowledge, and
that apart from knowledge life is insecure.

Nothing is said by this writer regarding the nature
of Christian worship except indirectly, by way of protest against the superstitions of the Jews. In these
are included their sacrifices, their scruples concerning
meats, their ideas of Sabbath observance, their notions about fasting and new moons and circumcision,
all of which are spoken of as ridiculous and unworthy
of notice. The use of seasons, some for festivities and

some for mourning, is no part of divine worship. But the mystery of the Christian *cultus*, it is said, cannot be learned from any mortal. The worship of the Christians, which distinguishes them from every people among whom they sojourn, is essentially a moral attitude toward God and toward man, — the love which is the fulfilling of the law. Hence, to sum up all in one word, " the Christians are in the world what the soul is in the body." They are diffused throughout all cities, in the world but not of it. As the soul is the principle which holds the body together, so Christians hold together the world itself.

In such an utterance as this may be traced the earliest and also the highest conception of the Catholic church, — the embodiment of humanity in its ideal aspect. Such a conviction of the absolute value and universal mission of the church, in the mind of a solitary thinker musing in the early dawn of Christian history, is a testimony that a new life has entered into humanity, which persecution cannot extinguish, and which is destined to overcome the world.

When we reach the age of Justin, who became a martyr in the reign of Marcus Aurelius (A. D. 166), the church is beginning to emerge from its hidden existence into the clear light of history. In the account of his conversion, we have a picture of the world of educated thought in the middle of the second century. The varieties and confusions of opinion are seen in contrast with the power of the new revelation slowly making its way to the conquest of the human intellect. Like Augustine, whom in other respects he also resembles, Justin had run through the different schools of heathen thought before finding that which his spirit craved. Beginning with Stoicism, he turned from it to Aristotle; he then made a trial of Pythagoreanism, and had at last adopted the Platonic philosophy as the only adequate explanation of the problems of life, when he was once more unsettled by the presentation of the Christian faith, in which he reached the complete satisfaction of his being, of his intellectual as well as his moral nature.

The nationality of Justin is unknown. After his conversion he passed much of his life in Rome, where he is said to have established a school for the philosophical explanation and defense of Christianity. But such an institution had little chance of success in the Eternal City, and it is not surprising to learn that the school ceased to exist after his death, having produced one unfortunate disciple, Tatian, whose career did little credit to his master. As a theologian, Justin must be regarded as a representative of that tendency which afterward gave birth to Latin theology. Through his familiarity with that phase of Christianity which prevailed at Rome where Jewish influence was especially active, he was led to adopt the current opinions of the church in Rome, to identify them with the Christian revelation, and to fall back for their defense upon the authority of the Jewish Scriptures. One can see from his mental history that he had a taste for philosophy rather than that high mental endowment which constitutes the genuine philosopher. His culture consisted in what he gained from this or that teacher, rather than in the attainment of the philosophic mind.

But in one important respect Justin differs from those who followed him as teachers of Christianity in the Latin church, — he did not turn his back upon philosophy as an evil thing when he became a Christian. Tertullian and Irenæus, and even Augustine in his later years, condemned philosophy as a source of danger and evil to the church, as the parent of all heresy. Justin on the other hand remained true to his old teachers. After his conversion he still continued to wear his philosopher's cloak, and maintained that Christianity was the only true philosophy. He recognized a continuity in his spiritual history. He had not accepted the gospel because he had found his pagan teachers to be false, — they were true, and had taught truly so far as they had conformed to that divine reason which is everywhere diffused throughout the world.[1]

In this attitude of Justin toward Greek philosophy may be seen the first great theological issue which divided the ancient church. Justin represents the class of educated minds who had been led to Christianity by another line of approach than that which lay through Jewish tradition, and who could not but maintain the continuity of their spiritual development. Although they had not been taught to believe, as had the Jewish Christians, in a Messiah foretold by Hebrew prophets, they saw behind them a long and glorious line of philosophers and teachers, through whose preparatory labors they had been enabled to enter into the heritage of the Christian faith. When Justin is obliged to meet the objection, that since Christ had been born only one hundred and fifty years before, all who lived previous to his advent were without the true light for the reason and the conscience, he rises at once to the idea of the spiritual essential Christ who is limited by no conditions of time or space. Christ is the Word of whom every race of men are partakers. Those who have lived in a manner conformed

[1] *Apol.*, i. c. 10.

to truth are Christians, even though they have been held as atheists.¹ Such were, among the Greeks, Socrates and Heraclitus and those who resembled them; and among the barbarians, Abraham, Ananias, Azariah, Misael, Elias, and many others of whom it is superfluous to mention the deeds or recite the names. Of Socrates and others, he further remarks, that like the Christians they were persecuted because of their devotion to the truth. For Socrates had known Christ,² though but in part, for Christ was and is the divine reason which is universally diffused. In all this Justin was only expanding the utterance of St. John, "He was the light that lighteth every man that cometh into the world." ³

Justin is the first writer among the ancient Fathers to assert the truth that God had revealed Himself to the heathen world as well as to the Jewish people, that He had done so not merely through some subordinate process in external nature, but through his Son, who is the divine reason in every man. In this comprehensive idea of revelation is revealed the influence of the Stoic philosophy which was still potent in the spiritual atmosphere of the age. The indwelling divine reason which Justin identifies with the Christ who in the fullness of time became manifest in the flesh, is no other than the immanent Deity of whom Seneca says that He is near to man, is with him and is in him, who not only comes near to men but comes into them, whose abiding presence in the soul alone makes goodness possible.⁴

[1] *Apol.*, i. c. 46. [2] *Apol.*, ii. c. 10.
[3] Cf. Abbot, Ezra, *Authorship of the Fourth Gospel*, in *Critical Essays, etc.*, for a discussion of the point, whether Justin was familiar with the Fourth Gospel.
[4] *Ep. ad Lucilium*, 41, 73.

But there is also to be discerned in Justin's thought the influence of the Platonic philosophy, leading him to another and widely different conception of Deity. The treatise of Plato which seems to have most powerfully affected the religious thought of the second century was the "Timæus," which deals more directly with theology than the other dialogues. Here the Deity appears withdrawn from the world into a distant heaven, distinct and separated from the creation, because of the evil with which matter is essentially connected.[1] Justin tells us that the Stoic idea of God was deficient in that it made Him responsible for the evil in the world by identifying Him too closely with the life underlying all phenomena. It was this sense of evil to which the conscience of Plato had become so sensitive, that was also operating upon the minds of thoughtful and earnest men in the second century, and was leading them to a renewed study of the Platonic philosophy. The consciousness of sin was banishing God from the universe; and it was becoming a question whether the Christian consciousness of redemption — the conviction that this world had been actually redeemed by Christ — was strong enough to reverse the tide of heathen thought, and to maintain its hold upon a God united to humanity in an organic indissoluble relationship.

In the writings of Justin we find the first traces of the conflict between these two tendencies, — a conflict which went on for two centuries before the church acquiesced in the theology of Athanasius. Justin does little more than reveal the conditions of the great issue. On the one hand, in accordance with what he has received from Plato, he speaks of Deity

[1] Cf. Jowett's Introduction to the *Timæus*, ii. p. 458.

as the unknown and the unknowable, the ineffable transcendent One, the absolute in the sense that He exists in His completeness and perfection apart from all relation to the world of finite being. But on the other hand his gaze is fixed in love and adoration on the immanent Deity revealed in Christ. He may be deficient, he undoubtedly was, when judged by the technical language of a later age, in his definition of the relation of Christ to the Father, but there can be no doubt in which direction his thought was traveling. The Christ whom he worshiped was the eternal Wisdom become incarnate, the indwelling God by whom the worlds were fashioned, whose existence is recognized in human souls, who mingles with humanity "as the perfume with the flower, as the salt with the waters of the sea."

It is unnecessary to allude here to the opinions on other subjects connected with the Christian faith, put forth by Justin as the orthodox teaching of the church. It may be said of them in passing, that they are for the most part in harmony with that theological tendency which was afterward more fully represented by Tertullian. It is vain to attempt to reconcile the contradictions in Justin's thought. Opposing currents of influence met in his mind, and while he was in some respects the forerunner of the Greek theology, he leaned in his practical conception of Christianity to the Jewish legal attitude which saw in Christianity a new law, and in Christ a second law-giver, after the analogy of the Mosaic dispensation. His conception of Deity after the Platonic idea, as the absolute and the incomprehensible, prevented his rising to the knowledge of God as the father, or his grounding the revelation in the divine love, as the inmost essence of the being whom Christ revealed. But despite his contradictions and his failures, the genuine Christian feeling in Justin was never overcome. His writings remain as a monument to that earlier, purer type of Christianity, when priesthood and altar, temple and sacrifice, were regarded as having been abolished in Christ; when as yet there was no observance of sacred seasons, for life was one perpetual Sabbath or day of rejoicing; when fasting was not an outward observance but an inward principle of restraint upon all evil.[1]

II.

Christian theology was the fruit of the Greek genius, and had its origin in the Greek city of Alexandria. It was here, in the second and third centuries, that the most favorable conditions existed for the development of Christian thought. Not only was the Greek genius still at the height of its powers, but it had renewed its life on this foreign soil. Alexandria had become more thoroughly Greek than Athens in the days of its renown. For the first time in history thought was absolutely free.[2] No dominant religious conviction could hinder the freest inquiry, no fear of persecution repressed the utterance of obnoxious tenets. The limits of thought were as boundless as the flight of the human imagination. In such an atmosphere it was inevitable that the largest hearing should be accorded to him who spoke most directly and powerfully to the heart, the conscience, and the reason of the age. In the presence of the truth, the oppositions of error tended ultimately to die away

---

[1] *Dial. cum Tryph.*, cc. 15, 21, 22, 117.
[2] Cf. Renan, *Conferences*, p. 22.

This rare conjunction of intellectual freedom, and of the intellectual capacity to improve it, was not of long duration; but before it vanished, to reappear again only when ages had rolled away, it had given birth to Christian theology. The Christian thinkers in Alexandria, at that favored moment in the history of thought, gave the outlines of a theology which for spirituality and Catholicity could never be rivaled or even appreciated at its true value, till, in an age like our own, the same conditions which made its first appearance possible, should make its reproduction a necessity.

The resemblance between the second century and the nineteenth has often been noted. The likeness is seen more especially in this, that the conquests of Rome had brought the then existing world together, had compacted it and made it more easy of comprehension, just as in recent times mechanical appliances in navigation and the quick communication of intelligence have again repeated the same result on a larger scale. The benefit of Roman conquests to later civilization has been fully acknowledged in the results achieved by Roman jurisprudence. The necessity of enforcing one common method of legal procedure upon a variety of peoples, each with its own conception of justice and of its practical administration, gave rise to the comprehensive spirit of Roman law and the endeavor to ground it in the nature of man. A similar necessity gave rise to similar efforts in the sphere of religious thought. If, on the one hand, the spectacle of so many religions dividing the allegiance of men created confusion and skepticism, on the other hand, there were those who sought to penetrate beneath the diversity to some underlying principle of unity, and by doing justice to all the elements of truth and spiritual thought wherever they might be found, attain the idea of a universal religion. Such an effort was made by Plutarch and other heathens who stand as the representatives of heathen faith in the midst of a prevailing skepticism. Such also was the role of some of the Gnostics, and at a later time of the Neo-Platonic philosophy. A similar duty devolved upon the Christian thinkers of Alexandria. They were forced, if they would address intelligently and successfully the inquiring mind of heathenism, to do justice to the truth in all systems of thought, to interpret their aspirations after the eternal light, to emphasize the value and importance of the divine revelation given in Greek philosophy, and always to keep prominently in view that feature of Christianity upon which rested its claim to be a universal religion.

The city of Alexandria represented in miniature the world of that distant age. In some respects it was a city more cosmopolitan than any other in the empire, in comparison with which even Rome was provincial. In its population were included large numbers of Greeks and Jews, Orientals and Romans. It had also become one of the great centres of the Christian church. The combination of these different types of religious thought stimulated the speculative mind to the highest activity. There the Jews came under the influence of Greek philosophy; the Greeks discerned in Judaism a moral force and directness in which heathenism was wanting. Each was impelled to the search after a universal principle in whose comprehensive grasp might be realized the unity of all things human and divine. There was also felt the subtle contagion of oriental theosophy, with its dark consciousness of sin and disorder in the world, with its dualism between God and some rival power for evil, to which the consciousness of sin, without the full light of redemption, has always and everywhere given birth.

No doubt there was danger to the faith of Christian thinkers in such a situation. The problem was indeed a complex one which the Greek theology in Alexandria was given to solve. To maintain the divine immanence, and yet not identify God with the world; to combat Gnosticism and oriental tendencies, and yet not underrate the evil and heinousness of sin; to insist upon the divine love as the essence of Deity, and yet enforce the judgments and punishments of sin; to assert the superiority of the Scriptures of the Old and New Testaments, and yet do justice to the divine revelation contained in Greek philosophy; to combat Jewish deism as an unworthy conception of God, to resist the tendency to reduce Christianity to a ritual in imitation of the Jewish ceremonial law, and yet not fail to acknowledge in Jewish history the preparation for a higher truth; to assert the importance of intellectual culture, and yet to recognize the power and value of simple faith, — such were the conditions under which Greek theology was developed.

Complex and difficult as was the environment of the church in Alexandria, yet this close contact with heathen thought in its various forms and its highest moods was necessary and unavoidable, if the Christian revelation was to be put to the severest test, if its essential principle was to be apprehended in its purity by the intellect as well as by the moral sentiment, if in a word Christianity was to make the conquest of the human reason. What the persecution of the church by the

Roman state was to the simple lives of Christian people, developing a heroism which the world had never seen before, demonstrating that no earthly force could subdue the power of faith, such also was the conflict in the intellectual sphere between heathen philosophers and Christian theologians. Christian thought, as presented by Clement and Origen and Athanasius, overcame the polemics of their heathen antagonists, and brought forth into the clear light of the reason the principle which bound heaven and earth together, and formed the basis of a universal religion. Alexandria, it is true, generated some of the worst heresies that endangered the Christian faith, but it also produced a Catholic theology in which those heresies were met as they were nowhere else in the church. No other writer overcame the principle of Gnosticism so completely as Clement of Alexandria: when Celsus assaulted by argument and by ridicule that which was most distinctively sacred in Christian belief, it was from Alexandria that the answer came; when Arianism would have reduced Christianity to a form akin to heathen polytheism, it was Athanasius, the Bishop of Alexandria, who fought for the doctrine of the incarnation, and secured its triumph.

Whatever may have been the deficiencies of Greek theology, it may be safely averred, that until its progress was arrested by the mysterious decline which paralyzed all intellectual activity and freedom, it did not succumb to the subtle spirit of heathenism, nor adopt unwittingly what was foreign to the Christian idea in Gnostic or Manichæan theosophies, nor was the principle of redemption neutralized by an oriental or Buddhist conception of human sinfulness, which divorced God from the world, and left humanity, in its isolation and weakness, a prey to the encroachments of an ambitious priesthood. These were the evils which befell the church, more especially in the West, where intellectual culture had come to be disowned as having no connection with Christian faith, where reason was separated from feeling and piety, and philosophy was denounced as the parent of all evil.

Clement of Alexandria may be called the father of Greek theology.[1] Of Pantænus, his predecessor in the theological school, but little is known; the important fact has been recorded, that he was an adherent of the Stoic philosophy, and Clement, who was his pupil, bears witness to the high value of his teaching. Very few details of the life of Clement have been preserved. The date of his birth may be fixed about the middle of the second century, while that of his death is unknown. The period of his greatest literary activity was when he presided over the school at Alexandria (A. D. 190–203), and when he must have been in the full maturity of his powers. As to his nationality, he was a Greek, possibly an Athenian, and his acquaintance with Greek philosophy and literature was thorough and extensive. The epithet "learned" belongs to him not merely in virtue of the courtesy which extends it to all the Fathers of the church; apart from their theology, his works are valuable to the classical student for their numerous quotations from books no

---

[1] Sketches of Clement's thought may be found in Presseusé, *Histoire des trois premiers siècles de l'église*, t. iii. — *L'Histoire du dogma*; Ritter, *Die Christliche Philosophie*, i. 300–310; *Studien und Kritiken*, 1841; Bp. Kaye, *Clement of Alexandria*; Freppel, *Clement d'Alexandrie*. A sympathetic study of Clement is contained in Neander, *Ch. His.*, vols. ii. and iii., Bohn ed.

longer extant, and for the light they shed upon the manners and customs of the ancient world. He had traveled widely in search of knowledge, and after he became a Christian he studied the new religion under several masters before he came under the influence of Pantænus, and heard a presentation of Christian truth which commended itself to his reason. That which attracted him in Christianity was its lofty ethical teaching, and the fruits which it bore in the practical transformation of the life. In the character of Christ, not in miracles or prophecy, did he find the highest evidence of His divine mission to humanity.[1]

We meet in Clement a more emphatic statement than in any other ancient father of the universality of the preparation in the Old World for the advent of Christ. As a Greek, it fell to him to vindicate the alliance between the Hellenic philosophy and the new religion. Such an alliance he does not regard as calling for an apology; it is a divine ordering of the world that Greek philosophy should have prepared the way for Christ, and to doubt that it did so would be to undermine belief in the possibility of a revelation, as well as to deny the providence of God.[2] Christianity, if the expression may be allowed, grew as directly out of Greek philosophy as out of Hebrew prophecy. The narrow conception that the only prophecy of Christ is to be found in Jewish anticipations of Messiah, belittles the subject of the divine dealings with humanity. The influence of Hellenic speculation in determining the true nature of the person of Christ is not a thing smuggled surreptitiously into the sphere of Christian thought, — an alien element, to be carefully

[1] Cf. Bp. Kaye, *Life and Writings of Clement of Alexandria*, p. 3.
[2] *Strom.*, vi. 17.

eliminated, if we would understand the original revelation in its simplicity and purity. It enters into the divine process of preparation for the advent of Christ as a constituent factor; it is essential to a right interpretation of the Christian idea in its widest and highest application.

What Clement asserted so eloquently as of vital importance to the understanding of the Christian faith, the Greek fathers who came after him accepted as an axiom without further discussion. The doctrines of the incarnation and the trinity, as developed by Origen, by Athanasius, and the Cappadocians, especially Gregory of Nyssa, rest upon the alliance with Greek philosophy, securely and serenely. In later times, when a meagre, mechanical notion of divine revelation obscured the earlier apprehension of its universality, the argument for the divinity of Christ's person came to rest almost exclusively upon Hebrew prophecies which found in Him their fulfillment, — a method which reached its legitimate result in a return to the Jewish deism from which it had derived its inspiration.

The following passages from Clement show how large and free was his conception of the methods of divine revelation : —

"To the Jews belonged the Law, and to the Greeks Philosophy, until the Advent, and after that came the universal calling to be a peculiar people of righteousness through the teaching which flows from faith, brought together by one Lord, the only God of both Greeks and barbarians, or rather of the whole race of men."[1] "And in general terms we shall not err in alleging that all things necessary and profitable for life came to us from God, and that philosophy more

[1] *Strom.*, vi. c. 17. The translation is that of the Ante-Nicene Library.

especially was given to the Greeks as a covenant peculiar to them, being, as it is, a stepping-stone to the philosophy which is according to Christ."¹ "Should any one say that it was through human understanding that philosophy was discovered by the Greeks, I find the Scriptures saying that understanding is sent by God."² "God was the giver of Greek philosophy to the Greeks, by which the Almighty is glorified among the Greeks."³ "The studies of philosophy therefore, and philosophy itself, are aids in treating of the truth."⁴ "Before the advent of the Lord, philosophy was necessary to the Greeks for righteousness. And now it becomes conducive to piety; being a kind of preparatory training to those who attain to faith through demonstration, — a schoolmaster to bring the Hellenic mind, as the law the Hebrews, to Christ."⁵ "By reflection and direct vision those among the Greeks who have philosophized accurately see God."⁶ "In the whole universe all the parts, though differing one from another, preserve their relation to the whole. So then the barbarian (Jewish) and Hellenic philosophy has torn off a fragment of eternal truth from the theology of the ever-living Word. And he who brings together again the separate fragments and makes them one, will, without peril, contemplate the perfect Word, the truth."⁷

In the second century Christianity was struggling against the tendency felt in all forms of religious and

¹ *Strom.*, vi. c. 8.
² *Strom.*, vi. c. 8.
³ *Strom.*, vi. c. 5.
⁴ *Strom.*, vi. c. 11.
⁵ *Strom.*, i. c. 5.
⁶ *Strom.*, i. c. 19.
⁷ *Strom.*, i. c. 13. Clement often asserts that Greek philosophy had plagiarized from the Hebrew Scriptures. But he takes this ground when trying to convince the Greeks, who boasted their philosophy to be sufficient, that the highest spiritual truth in Plato and others had been anticipated long before. There is no real contradiction in Clement's thought, however it may appear as such in his language. His highest meaning is clear, that Greek philosophy contained a direct divine revelation.

philosophical thought, to banish God from His creation, — to maintain the divine transcendence at the expense of an absolute divorce between God and humanity. The tendency sprang from a growing consciousness of sin, a conscience quickened to the perception of good and evil. All interest in other lines of human research was disappearing, and philosophy began to be characterized by an ethical purpose in comparison with which all else was unimportant.

It is perhaps the one most striking peculiarity of the religion of Christ, that it stimulates the keenest susceptibility to moral evil, and yet brings God close to humanity in an abiding eternal relationship. It does what no other religion has been able to do, — it develops the consciousness of sin, and yet maintains the consciousness of an actual redemption from sin. The most complete illustration of the gospel was given in one short sentence, when it was said of Christ that He sat down to eat with publicans and sinners, — a picture it may called of indwelling Deity in close contact and communion with humanity stricken with a sense of its debasement and guilt.

And yet in the "fullness of time" when Christ appeared, the world was witnessing the mightiest transition recorded in the spiritual life of man. The belief in immanent Deity was slowly yielding to the conception of a God removed to an infinite distance from the world and from all human interests. Wherever we look in the second and third centuries, we may see the transition in process of accomplishment. To enter upon its full description is here impossible. It must suffice to allude briefly to the causes which initiated so vast a revolution, and to the most significant indications of its progress, in order to get the key to the theology of the incarnation, as it was presented by the Greek fathers, before the world and the church had acquiesced in a change which was to alter the character of human civilization.

The leading cause which underlies and modifies the conception of God is the action of the human conscience under the conviction of sin and guilt. It was in the ancient home of the Aryan races that the primeval idea of Deity received its profoundest modification in the reaction of Buddhism. In the Buddhist mind, the consciousness of evil was so supreme, as to almost rob the world of anything answering to the idea of God at all. That which took place in India was substantially repeated, not long after, in the protest of philosophy against Greek religion in the time of Socrates and Plato. The religion of ancient Greece resembled that of India in resting on a pantheistic basis, where God and man and the external world are hardly distinguishable from each other. It is not necessary that Plato should have felt the direct influence of Buddhism, but it is certain that he was moved by kindred motives to those which had generated it. In the "Timæus" he pictures God as the passive Deity at an infinite distance in the heavens, unable to come into immediate contact with a world of which the very materials contain the conditions of evil. We may admire, as we study Plato, his high moral conception of the nature of God, while at the same time we discern in him how the quickened moral sense, when not enlightened by the Christian idea of redemption, perverts the true relationship between God and humanity.

In the subsequent course of Greek philosophy may be read, as in a register of man's spiritual life, the records of the variation of human thought as it studied the relation of God to the world. Plato did not willingly give up the world to absolute separation from its Maker: he strove hard to overcome the schism which his own thought had created. But the tendency of his theory of ideas was to reduce the creation to a pale reflection of the divine glory, a poor substitute for that beautiful vision which had haunted the dreams of earlier Greek religion. Aristotle combated Plato in the interest of redeeming the external world from the unreality which it tended to assume in his master's thought. In the religious estimate of Greek philosophy, he may be said to have prepared the way for the Stoic school, which appeared in the third century before Christ. The Stoic philosophy returned to the idea of God from which Plato had departed, and conceived of Him as indwelling in the world, penetrating everywhere and filling it with His presence. The world was thought to sustain the same relation to God as the body to the spirit; it was directed and controlled by an immanent life of whose beauty and glory outward nature is the direct manifestation, while the human spirit in its moral capacity and attainments expressed the highest revelation of the actual presence of the divine. That such a system of philosophy as the Stoic should have prevailed till the second century after Christ, and on the eve of its decline should have given birth to three such men as Seneca, Epictetus, and Marcus Aurelius, is a circumstance, the importance of which it is hardly possible to overestimate, when considering the influences which moulded the early teachers of Greek theology.

But in the second century of the Christian era, the tendency of thought was back again to Plato. Stoicism was failing to satisfy the dark mood of an age in which the sense of sin was once more becoming the supreme motive underlying all speculative thought. The world was no longer what it had been. The horizon seemed dark and forbidding to those who sought to read the future destinies of mankind. They saw everywhere the presence of gigantic evils, and no power at work adequate to redress them. Even to many Christian thinkers it required too much faith to believe that the world as they saw it had been redeemed. Hence the Gnostics reverted to Plato, with his idea of a distant passive Deity, and gave up the world to destruction, with the exception of a chosen few in whom kinship to God was sufficiently strong to enable them to secure salvation. Neo-Platonism had its forerunner in Plutarch (A. D. 120), who by one of the strange perversions which so often accompany the revival of an earlier thought, saw in Plato a principle for the renewal of the old mythology which Plato had done so much to bring into discredit.

Such was the spirit of the age when Clement was aiming to commend Christianity to earnest and inquiring minds. That he was to some extent influenced by the current sentiments of his time it is sufficient to admit. We should be misled, however, as to his real meaning and purpose, if we sought only in his writings for his formal concurrence with prevailing ideas. Like Justin, he sometimes speaks of God as the absolute and the unknown, or even as the incomprehensible, whose life is sufficient in itself without the creation. But he has no real interest in concessions like these to the fashion of the age; his higher utterances contradict and disprove them. He is mainly concerned in enforcing the immanence of God. Christ is everywhere presented by him as Deity indwelling in the world. The world is viewed as part of an organic whole, moving on to some exalted destiny in the harmony of the divine order. Humanity has its life and being in Christ, to whom also it is constitutionally related; the whole human race, not any elect portion only, is included under the operation of grace as well as of law; all human history is unified and consecrated by the visible traces of divine revelation.

Less than any of the fathers is Clement tempted to indulge in speculations about the mode of the divine existence. He is concerned with realities, not with mere speculative opinions. He attempts no formal explanation of how Deity in His immanence is to be reconciled with the transcendent and unknown essence of God. But there is no qualification in his belief, that Christ is in the fullest sense God indwelling in the world and in humanity. Language seems poor and inadequate as he struggles with it in order to assert and illustrate the workings of the present God.

Nor does Clement formally endeavor to demonstrate the connection between the historic personality of Jesus, and the Deity whom he held to have been incarnate in Him. This is the assumption which underlies his thought, that which he takes for granted, because, in his own exuberant faith, he feels no need of labored demonstration. But the connection, as it exists in his mind, may be clearly traced. He does not rely upon the display of omnipotent power, as seen in the miracles of the historic Christ, to confirm His divine character, but upon the life of the church of which He is the perennial source, in the transformation which His name still works in human character, in the self-sacrifice which is the reproduction of His example, in the boundless hope which has its spring in the love and devotion which He still continues to inspire, in the spiritual illumination of a soul who has acknowledged Him as its master.

Since Christ is the indwelling God, His incarnation is not a thing new or strange, an abrupt break in the continuity of man's moral history; it had not been decreed in the divine counsels, in order to avoid some impending catastrophe which suddenly confronted or threatened to disappoint the divine purpose; it was not merely an historical incident by which He came into the world from a distance, and, having done His work, retired again from it. He was in the world before He came in the flesh, and was preparing the world for His visible advent. As indwelling Deity, He was to a certain extent already universally incarnated, as the light that lighteth every man, the light shining in the darkness, the light and life of men in every age. Hence the prophecies of his advent enter into the organic process of human history, and in the spiritual life of man may be read the foreshadowings of Him who was the crown and completion of humanity, the fulfillment of the whole creation.

Because Deity indwelt in humanity, and the human reason partook, by its very nature, of that which was divine, Clement was forced to see in the highest products of the reason the fruit of divine revelation. He makes no distinction between natural and revealed religion, between what man discovers and God reveals. All that is true and well said in Greek philosophy was as truly given by divine revelation, as was the moral truth proclaimed by Jewish legislators and prophets. The higher activities of human thought and reflection are only the process by which the revelation of truth is conveyed to man,[1] and inspiration is the God-given insight which enables men to read aright the truth which God reveals.

The doctrine of indwelling Deity — of the Logos, as constitutionally or organically related to the human soul — may be called the theological principle in the teaching of Clement. Closely connected with it, and indeed the necessary inference from it, is his doctrine of man as made in the divine image. No other writer in the ancient church has presented this truth with so much clearness, or so insisted upon its importance as the ground of faith in God or of hope for man. With Clement it is the point of departure in treating of sin and of redemption, — the key-note, it may be called, of his anthropology.[2] The image of God in man is a spiritual endowment of humanity which is capable of expressing the inmost essence or character of God, — it is a moral or spiritual image, containing, as it were, in the germ, the highest and divinest qualities as they exist in God. It is that in the Son, which comes from being begotten by the Father. Because man's spiritual constitution is made after a divine type, it becomes the law of his being to fulfill its possibilities, and to rise to the full resemblance to God. The image of God in every man constitutes the warrant for believing that he may rise from the possibility into the actuality, that the image may develop into a living and speaking resemblance. It is because man is made in the divine image that his nature responds to the call of God, and his conscience reëchoes the commandments of God. But the law of God, according to such a view, is not conceived as a code of external command-

---

[1] *Exhort.*, c. vi.; *Strom.*, i. c. 19; also, i. c. 5.
[2] *Exhort.*, c. x.; c. xii.

ments, — it is a law written within the heart. Christianity, as compared with Judaism, is the passing from the stage where the law is presented from without on external tables of stone, to that in which it is discerned as written within man's nature; and when thus recognized, the hard sense of duty gives place to willing aspiration, and the attainment of character is set over against the fulfillment of formal ordinances. Such is the spirit of the new covenant in Christ as St. Paul discerned it, as the prophet Jeremiah described it, in the transition hour of Jewish history: "Behold, saith the Lord, I will make a new covenant with them in those days: I will put my laws in their hearts, and in their minds will I write them, and their sins and iniquities will I remember no more."

Clement does not speculate on the nature or the origin of evil. He knows nothing of the later dogma of the fall of man in Adam, nor of Adam as the federal representative of mankind; nor does it seem as if such opinions would have commended themselves to his mind as explaining the nature or the source of human sinfulness. He sees, rather, in Christ the normal man, the true head and centre of humanity; and in treating of sin and its ravages, never lets go his hold on the truth that man is constituted after the divine image. Hence he regards the will as free to follow out the divine purpose which is the law of man's being. The freedom of the will, which Clement held in common with all the Greek fathers, was not a temporary expedient in their thought in order to meet the fatalism of Gnostic theories; it was a necessary principle flowing from the importance assigned to the primary truth that man was created in the divine image. However much that image might have been obscured by human sinfulness, it still existed with its original endowment, and the work of Christ had consisted in revealing man to himself, in making known to him the divine constitution of his being, as well as in presenting the nature and character of God. The freedom of the will was not the freedom of a being independent of God or detached from Him, but rather allied to Him by his inmost constitution, and therefore retaining the capacity, through all the vicissitudes of his career, of fulfilling his appointed destiny.[1]

Like others of the Fathers who had come under the influence of Hellenic thought, Clement regarded ignorance as the mother of sin, and finds in revelation, considered as light, the divine remedy. But he does not view ignorance as the only difficulty to be over-

[1] It was not till Augustine had fallen back into the bondage of an essentially Gnostic or Manichæan fatalism, and accepted the principle of an arbitrary election common to all the Gnostic systems, that he gave up the freedom of the will. His denial of freedom was, indeed, a consequence of his doctrine of election, but beneath this notion of election lay the idea which conditioned all Gnostic speculation, that humanity had become separated from God, and, in its independence and isolation, needed the aid of a power foreign to itself in order to its restoration ; or, in theological language, the image of God forfeited by Adam must be restored by an external creative act, as in baptism. A recent writer has remarked on the impressiveness of the fact that the Greeks were never embarrassed as were the Latins by questions relating to free will and necessity. The fact does not lose its impressiveness, though no longer difficult to understand, when it is remembered that the Greek theologians regarded the image of God in man as an inalienable possession, and therefore regarded God and man as bound together by an organic tie ; while the Latins regarded mankind as having, through the fall of Adam, lost its spiritual kinship to God, while yet remaining susceptible to an omnipotent influence capable of bearing down all finite opposition. Cf. Maine's *Ancient Law*, p. 342.

come in the redemptive process; there is also in man the inability to follow righteousness, which springs from the weakness or disinclination of the will. Ignorance of the right, or the unwillingness to follow it, these are the two obstacles to be removed in order that man may rise to the free imitation of God, and share in that humanity which has been deified in Christ.

The history of man's redemption from sin becomes, according to Clement's conception, the education of the human race, under the tuition of indwelling Deity.[1] The divine teacher, whom he has portrayed in his work called the "Instructor," is, he tells us with constant reiteration, no other than God Himself. One can imagine that he had in view, as he wrote it, the prophetic language of Plato: "We must wait for one, be it a God or a God-inspired man, who will teach us our religious duties, and take away the darkness from our eyes." But the reality, in Clement's view, surpassed the prophecy and the anticipation. Such a divine teacher had come in the flesh and dwelt amongst us in visible form; but in his spiritual, his most real presence as the essential Christ, He remained here forever as the teacher of humanity; nor had there been a time since the world began when He was not present to superintend the education of the race. It was He who spoke through Moses and the prophets, and it was He who spoke in Greek philosophy. In the progressive education of humanity, He even gave the sun and moon to be worshiped, in order that men might not be atheistical; in order, also, that they might rise through the lower worship to something higher.[2] He is not the teacher of a few

[1] *Pædag.*, i. c. 9.   [2] *Strom.*, vi. c. 14.

only, in some favored time or place, but He comes to all, at all times and everywhere. He is the Saviour of all, for all men are His; "some with the consciousness of what He is to them, others not as yet; some as friends, others as faithful servants; others barely as servants."[1] As their teacher, He educates the enlightened by the inward intuition of truth, the believers by good hopes, and those who are hard of heart by corrective discipline through operations that can be felt.

The idea of life as essentially an education under the guidance of immanent Deity implies a divine constitution in man formed to receive the divine teaching. The idea of education involves capacity and ability in the pupil, and also an innate disposition to receive and follow instruction. To educate is to educe and develop the powers already implanted in the soul. The teaching of the divine Instructor follows the analogy of human methods, — it appeals to, it evokes and strengthens, the divine that is in man, those instincts of the soul which yearn after all that is true or beautiful or good. The gracious and benign Instructor of humanity possesses unwearied patience, and in accomplishing His task has at His disposal all the resources of God. His methods vary with the need of the pupil. He overcomes ignorance by setting forth the truth; He meets unwillingness to follow and obey the truth, by threatening, by censure, by discipline, by chastisement. He prefers the gentler methods, but never hesitates to follow severer measures when gentle ones do not avail.

Clement has much to say upon the function of fear as a motive to righteous action. He regards it as in-

[1] *Strom.*, vii. c. 2.

THE PURPOSE OF FEAR.

dispensable in this lifelong process of redemption from the power of sin, but he also refuses to consider fear apart from the work of the instructor. Fear is not a quality begotten in man in separateness and isolation from God, for in his view no human soul can escape the divine tuition. It is rather a necessary part of the divine method of education, that fear should be implanted in man in order to his protection from the evils that assault and hurt the soul, as well as from those that endanger the body. But if we may so speak, the ultimate objective ground of this saving fear in spiritual things lies in no being, no condition of time or place, save God Himself. God alone inspires the fear, and always for a disciplinary purpose.[1] In whatever forms the fear may be clothed by the human imagination, the only reality to be truly feared is God; and he has read rightly the true meaning of fear, who, in the words of St. Paul, works out his own salvation in fear and trembling, *because it is God that is working in him*, to will and to do of His good pleasure.

The Instructor has not only fear at his disposal as a means of education, but He inflicts judgments and penalties. The unbeliever who will not heed exhortation, or the believing Christian who still cherishes the inclination to sin, must experience the severity of God. The judgment is not conceived as the final assize of the universe in some remote future, but as a present continuous element in the process of human education. The purpose of the judgment, as of all the divine penalties, is always remedial.[2] Judgment enters into the work of redemption as a con-

---

[1] *Strom.*, ii. c. 7; *Pædag.*, i. 9.
[2] *Strom.*, i. c. 27; iv. c. 24.

structive factor. God does not teach in order that He may finally judge, but He judges in order that He may teach. The censures, the punishments, the judgment of God are a necessary element of the educational process in the life of humanity, and the motive which underlies them is goodness and love. They are at the disposal of a divine Instructor, who orders the course of the external world for a beneficent end, who has attested His love by coming into the world and dying for men.[1] There is no essential difference between justice and goodness (as Marcion had taught); justice resolves itself into love; even the divine anger — if it is proper to so term it — is full of love to man, for whose sake God became incarnate; "to Him alone it belongs to consider, and His care it is to see to the way and the manner in which the life of men may be made more healthy."[2]

The idea of life as an education under the immediate superintendence of a divine Instructor, who is God Himself indwelling in the world, constitutes the central truth in Clement's theology. Here lies his answer to the diverse Gnostic heresies with which his age abounded. To Marcion and others denouncing the heathen world before Christ came as under the dominion of demons, and as only ripening for destruction, Clement virtually replies that the divine Instructor had himself been speaking to the heathens, through their own recognized teachers, their poets and philosophers, by exhortations to the pursuit after righteousness; that these utterances, however imperfect, appealed to a humanity made in God's likeness, and endowed with a desire to reach forth after the divine. To Marcion, still further sharply dis-

[1] *Pædag.*, i. c. 12. [2] *Pædag.*, i. c. 12.

tinguishing between justice and love, and discarding
the Old Testament and Jewish religion, because in
them justice appears as the ruling principle, Clement
replies that justice is but another form or manifestation of the divine love, designed to act upon those
who are in the lower stages of the redemptive process; that the judgments of God, which are in all
the world, are purifying the spiritual atmosphere, and
adapting the earthly environment of man to his spiritual life.[1] Against those, on the other hand, who
saw in Christianity only the continuation of Jewish
religion, as in Ebionism, or the pseudo-Clementine
writings, Clement, while doing full justice to the
principle of historical and spiritual continuity which
binds together the two dispensations, asserts their
difference by showing that He who spoke through
Jewish prophets had in the fullness of time appeared
as God manifest in the flesh, and given to men to
know the truth, which in Judaism was but faintly
discerned, and enabled man, through Christ, to rise
to the imitation of God, to the contemplation of Deity
in His inmost nature. In opposition to the tendency
which showed itself in all the Gnostic systems to divide
the human family into fixed classes, the elect and the
non-elect, separated by impassable barriers, Clement
emphasized the spiritual oneness of humanity, its actual redemption as a whole in Christ, while each individual is necessarily related to God in virtue of his
constitution in the divine image. The idea of a distant Deity which underlies all the Gnostic theosophies,
— a God outside the framework of all human things,
and incapable of communicating Himself to humanity, — is met by the idea of God as indwelling in the

[1] *Pædag.*, i. c. 12.

world, a real and continuous presence of the Word made flesh, who is one with God, and who is God. The Gnostic conception of the world as an accident, in its nature evil, only by the renunciation of which a few rise to salvation, is everywhere contradicted in Clement's thought, by the conception of the world as organized throughout in accordance with a moral principle, and as lending itself to the higher interests of man. Salvation is not a physical process, but an ethical growth, through union with God; divine knowledge is no mere speculative insight into the origin of things, but an ever-growing perception of the true character of God, as it is revealed in Christ. Another ruling idea among the Gnostics, that in the process of redemption God remains passive and unconcerned, an idea which also lay at the root of all oriental theosophy, and at a later time became influential in Neo-Platonic thought, is met in Clement's theology by the truth, to advocate which was the object of all his writings, that God Himself initiates and indwells in the process of redemption; that God alone is the immanent force acting directly or immediately within humanity, dispensing with the necessity for mediators in heaven or in earth.

The doctrine of a sacrificial expiation for sin as commonly understood finds no place in Clement's view of redemption. There is no necessity that God should be reconciled with humanity, for there is no schism in the divine nature between love and justice which needs to be overcome before love can go forth in free and full forgiveness. The idea that justice and love are distinct attributes of God, differing widely in their operation, — a doctrine first propounded in all its rigor by Marcion, — is regarded by Clement as having its origin in a mistaken conception of their nature. Justice and love are in reality one and the same attribute, or, to speak from the point of view which distinguishes them, God is most loving when He is most just, and most just when He is most loving. Love constitutes the essential quality of God; not the love which in its inferior human manifestations appears as an indulgent, weak affection; but love in its highest sense, as that in God which seeks the perfection of all His creatures, and follows them with chastisements for the insurement of its end.

In the redemptive work of Christ, Clement sees no readjustment or restoration of a broken relationship between God and humanity, but rather the revelation of a relationship which had always existed, indestructible in its nature, obscured but not obliterated by human ignorance and sin. Humanity in the light of the incarnation appears as constitutionally allied with its Maker, as in its inmost being lovable and therefore loved by God. Truly to know Him who in love guides men to the life that is best, carries with it the recognition of duty and the obligation of obedience. The forgiveness of sin comes as by a spiritual law to those who respond to the divine Teacher speaking within the heart. In the life and especially the death of Christ lies the evidence of God's identification with man; the incarnation is in itself the atonement by which God reconciles the world unto Himself. God in Christ is seen sharing all that is darkest and most bitter in human experience, in order to the supreme manifestation of His love.[1]

According to Clement, faith is the inward response of a soul constituted for the truth ; it is the spiritual

[1] *Pædag.*, i. cc. 6, 8.

vision by which spiritual truth is discerned, corresponding in the sphere of spiritual things to the eye of the body in the world of external things.[1] It may be weak in its first ventures, but it grows stronger and clearer under the divine tuition; its tendency in the matured Christian is to pass over into that knowledge which is the absolute certainty of the things revealed, — the knowledge (Gnosis) of St. Paul when he said, "I know in whom I have believed." In this consciousness of the soul lies the principle of certitude. Back to it must be referred for final sanction, the teachings of philosophers, of apostles, and prophets. Clement admits no antithesis between faith and knowledge, between reason and revelation; knowledge enters into faith as one of its constituent elements;[2] reason and reflection are the avenues through which the divine revelation comes. What is called "culture" has therefore a close relationship to faith,[3] and human knowledge in all departments of inquiry is necessary for the comprehension of the Scriptures.[4] As Clement recognizes no schism in the divine nature between justice and love, so neither is there an antagonism between the faculties of the human soul. Those are wrong who make faith an exceptionally supernatural gift, as if it were sufficient in itself apart from the intellect or reason; faith in its highest aspect is truly natural, springing from the endowment of our constitution with God's image. But if Clement exalts what some have called the human element in religion and revelation, he does not fall into the error of thinking that man originates a revelation, or evolves the truth

[1] *Pædag.*, i. c. 6.
[2] *Pædag.*, i. c. 6; *Strom.*, i. c. 8; also vii. c. 10; and ii. c. 4.
[3] *Strom.*, i. c. 6.   [4] *Strom.*, i. c. 9.

by some internal process apart from God; for he cannot conceive of man except as under a continuous divine influence, under an education which binds him closely to those objective facts in human history through which the divine Instructor speaks to the reason, above all to the supreme historic fact of the incarnation of the Word. It is for this reason that Clement attaches the highest importance to the Scriptures both of the Old and New Testaments; he has grasped the principle which makes the Bible to be the word of God; everywhere he sees in the written Word the traces of the divine Instructor, exhorting and teaching, reproving and correcting, disciplining men by judgments and punishments, presenting Himself in the body as the consummate model of life, using all the events of life as the instruments of that spiritual education whose end is conformity to His own likeness.

But Clement's use of Scripture is also in harmony with the principle that all authority for spiritual truth lies in its last analysis, within the consciousness of man. He does not adduce scriptural proof as having an independent value for the support of tenets obnoxious to the reason, which must be received if at all on evidence external to the reason. Although he has given no formal definition of inspiration, it is clear that he regards it as having the same general character in the sacred writers that it has among the best of Greek philosophers;[1] it is no arbitrary action of God upon the human faculties, but rather the high exhibition of that capacity with which the human constitution is endowed in virtue of its divine affiliation, and by which is discerned the revelation which God is

[1] *Strom.*, i. c. 13; *Ibid.* vi. c. 17.

always making to the world;[1] in its highest action it still corresponds in principle, however it may differ in degree, with the humblest insight of faith.[2] Hence the verification of Christian truth is dependent upon no line of hierarchical descent; the apostles are to be revered and followed, not so much because they were apostles, but because and in so far as they have penetrated into the divine treasures of the incarnate Word; the true successors of the apostles[3] are they who like them live perfectly in accordance with the highest reason.

In his relation toward heresy the position of Clement differs greatly from the attitude of the Roman church in his own day, or that of the later degenerate church of the East. Although he lived in the centre from which most of the heresies proceeded, and was familiar with them in their worst forms, yet such is his faith in the power and invincibleness of the truth, that he believes in the freest examination, and boldly urges upon the heretics themselves the necessity for a deeper study of the faith as the remedy for false opinions. He does not fall back upon a creed or rule of faith to be received on the external authority of the church or of tradition; he does not appeal to any tribunal to cut off the heretics from the communion of the faithful; he does not denounce them in extravagant language in order to show a becoming horror for their tenets. From some of his allusions to the heretics, it appears that he regarded them as men earnest and sincere in the pursuit of truth. When those outside of the church urge the diversity of opinion within its ranks as an argument against joining the Christian

[1] *Strom.*, i. c. 19.
[2] *Strom.*, i. c. 4; *Ibid.* c. 9.   [3] *Strom.*, vi. c. 13.

communion, he replies that there are many sects in philosophy, and yet one does not refuse for that reason to philosophize; that there are many opposite opinions in medicine, and yet one does not decline to call in a physician.[1] Heresies call for a deeper and more searching inquiry, they entail a greater labor on the seeker for truth, but for this very reason they are aids to the discovery of the truth.[2] As to the heretics themselves, if their errors proceed from vanity or self-will, or any other evil root, the remedy lies with the divine Instructor, the living present Christ, whose discipline and chastisements alone can wean them from their evil state to the knowledge of Himself.[3] So far as their errors proceed from a superficial use of the reason, the remedy lies in a fuller use of the reason. If they have mistaken the sense of Scripture, they are to be invited to its more thorough study. Clement wrote no books, as did some of the fathers, "against all heresies," for the purpose of a detailed exposure of error; but he did that which was better: he combated the errors most effectively by writings whose object was to exhibit the truth in the fullness of its attraction and adaptation for man; indeed his entire literary activity may be regarded as one great apology for the Christian faith by showing what the faith really was.

Clement does not give any formal definition of the church, nor are his few allusions to the subject of a kind to satisfy those in search of a historical *catena* by which later notions regarding the church may be supported. There are no traces in his writings of the doctrine of apostolic succession; the unity of the church is nowhere made to depend upon unity with

[1] *Strom.*, vii. c. 15.
[2] *Ibid.*
[3] *Strom.*, vii. c. 16.

the bishop; baptism is not presented as essential to salvation; nor is salvation limited to those within the visible organization. The clergy are not regarded as having any special priestly character; in the current acceptation of terms, there is in the church neither priesthood, sacrifice, nor altar. Everywhere the Scriptures are placed above the church as well as before it, and Scripture is not intrusted to the hierarchy for preservation or interpretation, but to the Christian conscience. And yet the church which Clement portrays has its *notes*. Its main characteristic is ethical. It is composed of those who realize their calling as the children of God, who have put aside the old man and stripped off the garment of wickedness, and put on the immortality of Christ. The church has also organic life; it is a community of men who are led by the divine Logos, an invincible city upon earth which no force can subdue, where the will of God is done as it is in heaven. The church is like a human being,[1] consisting of many members; it is refreshed and grows; it is welded and compacted together; it is fed and sustained by a supernatural life, and becomes in its turn, in the hands of the divine Instructor, a means of leading humanity into life. The bond of the church's unity, the secret of the church's life and growth, is the living personal Christ, whose immanence in humanity is the only force adequate to its deliverance from sin, and its final perfecting according to the original purpose of its creation.

The sacraments, and, in general, the rites of worship, do not meet any extensive treatment in the writings of Clement. What is said on these topics is always in the way of incidental allusion rather than

[1] *Pædag.*, i. c. 6.

of direct exposition. In Clement's thought, the real presence and the divine activity of the living personal Christ is organically related to the soul, in all times and places, in all the conditions and circumstances of life. He alone purifies man from sin, leads him to repentance, and prepares him for that supreme moment when, in the waters of baptism, he takes the vow of self-consecration to the divine will. He alone everywhere and always gives Himself to humanity as the bread of life. Hence the sacraments became symbols of great spiritual processes; they are signs, and effective signs, of an actual purification and an actual sustenance. But the vast spiritual reality is never limited, diminished, or materialized by identifying the sign with the thing signified. The water of baptism is charged with no magical potency; the bread and wine are not transmuted into spiritual power operating as by a mechanical law; the bread and wine stand as metaphors [1] of that eternal Word of life conveyed by God in Christ to those who know to receive it, by the many and diverse channels of approach to which the soul lies open. The idea of a sacrifice in the eucharist which the church pleads before God, or which propitiates the divine favor, is disavowed : " Neither by sacrifices nor offerings, nor, on the other hand, by glory and honor, is the Deity won over, nor is He influenced by any such things ; " " we glorify Him who gave Himself in sacrifice for us, we also sacrificing ourselves." [2] There is in the nature of spiritual things no other sacrifice than that of self to do God's will, which man can offer to the Eternal.[3] "The altar that is with us here on earth is the congregation of those who devote themselves to prayer, having, as it were, one common

[1] *Pædag.*, i. c. 6.   [2] *Strom.*, vii. c. 3.   [3] *Strom.*, vii. c. 6.

voice and mind." "The sacrifice of the church is the word breathing as incense from holy souls, the sacrifice and the whole mind being at the same time unveiled to God."

In the lifetime of Clement, the contagion of a false asceticism was beginning to spread in the church, although its recognition as a principle of the Christian life was still chiefly confined to the heretical sects, such as the Montanists and the Gnostics. In opposition to those who advocated voluntary poverty or the abandonment of property, by a misunderstanding of the teaching of Christ, Clement reasons that it is the inordinate love of money which the Saviour condemns; that the abuse of riches, not their possession, hurts the soul. What Christ desires is the conversion of the inward man to Himself, and this can be accomplished by no external procedure. It is God's design that property should be unequally distributed; the divine education of humanity includes the right use of riches; they are the stewardship of a trust for one's own benefit, and that of others. Hence the doctrine of the community of goods appears to him to controvert the divine will.[1] Clement does not conceive of fasting as consisting in abstinence from meat and wine; such an idea prevailed in heathen religions, and has no essential relationship to Christian culture.[2] There is a true fasting,[3] which lies not in the mortification of the body or the endeavor to extirpate the physical appetites, but in obtaining the mastery over sin; the abstinence from all evil in thought, word, or action, — from covetousness and voluptuousness, from which all vices flow. The only true fasting is that

[1] *Strom.*, iii. c. 9. [2] *Strom.*, iii. c. 7.
[3] *Pædag.*, vii. c. 12; *Strom.*, vi. c. 12; *Ibid.* vii. c. 12.

which God has appointed, — to loose the bands of wickedness, to dissolve the knots of oppressive contracts, to let the oppressed go free, to cover the naked, and to shelter the homeless poor. Against those who urged the celibate life as preferable in itself, on the ground that thus a greater work could be done for God, or the salvation of the individual soul more perfectly secured, Clement maintained that marriage is a divine ordinance, given to subserve the loftiest purposes of human education and discipline, and not a concession to the flesh. He who is married is more of a man and fitted for a larger work for God, in that he receives thereby the fuller, more complex discipline of life, in his solicitude for wife and children, home and possessions, remaining faithful through all temptations, and inseparable from the love of God.[1] In Clement's application the words of Christ, "There am I in the midst of them," apply to the family, where father and mother and children gather together in his name.[2]

The principle which made Clement strong to resist the sinister tendencies of asceticism sprang from his idea of God and of His relationship to the world. The world is sacred as a divine creation, — the abode of indwelling Deity; the human body is the temple of a Holy Spirit, and becomes a very sanctuary by consecration to the will of God. The outward world is ordered in the divine purpose for the well-being of man, its beauty is the reflection of a higher, diviner beauty; it belongs to one organic whole, the disowning of which in any part is to distrust God and contemn His wisdom. While the power of self-restraint is one of the divinest gifts of God to man.

[1] *Strom.*, vii. c. 12. [2] *Strom.*, iii. c. 10.

and temperance and moderation are to be followed in all things, so that the life of the senses does not entangle and weaken the higher energies of the spirit, yet every creature of God is good and to be received with thankfulness; "The economy of creation is good, and all things are well-administered: nothing happens without a cause. I must be in what is thine, O omnipotent One; and if I am, then am I near Thee."[1] Man, it is true, is in this world as in a pilgrimage; yet he uses inns and dwellings by the way; he has a care of the things of the world, of the places where he halts. The wise man is ready to leave his dwelling-place and property without excessive emotion, he gives thanks for his sojourn, and blesses God for his departure. We are sojourners in the world, but we are also at home in the world. No one is a stranger to the world by nature, for their essence is one, and God is one.[2]

Clement has expressed himself sparingly in reference to the future life, and what are called the "last things." Either he is not interested in questions which cannot be solved, and avoids the sphere of mere opinion, or his mind is preoccupied with the theme of redemption, as calling out and satisfying the highest energies of the soul. The opinion once so generally held, especially among Jewish Christians, and still prevailing among the Christians in the West in Clement's own time, that Christ was soon to make a second personal coming in the flesh, in order to introduce a millennium for the faithful and to take vengeance upon his adversaries, is to his mind irrational, for it contradicts his supreme conviction that the essential spiritual Christ is already here in the fullness of his

[1] *Strom.*, iv. c. 23. [2] *Strom.*, iv. c. 26.

exalted might, and has already begun to witness his triumph "at the right hand of the Father." The judgment of the world is not viewed as a fixed event in the distant future, but as now forming part, an integral part, of the process by which the human race is educated under its divine Instructor. The motives and sanctions of the higher spiritual life are not the rewards of future bliss; but the service and imitation of God for His own sake is the inspiration and reward of the truly enlightened Christian.[1] Clement did not accept the opinion regarding the resurrection, which was received in the West, and sustained by Tertullian, that the identical flesh of the body which had been laid in the grave would be reanimated; the resurrection was the standing up again in immortal life; it was not the same body, but a reclothing in some higher form of the purified spirit. The future life is conceived as existing in different stages of blessedness on the principle of a progressive development. "God works all things up to what is better."[2] The beneficent work of the Saviour is not restricted by any accidents of time or place, but He operates to save at all times and everywhere. "If in this life there are so many ways for purification and repentance, how much more should there be after death. The purification of souls when separated from the body will be easier. We can set no limits to the agency of the Redeemer; to redeem, to rescue, to discipline, is His work, and so will He continue to operate after this life."[3] It may be that Clement had limited notions of the immensity of the universe, as modern astronomy has revealed it; but

[1] *Strom.*, iv. c. 22.
[2] *Strom.*, iv. c. 26.
[3] *Strom.*, vi. c. 6; cf. Neander, *His'ory of Doctrine*, p. 254.

even had he known all that we know, one cannot think that it would have shaken his faith in the doctrine of the incarnation, — that the insignificance of this planet among the millions of the spheres would have been to him a reason why God could not have walked it in human form. His belief in the inherent worth of the individual soul, as constituted after the divine image, would not allow him to succumb to the thought that man was created practically an animal only, with the possibility attached of some time receiving an immortal spirit in virtue of his own exertions; or, on the other hand, that any soul could continue forever to resist the force of redeeming love. Somehow and somewhere, in the long run of ages, that love must prove mightier than sin and death, and vindicate its power in one universal triumph.

The theology of Clement has been presented at some length, because, as the first of the great Greek fathers, he stands in the same relation to those that came after him that Augustine sustained to the Latin theology of the Middle Ages, or Luther and Calvin to the later Protestantism. The modifications of his thought by later fathers were considerable; but as in the mediæval church the type of Augustine's theology continued to prevail though some of his tenets were discarded, or as Lutheranism and Calvinism, while abandoning much that was essential in the attitude of their leaders, still retained a certain faithfulness to them which continued to manifest itself in their history, so the Greek theology, as presented or developed by Origen, Athanasius, Basil, and the two Gregories, remained substantially true to the spirit of Clement's teaching.

In one respect, Clement had an advantage over all that followed him. He lived in a fresh creative epoch; his age witnessed the production of the ancient creeds, those spontaneous utterances welling forth from the heart of the church, which, as summaries of great convictions by which the soul of man was possessed, have an enduring freshness and value which no lapse of time can impair. It was Clement's peculiar merit that he kept himself so free from entanglement with mere opinions. He never lost sight of the distinction between God as the great reality and all human speculations about Him. In his own words, "there is a difference between declaring God and declaring things about God." To declare God was the ruling purpose of his life. He held, or rather was held, by a supreme conviction, that God and humanity were bound together in one through Christ; that God did not leave men to themselves in the search after Him, but was forever going forth in Christ to seek after men and to lead them into life.

It was some such truth as this for which Plutarch had been yearning, which he and many other noble heathens were in vain trying to extract from the old polytheism. Had Marcus Aurelius known of such a teacher as Clement described, it would seem as though the inmost need of his being must have been met and satisfied.

The history of the age in which Clement lived yields no traces of the extent of his influence, vast as we may feel that influence must have been. It is strange how almost all knowledge of the man himself has disappeared. Only his books remain to show us what he was like. Judging from these, said the late Mr. Maurice, "he seems to me that one of the old fathers whom we all should have reverenced most as a teacher and loved as a friend." [1]

III.

Clement was succeeded in the headship of the school at Alexandria by Origen (186-254), who had been his pupil, and whose brilliant genius eclipsed the reputation of his teacher. The fame of Origen surpasses that of any other ancient father for the extent of his learning and the range of his mental powers. So profound was the impression which he left upon his own and succeeding ages, that he became the starting-point from which later directions of thought took their departure, while still acknowledging their indebtedness to his influence. Systems even that were hostile to each other, the right and the left wing in the trinitarian controversy, each claimed the sanction of his name. If Arius appealed to his authority, Athanasius was eager to vindicate his reputation for orthodoxy. For these reasons, Origen has been often taken as the best representative of the Greek theology, while the name of his master has been allowed to sink into neglect. There was another reason why Origen rather than Clement should have been identified so exclusively

---

[1] *Eccles. History of the First and Second Centuries*, p. 239. The name of Clement was retained in the calendar of the Roman Catholic Church as a saint until the close of the sixteenth century, when it was omitted under the pontificate of Clement VIII. (1592-1605). Pope Benedict XIII. (1724-1730) justified its omission, on the grounds that little was known of his life, that no popular cult had gathered round his memory, and that there were divergent estimates of the value of his teaching. It was manifestly an oversight that his name should have remained so long in the Roman calendar. Cf. Freppel, *Clement d'Alexandrie*, p. 65.

with Alexandrian theology. Coming as he did a generation after Clement, he fell upon an age which was seeking to define and justify, in speculative terms, the doctrine of the Christian trinity. When this great issue began to absorb the energies of the church, an earlier writer like Clement, who had not approached the problem on its purely intellectual side, nor contributed anything definite to its solution, would fall outside the circle of living interests.

But notwithstanding the different requirements of his age and his own mental independence, Origen was in substantial sympathy with the theology of his teacher. In his interpretation of the Christian faith, Clement reappears, often in greater clearness and fullness, as well as beauty of expression. It is therefore as unnecessary as it would be impossible to attempt a résumé of his complete thought. It is in his relation to philosophy that Origen diverged most widely from Clement, and to this divergence were owing the fanciful opinions which have disfigured his teaching, and which the common sense of the church, even in his own time, repudiated. Like Clement, Origen believed that philosophy was a divinely appointed means for attaining the truth. But Clement adhered to no one system of philosophical thought as containing the absolute truth, and possessed an inward vigor of spirit, by which the heathen elements in the systems of Plato or Aristotle or Zeno might be eliminated or transmuted by a higher method. "By philosophy," he says, "I do not mean the Stoic or the Platonic or the Epicurean or the Aristotelian, but whatever has been well said by each of those sects which teach righteousness along with a faith pervaded by piety."

Origen, on the contrary, came under the influence of the rising Neo-Platonism, and was inclined to receive it as a whole, to adopt its methods for the explication of the more recondite principles of Christian theology.[1] The principle of the Neo-Platonists, whose object was to create an eclectic system in which all forms of philosophy and religion might be harmonized, commended itself naturally to a mind like Origen's, with its vast capacity for generalizations, with its insatiate thirst for a system which should embrace all things in heaven and earth. Thus are explained his notions about the origin of evil, a fall in celestial circles, the preëxistence and transmigration of souls, the design of the body as a prison-house of the spirit, the prominence assigned to angels as corresponding somewhat to the demons of the old polytheism, and also his principle of biblical interpretation which led him to neglect the literal teaching of Scripture in the interest of some fancied higher truth discerned beneath the letter.[2]

While Origen was to some extent unfavorably in-

[1] After Origen had begun his career as a teacher in the Christian school in Alexandria, he placed himself under the instruction of Ammonius Saccas, the first of the long and distinguished line of Neo-Platonic philosophers. Euseb. *H. E.*, vi. 19. See, also, Mosheim's *Commentaries*, ii. sect. 27; Redepenning, *Origenes*, p. 230; Ritter, *Die Christliche Philosophie*, i. 340.

[2] Origen, it should be said, recognized a wide difference between his speculative fancies and the essentials of Christian revelation. Nor did the purity of his faith or the simplicity of his Christian character suffer from his intellectual vagaries. Mosheim, who had great contempt for his philosophical aberrations, says of him: "Certainly, if any man deserves to stand first in the catalogue of saints and martyrs, and to be annually held up as an example to Christians, this is the man." — *Commentaries*, ii. 149.

fluenced by Neo-Platonic thought, yet in his attitude toward the fundamental issues which it was the aim of that philosophy to explain, he rests upon the Christian revelation, and brings out the truth of the incarnation as that which can alone meet the needs of speculative inquiry or the wants of the religious life. In some respects, it is true, the Neo-Platonists had before them the same problem which confronted the Christian theologian. That problem was no other than to bind together in close organic unity the world and God, — to overcome the tendency to separation derived from oriental theosophies which was exerting its influence upon Greek philosophy as well as upon Christian thought. The dying words of Plotinus have been often quoted as expressing the ruling idea of his philosophy: "I am striving to bring the God which is in me into harmony with the God which is in the universe." One difference between the Christian thinker and the pagan philosopher lay in this: that the one started with the conviction of the divine immanence in the world and in humanity, while the other could not escape from the notion of God as primarily existing at an infinite distance, in an absolute isolation from the world. The problem of the Neo-Platonic philosopher had been already solved indeed, had he but known it, in the theology of the incarnation. Hence, however Origen may seem to approximate to the position of heathen thought, the appearance is but superficial; he may admit the heathen postulate of a distant and unknown Deity, and the admission may involve him in contradiction and confusion, but he never yields his conviction of the indwelling God as revealed in Christ. In Him the visible creation in all its grades of existence lives and moves and has its being; in Him it is the prerogative of humanity by virtue of its constitution to participate.[1]

The contribution of Origen toward the great question of his age was of the highest value to all who followed him. He did not indeed reach the true formula of the Christian trinity, but he made it possible for his successors to do so by his well-known doctrine of the eternal generation of the Son. When interpreted by the light of his age, that doctrine was the effort to bind together Father and Son and Holy Spirit in a necessary organic communion and fellowship. The result of the heathen belief invading the church was not only to separate God from man, but to separate also between the Father and the eternal Son; to reduce Christ to the rank of creatures brought into existence by the absolute will. In the doctrine of the eternal generation of the Son, Origen was resisting the heathen principle which makes God the absolute incommunicable Deity. From all eternity, so Origen reasoned, by a necessary law of His being, God communicates Himself to the Son, — the light which is the life and blessedness of the whole creation goes forth eternally from the source of light, as the rays go forth from the sun. To exist in relationship is the essential idea of God. To think otherwise would be to rob Deity of His true glory. If He existed alone in simple unity and solitary grandeur, apart from some object upon which from all eternity to expend His love, in whom He forever delighted to see Himself reflected, then He was not from all eternity God; His fatherhood, His love, His infinite power would be accessions to His being in the course of time. There would have been a time, therefore, when He was imperfect, when love

[1] *De Princip.*, i. c. 3.

did not go forth, when the light did not shine, when the righteousness and power of Deity lay idle and ineffective.[1]

Beyond this, Origen did not go. There remained another step to take, the nature of which could be seen, and its necessity demonstrated only when the logic of events should have ripened the mind of the church, and exposed more clearly the danger to which the Christian faith was exposed from the inroads of the heathen principle. To this end even the errors of Origen contributed. It was seen that his thought must be supplemented if the truth which he had reached was to be retained. For while Origen had asserted the eternal generation of the Son from the Father, he did not resist successfully the prevailing oriental notion that what is generated must be in some way inferior to the source from which it proceeds. Hence he had so subordinated the Son to the Father and the Spirit to the Son, that his conception of the trinity might be regarded as akin to the principle by which Neo-Platonism was seeking to revive the old polytheism.

Two directions in thought lay open to the church after Origen's departure, both of which claimed the authority of his reputation: the one, neglecting his doctrine of eternal generation, pushed to an extreme the principle of subordination; while the other dropped the idea of subordination, and asserting the coequality of the three distinctions in the divine name, sought to carry out all that was implied in the positive principle of a Son eternally generated from the Father. Long before Arius appeared the divergence had begun to be manifested. In what was known as Sabel-

[1] *De Princip.*, i. c. 2.

lianism may be read the protest of the Christian consciousness against the separation of the Son from the Father, or of the infinite Spirit from both. But this protest against separation and subordination was carried so far as to obliterate the eternal distinction between them. The tendency of what is known as Sabellianism, if it had prevailed, would have so enfeebled the Christian doctrine of the trinity as to make Father, Son, and Holy Spirit merely names for the diverse operations of God, and thus eventually have substituted for the complex and fruitful idea of Deity as given in the Christian revelation the single or simple essence of Jewish or Mohammedan deism. To this result the Arianism of a later age was also tending, though by a different process.

The situation was a difficult one, — to maintain the distinct and eternal existence of Father, Son, and Holy Spirit, while not denying the unity of the one God, and on the other hand to emphasize the divine unity without endangering with Sabellius the eternal distinctions within the bosom of Godhead. Jewish deism on the one hand, and polytheism on the other, were the Scylla and Charybdis between which the church was moving. Either of them was an easy and simple solution of the difficulty, and either of them was alike fatal to the Christian revelation. The issue became a clear one in the early part of the fourth century. The church was profoundly moved at the voice of Athanasius proclaiming, as the doctrine of God, the one essence within which coexisted, and as it were circulated from all eternity, the three vital and coequal forces or distinctions of Father, Son, and Holy Spirit.

IV.

Athanasius was born in the city of Alexandria in the year 296, and follows Origen as the next most illustrious representative of Greek theology. But it is not to Athanasius in his capacity as a theologian only that the church has decreed the highest honors. He has been designated the father of orthodoxy, but he is also the ecclesiastical hero in the supreme crisis of the church's career. He was great in himself, but he also owed his greatness to the environment of his age. What he might have been had he lived at an earlier period or under different circumstances it is useless to conjecture. The external events of his time developed in him a character not seen in the church before, — that of the statesman or ecclesiastical politician whose object it was not to attain martyrdom but triumph, who exposed himself to danger in order to secure success, who fought in order to conquer. It is sometimes forgotten in ecclesiastical circles, where it most needs to be remembered, that he fought not only the world in the shape of an intriguing imperial court, but his hardest conflicts were with the church itself, his greatest victory over the oriental bishops arrayed against him in a large majority. His name stands for the encouragement of those who resist the church in the interest of some higher truth which it has not yet learned to appreciate; his experience illustrates that one man standing out against the church may be right and the church may be wrong; and further, his life demonstrates how at all critical moments the faith takes refuge, not in institutions but in individual men. To Athanasius, with his clear insight and his unconquerable purpose, is it owing that the church was saved to the doctrine of the Christian trinity.

But all this belongs to the history of the church as an institution. We are concerned now only with the place of Athanasius in the history of Christian thought.

Born and brought up as he was in the home of Greek theology, he had drunk in the influence of that culture whose aim it has been said was the discovery of the highest beauty and the divinest wisdom. The traces of Greek philosophy are apparent in his writings, and the principles drawn from Greek philosophy underlie his controversy with the Arians. "He was a Greek by birth and education; Greek also in subtle thought and philosophical insight, in oratorical power and supple statesmanship." [1] In his theology the habit of spiritual thought seen in Clement and Origen is everywhere visible; all that was distinctive of Greek theology in its contrast with the later Latin belongs to him, not merely by way of traditional acceptance, but through the free concurrence of independent and original reflection.

The greater part of Athanasius' writings are of a controversial character. But in two small treatises written before Arius arose, we have the groundwork of the theology which served him in his long struggle. They are entitled, "A Treatise against the Greeks," and "The Incarnation of the Word." The value of the first treatise lies in the manner in which he conducts his polemic against heathenism. He broke away from the tiresome and fruitless method of former apologists, and addressed himself directly to

[1] Gwatkin, *Studies of Arianism*, p. 67; Fialon, *Saint Athanase*, 284-291.

the great issue between Christianity and polytheism. The class of educated men to whom he spoke no longer believed the absurd and immoral myths which the traditional apologist from force of habit continued to expose and ridicule. But while discarding the absurdities of mythology, men like Porphyry and Jamblichus still maintained that the world was created and governed by intermediaries, lower deities, who were the beneficent forces of nature, whose dwelling-place was in the sun or planets, in the ocean, in rivers, in forests and groves, or in the human mind. To worship them, they thought, was only to recognize through them the higher Deity from whom they proceeded. This was the point to which the controversy between Celsus and Origen had reduced itself. The emperor Julian, in a treatise now lost, in which he was combating Christianity, expressed the most deep-rooted conviction of heathenism when he said that what hindered him from giving his assent to the new religion was the impossibility, to his mind, of conceiving how the one and infinite God was able to govern the world without a retinue of intermediate deities.

Athanasius met this position in his discourse against the Greeks by asserting that there was no necessity for such intermediaries, since God Himself was dwelling in the creation, and that all things had been made directly or immediately by Him. The principle upon which he rested was the Stoic doctrine of the divine immanence. "The all-powerful and perfect reason of the Father," so he wrote, "penetrating the universe, developing everywhere its forces, illuminating with His light things visible and invisible, made of them all one whole and bound them together, allowing nothing to escape from his powerful action, vivifying and preserving all beings in themselves, and in the harmony of the creation." "In the light of the divine Logos, everything lives upon earth while all is organized in the heavens. There is nothing of that which is and which each day appears which has not its being in Him, and by Him, its place in the universal harmony." [1]

In his treatise on the incarnation one can see the inner process in Athanasius' mind as he labors to retain the Stoic principle of immanent Deity without confounding God with the world. Like his predecessors Clement and Origen, he builds his thought upon the divine immanence, not on the transcendence of God. "This divine Logos, a being incorporeal, expands Himself in the universe as light expands in the air, penetrating all, and all entire, everywhere. He gives Himself without losing anything of Himself, and with Him is given the Father who makes all things by Him, and the Spirit who is His energy." He unfolds Himself in all things without merging Himself in them. The Deity communicates Himself to His creatures, penetrates them, animates them, while yet remaining distinct from them, — the true God of humanity whose presence and love we feel, the vivifying intelligence which mingles and circulates in the great body of the universe.[2]

In order to know God He must be looked for within the soul.[3] The soul contemplates shining within itself as in a mirror, the image of the Father, the Word incarnate, and in itself it conceives the Father.[4] Upon

[1] *Contra Gentes*, c. 42.
[2] *De Incar. Verbi*, cc. 8, 17. Cf. also Dorner's *Person of Christ* Eng. trans. Div. i. vol. ii. p. 250.
[3] *Contra Gentes*, c. 33.   [4] *Contra Gentes*, c. 34.

this point, the way to the knowledge of God, the thought of Athanasius reproduces the teaching of Greek philosophy, and more especially that of the Stoic school. The revelation of God is written in the human consciousness; the ground of all certitude is within man, not in any authority external to his nature. "In order to know the way which leads to God and to take it with certainty, we have no need of foreign aid, but of ourselves alone. As God is above all, the way which leads to Him is neither distant, nor outside of us, nor difficult to find. The kingdom of God is within us. Since we have in us the kingdom of God, we are able easily to contemplate and conceive the King of the universe, the salutary reason of the universal Father. If any one asks of me, What is the way? I answer, that it is the soul of each and the intelligence which it encloses." [1] The wise man has no need to seek without himself, or to infer the divine existence from the external world. He sees God within himself, who is His image and as it were His shadow.

The preparation of a soul for seeking and knowing God is in its own purification. In order to rise to the knowledge of the truth, it is necessary to unite with the intelligence a virtuous life and purity of heart. It is the soul itself which of itself and by itself disengages itself from that which stains it, and is thus rendered worthy of entering into communion with Him who is purity. It is not through grace coming from without, but by a voluntary purification within, that man can see God. In thoughts like these, Athanasius was only asserting the principles implied in the doctrine of the incarnation. As he reasons in his discourse against the Greeks, it is through the revelation

[1] *Contra Gentes*, c. 30.

of God in Christ that man comes to know his real nature, and the power with which he has been invested. The revelation is a disclosing to man of his true constitution. Christ has come to break down the barriers of ignorance and neglect by which man is hindered from knowing himself in the capacities and destiny imprinted upon his nature in the first creation. Hence, with Athanasius as with his predecessors, the freedom of the will is an inalienable heritage in virtue of the human constitution in God's image; it still exists as the ability to turn to what is good, even after man has turned away to the evil; it cannot be forfeited or lost because it is the endowment of a constitution which is divine.[1]

If in any respect in his view of the incarnation, Athanasius advances upon the teaching of his predecessors, it is in the more emphatic assertion of the solidarity of the human race in Christ. Christ is the head and representative of all mankind, and through His organic relationship with humanity all that He was, all that He did, belongs to the race of man. From Him mankind inherits a glory and distinction in which all its members share; from Him a Spirit flows forth upon all, anointing them as with a precious ointment; or, in other words, humanity has been actually redeemed in Christ. He took upon Himself the sin and guilt of men; in Him all men died to sin; in Him all men suffered the consequences of sin; in Him all men share in the punishment of sin; all men inherit the blessing which through Him comes from the fulfillment of the law of righteousness, and all are clothed with incorruption through the power of the resurrection. The saving force which was in Him becomes

---

[1] Maurice, *Philosophy of the First Six Centuries*, pp. 85–90.

henceforth through Him inherent in the life of humanity and is diffused through all its members.[1]

No better illustration to set forth his thought can be found, than that which Athanasius himself employed: "As when a mighty king entering some great city, although he occupies but one of its houses, positively confers great honor upon the whole city, and no enemy or robber any longer throws it into confusion by his assaults, but on account of the presence of the king in one of its houses, the city is rather thought worthy of being guarded with the greatest care. So also is it in the case of Him who is Lord over all. For when He came into our country and dwelt in the body of one like ourselves, thenceforth every plot of the enemy against mankind was defeated, and the corruption of death that formerly operated to destroy men lost its power." [2]

In defending the truth of the incarnation against those who maintained that such a doctrine implied what was absurd and impossible, Athanasius draws his argument from Greek philosophy, and urges the Stoic principle of the divine immanence, as lending rationality and probability to the conviction that the Word became flesh and dwelt among men. "For the world itself may be thought of as one great body in which God indwells; and if He is in the whole, He is also in the parts. It is no more unworthy of God that He should incarnate Himself in one man, than it is that He should dwell in the world. Since he abides in humanity, which is a part of the universe, it is not unreasonable that he should take up His abode in a man who should thus become the organ by which God acts on the universal life."[3]

[1] *De Incar.*, cc. 8, 9, 20; *Oratio contra Arianos*, i. 46–48.
[2] *De Incar.*, c. 9.   [3] *De Incar.*, c. 41.

The process by which the historical Christ who lived and taught in Judæa is identified with the eternal Word of God made flesh, does not for Athanasius depend primarily upon any external evidence for its verification. Miracles in his view illustrate the intimate relationship of Christ to the physical world as its Lord and Master, and given the Christ, they are results to be expected by way of confirmation of that which is already perceived and believed. But the greatest miracles are wrought in the sphere of the spiritual life, and it is by these that the miracle in the outward life of nature is corroborated. For example, the evidence of the resurrection of Christ is to be found mainly in the reality of the church's life. When the darkness of the material world gives way to light, it is proof that the sun has appeared. So also in the spiritual world, the light which is diffused where before there was darkness is evidence that Christ still lives. Once men lived under bondage through fear of death; now death has lost its sting; even women and children voluntarily submit to it. In the power which effects the conversion of the heathens, in the influence which transforms the life, in these and results like these lies the evidence that Christ is not dead, that He is risen from the grave. The Saviour Himself continues to offer the proof of His resurrection in the works which He still accomplishes for the salvation of men.[1]

Such had been the teaching of Athanasius before the year 318, when Arius arose in Alexandria. Arius had had his precursors in the history of the church. In the sect of the Ebionites, and in the pseudo-Clementine writings of the second century, may be seen a view of Deity struggling for recognition, which, at a later

[1] *De Incar.*, cc. 27–32.

time, was to find its full development in the teaching of Mohammed. The Jewish faith was so popular in the second century throughout the Roman empire that it threatened to break the bonds of national exclusiveness, and expand into an universal religion.[1] Had it done so, it might have anticipated by centuries the system of Islam, which like Judaism commended itself to deep-rooted instincts in the oriental mind.

Arius had received his training, not in Alexandria, but in Antioch, a city which, located as it was on the eastern confines of the empire, had not been able, despite its attachment to Hellenic culture, to overcome the preponderating influence of orientalism. Here toward the close of the third century was growing up a school of Christian thought, antagonistic in its spirit to that which had constituted the ruling idea of Greek theology, — a school which was destined also to leave its impression on the Christian church. The leading characteristic of the school of Antioch was the oriental tendency it displayed to separate the human from the divine. The tie which united them, however it may have been viewed, did not spring out of the natural kinship of the human with the divine, — a kinship always existing, but revealed in the splendor of its perfection in Christ. In the Antiochian theology there was a disposition to regard the *nexus* between the Deity and humanity as the arbitrary exertion of the divine power, by which natures incongruous and incompatible in their essence had been brought together in an artificial alliance rather than a living union.

Beneath this conception of the relation of the human to the divine lurked the oriental idea of God as the absolute and incommunicable, for whom contact

[1] Renan, *Le Judaisme comme Race et comme Religion*, p. 20.

with humanity or with the world was by his very nature impossible. From such a point of view, the incarnation of God in Christ was not only inconceivable by the reason, but seemed also to endanger the well-being of true religion.

Arius was the first to formally advocate such a view of Deity, and to follow it out in its logical consequences to the denial of the incarnation. Of his sincerity there can be no doubt, nor of his high moral character. It does not surprise us to learn that he was a strict ascetic, surpassing in this respect his Christian contemporaries; for asceticism was a necessary concomitant of oriental religion, and had *at first* appeared in those sects and heresies claiming an oriental origin before it made itself at home in the church. The time in which Arius lived was favorable to the spread of his thought, for the Roman emperor had just professed himself a Christian, and the world was willing to follow in his train if only the one obnoxious tenet of the incarnation could be so modified as to reconcile Christianity with the principle of heathen religion.

To this task Arius addressed himself in all earnestness, and with singular powers of influence and even fascination. In his theology God is conceived in his absolute transcendence as at an infinite distance from the world and humanity, and in his solitary grandeur forever abides beyond the possibility of communion with any creature. For the purpose of creating the world He calls into existence a highly endowed supernatural being of a different essence from His own, who yet participates to some extent in the attributes of Godhead, and is therefore worthy of being called a god. In reality He is neither God nor man, but stands midway between the two, as far below the one as He is exalted above the other. Because of the inferiority and limitation of his nature compared with that of Deity, He is not able to perfectly comprehend the character of God. What He sees and knows of God is after a measure proportionate to His capacity, and the revelation which He imparts to man is still further reduced and limited by the weakness of human faculties. God therefore remains in His inmost character unknown and unknowable; revelation becomes a regulative principle of conduct, but is no longer a ground for communion between the human and the divine. Union with Deity, according to such a theology, is impossible. The supernatural being whom Arius sets forth as a mediator between God and man, does not unite but separates them, for He serves to reveal the infinite impassable gulf that lies between them.

The system of Arius was in its principle a reversion to Jewish deism, as if it had been the highest type of human thought concerning the nature of Deity. But it was also a system inferior to Judaism and even to Mohammedanism, for it was weakened rather than strengthened by its adherence to Christ at all. In Jewish and Mohammedan theology the world is at least created directly by God Himself, whereas according to Arius, creation is the work of a being inferior to God. The door was thus opened for a return to polytheism, and there was no obstacle to the introduction of many such beings, inferior to God and yet higher than man, who should serve as intermediaries in the economy of external nature or of the spiritual life.

If it seems strange that a system like this could have grown up within the church and have spread far and wide, it is only necessary to recall how strong was the hold of the dying heathenism over the imagination, or how, at a later time, Islamism snatched away a vast Christian population and took possession of what had once been the fairest possessions of eastern Christendom. In both cases the rationale of the process was the same. Humanity, overcome with the sense of sin, and struck with fear and terror as it contemplated the judgments of God in the world, was under the control of motives bred by a diseased and guilty conscience in its thought of God, and could not accept the pure consciousness of Christ, with his filial love and perfect trust toward the Father, as the normal principle of true religion. Rather than accept it, men adopted methods of their own by which to overcome the divine wrath, or acquiesced in any arrangement, however superficial, by which the consequences of sin might be evaded. Such was the principle of Judaism, in its popular aspects a religion in which God was believed to be propitiated by sacrifices. Such was Mohammedanism, with its doctrine of election, in which the followers of the prophet took refuge as a shelter from the waves of the divine anger; and akin to them was Arianism, — a symptom that the popular Christianity was shifting its basis from love to fear, and was thus endangering what was highest and most distinctive in the religion of Christ. Whether God was present or absent, whether humanity had been redeemed or still lay under the curse of sin, whether the incarnation had revealed the inmost nature of God, as written in the nature of man, or the revelation made by Christ was an official code of duty promulgated by some high celestial ambassador, — such were the issues involved in the Arian controversy.

The excitement which shook the church as if to its

very foundations, and which threatened to destroy its unity, on which Constantine rested his hopes for the consolidation of the empire, indicates the gravity of the crisis which the teaching of Arius had precipitated. In this critical hour, it was not Rome that came to the rescue. She was as silent, it has been said, as St. Peter at the door of Caiaphas when Christ was delivered up to the power of the High Priest. It was a Greek theologian, going forth from the home of Greek theology, who uttered the word to which the heart of the church ultimately responded.

According to Athanasius, the Christian revelation is summed up in the divine name of the Father, the Son, and the Holy Spirit. Into this name, and into the actual and living relationships which it implies, those who accept the religion of Christ were to be baptized. It was the formula of benediction, the ever-recurring refrain in the solemn and inspiring worship of the church. It declared of God that His essential character was love. Deity in the inmost recess of His being, in that mysterious background of existence, as ancient thought conceived it, whence sprang the divine consciousness and thought and will, was henceforth known truly and absolutely as the Father. The deepest and most endearing of human relationships found its basis in the divine nature, and received its consecration from an eternal prototype.

The revelation of God as the Father was made through the Son. He who became incarnate in the fullness of time had been from all eternity with the Father, as His second self, in whom the Father knew Himself and saw Himself reflected. By Him the world had been created; upon its constitution had been stamped the impress of the divine nature; and in humanity was implanted the image of God, through which it was made capable in its totality of attaining the divine likeness. All things in heaven and earth live and move and have their being in Him, — the indwelling God, who is all and in all. In the incarnation God not only reveals Himself to man, but also makes known to man his true nature and constitution. The incarnation is the union of humanity with Deity, and the divine life of Christ, who is the head and representative of humanity, is diffused through all its members. Humanity, in all its fortunes and aspects, is one whole, and as such has been redeemed in Christ, who carries it, as it were, in Himself, — in its sin and guilt as well as in its exaltation and glory. In Him the human race has died to sin and risen again to life and immortality. Life has been shown stronger than death, righteousness mightier than sin. In Him has been manifested the apotheosis of humanity, its redemption, salvation, and deification.

The incarnation made possible the life of the Spirit, through whom mankind becomes increasingly conscious of its relationship to the Father and the Son. The holy and infinite Spirit is the life of the Father and the Son as they are bound together in perfect communion and fellowship; the work of the Spirit is to lead men to participate in this life which is in God. The Spirit abides in humanity as the law of its progress; He acts upon all men; but He indwells only in those who have been renewed after the image of Him that created them.[1]

Such a conception of the nature of the triune Godhead as existing from eternity and manifested in time,

[1] On the immanent trinity, cf. Voigt, *Jahrb. für Deutsche Theol.*, 1858.

demanded that its members should be regarded as in their essence one and coequal, and as forming together the one absolute or infinite personality whom we call God.[1] It was a result of Arianism that it showed to Athanasius the nature of the danger which threatened the integrity of the Christian revelation, and the step also which must be taken to guard against it. As the tendency of Arianism was to separate between Christ and the Father, between the world and God, so the aim of Athanasius was to present them as sharing alike in the one divine essence, and thus retain the world and humanity in close organic relationship with Deity. The word which he used for the purpose of defining the relation of the Son to the Father, — the ὁμοούσιος, — was, to the minds of many even who did not sympathize with Arius, a damaged and suspicious word. It had been first used by Sabellius, and then by Paul of Samosata, and had thus been identified with the heresies of a past age which the church had condemned. To the minds of the majority of Eastern bishops[2] it still savored of the pantheism with which it had been first associated. It was the one word which was most obnoxious to the Arians, the significance of which their dialectic could not evade. It was irreconcilable with the Arian trinity, in which three beings were loosely associated in polytheistic fashion. It presented God in the richness of a complex nature, triple in His unity and one in His triplicity, in opposition to Judaism, with its meagre, impoverished notion of unity as identical with singleness of essence.

[1] Liddon, *Bampton Lectures*, p. 37.
[2] For the attitude of the Asiatic bishops to the Nicene controversy, see Gwatkin, *Studies of Arianism*, pp. 90–92.

The ὁμοούσιος was admitted into the creed of the church at its first general council; but it was not on the authority of the council that the church received it. The synod of Nicæa was the beginning of a long controversy, in which Athanasius bore the principal part, and in which the question was argued with all the subtilty of the oriental mind, — whether Christ was of the same essence with the Father, or of a similar essence, or of a different essence. The victory of the ὁμοούσιος was at last a victory of the reason; it was the triumph of the Greek theology over oriental theosophies, whether Jewish or heathen; it stood for the sign by which the church had overcome the heathen mind, as Christian faith had already overcome the force of persecution and the sword.

But the Christian doctrine of the trinity could not have triumphed over heathen thought, had it not also been the fulfillment of all that was true in Greek philosophy. In the formula of Father, Son, and Holy Spirit, as three distinct and coequal members in the one divine essence, there was the recognition and the reconciliation of the philosophical schools which had divided the ancient world. In the idea of the eternal Father the oriental mind recognized what it liked to call the profound abyss of being, that which lies back of all phenomena, the hidden mystery which lends awe to human minds seeking to know the divine. In the doctrine of the eternal Son revealing the Father, immanent in nature and humanity as the life and light shining through all created things, the divine reason, in which the human reason shares, was the recognition of the truth after which Plato and Aristotle and the Stoics were struggling, — the tie which binds the creation to God in the closest organic relationship.

In the doctrine of the Holy Spirit, the church guarded against any pantheistic confusion of God with the world by upholding the life of the manifested Deity as essentially ethical or spiritual, revealing itself in humanity in its highest form, only in so far as humanity realized its calling, and through the Spirit entered into communion with the Father and the Son.

It is true, as has been often noticed, that the ancient church dwelt chiefly upon Christ as the indwelling Deity who manifested the Father, and that the idea of the Holy Spirit is not formally presented with equal prominence.[1] But it was necessary that the incarnation should become the full possession of the Christian consciousness before the life of the Spirit could be understood or appreciated. To the infinite Spirit it belongs, in the economy of the trinity, to lead humanity into all truth. But the "ways of the Spirit" had yet to be disclosed more fully to the reason in the long and painful process of human experience, — the world that then was had to pass away, and a new world to arise, and grow, and reach maturity, before the life of God as the Spirit could be revealed in humanity as its actual possession, by which it shares while on earth in the glory of the eternal trinity, and moves forward to its destiny in attaining the fullness of Christ. It has been given to us to read in the church's history, since the new world in western Europe began its career, the larger record of the continuous divine revelation, and to trace the process by which the Spirit has been convincing of sin, and of righteousness, and of judgment. As we survey our inheritance in the past, we

---

[1] For a summary of the views of "thoughtful men" upon the subject of the Holy Spirit, see Greg. Naz., *Oratio* 38, *De Spiritu Sancto.*

are unrolling what to the Fathers of the ancient church was a future hidden from their eyes. In the fresh enthusiasm of a great conviction, they dwelt upon the glorious consummation of all things in Christ, and were inclined to foreshorten the long perspective of human history. It is as though to them the words of Christ were more especially addressed: "I have many things to say unto you, but ye cannot bear them now."

THE LATIN THEOLOGY.

Etenim cum deberetis magistri esse propter tempus: rursum indigetis ut vos doceamini quæ sint elementa exordii sermonum Dei.—HEB. v. 12.

CHRONOLOGICAL TABLE.

A. D.
14. Death of Augustus Cæsar.
150. [c.] Montanism and Gnosticism.
160. Apuleius flourished.
201. (?) Tertullian becomes a Montanist.
202. Irenæus died.
235. Hippolytus died.
249-251. Decius, Emperor.
258. Cyprian died a martyr.
306-337. Constantine the Great.
311-415. Donatist Controversy.
312. Toleration granted to the church.
323. Constantine sole Emperor.
331-420. Jerome.
333. Jamblichus died.
374-397. Ambrose, Bishop of Milan.
379-395. Theodosius the Great, Emperor.
387. Augustine's Conversion.
396-430. Augustine, Bishop of Hippo.
397-407. Chrysostom, Patriarch of Constantinople.
412-431. Pelagian Controversy.
412-444. Cyril, Patriarch of Alexandria.
429. Nestorius, Patriarch of Constantinople.
429. Theodore of Mopsuestia died.
431. Third General Council.
440-461. Leo the Great, Bishop of Rome.
451. Fourth General Council.
485. Proclus died.
553. Fifth General Council.
622. Flight of Mohammed.
680. Sixth General Council.

THE LATIN THEOLOGY.

In the Latin church, theology was subordinated to the requirements of an ecclesiastical hierarchy. The Roman church gave birth to no system of theology. It devoted its energies from the first to the work of perfecting its organization and of exercising its capacity for discipline and control. The foundations of the later primacy of the Bishop of Rome date back to a very early stage of Christian history. Roman controversialists have not been very far wrong in making the preparation for the Roman supremacy almost coeval with the birth of the Roman church.

During the second century, the Latin church was under the influence of Greek thought, and for some time longer the echoes of Greek theology continued to be heard in its principal writers. It was rather as souvenirs of a culture which had been abandoned, than as living and profound intuitions of thought, that Greek ideas appear among the Latin writers of the second and third centuries. However this may be, Christianity had come to the West from the East. It was Greek missionary enterprise and not Roman that carried the Christian faith to Gaul. The writings of apostles, the narratives of the life of Christ, had appeared in the Greek language; even the ritual of the Roman church, so far as one existed, may have been in Greek, and the circumstance mentioned by the historian Socrates, that during the first centuries there was no public preaching in Rome, may be explained by the absence of the vernacular in the Christian assemblies. But it was impossible that the Greek influence should long dominate over a spirit so deeply imbued with native characteristics as the Roman. In the course of the third century, the Latin language was generally substituted for the Greek, and the process began by which the two churches were to grow more widely apart, until all Christian fellowship between them should come to an end.

As in the history of Greek theology the continuity with Greek philosophy was not broken; so in the history of Latin Christianity the continuity may be traced with pagan Rome in its religious as well as its political aspects.

I.

The early religion of pagan Rome discloses no principles which distinguish it in any marked way from other local religions. It has enriched in no way our knowledge of the religious consciousness of man. It was essentially a borrowed product, with no traditions of its own running back to the origin of things. It was a formal thing, consisting mainly in the scrupulous performance of a ritual. It did not stimulate devotion, or give rise to hymnody, or lead to mystic excesses. It rested on a belief in the power of the gods which, by the use of right methods, might be made available for the requirements of Roman ambition. It was a religion grounded on fear as its motive and sanction. The Romans did not cultivate friendly or intimate relations with their gods as did the Greeks; there was no sense of the constant nearness of a divine benignant presence as is seen in Greek mythology. The Roman kept his gods at a distance, and avoided as a calamity the actual vision of a supernatural being. The chief innovation which Rome introduced into religion was in illustrating its connection with the fortunes of the state. Religion became an affair of the government, to be administered chiefly in its interest. When the conquests of Rome had demonstrated the value of Roman deities to the state, it was only natural and fitting that the highest officer of the state should assume a religious character, and, as Pontifex Maximus, preside over the administration of the sacred deposit by which the priesthood deciphered the secrets of the future.

The religion of ancient Rome, despite its lack of interest in theology, could not remain apart from the larger movements of thought, at a time when the human mind was so widely occupied with religious issues. From the time of Augustus it had begun to recover from the disintegrating effects of the rationalism which had prevailed in the last days of the republic.[1] To some extent it had been clarified and elevated by the Stoic philosophy, so that it seemed not unworthy of the respect and devotion of a man like Marcus Aurelius. But the Stoic interpretation of polytheism, attractive as it might have been to poetical minds or to the highly educated, must have seemed to the mass of ordinary men like explaining religion away. The gods, as the Stoics viewed them, were no longer personal beings, but rather impersonal manifestations of the presence of the universal spirit which penetrates and fills all things, so many different names, as it were, for the activity of the divine soul of the uni-

[1] Boissier, *La Religion Romaine*, ii. c. 7.

verse. It was through the influence of Platonism, which had been made popular in Rome by the writings of Apuleius during the second century, that polytheism became once more a living belief affecting profoundly all classes of society. Apuleius proclaimed the Platonic notion regarding the nature of Deity and His relation to the world, a being who exists in solitary majesty outside of the world, who, having accomplished creation by an act of omnipotence, secludes Himself at a distance from all communication or connection with it. Thus the tie which unites God to nature is broken: on the one side is God, and on the other man, and a vast abyss lies between them. To bridge this abyss, Apuleius employed as intermediaries the gods of ancient religion, — no longer names only for spiritual functions as the Stoics thought, but real existences, who from their lowest form, as the demons standing near to men, rise by gradations to the throne of infinite Deity. This was the underlying principle which everywhere quickened polytheism into activity, the spirit in the air when the writings of the first distinctively Latin fathers were beginning to appear.

It was inevitable that in the transition from heathenism to Christianity, the influence of such tendencies should be perpetuated, and in some degree modify the character of the new religion. The practical bent of the Roman mind, the love of order, the genius for government, were destined, like the Greek love for philosophy, to find a home in the Christian church. The Roman Christian may have begun very early to dream of the possibility that his new worship might be a substitute for the pagan state cultus, — the Christian hierarchy standing in the same close relation to the empire, usurp the place of the sacerdotal machinery of paganism. For the empire itself the Christian converts continued to cherish admiration and reverence. To their minds it was doing a divine work in breaking down the barriers of a selfish individualism, bringing the nations into a common fellowship, and consolidating them into one great people; extending to all, rich and poor, equal privileges under a system of uniform law. This was also, as the Roman Christian conceived it, with the necessary modifications, the idea of Christianity itself. The religion of Christ was to him the "new law," and in obedience to rightful authority lay the principle of redemption. Latin Christianity gravitated naturally, as if by instinct, toward that conception of the church as an external kingdom which sprang out of the Jewish conception of Messiah, and of which the apostles of Christ had dreamed while they were striving about the places of honor which it offered. It is possible that a similar idea underlay the organization of the church in Jerusalem, where James, in virtue of his relationship as the brother of Christ, became His successor in the headship of the messianic kingdom. Certainly thoughts like these were current in the Roman church of the second century. The Clementine recognitions, — the first Christian romance, as it has been called, — even though of heretical origin, is valuable as bearing witness to germinal ideas which were afterward to expand into institutions. Its unknown writer makes Rome take the place of Jerusalem as henceforth the sacred centre of Christendom, and St. Peter take the place of St. James as the visible head of the new society.

Ideas not dissimilar, though in some respects more limited in their range, had occupied the mind of Ignatius, the Bishop of Antioch. Though not a Roman by birth or education, he had the same conservative anxiety for the welfare of the church as an organized society. In his desire for unity, the only guarantee of strength, he conceived each local church as having its hierarchy and its primate. He may be said to have given the first rough outline of what was later known as the apostolical succession, as well as of the Roman supremacy. In his scheme of the hierarchy there are bishops, presbyters, and deacons; but the bishops are regarded as the successors and representatives of Christ, while the presbyters hold the rank of apostles. Each local church was thus to reproduce the picture of Christ and his apostles; to the bishop was due the absolute submission of conscience and will, as if to Christ in person, and the presbyters were to be attuned to the bishops as the strings to the harp. Ignatius (ob. 115) lived before the idea of a Catholic church had been fully recognized, and his conception of the church implied only an aggregation of highly organized ecclesiastical atoms, each one complete in itself, but without any visible tie binding them organically to each other. This defect in his scheme was supplied by the Roman conception of a hierarchy for the universal church, with the Bishop of Rome as the representative of Christ to the whole body of believers.

The Roman Christians not only saw no incongruity in the church or kingdom as having a visible head, but could not understand the existence of a visible society without it. To think of the church as having an invisible king with no delegated representative on earth, was to the Roman mind to leave it in an indefinite, intangible condition. It was not enough to talk of the real, though spiritual, presence of the invisible Christ as a bond of unity, the principle of all life and growth; a divine-human fellowship of Christian disciples, — a school for learners under an invisible instructor, — was to the Roman mind no church at all. The church must have a visible centre and a visible circumference: the terms of admittance and of exclusion must be exactly defined; the nature of the powers delegated to its officers must be explicitly determined; there must be uniformity of practice and uniformity of opinion as well; there must be stringent methods of securing obedience and subordination, — all this, and even more, if the church was to be the kingdom of God, a power of God unto salvation.

Such was the spirit and aim of the Latin church as traced in the Christian literature of the first three centuries. If we compare the Epistle to Diognetus with the Epistle of Clement of Rome, contemporaneous as they were among the earliest writings of the post-apostolic age, we may note the divergence between Greek and Latin Christianity as clearly marked as at any later stage in history. The author of the Epistle to Diognetus is occupied with the work and person of Christ, with the endeavor to read the new revelation in its largest, most spiritual relationships. In the Roman Clement's writings, we recognize the familiar strain so often repeated in later literature down to our own age, how Christ had sent apostles, and apostles had appointed bishops and deacons, and how all this had been done to prevent strife about ecclesiastical offices. The supreme question in Clement's mind concerns orders in the ministry, the necessity of obedience, and subordination. The contrast is further seen if we compare Tertullian with Clement of Alexandria, Cyprian with Origen, or Ambrose with Athanasius.

With the one class of writers the constantly recurring burden is the divine authority of the established order, the necessity of uniformity in opinion, the claims of tradition, the need of some centre of authority, the terms of entrance into the church or of exclusion from its fold, the power of the keys; in a word, all that is implied in ecclesiastical administration. For these things it is not to the theologians of the Greek church in the second or third century that we must go, if one is impressed with their importance or in search of weapons in ecclesiastical controversy. In the Greek church we are in a different atmosphere altogether.

By the middle of the second century a great advance had been made in the work of organizing and consolidating the Christian communities scattered throughout the empire. The idea had taken root of a Catholic church which, in its earliest form, as it appeared in Greek thought, was the fellowship of those in whom Christ had been revealed, or in whom He was unconsciously active; in the Latin mind, an organization which was not to be cut short in its career by the sudden reappearance of Christ, but as destined to grow and spread throughout the empire, was worthy of the highest efforts of the Roman genius for administration. By this time also it is evident that the principle which inspired the Latin method must have already begun to yield its fruits in the separation of the clergy from the body of the people, in the growing tendency to regard them as a sacred caste, as rulers of the church by some external law of divine right, instead of ministers and organs of the Christian community in whose recognition lay the foundation of all authority. Already men were beginning to identify the church with the clergy, to regard the most precious promises of Christ as made to the apostles, in their capacity as ecclesiastical administrators handing down a deposit to their successors in office.

That such a view of the church was repugnant to many, and especially to the oriental communities, is apparent from the protest made in the Montanistic movement which originated in the East about the middle of the second century, and whose influence was felt, not only in Asia Minor, but in North Africa and Gaul. It is not necessary here to enter into a discussion of its character, or seek to disentangle its original purpose, so much obscured by the angry declamations of its opponents. That the movement was in some respects a retrograde one; that it cherished principles which would have hindered the spread of genuine Christianity, — all this may be at once conceded. It revived the old belief, which was fast dying out, that the coming of Christ in the flesh was near at hand, as the most fundamental tenet of Christian faith and practice; it introduced a rigid and gloomy asceticism as a preparation for the disasters which would precede His advent, and by its false enthusiasm gave birth to much disorder. But the main significance of Montanism in this connection was its assertion of a truth to which the church had not yet awakened, or which was lost sight of under the increasing activity in the development of ecclesiastical order. The Montanists declared the active presence in the church of a Holy Spirit who, since Christ's departure, had come to carry on His work. It was the Holy Spirit, and not apostles, who was the true and only successor of Christ, the only prelate, because He alone succeeds Christ.[1] It was the work of the Spirit

---

[1] Tertullian, *De virg. vel.*, c. i.

to lead men into all truth, to truth which had not yet been discerned, to break down the power of custom and tradition when they obstructed the process of a fuller revelation. The organs through which the Spirit spoke were not necessarily the clergy; any man or woman might be chosen to declare the Spirit's message to the churches. So far did the Montanists carry their opposition to the encroachments of the hierarchy, that women rather than men were their favorite oracles, and it is even possible that women may have been set apart to the sacred offices of the church.

The movement was welcome to different people for different reasons. Irenæus plead in its behalf because its doctrine of the coming of Christ commended itself to his judgment. Tertullian, after having been a Catholic Christian, became a Montanist, and found in the exclusiveness of the sect, with its rigid protest against the world and the flesh, elements that were congenial to the fierce vehemence of his natural temper. He never seems to have got on well with the Roman clergy, and in the freedom of the Spirit, as the Montanists proclaimed it, may have found an inward satisfaction never experienced in the Catholic church as he had known it. But Montanism was doomed to failure from its origin. Too many false conceptions mingled with the truth which it held: it lacked a spirit of soberness and self-control; in its idea of the church as a faithful few, holding together till Christ should come to claim them as His own, there was no working theory to oppose to the ambition of an aspiring hierarchy. The church, however, did not fail to take lessons from a movement which, as a sect, it opposed and crushed. Some of the ascetic regulations which the Montanists were the first to advocate, and more particularly the dislike to science and art, were domesticated in the Catholic regime. After the strong protest in behalf of the Holy Spirit, the doctrine could no longer remain unheeded. But Rome economized the doctrine to its own advantage. It was a crisis in the history of ecclesiastical development when it came to be admitted that such a Spirit as the Montanists described did indeed continue to bring gifts to the church, but connected with this admission was the strenuous assertion of Rome that the Holy Spirit was tied in His action to the hierarchy, and spoke only through its accredited representatives. The bishops thus came to be regarded as the sole depositories of the Spirit's presence, and in accordance with this belief grew up a theory that the decisions of councils composed of bishops were directly given by the Holy Spirit, inasmuch as they were given by the voice of the united episcopate.

It was Cyprian, the famous Bishop of Carthage (ob. 258), who first enunciated this theory explicitly, who first distinctly taught the doctrine of apostolical succession, giving to it a form that made it easy of comprehension, as well as adapted to the needs springing out of the growing recognition of the Catholicity of the church. His well-known treatise, entitled "The Unity of the Church," may be regarded as the charter of the institution which was to be known in history as the Latin or Roman Catholic church. In Cyprian's view, the episcopate, which in reality constitutes the church, is conceived as an organic whole complete in itself, everywhere diffused and endowed with the divine powers necessary for the salvation of men. To be in unity with the bishop has, according to this conception, a wider significance than it had in the mind of Ignatius, — it implies the larger relationship with the universal body of the episcopate, of which the local bishop is the organ or representative.

The theory of Cyprian had its defects as a working policy, however it may for a time have commended itself to Christian sentiment. It did not meet the rising demand for a head and centre of the church which should give to the episcopate an actual and visible unity. It asserted the equality of the bishops as the representatives of the apostles, but there was a conviction in the mind of the Roman people that the church was entitled to have not only representatives of the apostles, but, as Ignatius had thought, a representative of Christ as well. Cyprian's theory called attention, and that in a conspicuous way, to the majesty of the vacant place which in the days of apostles had been filled by the divine Master. The same method of argument which Cyprian had used, in demonstrating the apostles to have been the divinely ordered rulers of the church, was employed by the Roman church to prove that St. Peter had been the supreme prince or pontiff of the apostolic college. Why else should it have been said that the church was built upon Peter, why should the power of the keys have been imparted to him alone, with the commission to feed the flock of Christ, and how otherwise explain his prominence in the first days of the church, and the grandeur with which his memory still filled the Christian imagination? Cyprian could not easily meet such an argument. In his view, the words spoken to Peter were addressed to him simply as a representative of all the apostles. But if Peter was a representative of the apostles, why should not the apostles themselves be regarded, not merely as the princes or divinely ordered rulers of the church, but as the representatives of a sanctified humanity which was larger than they; and why should not the promises and commissions given to them have been given in their name to all Christians in virtue of their membership in the body of Christ?

If we may characterize the Cyprianic and Roman theories in the well understood language of political institutions, it may be said that Cyprian was arguing in behalf of the government of the church by an oligarchy, while Rome was urging the principle of ecclesiastical absolutism,— the need of the impersonation of authority in one man. An analogy may be found for the relation of Cyprian to the Bishop of Rome in the earlier political history, when Cicero, in behalf of the senatorial oligarchy, disputed the advances of Cæsar to supreme authority. The same reasons which justified imperialism in the state might be applied with equal force in behalf of its adoption by the church. The oligarchy of the Roman senate succumbing to the fascinations of Cæsarism was a type of the episcopal oligarchy yielding its claim to the Roman papacy.

II.

In order to a fuller understanding of the work of the Latin genius, as inspired anew under Christian auspices it sought to create another empire and to go forth a second time upon a career of conquest, it will be necessary to dwell for a moment upon the Latin church in the presence of the intellectual and moral vagaries of heresy, and also to inquire what shape the object and goal of Christianity assumed to the Latin mind. To what end was the authority which she created subservient? What motive inspired the growth of the hierarchy and the submission to its rule ? What was the object in view of this vast elaboration of ecclesiastical machinery known as the Roman Catholic Church?

The one typical heresy which confronted the Christian faith in Rome, as elsewhere throughout the church, was known as Gnosticism. Whatever the date of its origin, it was at its height as a phase of religious thought by the middle of the second century. While it is difficult to speak of the movement as a whole, since it comprised so many different systems, yet in its general outline it was unmistakably a reflection of that oriental tendency whose embodiment may be seen to-day in Buddhism. The sense of weariness of human life, the despairing pessimism which saw no hope for the future of humanity in this world, the contempt for external nature, the deification of asceticism as the principle of salvation, — such were the external features of oriental religion as it began to be reproduced in the West, and which in Gnosticism threatened to combine with the religion of Christ. In the second century the Gnostic Christians were asking themselves the same questions that Buddha had propounded in his long reveries before he came forth a religious reformer. They were so impressed with the magnitude of the evils and the miseries of life, that they questioned the divine omnipotence, and wondered why the world should have been called into existence. All the Gnostics were agreed that God could not have been its creator. He stood in their imagination at an infinite distance from such a scene as the world presents. But having severed the world from God, the Gnostics, like the Neo-Platonists, endeavored to reunite them by a long series of potencies or beings who stretched themselves across the abyss which lay between humanity and the supreme Deity. The lowest being in this line of intermediaries, in whom the evil was conceived as predominating over the good, was selected by the Gnostics as fit to be the creator. Since the world-maker is not wholly evil, for he has some remote relationship to the heavenly sphere, there is still something in his creation which is capable of redemption, though he himself is not able or disposed to assist in the process. In order to rescue the few souls who have an affinity for the divine, in whose composition the good outweighs the evil, one of the higher beings known as the Christ descends into the world and makes known the method by which their salvation is to be accomplished. But inasmuch as the very nature of matter is evil, it was impossible for the Gnostics to admit an incarnation, — to believe that Christ had really taken a human body and died upon the cross. The historical aspects of Christ's earthly life were explained away as unworthy of a being who was divine. He appeared to have a human body in order that he might proclaim his message; and the essence of his teaching is, that by ascetic practices a few may rise into the sphere of the higher, spiritual world, — the majority of men are doomed to annihilation or perdition, and the physical world to be finally consumed in a great conflagration.

What is known as the "Apostles' Creed" is the simple but emphatic protest of the church against the Gnostic heresies, — the summary of that which was believed or felt to be true as recorded in history or verified in Christian experience. There were other summaries of a similar character, which, like the Apostles' Creed, had grown up after the middle of the second century; while differing in detail, they agree in their substance as expansions of the baptismal formula, and the explanation of their appearance is due to the energy with which the heart and common-sense of the church resisted the errors which were fatal to its existence. As we examine the Apostles' Creed with reference to its historical interpretation, the antagonism is apparent at every point. In the first clause, — "I believe in God the Father Almighty, Maker of heaven and earth," — it is affirmed that God is not limited or hampered by an evil power in the universe which acts contrary to His will, and that this earth as well as the heavenly sphere is created by supreme Deity, and not by some inferior or malignant being. In the second article of the creed, the words referring to Christ as "His only begotten Son our Lord," imply a rejection of the long line of Gnostic intermediaries who do not so much unite as separate God from humanity. The Gnostic notion that the Saviour did not have a real body is met by the assertion that He was born of a human mother whose name is preserved in history; against the Gnostic denial of the fact of His death, the time of His suffering is fixed by the mention of the Roman procurator in Judæa; and in order to make emphatic the church's belief in the reality as well as in the importance of his death, it is declared with a threefold reiteration, — "He was crucified, dead and buried." The creed which thus arose as a protest against Gnosticism was afterwards extended to meet other needs of the church as they appeared in later ages.[1] As a confession of faith, it shows how strong

[1] At what time the clause, "He descended into Hell," was added to the creed is not known. The clauses, "The Holy Catholic Church, the Communion of Saints, the Forgiveness of

was the hold of the essential truth upon the Christian consciousness, in the presence of the worst skepticism which it could be called upon to encounter. In its Eastern or its Western form, it is simply the emphatic assertion of the incarnation as the essence of the church's faith.

But there were profound issues that lay back of the creed, which the creed does not mention. To these Greek theology had addressed itself in order to overcome the principle which made Gnosticism possible. The Greek theologians were optimists, not because they shut their eyes to the darker side of life, but because they had exhausted pessimism at its source by refuting the principle in which it originated. They were not given to raising the cry that the church was in danger; they were not alarmed at the rise of heresies, nor had they fears for the safety of the church, because they accepted the incarnation not only as an historical fact which had taken place in the past, but as a living present reality, and saw the essential Christ always and everywhere exerting his spiritual force in

Sins," were probably inserted in the West in connection with the Novatian schism after the middle of the third century. None of the above expressions are to be found in the rule of faith as recited by Irenæus (i. c. 10, and iii. c. 4), or Tertullian (*De præs. hæret.* 12, and *De vir. vel.*, i.), nor were they contained in the creed as recited at Nicæa. The clause, "the resurrection of the body," is given by both Irenæus and Tertullian, but is wanting in the Nicene Creed, where it reads "the resurrection of the dead." The doctrine of the resurrection of the flesh lacks the sanction of the Catholic Church, — the Apostles' Creed being unknown in the East. The interesting legend that the Apostles' Creed was the verbal composition of the apostles themselves, each of them contributing a clause to the joint result, was first mentioned by Rufinus in the fifth century. As a legend it embodies the Latin idea of tradition as the sole authority of faith.

order to make manifest the redemption which He had wrought in the flesh.

The Latin church had no more aptitude for theology as a science than the Latin people had for philosophy throughout their history. Literary men could borrow to a certain extent from the philosophy of the Greeks, or adapt it to their own conceptions; but as the Roman people created no philosophy, so the Roman church gave birth to no theology. A deep and instinctive aversion to all speculative thought, a desire for a definite faith firmly grounded on tradition as the only stable basis, a faith that could be as exactly formulated as a code of law, the slightest variation from which could be easily detected and exposed, — such was the characteristic, the ideal and ambition of the Latin church in the second and third centuries, and such they have remained throughout her entire career.

As a matter of fact, it does not appear that the heresies of the second century particularly disturbed the peace of the Latin church, or that they were disseminated to any great extent. For the most part they originated in the East, and after they had become full-fledged were taken to Rome. What principally disturbed the Latin church was the existence of heresy at all, whether near or remote. It seemed to the genuine Roman mind a contradiction or violation of the Christian principle that heresy should dare to assert its existence. That principle, as the Roman Christian understood it, was an explicit and implicit obedience, which included within its range the intellect as well as the conscience. Heresy in its last analysis was simply self-will setting itself above the authority of the church, and thus endangering the external unity of the Christian empire. Hence it was above all necessary to proclaim a definite faith, and to maintain it by some tangible authority which could not be misunderstood or evaded. This was the problem to which Latin ecclesiastics devoted their energies.

At first, as has been already remarked, the Latins received their theology from the Greeks as submissively as their ancestors had received their philosophy. But after the Latin language had become the vehicle of religious thought in the West, and the two churches had begun to grow apart, it became difficult to follow the development of Greek theology. And even if it had been understood and intelligently followed, it would not have been congenial to the Latin spirit, which so profoundly distrusted the human reason. What could Roman ecclesiastics, dreaming of a great Christian empire, do with a theology which rested for its sanction on so vague a basis as the Christian reason or consciousness, or how with such a principle could they meet the Gnostic and other heretics? Even the "rule of faith" was of little value unless it were based on some more material foundation than Christian experience enlightened by a divine spirit. If the appeal was made to Scripture as the final authority, the case was not helped, for Scripture was capable of varied interpretations, and had been already discredited by the heretics who had been the first to use it as a refuge from their opponents.

Irenæus (ob. 202) was the first among western writers who combated the Gnostic heresies.[1] He had been

[1] In his conception of the incarnation Irenæus is in full sympathy with the spirit of Greek theology, and has set forth the doctrine with great force and beauty of expression. He has been sometimes regarded, together with his pupil, Hippolytus, as representing a distinct school in which a liberal theology was com-

born in the East, and was to some extent familiar with Greek philosophy. Yet in his distant home in Gaul he had felt the influence of the Roman spirit, and his writings reveal that in the compromises of his thought the Roman principle was predominant. He used his knowledge of philosophy in reasoning with the Gnostics merely to point a moral. He had no faith in philosophy as such — in the reason as a divine gift through which God reveals His truth. To be able to trace a Gnostic opinion to its supposed origin in the teaching of some philosopical sect was sufficient evidence of its falsity. It is not surprising, therefore, that he should fall back upon the tradition of the church, descending through the episcopate from the apostles, as the best bulwark that could be raised against the danger of heresy. He formulated the idea of tradition so forcibly, that his memorable words have been regarded by the Latin church ever since as an axiom in dealing with the divergences of religious belief. It is possible that he did not intend to convey the meaning which later generations attached to his language, but as to the general bearing of his argument there can be no doubt. While he admitted that

bined with an ecclesiastical tendency. While in some respects he stands by himself and cannot be classified, his real affinity was with the West and not with the East. He had no confidence in the reason as an organ of the truth, and accepted the Latin idea of the episcopate as possessing the *charisma veritatis*. His tendency was toward a legal apprehension of Christianity. Cf. Art. Irenæus by Lipsius, *Dic. Chris. Biog.* The difference between Origen and Hippolytus has been clearly stated by Martineau, *Studies of Christianity*, p. 246. In meditating on the conjunction between Father and Son, Origen would think of the relation between *thought* and *volition;* Hippolytus of that between volition and execution.

the "deposit" of the faith might have been preserved in every church in which an unbroken descent of the episcopate from the apostles could be traced, yet, as he argued, it was preëminently the church of Rome by which the tradition of every other church must be regulated, because of its high importance as the capital of the empire and as founded by the two most glorious apostles, St. Peter and St. Paul. The apostolic tradition, he further reasoned, must have been faithfully preserved at Rome, because any departure from it would there have been most easily detected among believers from all parts of the church who were in the habit of meeting there; and, therefore, since the tradition had been maintained in its purity at Rome, all other churches are in possession of the faith so far as they are in agreement with the church in Rome.[1]

The same line of reasoning was also adopted by Tertullian (Ob. circ. 220) in his famous treatise on the "Prescription of Heresy." He had been a Roman lawyer before his conversion to Christianity, and the legal attitude is everywhere apparent in his writings. He was always the advocate, holding, as it were, a brief for Christianity as he understood it, not concerned so much for the truth as for overthrowing the adversaries that rose up against it. From his point of view the church's faith was its property, and the aim of heresy was to weaken the church's sense of security resulting from long possession. Hence the receipt for dealing with the heretics was the legal argument that the church had a presumption in its favor springing from long and undisputed possession, which constituted its prescription against all new claimants. Or, to drop

[1] iii. c. 3. "Ad hanc enim ecclesiam propter potiorem principalitatem necesse est omnem convenire ecclesiam."

the figure, heresy is simply self-will, and is instigated by philosophy, — the one source of evil against which the church must be always on its guard. Athens has no connection with Jerusalem, the academy with the church, or heretics with Christians. "Away with all efforts to produce a mottled Christianity of Stoic, Platonic, and dialectic composition." Truth does not call for continual research and inquiry, — it is a definite thing, to be sought after until it has been found, and then all inquiry should cease ; just as the woman in the parable did not go on looking for the piece of silver after she had found it. Away with the man who is ever seeking because he never finds ! The creed or rule of faith is the summary of all truth, and curiosity should not attempt to go beyond it. Nor should the church condescend to support the rule of faith by arguing with the heretic from Scripture, for the Scripture belongs to the church alone, and heretics should not be allowed its use, since they have no title at all to the privilege. The appeal, therefore, does not lie to Scripture, but to the authority of tradition handed down through the apostles and apostolic churches. Here lies the test of truth, the principle of certitude. Since Christ gave a "deposit" to the apostles and sent them forth to preach, no others ought to be received as preachers than those whom He appointed. Having been under the teaching of Christ, the apostles must have been fully instructed in all things, and were quite competent to transmit safely the truth as they had received it. The fact that St. Paul rebuked St. Peter for his inconsistency or cowardice does not at all invalidate the teaching of St. Peter. Nor did St. Paul have any superiority, as a preacher of truth, to St. Peter. The apostles did not keep anything back, as the heretics pretend, but handed on the entire "deposit" to their successors. It is inconceivable to imagine the churches which they founded as capricious or unfaithful stewards of a treasure held in trust for those that came after them; nor is the value of this argument affected by the circumstance that the apostolic church of Galatia fell away from the truth, and "was so soon removed to another gospel" than that which St. Paul had preached; or that the church in Corinth required to be fed with milk because it was not able to bear strong meat; for if these churches were rebuked for falling away from the truth, were they not also corrected by the apostle? That the transmission of the "deposit" has been faithfully accomplished is shown by the substantial agreement in the churches everywhere. Variations and diversities indicate a corruption of the faith, and are the essential mark of heresy.

The heretics are therefore challenged to display their record; let them unfold the roll of their bishops, coming down in due succession from the apostles, so that the first in the line of descent can show that he was ordained by some apostle or apostolic man. Here lies the strength of the Catholic church, that it has apostolic sees which utter the voice of the apostles themselves. There is Corinth, Philippi, Thessalonica, and Ephesus. In Italy there is Rome, which may boast a threefold apostolic authority. How happy is its church on which apostles poured forth all their doctrines along with their blood, — where Peter was crucified, and Paul beheaded, and John came forth unharmed from immersion in boiling oil. So, then, to conclude, the heretics are trespassing on a domain which is not theirs. It may be fairly said to them, Who are you? When and whence did you come? As you are none of mine, what have you to do with that which is mine? By what right do you hew my wood, or divert the streams of my fountain, or remove my landmarks? This is my property. Why are you sowing and feeding here at your pleasure? This is my property; I have long possessed it; I possessed it before you; I hold sure title-deeds from the original owners themselves to whom the estate belonged; I am the heir of the apostles. As they carefully prepared a will and testament and committed it to a trust, even so I hold it.

Such was the argument of Tertullian in his "Prescription of Heretics." The book was probably written in the early part of his life; after he became a Montanist he ceased to make so much of apostles as successors of Christ, and dwelt upon the work of a divine spirit, whose office is to break down custom and routine as the sanctions of truth, and to lead men into a deeper knowledge of the things of God. But the argument of the Prescription was too clear and valuable, too much in accordance with the genius of the Roman church, to be laid aside because its author had become recreant to its significance. Of all the writings of Tertullian, it was the one most deeply studied in later ages, the favorite treatise with ecclesiastics who have aimed to revive the authority of the church or resist the encroachments of the reason. In the early church it marked an important step in the process by which the authority of the episcopate was created as a means of overcoming heresy. Like the argument of Irenæus, it tended naturally to build up the supremacy of the see of Rome, for it was a method which found its most emphatic illustration in pointing to the one church which was believed to concentrate in itself the united labors of the most eminent of the apostles.

The desire to rid the church of heresy was one of the causes which stimulated the growth of the ecclesiastical organization in the West, and gave direction to the peculiar genius of Rome. But back of this desire may be seen the operation of a yet more powerful motive. The practical purpose for which the church had been established, or for which Christianity existed, was not to the Latin mind primarily an ethical one; even the obedience which the church required, or the morality which the gospel enjoined, were not an end in themselves but a means to a remoter end, — the salvation of the soul from the consequences of sin in the future world. The doctrine of an endless punishment for all who rejected the claims of Christ must have been from an early period the underlying belief which gave the strongest sanction to the church's authority.

At first the church had appeared as the community of Christian disciples held together by their love for the Master, and waiting for his return in order to be reunited to Him in His millennial kingdom. The fate of those outside its limits, who had not repented of their sins or abandoned the worship of idols, and especially of those who persecuted the church, is portrayed in the gloomy visions of the Apocalypse. All that the human imagination could conceive as most awful was the punishment in store for these when the seals of the future were broken, when the angels should sound the successive trumpets of human doom. This belief in a millennial kingdom soon to be established grew weak in the second century, and in the third may be said to have disappeared. But the vision of a lake that burned with endless fires for the enemies of Christ, the tortures in reserve for those who persecuted his faithful followers, still appealed to a church that existed in the face of a perpetual hatred and scorn on the part of the heathens. It was impossible that recriminations should not be heard from heathens and Christians alike. The latter told their adversaries of a day of judgment, when the punishment which had been withheld in this world should fall upon them in awful severity, — when the final sentence should be pronounced which remanded them to the tortures of endless suffering. Tertullian grows eloquent as he describes the scene which he shall witness when that last judgment day, with its unlooked-for issues, shall be over. The vast spectacle which will then burst upon his gaze will excite his admiration, his derision, his joy, his exultation. He will see illustrious monarchs who had been deified on earth groaning in the lowest darkness with great Jove himself, and with them the governors of provinces, in fires more fierce than those which they lighted on earth for the followers of Christ. The world's wise men and philosophers, who had taught falsely, and among them those also who had denied the resurrection of the same identical body which they had left, these will be there, to be consumed in the body, covered with shame, in the presence of those whom they had deceived. The poets who had sung of a judgment seat of Rhadamanthus or Minos will appear at the unexpected judgment seat of Christ. There will then be a better opportunity than he has cared to avail himself of here, of witnessing the tragedians and the play-actors declaiming in a real calamity, the charioteers glowing in their chariots of fire, the wrestlers tossing in their fiery billows. Or if he should not find interest enough in such a spectacle, he is sure to turn with eager and insatiable gaze upon those who vented themselves in fury against the Lord. These are sights which no quæstor or priest can now procure a Roman audience the pleasure of beholding, but the Christian can even now by faith behold these things in the pictures of the imagination.[1]

When Christian apologists like Tertullian were thus proclaiming to their heathen brethren a day of final judgment, in which they were to receive the never-ending penalty of their madness, we may admire the boldness which their speech displays, but we can no longer wonder at the growing indignation which was soon to culminate in the Decian persecution, in one supreme effort to root up and exterminate the Christian church.

A certain unhealthy and morbid tone characterized the spirit of both Christians and heathens in the third century. The decline of the Roman empire since the death of Marcus Aurelius (A. D. 180) was attended by disasters of varied kinds, often on an immense scale, — pestilences, famines, earthquakes, frequent defeats of the Roman legions. The feeling that something was wrong, that more fearful judgments were impending, took possession of the public mind. Under such circumstances it was becoming difficult to maintain the conviction of the love of God. The heathens were cherishing a fatal conviction that the gods were angry because the Christians neglected their worship, and were visiting their wrath upon the empire. Cyprian replied in the same strain, that God was angry with the heathens because they did not turn from

[1] *De Spec.*, 30.

their idolatry. The writings of Cyprian reveal how the popular theology of the Latin church was taking shape in one of the darkest moments in its history. The Decian persecution (249-251) had been followed by a calamity even more awful in the great plague which reached Carthage in the year 252, and is said to have destroyed half of the population of Alexandria, and for a time to have carried off at Rome five thousand people daily, lasting for some twenty years before its ravages were over. An event of this kind must have gathered additional horror when we consider how society was sharply divided against itself, Christians and heathens accusing each other of being the cause of the calamity.

Cyprian sought to improve the moment by calling the heathens to repentance, but his method of appeal was calculated to embitter rather than appease the pagan mind. Like Tertullian, he portrayed the sufferings of the future world endless in their duration, of which the present disasters were a warning and a prophecy. He did not, indeed, exult in the prospect, but still thought it would be a compensation to the Christians for what they endured at the hands of their persecutors. In the history of theology his letters and treatises possess a peculiar value as bringing out his theory of life, — a theory now for the first time announced with dogmatic clearness and precision. The world, he declares in his "Address to Demetrian," is nearing its end, and the coming of Anti-Christ is at hand. The earth has grown old and exhausted, life is failing at its sources, the sun is losing its heat, the rain diminishes, the harvests grow thin, the disemboweled mountains no longer yield the precious ores, young men are born prematurely old, — everywhere he looks he reads the signs of decay and approaching dissolution. Meantime the church remains as an ark of deliverance from the wrath of God. The Christians may seem to share with their neighbors in the troubles of the time, but they who have a confidence in the good things that a future life will bring do not in reality suffer from the assault of present evils. To the pagans the church offers a refuge, if they will turn to it. But the opportunity is brief, the end is near; after this world is over there is no hope, no possibility of repentance. The pain of punishment will then be without the fruit of repentance, tears and prayers will be of no avail. Here life is either saved or lost. So long as one remains in this world, no repentance is too late. Death constitutes the line between hope and despair; it puts an end to human probation. Hereafter a punishment devouring with living flames will burn up the condemned in an ever-burning Gehenna; to their agonies will be neither end nor respite. Souls with their bodies will be reserved in infinite tortures for suffering.[1]

When Christianity was presented in ways like these to the heathen world, when fear was becoming the motive to the worship of God and the communion of the church, and salvation was escape from impending wrath, it was only a question of time how long the Christians themselves could maintain their faith in their own salvation. Cyprian's theory made life a probation for the heathen world, while those within the church had already entered by anticipation upon an assured inheritance. But how were the Christians to retain this assurance when they saw the great ma-

[1] *Ad Demetrianum*, 23–25.

jority of their heathen brethren passing to endless perdition, when religion was no longer grounded in love, and God had become a passive spectator in the struggle where endless issues depended upon the decision of an hour? To such an inquiry the answer may be read in the changes which were coming over the church after the middle of the third century, some of them in Cyprian's lifetime. The world was becoming, in the Christian imagination, a theatre for the activity of malignant supernatural forces. The heathen deities ceased to be regarded as mere phantoms; they became real existences, demons in the air, which lurked in wait for unwary souls. Baptism assumed the character of a magical rite, by whose waters the soul was rendered invulnerable against the assaults of evil spirits. Connected with baptism from this time, as an indispensable preliminary, was the rite of exorcism, by which the evil spirit was first banished before the formula of the sacred name could be repeated. The sign of the cross was thought to be a safeguard against the thousand shapes in which the deities of heathenism sought to regain possession of the Christian convert. The dread and terror which had fallen upon this world began to extend to the next, and when men began to pray for their dead it was a sign that the old assurance had departed which regarded them as safe in the bosom of God. So far had God retreated from man that the gulf which divided them began to be bridged with saints and martyrs and confessors, to whom prayers might be addressed, through whose mediation with Christ prayers stood a better chance of being heard and answered. Influences like these began thus early to transform the Lord's Supper into a sacrifice after

Jewish and heathen types, by which the favor of God might be propitiated. The clergy were a priesthood after the same analogies, whose function was to stand between God and the people, as the mediators through whose intercession heaven remained open, and the favor of God descended to man.

The course of events in the third century tended to confirm the Roman idea of the church by determining how its catholicity was to be conceived as a working principle. A brief allusion to the controversies which were connected with this result will be sufficient. After the Decian persecution it became an important question what should be the method of treatment adopted toward the large number of Christians who had apostatized or denied their faith. Should they be received back into the church on easy terms after professing repentance, or should they be subjected to a severe, protracted discipline, or was it proper that they should be received back into the church on any terms, so heinous was the offense which they had committed? Another kindred issue was whether the baptism performed by heretics possessed validity, or whether the rite must be repeated in the case of those who, rejecting their heresy, sought the communion of the church. The position of the African church differed in both instances from that of Rome. The Montanist influence still lingered in Carthage, and even Cyprian, who had been a pupil and admirer of Tertullian, retained something of that stern old Montanist's exclusive zeal for the purity of the Christian community. He was a Protestant at heart, despite his sympathy with the Roman spirit for order and administration. While he condemned the extreme attitude of those who said that forgiveness was impossible for those guilty of apostasy, and therefore forbade their return to the church on any condition, yet he insisted on a penitence and discipline which to many seemed too severe. In his controversy with the Bishop of Rome about the rebaptism of heretics, he vehemently assailed the validity of heretical baptism.[1] The purpose of Cyprian was to keep the church as pure as possible, even though such a policy should hinder its extension. Two theories of the

[1] The Bishop of Rome maintained, on the ground of tradition, that baptism in the name of Christ only, by whomsoever administered, possessed validity (Cyprian, *Ep.* 72, c. 18); while Cyprian held that a true baptism required the name of the trinity, as well as its performance in the Catholic church. But how could the Bishop of Rome, so early as the middle of the third century, have made a mistake in so important a matter as the tradition concerning baptism, especially when, if Irenæus was right, Rome was the one place where any departure from the tradition would be most easily detected, and whose possession of such safeguards made the Roman church the best custodian of tradition? Firmilian, Bishop of Cæsarea, in a letter to Cyprian, gets over the difficulty by alleging that Rome was not specially distinguished for maintaining the traditions of the apostles. But if Rome did not keep the traditions, what apostolic see could be depended upon to do so; and then what becomes of the argument from tradition? Firmilian went on further, in the same epistle, to say that the Bishop of Rome, not content with the one rock on which the foundation of the church was laid, had introduced many other rocks, and indeed, by his innovations, had abolished the rock on which he claimed to rest as the successor of Peter. For this famous epistle, which patristic scholars in the Roman church have never sought to make easily accessible, see Routh, *Scrip. Ecclesiasticor. Opusc.*, i. pp. 235, 243.

It is a curious fact in the history of baptism, that in the ninth century Pope Nicholas I. should have again taken the ground of the Roman bishop in the third century and have declared baptism in the name of Christ only to be valid. Labbé, *Concilia*, viii. p. 548.

church were contending in his mind, one of which made it consist in the clergy, the other in the body of the faithful, and to neither view did he give unqualified approval. It was quite otherwise with the authorities at Rome. They rejected by a sure instinct whatever conflicted with the idea of the church as an entity in itself existing independently of those within its fold. A stable, divinely ordered society, as Rome conceived it, could only exist and grow on condition that the mode of entrance should be easy and the gates of admission stand open to all postulants. The demands which it made upon its members should not be too rigid or exacting, and in case of failure or apostasy the terms of restoration must not be severe. Against the restrictions which Cyprian imposed, the Roman church contended, in the interest of a more comprehensive and flexible organization, though at the expense of the spiritual claims which marked the early Christian communities. The Roman policy was bringing the church nearer to the world by lessening the difference that divided them, — its result was to make the church accessible and attractive to the great multitude of pagans who were incapable of discerning its spiritual heritage.

III.

The accession of Constantine in the early part of the fourth century marks a new era not only in the history of the church but also in the fortunes of theology. No greater change can be conceived than took place when the once persecuted and despised Christian community first realized that it had superseded the old paganism, that the Roman emperor was henceforth to stand in close relationship to the church as its protector and highest representative. Constantine bestowed a great favor upon the church by giving to it the recognition of the law. The church fell heir to the old pagan temples and their revenues; it was freed from the burden of taxation; its representatives became a privileged class by exemption from the disagreeable duties which rested so heavily upon Roman citizens. There were no formal terms of alliance between church and state, but it was understood that the church made some return for these favors so generously bestowed. Constantine wanted unity above all things, and saw in the Christian communities a comprehensive method of organization capable of being utilized for the restoration of unity to a distracted empire. It was his policy to exalt the bishops as the representatives everywhere not only of the church but of the state. One of the first effects of his reign was the realization of the external unity of Christendom in a formal and imposing manner. When the controversy arose over the teaching of Arius, and it seemed as though the empire itself was shaken in the excitement which rent the church, a great synod of bishops was held at Nicæa (325), which not merely disposed of the question in dispute, but illustrated the glory of the church's external unity in a way calculated to forever enthrall the Christian imagination.

It had been the work of the Latin church to perfect and establish the ecclesiastical organization, and the church in the East had received and exemplified the theory which Cyprian had been the first to enunciate, of the solidarity of the episcopate. The doctrine of the trinity, the formula of which had resulted from the alliance of Greek philosophy with Christian thought, had on the other hand been received by the

Latin church from the hands of Greek theologians.[1] The doctrine came to the Latin church in the shape which it preferred, — a dogma put forth upon authority. It is doubtful whether the Latins appreciated always the process of speculative thought by which the doctrine of the trinity was maintained by Greek thinkers. The opposition to the doctrine did not come from the West, but from oriental countries where the bishops were in bondage to notions about emanations, which prevented them from accepting easily the idea of the coequality of Christ with the Father. When this doctrine had once received the sanction of a reputable authority, the Latins not only accepted it but became its strongest supporters. In the long controversy that followed the Council of Nicæa, before its decision gained the voluntary recognition of the oriental bishops, it was mainly by a process of reasoning that the Nicene formula won its way in the East to acceptance. Athanasius declined to rest upon the authority of the council when urging its claims. But the Latins, who wished a definite faith set forth upon unquestioned authority, sustained from the first the decision of Nicæa as final and unchangeable. What indeed to the Latin mind would become of the faith itself, if a decision once solemnly rendered under the inspiration, as it was believed, of the divine Spirit, could be rescinded or modified by a subsequent discussion. There may have been deeper reasons for the acceptance of the dogma, but with the Latins it was a question of life or death that the authority of the Council of Nicæa should be maintained. And it may

[1] The only Western writer who took an important part in the trinitarian controversy in the third century was Dionysius, Bishop of Rome, and he was Greek by birth and education.

be regarded as providential in the divine ordering of history, that the one doctrine which contains the essential and comprehensive principle of the Christian faith should have met with such powerful and unquestioning support in an age when reason and philosophy were so soon to abdicate their throne.

The fourth and fifth centuries have been idealized by the worshipers of catholic antiquity as the halcyon age of the church — as the actual fulfillment for once in its history of the promise which attended its birth. The church developed to a fuller extent its organization by following the new political divisions of the empire, and a graded hierarchy of bishops arose corresponding to the grades of the civil service. As the state borrowed from the debased courts of oriental despots a ritual of great magnificence, attaching an exaggerated importance to form and etiquette, and by the symbolism of pomp and luxurious display endeavored to impress the people with the sacred majesty of the emperor's person, so the church also developed a ritual of extraordinary beauty and splendor. The church grew rich and powerful. Her coffers were filled with the voluntary offerings of the people or with the property of a declining paganism. Her bishops became personages of so great distinction that no officer of the state could rival them in power and consideration, and even emperors stood in awe of them as wielding a power which was greater than their own. Certainly there was something in the spectacle of such a church to awe the mind of the multitude into submission. It is not to be wondered at that paganism hastened to abandon its discredited deities, that the Roman world became a nominally Christian one. But there is a dark side to the picture. The morality of the age was no better under Christian emperors than it had been under pagan; the church had lost much of the simplicity, the purity, the self-sacrifice which had marked the era of her depression and apparent weakness. The records of the period are full of incidents connected with the ambition and rivalry of bishops; schisms, intrigues, and scenes of cruelty and bloodshed attendant upon episcopal elections were far from being rare occurrences. We read of them in Rome, in Constantinople, in Alexandria, in Ephesus, in Antioch, in Jerusalem. If they happened in the great centres, we may be sure that smaller towns and cities were not exempt from the same disgrace. These things constitute the scandals of church history. There have been times when it was thought a Christian duty to pass over them in silence. They are alluded to here because they have a close connection with Christian theology. The want of charity, the hardness, the almost systematic cruelty which had invaded the church, which were the invariable accompaniments of general councils, — these things hurt the Christian ideal. More than anything else, they were insensibly modifying human convictions about the character of God and His relation to humanity. The high officials of the church claimed to represent Deity and to act as His ambassadors or delegates. In one sense, and that the highest, all men are called to the performance of the same function. Men represent God to each other, and if they fulfill their task unworthily the idea of God is degraded in human estimation. When justice and charity and humanity prevail in the life of society, then God is most truly worshiped as He is. It is hard to believe in the divine love or in a righteous order in the world, when these qualities cease to be reflected in the institutions which have the moulding of human character.

The moral deterioration which marked the fourth and fifth centuries had affected the state before it reached the church. It may not have been possible for the church to resist the fatal influences which were undermining the strength of the ancient civilization. Roman imperialism from the time of Constantine, and largely in consequence of his policy, had become an increasing burden, crushing out the life and spirit of the people. It had destroyed all vestiges of self-government, and had substituted an elaborate machinery which had to-be maintained by force and at great expense, and which had become identified in the public mind with an odious, exacting tyranny. The conditions of human life under such a régime were growing cheerless and unattractive. The future held out no prospect of improvement. The dark cloud which had hovered over the empire for two centuries was now closing in around it and was portentous of fearful disasters. The barbarians had already, in the latter part of the fourth century, gained a footing within the empire, and no occasional victories on the side of the Roman armies did more than postpone the evil day.

It is not surprising therefore that Christian people should have fled from the cities into the desert, in the hope of realizing there a vision of the kingdom of God. They fled from a church that was becoming corrupt, from a civilization that was dying, from a state of society of whose improvement they despaired. But it does not appear that they carried with them in their flight any higher or truer conception of the Deity by whose fear they were moved, to whom they wished to render a more acceptable service. The true fear of God, which constitutes the motive of the religious life, was assuming the shape of a wild and superstitious terror, such as afterwards fell upon the races that responded to the call of Mohammed.

The process of decline may be seen in the famous school of heathen philosophy at Alexandria. The earlier Neo-Platonists had resisted bravely the encroachments of orientalism when they first appeared in the Gnostic sects. In the spirit of Plato, they had tried to view the world as everywhere instinct with a divine life. Inheriting as they did the peculiar quality of Hellenic culture, nothing could be more obnoxious to them than the anathema which the Gnostics flung upon the whole creation. Jamblichus and Proclus, their successors, not only failed to sustain the high intellectual tone of their predecessors, but showed the debasing influence of the age in their disposition to put magic and theurgy in the place of the ethical and intellectual effort by which, according to earlier Neo-Platonism, elect souls might rise to the vision and communion of the gods. Christian theology shared in the decline which had overtaken Greek philosophy. The theological school of Alexandria, which had maintained itself in great wealth of intellectual and spiritual power for more than a hundred years, ceased to lead the church in the East after the fourth century. As Alexandria declined there was rising in Antioch another school, marked by a different tendency and occupied with other issues. Its leading theologians, Chrysostom, Theodore of Mopsuestia, and Theodoret, still bore the impress of their Greek teachers, and still held in reverence the name and labors of Origen, however much they differed in their methods. But they lived in an age when tradition was fast usurping the place of free inquiry in theology.[1] The false and superstitious reverence which haunted the church as intellectual activity declined, — the last expiring influence, it may have been, of the old Egyptian love of the mysterious for its own sake, — led the representatives of the school of Antioch in a rationalistic direction,

---

[1] The time when tradition was first formally adopted in the East as a better method than free theological discussion for determining disputed points, dates back to the year 383, if we may trust the historian Socrates. At this time the Emperor Theodosius, thinking that a mutual conference of the bishops would heal the dissensions in the church, sent for Nectarius, the Bishop of Constantinople, in order to advise with him on the best method of procedure. In the emperor's opinion a fair discussion was the best means for the detection and removal of the causes of discord. The emperor's proposition gave Nectarius the greatest uneasiness, for he was a man unacquainted with theology, who had been suddenly transferred from the army to the episcopate, and in whose case it had been necessary to hastily run through the sacred offices from baptism to consecration as bishop, in order that he might occupy his see without delay. Nectarius therefore referred the matter to Agelius, his friend and sympathizer, and he turned it over to Sisinnius. This Sisinnius was said to have been just the person to manage a conference. He was eloquent and possessed great experience, well read in Scripture and in philosophy, and above all was aware that free discussions, far from healing divisions, generally make them worse, and even create new heresies of a most inveterate kind. He therefore advised Nectarius to fall back upon the testimonies of the ancients instead of entering into logical debates. Let the emperor, he said, ask the representatives of the different sects if they had any respect for the fathers, who flourished before divisions arose, or whether they rejected their teaching as that of men alienated from the Christian faith. If they took the latter course, they were then to be called upon to anathematize them, and the moment they should do this, the people would arise and thrust them out. This plan commended itself to the bishop, and the emperor perceiving its wisdom and propriety carried it out with consummate prudence. Socrates, *Hist. Eccles.*, v. c. 10.

and in opposing what was superstitious or irrational, they were in danger of limiting the truth of the incarnation as it had been apprehended by the masters of Greek theology.

Toward the end of the fourth century there appeared the first traces of a controversy destined to endure with varying fortunes for three hundred years before its issue was finally determined. It is strange that a controversy of such duration, absorbing so much of the thought of Christendom, and attended by such grave consequences, should have awakened so little interest in the modern theological mind. The long discussion about the two natures of Christ, in which the opinion of the ancient church was so widely and deeply divided, occupied the attention of four successive general councils, while three schisms existing to this day, two of them of large extent, in Oriental Christendom, attest the inefficacy of conciliar decisions resting upon external authority to promote the harmony of the church.

The christological controversies, as they are called, turned upon the question whether Christ had one or two natures: or more exactly whether the human and divine natures were in Him so closely united as to form but one nature, or whether they still remained in their distinctness, conjoined, but not in themselves united, and always capable of being discerned the one from the other, not only in thought but in the historical incidents of His human career. Two tendencies can be seen running through the ages during which the church was occupied with the solution of this problem. One of these tendencies, which proceeded from the home of Greek theology, where the influence of Athanasius still lingered, regarded the human nature as in its constitution so closely akin to the divine, that when Christ assumed humanity He did not take something in its nature foreign to the divine principle: He rather by His incarnation revealed the kinship of the human with the divine, and the perfected human was therefore declared to be identical with that which was most divine. Christ did not exist in two distinct natures formally united or combined by some bond external to either of them, but there was one nature only of the God-man, and in His sacred person the human and the divine were no longer to be distinguished even in thought, much less in the reality of His earthly life. He willed and acted, He spoke and thought, in the undivided consciousness of His unique personality, — a consciousness in which human nature was deified and identical with the divine. The other tendency, which proceeded from the school of Antioch and was most acceptable to the Western mind, was grounded in the conviction that the human and the divine were incompatible with or alien to each other, and were therefore incapable of a real unity, and remained forever distinct, however firm the conjunction into which they had been brought by the incarnation.

It is hardly necessary to remark that the age was no longer a favorable one for the discussion of a theme which implied so profound an issue as the innermost significance of the human in its relation to the divine. The controversies upon the subject were embarrassed by the passions and local excitements, so easily generated in the bosom of a declining society. As the empire grew weaker, the fragments of which it was originally composed tended to fall back into their original isolation, and national jealousies combined with theological differences to make Syria and Egypt so tenacious of their respective attitudes as to render a common understanding impossible. The controversies were further complicated by imperial or ecclesiastical intrigues and combinations. Popular instincts were invoked against theological distinctions. Such important terms as nature and person were not defined or carefully distinguished. While some held that a nature necessarily implied a person or personality, others contended that personality was distinct from the nature. To some it appeared as though to assert two natures in Christ was to teach a double personality, while their opponents maintained that one personality might be the tie which bound the natures together.[1] The general councils, as might have been expected, fluctuated in their decisions, leaning now to one side, now to the other. The third general council held at Ephesus in the year 431 — to whose acts no moral value attaches in consequence of the spirit in which it was conducted — gave its support to the doctrine of one nature in Christ as it had been expounded by Cyril; the fourth general council held at Chalcedon in 451 decided that there were two natures in Christ remaining forever distinct; and although it protested against their separation in the unity of the divine person, it did not attempt to explain their inner relationship or the mode of their union. The fifth general council held at Constantinople in 553, although unable

[1] It is important to bear in mind that the defect of ancient thought, as Dorner has pointed out, was the lack of the modern idea of personality — the ego as self-conscious spirit moving toward the fulfillment of its existence. The ancient fathers were feeling their way toward this conception in the use of such terms as essence, being, nature, hypostasis, prosopon, etc. Cf. Dorner, *Person of Christ* (Eng. trans.), A. ii. p. 510.

to set aside the action of the fourth council, did what it could to discredit the decision reached at Chalcedon by condemning the great leaders of the Antiochian school, of whose attitude the Council of Chalcedon was but the reflection. And finally, the sixth general council in 680 reasserted in another form the decision of the fourth council, by declaring that as there were two natures in Christ, so also there were two wills, the human and the divine; but following Chalcedon it did not recognize their ethical oneness, and contented itself with declaring that the human will followed and was subject to the divine.[1]

[1] If, as is generally admitted, the anathemas of Cyril against Nestorius received the approval of the Council of Ephesus, as the letter of Pope Leo received the approval of the Council of Chalcedon, it is plain that Leo committed the error which the fourth anathema of Cyril condemned. The two passages here given — the fourth of Cyril's anathemas, and the sentences from Leo's letter — are certainly in downright opposition to each other. The original texts are given in Labbé, *Concilia*, tom. iii. p. 958, and iv. p. 1222. They may also be found in Gieseler, *Eccles. Hist.*, i. pp. 349-357.

Εἴ τις προσώποις δυσὶν, ἤγουν ὑποστάσεσι, τάς τε ἐν τοῖς εὐαγγελικοῖς καὶ ἀποστολικοῖς συγγράμμασι διανέμει φωνὰς, ἢ ἐπὶ Χριστῷ παρὰ τῶν ἁγίων λεγομένας, ἢ παρ' αὐτοῦ περὶ ἑαυτοῦ, καὶ τὰς μὲν ὡς ἀνθρώπῳ παρὰ τὸν ἐκ θεοῦ λόγον ἰδικῶς νοουμένῳ προσάπτει, τὰς δὲ ὡς θεοπρεπεῖς μόνῳ τῷ ἐκ θεοῦ πατρὸς λόγῳ, ἀνάθεμα ἔστω.

(If any one portions out to the two persons or hypostases the expressions in the evangelical or apostolic writings, or the expressions used by the saints concerning Christ, or those put forth by Him concerning Himself, and shall assign the one class of expressions as especially belonging to the man as distinct from the divine Logos, and the other class as divine to the Logos only, let him be anathema.)

Quem itaque sicut hominem diabolica tentat astutia, eidem sicut Deo angelica famulantur officia. . . . Ita non ejusdem naturæ est dicere; *Ego et Pater unum sumus* (Joan. x. 30); et dicere; *Pater major me est* (Joan. xiv. 28).

As we review these long-enduring controversies about the person of Christ, it becomes apparent that their varying moods and results are the visible signs of a profound inward transformation going on within the church, which is to determine the character of Christianity for a thousand years until another transformation, equally profound and far-reaching, shall reverse the spirit and the bent of centuries. From the time of the Nestorian controversy, when the unfortunate patriarch of Constantinople protested in vain against the application to Mary of the title, Mother of God, a title heathen in its origin, and in its Christian use obscuring the meaning of the incarnation,[1] it is increasingly evident that the earlier and more spiritual conception of Christ as the divine immanence in humanity is disappearing from the church. The vision of the essential Christ as He existed from eternity, and as He still revealed Himself to the world, was giving way to a limited portrait of His historical existence in which His mother and His brethren, according to the earthly relationship, were rising into a prominence which Christ Himself had not countenanced. The woman who lifted up her voice in the crowd and exclaimed, *Blessed is the womb that bare Thee and the paps which Thou hast sucked*, was now becoming, as

(Therefore just as diabolical subtilty tempts Him as man, so also angelical ministrants wait upon Him as God. . . . It does not belong to one and the same nature to say, *I and my Father are one*, and to say, *My Father is greater than I.*)

[1] Upon the phrase, "Mother of God," as applied to Mary, Coleridge remarks : "An epithet which conceals half of a truth, the power and special concerningness of which relatively to our redemption by Christ depend on our knowledge of the whole, is a deceptive and dangerously deceptive epithet." — Coleridge, *Works*, v. p. 60, Am. ed.

it were, the typical spokesman of the church, whether in Alexandria or Asia Minor, in the East or in the West. The spiritual relationship was becoming subordinated to the relationship after the flesh, and the words of Christ were becoming unintelligible, — *Nay, rather blessed is he that heareth the will of God and keepeth it : he that doeth the will of my Father which is in heaven the same is my mother and sister and brother.* In proportion as Christian faith was losing its hold on the essential Christ, with greater tenacity did it cling to the historical Christ. In proportion as men ceased to realize the divine immanence in humanity, they emphasized the fact that God had once blessed the world in visible form, and dwelt with increasing devotion upon the historic environment of his earthly life. The worship of Mary, the cultus of apostles, became a means to this end by enabling the lower intelligence to realize more easily the historic fact of an incarnation, or to deepen the vividness of its apprehension. From this time the Latin church began to realize more distinctly her peculiar mission, — to impress upon the new races that there had once been a manifestation of God in the flesh. So long as that belief remained, the world was the richer for it; and though humanity went on its way groping in the dim light of an eclipse of the fuller faith, yet it could never again become so helpless or forsaken as before the advent of Christ.

Whatever weight is to be attached to the conflicting utterances of the general councils on the subject of the person of Christ, one thing is clear — that they did not and could not control a mighty sentiment silently operating in the church, whose growth was stimulated by causes, the influence of which could not at the time be detected or measured. While theologians in the councils were carefully selecting their language in order to express some delicate shade of meaning, or were devising compromises by which the peace of the church might be obtained, the sentiment of Christendom was slowly gravitating to the conclusion that the human and the divine were not only distinct from, but alien to, each other; and no assertion, however carefully balanced, in regard to their union in Christ, could overcome the conviction that an infinite impassable gulf divided and separated humanity from God. The doctrine of the two natures which Rome and Antioch agreed in asserting at Chalcedon in opposition to Alexandria, when it had been filtered through the experience of later ages, became a principle of dualism which sanctioned the divorce between the human and the divine, the secular and the religious, the body and the spirit. The dualism of the two natures runs through all the institutions of the Middle Ages, affecting not only the religious experience, but the political and social life of Christendom. As a theological principle, it underlies asceticism in all its forms; it creates and enforces the distinction between sacred and profane things, holy days and common days, between the clergy and the people, the church and the world, the pope and the emperor, the city of God and the city of man. As a theological principle it reigned supreme from the time of Augustine till the age of the Reformation.

IV.

The most important event in the history of the Latin church was the conversion of Augustine in the year 387. It was the mission of Augustine to personate the crisis through which the church and the world of his time were passing. In his experience we may read as in a mirror the inward moods of the darkest and saddest age in human history. All the sinister tendencies which had been gathering strength for generations met in his mind. The decline of the Roman empire, which had become so evident that men of great capacity no longer looked to it as a sphere in which the highest ambition for usefulness might be gratified; the decline of intellectual activity, accompanying necessarily the decadence of human hopes for this world; the skepticism which looked upon philosophy as a vain struggle for the attainment of truth; the feeling that things were out of joint, that evils whose horror and extent the mind could not fathom were at hand, and could not be postponed much longer; the sense of sin, which, in its crudest shapes as it appears in history, is the inward conviction that something is wrong in the relation of the world to the unseen powers, and is drawing down upon it the divine vengeance, — these were the dominant moods of the age which gave birth to Augustine. He lived them out in his own experience, and became therefore the type of his time; he reveals how other men were thinking, how the age itself was tending; he discloses the inner process of transition from heathenism to Latin Christianity. He was as truly a prophet to the Roman world as was Mohammed, two centuries later, to the Arabian races, — both of them struggling with the same great issues of human destiny.

The conversion of Augustine is an event inexplicable unless we go beneath the surface of the conventional language used in describing it. One may read his "Confessions," and feel that the secret of the change has evaded him. As in all similar cases, whenever they occur, the actor himself is not capable of giving an intelligible explanation of that which has befallen him. The full significance of Augustine's conversion becomes apparent only when we follow his career to its close, or interpret it in the institutions upon which he impressed his convictions.

The outward life of Augustine before his conversion was the ordinary life of a young and ambitious Roman, looking forward to success and distinction in the customary ways, except that he possessed extraordinary talents which seemed to promise an unusually brilliant career. Despite the sins of his earlier years and of a certain want of honor and sensitiveness in his relationships which still appears strange to us, notwithstanding our allowance for the social usages of an age very unlike our own, there was also something in Augustine's early life which represents the serious bent of his nature. He was interested in the search for truth and studied Greek philosophy as a means to its attainment. That which most of all attracted him in the problems of human thought was the question concerning the origin of evil. It was therefore a significant fact that in his early life he became a Manichæan and for nine years remained a member of this sect, or till he had reached the age of thirty. In the dualism of the Manichæan theosophy, which explained the predominance of evil by the existence of an evil deity, who from all eternity combated the good deity and who furnished the larger part of the material out of which the world had been made, there was something which appealed to the darker moods of thoughtful men in the fourth century. Manichæism was in no respect a Christian system of thought, although it had adopted a Christian nomenclature, and it showed its divergence from the Christian idea in another respect by denying the redemption of humanity in Christ. Such a world as this was incapable of being redeemed, — the only hope was in a principle of election by which a few might be saved.

Even though Augustine turned away from such teaching and believed he had renounced it, it was impossible that it should not have left its traces stamped indelibly upon his mind, to reappear again under other forms, in different combinations. The next stage in his mental career was one of skepticism, in which he doubted if the reason was capable of attaining the truth. It was in this mood, which extended over some five years of his life, that he went to Milan about the year 384, in the exercise of his profession as a teacher of rhetoric. So far, his life from a human point of view had not been successful; he had not achieved the wealth or the honor which he was entitled to expect; his mind was in a perturbed unsettled condition, ready to receive the strongest influence that could be brought to bear upon it. His familiarity with different phases of thought, the various changes which he had already gone through in his mental experience, the profound dissatisfaction which he felt with himself and with the world, — these things were undermining his intellectual integrity. For such a man whose will was weak and whose passions were powerful, whose strength lay chiefly in the life of the emotions, who had no canon for the recognition of truth, whose intellectual stability had been shaken by so many changes of opinion, there was but one resort at last, — to fall back upon some external authority, if any such existed, powerful enough to subdue the intellect, to open up a channel for the emotions, and to hold the will to a definite purpose.

Hitherto Augustine does not seem to have had much respect for the church; it probably appeared to him as to most educated Romans as offering no sphere for thoughtful persons. That it had been the object of his mother's devoted love was no recommendation in his eyes, for it had been one of his principles to refuse to be led by a woman's influence. But at Milan, where the church was administered by Ambrose, it was impossible that a genuine Roman should not be impressed with a profound respect for the power which it exerted and the future which awaited it. In the fact of Ambrose turning away from the service of the state to what must have seemed a nobler opportunity, was an indication that far-sighted men had ceased to expect anything from the empire and were looking elsewhere. The church was already undergoing a momentous change, — it was beginning to grow into the state, as the state was tending to become a mere function of the church. Already the church must have appeared as stronger than the state when a bishop like Ambrose could successfully defy a Roman empress and humiliate under his spiritual authority an emperor like Theodosius. Augustine could not remain insensible to the spectacle of such a church and of such a bishop, — a predecessor in all but the name of the greatest popes of the Middle Ages. His contempt for the church gradually gave way to a feeling of reverence. As he attended its services and was moved by the eloquence of the great bishop, as he wept silently by the side of his mother during the singing of the hymns by the great congregation, a change was coming over his spirit. He was renouncing himself, his reason, his whole past life, in the presence of an external authority, whose power and splendor awed while it charmed his imagination, — a church in which truth assumed a concrete, tangible form for the practical control and guidance of life.

There was an important step in the process by which Augustine's conversion was accomplished which deserves a moment's notice. It is a phase of his mental or religious history upon which he does not dwell in his "Confessions," nor is it difficult to understand why in his later life he should pass it over so lightly.[1] While he was still in Milan under the influence of Ambrose, he was also studying the Platonists as he called them — the Alexandrian school of philosophers — and was coming to understand how, by the application of their method to Christian theology, there might be a more rational and liberal way of interpreting the doctrines of the church than he had hitherto met. He admits, for example,[2] that there was one difficulty which he had to overcome before entering the church, — the crude anthropomorphic conception of Deity as localized in space, which he had always supposed was the Christian idea of God, — an idea which Tertullian had advocated and which was certainly the popular view. The traces of this earlier theology, by means of which Augustine sufficiently satisfied his reason while yet making the sacrifice of reason, are to be found in those of his writings which were produced in the years immediately following his conversion, — before the necessities of ecclesiastical administration in the see of Hippo had revolutionized his intellectual methods or led him to economize the truth in the interest of the

---

[1] *Confess.*, vi. 5, and viii. 2. The *Confessions* were written after Augustine became Bishop of Hippo. Cf. Owen, *Evenings with the Skeptics*, ii. p. 173.

[2] *Confess.*, vi. 4.

church, or to adjust it to the comprehension of a barbarous people. In these treatises [1] he speaks like Athanasius, of Deity as immanent in the world, of the incarnation as the necessary mode of the divine manifestation,—a necessity inherent in the divine nature, of the love of God as the ground or determination of His will, of man as having power to read the divine character because of an inward light in the reason which is the evidence of the indwelling God, of the will as free and having power to follow the right, of the purification of the soul as the way to the knowledge of and union with the divine. But thoughts like these only served Augustine in the epoch of his transition; in his later writings they disappear, giving way to a set of dogmas more congenial to the Latin mind, or more in harmony with the aim of the Latin church as Augustine construed it.

For it was to the church as it had grown up in Latin Christendom that Augustine had been converted, and great as were the innovations which he sanctioned upon the theories of his predecessors, it was still to the Latin church as an institution that he consecrated the labors of his life. As he came in contact with sects or heresies which denied its authority or rejected its essential principle, his conception of it became more clear and dogmatic; [2] and it may be said of his life-

[1] Among them are the works entitled *De moribus ecclesiæ Catholicæ et Manichæorum*, *De vera religione*, *De libero arbitrio*, and *De utilitate credendi*.

[2] It was a characteristic of Augustine that he depended so largely upon controversy to determine his thought. He had not the constructive power of a consecutive thinker. The late Canon Mozley, who had made a special study of his controversial writings and was regarded as having an unusual gift for analyzing character, says of him as a controversialist: "In argument he

work as Bishop of Hippo, that its predominant aim was to adjust social institutions and even humanity itself to the claims of a hierarchy divinely appointed to teach and to rule the world.

Against the Manichæans, with whom he conducted his first controversy, Augustine maintained the authority of the church to teach. The same argument which Tertullian and Irenæus had employed is again brought forward, but with the increased weight which two centuries of growth had given to the power and magnificence of the hierarchy. Truth is a "deposit" intrusted to the episcopate for preservation; it is to be found only within the church, and to the sanction of the church even Scripture owes its authority.[1] The church for which is claimed such supreme authority is not the consentient reason of those who are enlightened by a divine teacher speaking within the soul, — it is the institution of which the episcopate holds the charter, which is possessed of a "deposit" intrusted to it by a power external to itself. The leading *notes* of such a church, as they were presented by Augustine to the

---

was not too deep; to have been so would have very much obstructed his access to the mind of the mass, and prevented him from getting hold of the ear of the church at large. He undoubtedly dealt with profound questions, but his mode of dealing with them was not such as to entangle him in knots and intricacies arising from the disposition to do justice to all sides of truth." In some parts of the Manichæan controversy "he returned neat answers rather than full or final answers." In the Pelagian controversy, "he did not allow the unity and simplicity of his answers to be at all interfered with by large and inclusive views of truth. To the extreme contradictory on the one side, he gave the extreme contradictory on the other." — *Ruling Ideas of Early Ages*, p. 255.

[1] *Contra Epistolam Manichæi*, c. 6: "Ego vero evangelio non crederem, nisi me catholicæ ecclesiæ commoveret auctoritas."

Manichæans, are its power, its splendor, its miraculous gifts, its vast extension, its long succession of bishops coming down through the ages from the see of Peter.[1] Unless it had possessed these credentials, its authority would have gone for little or nothing with Augustine.

In his controversy with the Donatists, the progress of Augustine in fixing the idea of the church is still further manifest, and there is also revealed the change in his conception of Deity which such a view of the church necessarily implied. The Donatists had already existed as a sect in North Africa for nearly a century when Augustine was led to take up the controversy against them. They had their origin in a protest against the laxity which allowed the apostates, in the Diocletian persecutions, to be received back again into the communion of the Catholic church, and, in accordance with the view which had been held by Montanists and Novatians, they contended that the church consisted only of those who were known or believed to be faithful. Hence they had organized as a separate community, calling themselves the only true church, and, toward the end of the fourth century, when Augustine came as bishop to Hippo, they were a formidable body in numbers and influence. In consequence of the persecution which they had encountered from the Roman emperors, who had endeavored to extirpate a sect which disturbed the external unity of the church, the Donatists had assumed another principle, — that it was sinful for the church to depend upon the state for protection; that between church and state there should be no connection whatever. A sect with such tenets could not but be obnoxious to

[1] *Contra Ep Man.*, c. 5.

one, like Augustine, bent on maintaining the undisputed authority and unity of the church, and who, as a practical administrator of a diocese, was constantly witnessing the confusion and weakness which its presence created. He was moderate at first in his opposition, and endeavored by conciliatory measures to meet the evil. But it was a feature of Augustine as a controversialist, as it was, also, of Tertullian, that he always appeared as a lawyer holding a brief for the church; and it became his object to find some principle which would completely subvert the position of his adversaries. If it was successful, if it shut the mouths of opponents, such a principle was to him its own verification. In the case of the Donatists, it was necessary to assert, if they were to be overcome, that the church, by its very nature, must include the unfaithful and the wicked, — the chaff was inseparable from the wheat in this world, the tares must grow until the harvest.

But such an attitude could not be maintained without going further, and Augustine seems to have hesitated before taking a step which, when once accepted and avowed, entailed momentous consequences. Augustine could not conceive of the church otherwise than he had first known it, — the majestic institution which had borne down his doubts and commanded the surrender of his reason, his conscience, and his will. He had taken the church as he found it; he had accepted unhesitatingly the *dictum* of Cyprian, that outside of this church there was no salvation, — that he who had not the church as his mother could not have God as his father. It was not enough, therefore, to assert against the Donatists the divine right of the hierarchy to an authority which required implicit obedience on the part of those only who acknowledged that authority. The nature of the church demanded that all men should submit to its sway. The church was not placed in the world in order to offer a probation to men, as Cyprian had thought. The idea of probation was becoming repugnant to the mind of Augustine. There was rising in his soul the idea of God as a being who intended to rule this world, and did actually do so. To leave men to decide for themselves the great issues of their destiny was to leave God out of the question. The church was here by divine appointment, and if so it was the divine will that all men should come into it; and if they would not come of themselves, they must be forced to do so; and if the church lacked the power of compulsion, it was the sacred duty which the state owed to the church to come to its rescue, and by the might of the sword "compel them to come in," that the church might be filled.[1]

The Manichæans denied that the Catholic church was the sole depository of truth; the Donatists denied that it had a divine right to rule the conscience; but there was growing up a third tendency which, as Augustine and others clearly perceived, denied that the church had any real motive for existence. In the system of Pelagius such a church as Augustine so rigorously and devoutly upheld was simply unnecessary; it subserved no indispensable purpose in the process of salvation; man could be saved without it; the human will was sufficient to itself; it had power to turn away from evil and follow righteousness; or, if necessary, God would vouchsafe His special aid to its assistance. Exactly what the Pelagians held, it may be difficult to

[1] *Epistola* (93) *ad Vincentium.*

determine,[1] but it is clear what their opponents thought they held, or ought to hold, and this is more important to the course of the history than the actual belief of the famous heresiarch who personated to the Latin mind the lowest stage of intellectual and religious depravity.

When we recall the prominence of the church in

[1] If the Pelagians were resting upon the same principle that Augustine had adopted, — the absolute separation of humanity from God, and yet held man to be capable of attaining salvation by his own unaided efforts, — their views were certainly most pernicious, and would have substituted a sort of Confucian morality in the place of the religion of Christ. But it is more likely that their teaching was the echo of an earlier and higher theology imperfectly apprehended, if, indeed, it was any longer capable of apprehension by the Latin mind on account of its inversion of the true relationship between Christ and the church. The contemporary Greek theologians could see no harm in Pelagius's teaching, and Greek synods declined to condemn it, — a fact which the Latins could only explain on the supposition that Pelagius dissembled his opinions. The third general council, it is true, condemned Pelagianism; this seems to have been the result of an understanding between Cyril and the Bishop of Rome, by which Cyril anathematized the Latin heretic, while the pope gave his voice against the Greek heretic, Nestorius, who had also incurred his displeasure by sheltering the Pelagians who fled to Constantinople. Because they were condemned together, it has been thought by some that there was a subtle connection between Pelagianism and Nestorianism; but there was in reality a closer connection between Nestorianism and Augustinianism. If the third council condemned Pelagius, it did not undertake to say in what his error consisted; and the two tenets of Pelagius which were most obnoxious to Augustine, namely, that original sin implies no guilt in Adam's descendants, and that the will of every man is free to choose good or evil, have remained the teaching of the Greek church to this day. A summary of what the Pelagians asserted against Augustine, as shown by their own statements, and not those of their opponents, is given in Gieseler *Eccles. Hist.*, i. 383.

the history of Latin Christendom from the time of Clement of Rome to Augustine, we are forced to admit that the same idea underlay the famous Pelagian controversy. Consciously or unconsciously it was the church, as the Latins conceived it, which formed the determining motive in the doctrines concerning the nature of sin and redemption, of grace and free-will.[1] When it is remembered that the result of Augustine's teaching upon these points was to subject men to the absolute authority of the Latin church, it is evident that this must have been also the intention which, however veiled, or subtly mixed with other tendencies, controlled his thought and influenced his conclusions. The church had already, before Augustine's time, taken shape in the Latin mind as a vast, pervasive, mysterious entity, a personification as it were of the hierarchy or episcopate, a living corporate existence endowed from without with all the powers, the supernatural gifts and grace for the salvation of men. In one sense, it is true, all men who were in communion with the Catholic episcopate were spoken of as the church. But in the most important sense, the church, as teaching and ruling the world, was not the people but the hierarchy; the grace that saved was deposited primarily not in the congregation, but in the bishops, by whom it was administered to the people. Thus the church had taken the place of Christ as the way of redemption, and had become the mediator between God and man. Such a view of the church implied that the departure of Christ from the world was real

[1] "The Augustinian theology coincided with the tendencies of the age towards the growth of the strong sacerdotal system; and the sacerdotal system reconciled Christendom with the Augustinian theology." — Milman, *Latin Christianity*, i. p. 172.

and complete; that the episcopate was appointed to teach and to save as vicars of the absent Lord. The church moulding itself by a natural instinct after the empire, and reaching out toward the centralization of authority in the most convenient and practical form, must, like the civil government vested in the emperor, regard its power as derived not from the people as their representative, but as coming from a source external to and above them. In other words, Latin Christianity had reverted to a deistic basis, in which God is conceived as existing apart from the world in the distant heavens, regulating human affairs from without through the agency of commissioned delegates.

To this church it was that Augustine had been converted, although the full significance of his conversion was not at once apparent, and for years his thought was in confusion in consequence of the lingering influence of a higher theology. But from the time when he became Bishop of Hippo, the ecclesiastical leaven began to work most powerfully, and truth, as such, was no longer the object of his life. Before the Pelagian controversy began, he was seeking for some dogmatic basis by which to justify the claims of the church as a mediator between God and man, without whose intervention salvation was impossible. In so doing he was laying the corner-stone of Latin theology. When the Pelagian controversy was over, the Latin church was for the first time in possession of a theology of its own, differing at every point from the earlier Greek theology, starting from different premises and actuated throughout by another motive.[1]

[1] It is in his famous treatise *De Civitate Dei*, and in his anti-Pelagian writings *passim*, that Augustine's matured theological convictions are to be found in their complete form.

The foundation of that theology was the Augustinian dogma of original sin. That doctrine was alone adequate to explain the existence and mediatorship of the church, or to justify its claim to teach and to rule with supreme authority. The dogma of original sin was unknown to Greek theology as well as an innovation also in Latin thought, though it had been vaguely broached by Tertullian and Cyprian, and intimations looking toward it are to be found in the writings of Ambrose. According to this dogma, humanity is absolutely separated from God in consequence of Adam's sin. In the guilt of that sin the whole human race is implicated, and has therefore fallen under the wrath and condemnation of God, — a condemnation which dooms the race, as a whole and as individuals, to everlasting woe. So deeply is Augustine interested in establishing this position, that the redemption of the world by Christ inevitably assumes a subordinate place, and is practically denied. Adam and not Christ becomes the normal man, the type and representative, the federal head of the race. There is a solidarity of mankind in sin and guilt, but not in redemption, — a solidarity in Adam, not in Christ. There stands, as it were, at the opening of the drama of human history a quasi-supernatural being, whose rebellion involves the whole human family in destruction. Endowed with a supernatural gift, — the image of God in his constitution which united him closely with his maker, — he lost it for himself and his descendants by one sinful act, and thus cut off humanity from any relationship with God. In this catastrophe, the reason, the conscience, the will of man suffered alike; the traces of the divine image in human nature were destroyed.

How then is the sundered relationship to be restored? What is redemption, and how is it to be applied? The place of Christ in Augustine's scheme is not a prominent one, for humanity has not been redeemed. Augustine continues to speak of Christ, it is true, in the conventional way, but he no longer finds in His work any bond which unites God with humanity. The incarnation has become a mystery, — God chose to accomplish human salvation in this way, but so far as we can see He might have adopted some other method. It almost seems as though, if Christ were left out altogether, the scheme of Augustine would still maintain its consistency as a whole and retain its value as a working system. The reasons which led Augustine to deny the universality of redemption were the same as had influenced Gnostics and Manichæans, — he was oppressed by the sense of sin in himself, the knowledge of it in others, the appalling extent and depth of human wickedness; these things to the mind of a practical Roman made it meaningless to think or act as if humanity were redeemed to God. But when the Christian principle of redemption had been abandoned, there was only one other alternative, and that was to follow still further in Gnostic and Manichæan footsteps, — to adopt the principle of an individual election by which some souls were saved out of the great mass doomed to destruction. The bond of union between this world and God is the divine will, — a will not grounded in righteousness or love, into whose mysterious ways it is vain for man to inquire, the justice of which it is presumptuous for him to discuss. That will whose arbitrary determinations constitute right, chooses some to salvation and leaves the rest to follow out the way to endless misery. In one respect the Augustinian idea of predestination diverged from the Gnostic and approximated the later Mohammedan conception, — it is a predestination which acts here and there in an arbitrary way without reference to human efforts or attainments. The clearest manifestation of the divine will in the world, which is open to the gaze of all, is the Catholic church, the one divinely appointed channel through which God has decreed that the elect are to be saved. Predestination is to a process within the church. For although Augustine believed that outside of the church none could be saved, he by no means held that all within the church would escape damnation. Although all are to be compelled to enter the church, this is only in order that the elect among them who are known only to God may obtain the grace to be found alone in the church, by which they make their election sure.

According to Augustine, sin has its seat in the will. The effect of original sin has been to so enfeeble or corrupt the will, that it has become powerless in every man to turn away from evil. The will is so firmly set toward evil, that only a divine creative act can renew it again after its original character. In this respect each man is isolated, and no man can help his brother; exhortations and example go for nothing; the enlightenment of the reason is in vain, — only God Himself acting upon the will from without, by His omnipotent power, can break down its opposition to what is good, and recreate it after the divine image which has been ruined in Adam's fall. This creative act takes place in baptism. In this rite, the image of God is restored, and the soul becomes possessed again of that supernatural gift which united man originally to his Creator. Hence, in the system of Augustine, baptism acquired a dogmatic significance which it had not hitherto possessed, great as was the importance which had always attached to it. For unless the divine image is replaced, it is impossible, in the nature of the case, that any one should be saved. Man, without baptism, is only a highly gifted animal, lacking the one essential quality which makes him capable of salvation, — of the divine communion here, and of the divine presence hereafter. Hence, for heathens and for unbaptized children, there is no hope in the world to come of ever seeing God. Their punishment may be a thing of degrees, for those who have not actually sinned it may hardly be punishment at all, — Augustine was willing to be lenient where his theory did not suffer, — but it will be endless, and the essence of their loss consists in this, that they can never to all eternity come to the knowledge of God, in which consists supernatural blessedness. The result of this belief was to make general the practice of infant baptism, which was not before Augustine's time the universal custom.[1]

Augustine's doctrine concerning original sin and its remission by baptism, as well as his views upon predestination, were regarded at the time as innovations, as well as a dangerous disturbance of the faith of the church. There is no doubt that the bishops of Rome were in sympathy with Augustine's policy; but in the course of the controversy there was one exception

[1] Some of the most eminent fathers of the fourth and fifth centuries, though born in Christian households, were not baptized till they reached maturity. Such were Basil, Gregory of Nazianzus, Gregory of Nyssa, Jerome, and also Augustine himself. Gregory of Nazianzus would have still further postponed the rite, had it not been a prerequisite for ordination. The custom of postponing baptism continued in the East for some time after infant baptism had become the rule in the West.

among them in the person of Zosimus, before whom the case of the Pelagians was laid, and who declared that their confession of faith revealed no taint of heresy, and that the whole discussion arose from a childlike love of innovation. Zosimus may have been, as is generally thought, a Greek, but he could not have called the doctrine of original sin and its remission by baptism, in the case of infants, a novelty, if it had formed a part of the Roman tradition and usage.[1] Theodore, of Mopsuestia, the greatest among Eastern theologians in the fifth century, charged Augustine's lack of insight into the nature of the Christian faith to his ignorance of the Scriptures ; he called his doctrine of original sin a novelty recently set forth ; he reflected upon his lack of reverence and of true fear, in asserting things about God which human justice would condemn, and with which no wise man could agree.[2] But the most remarkable opposition to the Augustinian theology came from the remoter West, and was formulated by Vincens of Lerins, in his famous motto, by which he sought at once a principle of Christian certitude, as well as a convenient test for detecting the innovations of error : " That should be held for Catholic truth which has been believed everywhere, always, and by all." [3] Judged by this stand-

[1] Cf. Labbé, *Concilia*, tom. iii. pp. 401, 403, for the letters of Zosimus to the African bishops.

[2] Gieseler, *Ec. Hist.*, i. 339.

[3] *Commonitorium pro Catholicæ fidei antiquitate et universitate*, etc., c. 2, Migne's *Patrolog.*, tom. 50, p. 640 : "In ipsa item Catholica Ecclesia magnopere curandum est, ut id teneamus quod ubique, quod semper, quod ab omnibus creditum sit." A partial translation of the *Commonitorium* was made by John Henry Newman, in *Tracts for the Times*, vol. i. p. 592, where it is intended to form a companion for Tertullian's *Prescription of Here-*

ard, the teaching of Augustine lacked each one of the three essential marks of truth. That it was the object of Vincens to controvert the great African father, though he does not mention him by name, is generally admitted; but the latter part of his "Commonitorium," in which he enforced the application of his principle, has been lost, and is said to have been stolen in his lifetime. The first part has ever since remained a standard exposition of what is called the "great Catholic principle." It is one of the curiosities — not to say variations — in the history of Latin theology, that the Roman church has accepted the principle of Vincens, and at the same time approved the theology which that principle was set forth to condemn.

No point more clearly illustrates the degradation which Christian theology underwent at the hands of Augustine than his doctrine of grace. Christ as the invisible teacher of humanity, whose presence in the world, in the reason and conscience of man, is the power by which men are delivered from sin and brought into the liberty of the children of God, gives way in the system of Augustine to an impersonal thing or substance which is known as grace. However it may be defined — and Augustine's use of the word varies — it is grace that constitutes the beginning, middle, and end of the way of salvation. There is prevenient grace that makes man ready to receive the gospel, there is grace that *operates* to renew the will, grace that *coöperates* with the will restored, irresisti-

tics. The notes attached by the illustrious translator have still a melancholy interest. A valuable criticism of the "Quod ubique," etc., may be found in Sir G. C. Lewis's *Authority in Matters of Opinion,* c. iv. The history of theology, however, is the best criticism upon this much vaunted test of truth.

ble grace that insures the final triumph. In one aspect, this grace may be defined as the will of God decreeing the salvation of the elect; in another aspect, it is a quality or spiritual potency deposited in the church or hierarchy and distributed to the people by the priesthood in the sacraments. What is sometimes called the sacramental theology is based upon the Augustinian notion of grace, — the principle that man is built up in the spiritual life by a subtle quality conveyed to him from without through material agencies, rather than by evoking the divine that is within. For such a system Augustine laid the foundation upon which the Latin church in the Middle Ages reared the elaborated structure.[1] Even in Augustine's time, it

[1] Augustine laid the dogmatic foundation of the sacramental theology by his doctrine concerning grace; but he did not connect the doctrine with the sacraments in the same way or to the same extent as was done in the mediæval church. According to Baur, his theory of the nature of a sacrament implied some supernatural affiliation between the sign and the thing signified: "Das Wesen des Sacraments setzte er in die Unterscheidung eines doppelten Elements, eines sinnlichen und übersinnlichen, welche beide sich nur wie Bild und Sache zu einander verhalten können. Das Vermittelnde dieser Beziehung ist das Wort." *Dogmengeschichte*, § 49. But the predominance of the idea of election in his system forced Augustine to modify what might otherwise have been a tendency to the lowest form of sacramentalism. Cf. *Epist.* (98) *ad Bonifacium* for the famous passage in which he seems to endeavor to speak plainly, but of which the apparent meaning can of course be disputed. Augustine certainly did not teach that all were regenerated in baptism, but only the elect; in the Lord's Supper also, only the elect, in virtue of their faith, participated in the body and the blood of Christ, while to all others it was but an empty sign. Such substantially was the teaching of Calvin. The leaders of the Tractarian movement in the Church of England were unconsciously asserting the mediæval view of the sacraments and not the Augustinian. In-

was felt to be desirable that the number of the channels or avenues of grace should be increased beyond the original two which Christ had appointed; and had the sacraments expanded until they included every agency for good with which human life abounds, the evil in the system would have been in some measure neutralized. But here also, as in the sphere of doctrine, the ecclesiastical idea was the controlling influence, and the sacraments were ultimately limited to those rites which bound men in absolute dependence upon the church for salvation.[1]

The effect of Augustine's views concerning the nature and consequences of original sin was to create a new dogmatic basis for the relationship between God and humanity, for the church, the priesthood, and the sacraments. The effect of these views is further seen in all that relates to human destiny in a future world. The doctrine of endless punishment assumed in the writings of Augustine a prominence and rigidity which had no parallel in the earlier history of theology, which had no warrant in the New Testament, and which savors of the teaching of Mohammed more than of Christ. Hitherto even in the West, it had been an open question whether the punishment hereafter of sin

deed it was the recognition by the Privy Council of the Augustinian view of baptism, as held by Mr. Gorham, that occasioned the stampede to the Church of Rome in 1852.

[1] The development of the sacraments in the Greek church followed in appearance somewhat the same course as in the Latin church, but was chiefly influenced by the teaching of the pseudo-Dionysius and not by the Augustinian idea of grace. The sacraments have never been to the Greek church quite what they are to the Latin, because they are viewed in their connection with the living and ever present Christ, rather than as channels through which the priesthood distribute an impersonal grace.

unrepented of and not forsaken was to be endless. Augustine has left on record the fact that some, very many indeed,[1] still fell back upon the mercy and love of God as a ground of hope for the ultimate restoration of humanity. Tertullian and Cyprian, as we have seen, had used harsh language in depicting the endless punishment of sin hereafter, but they may be said to have been speaking rhetorically and under the influence of excited emotion — under the conviction that only such a motive was adequate to move their cruel and hardened persecutors. But no such possible extenuation can be pleaded for Augustine. He is the first writer to undertake a long and elaborate defense of the doctrine of endless punishment and to wage a polemic against its impugners. In the 21st book of his "City of God" he seeks to establish it by Scripture, by analogy, by dialectic, by its inner necessary relationship with the scheme of God's government of the world. He rallies the "tender hearted Christians," as he calls them, who cannot accept it. The spirit in which he conducts his argument against the various classes of opponents whom he mentions, reveals how to his mind the doctrine entered as a necessary factor into the divine government, and was indispensable to the existence and work of the church on earth, which had been invested with the divine vicegerency.

[1] "Frustra nonulli, immo quam plurimi, æternam damnatorum pœnam et cruciatus sine intermissione perpetuos humano miserentur affectu atque ita futurum esse non credunt." *Enchirid. ad Laurentium*, c. cxii. "The belief," says Gieseler, "in the inalienable capability of improvement in all rational beings and the limited duration of future punishment was so general even in the West and among the opponents of Origen, that even if it may not be said to have arisen without the influence of Origen's school, it had become entirely independent of his system."- *Eccles. Hist.*, i. 321, Am. ed.

The allusions in Augustine's writings to the purifying fires which await the elect in another world,[1] have been sometimes regarded as hardly sufficient to warrant the mediæval doctrine of purgatory which was deduced from them. But Augustine is the father of the system, and its later modifications do not affect the substratum of the doctrine as announced by him. For if here on earth humanity is absolutely separated from God by Adam's fall, and the incarnation reveals no essential kinship between them, but is a device to overcome human sinfulness, and otherwise would not have been necessary,[2] why should the mere incident of death bring man at once into the presence of God and the enjoyment of his felicity. The causes which have operated here to maintain humanity in its isolation, may and even must continue in force to a certain extent hereafter. One can see that the dogmatic basis of thought and sentiment upon which the church was resting required, so to speak, that the church's influence and control should follow men into another world, before they were made quite ready to endure the beatific vision. Hence Augustine's hint, that the elect might remain for an indefinite period after death under the same penal system which held, during life, was no mere casual remark, but rather an inevitable logical deduction.

. The doctrine of purgatory followed naturally another belief which had prevailed chiefly in the Latin church, known as the doctrine of the intermediate state. This latter doctrine in its turn was dependent on those opinions concerning the resurrection of the body which had been advocated so vigorously by Ter-

---

[1] *Enchirid.*, c. 69, and *De Civitate Dei*, xx. c. 25.
[2] *Enchirid.*, cc. 33 and 48.

tullian, and which in the main Augustine accepted. When the doctrine of the resurrection was understood, as by Clement of Alexandria and others, to be an immediate standing up again in greater fullness of life, there could be no such conception entertained as that of an intermediate state; life here and hereafter was a regular and orderly progression under the guidance everywhere of the divine in-dwelling Word. But the belief in the resurrection as implying a restoration of the same identical body which had been laid in the grave, to which body all the particles which had composed it were essential, postponed the day when the dead should rise to the distant future. In the mean time the great host of the departed remained in a waiting attitude for the ultimate consummation. The idea, therefore, of a purgatory was, from such a point of view, an effort to occupy this waiting period with some definite purpose, and in some intimate way connect it with the life and work of the church on earth. In some respects, the belief in purgatory was an advance on the views of the future life which had prevailed among Jews and heathens, for it involved a moral principle and aim; and further, the imprisonment was not a final one, — at some time the doors were to be opened and souls to be received into their everlasting home. But both the doctrine of purgatory and that of the intermediate state have a close analogy with pre-Christian views, whether Jewish or heathen, and bear witness to a lower continuity between Christianity and the systems it supplanted. Apart from the element of hope which inheres in the Christian belief, the future life, whether of the intermediate state or purgatory, recalls again the Jewish Sheol and the world of the dead in Homer or in Virgil, — a place where souls exist in a disembodied condition wanting the richness and attractiveness of terrestrial life. To their brethren on earth their condition seemed one appealing to sympathy and pity. Augustine thought they might be helped by the sacraments and by the alms of their friends on earth. Certainly, with such a belief, it was not strange that men should pray for their dead; it would have been inhuman for them not to do so. But "prayers for the dead," as they were now offered, differed widely in spirit from that devout remembrance and giving of thanks for the departed which had characterized the higher and purer faith of the early church. Then it was believed that they were safe in the bosom of God, in joy and felicity; in the communion of Christ they had gone upwards to be with Him; and even the lower Hades, since Christ had penetrated its gloomy recesses, could no longer hold its own, but yielded up its inmates to the superior world of spiritual light and life. In the change of belief on this subject alone is sufficiently indicated the profound transformation which the Christian faith had undergone in Latin theology.[1]

In this brief sketch of Augustine's theology, his life has been alluded to only so far as it was connected with that system of opinions which he matured in his later years. In no ancient writer, however, does Christian experience seem to stand in such sharp con-

[1] It has been shown by De Rossi that none of the earlier expressions of confidence and hope, which are common among the few epitaphs of the second and third centuries, are to be found among the fifteen hundred inscriptions which belong to the fourth and fifth centuries. In their place appear the cold conventionalities of the obituary record, and utterances sometimes more pagan than Christian. Cf. Northcote, *Christian Epigraphy*, pp 74-76.

ESTIMATE OF AUGUSTINE'S WORK. 169

flict with formal opinion. When he writes from the heart, he still speaks to the Christian world to-day, as he has spoken through the ages, with an appeal in his tone which we are powerless to resist, with an exquisite charm in his language which we cannot forget. He lived in an age of transition, when the civilized world was passing in the West into a state of barbarism, and in connection with that fact his work as a theologian should always be remembered. He made the transition possible from the Roman empire of his day to the papal empire of the Middle Ages. The history of nearly a thousand years is summed up in his experience; but it was, on the whole, a history which the world does not care to see repeated, valuable as may be the results which it has contributed to secure to Christian civilization. It may have been necessary that the world should go back again to the " beggarly elements " from which it seemed to have escaped; but if so, it was because new races had come forward to carry on the line of human progress, who, before they could appreciate the Christian revelation, must undergo the preparatory training of tutors and school-masters, — who must pass under the yoke of the law before they were ready for the spirit of life and liberty. The work of Augustine ministered to this end. All through the Middle Ages his writings were the supreme authority in the study of theology. In one respect his books served a larger purpose than the aim of their great author, for they contained the germs of more than one system of theology, and from him the scholastic theologians, who knew no distinction between his earlier and his later writings, gained glimpses of a higher and vaster system of Christian thought than that which came down in tradition with the sanction of his name, — a system which they were debarred by their ignorance of the Greek language from studying in its original sources. He has been enumerated among the four great doctors of the Latin church; but he stands *facile princeps* among them. Ambrose was a distinguished administrator and popular orator; Jerome gave to the church its translation of the Scriptures; Gregory the Great illustrated, in a brilliant way, what service a pope might render to Christendom. But Augustine was great in that he may be said to have made possible the career of the Latin church. For a thousand years those who came after him did little more than reaffirm his teaching, and so deep is the hold which his long supremacy has left upon the church, that his opinions have become identified with the divine revelation, and are all that the majority of the Christian world yet know of the religion of Christ.

The question is sometimes asked why Mohammedanism, which swept over the East, should have halted at the gates of Rome, and never have succeeded in gaining anything but a precarious foothold in Western Europe. The answer to the question must take into consideration the work of Augustine. His doctrine of the church with which he inspired Western Christendom proved the impregnable rock to the irresistible wave. The belief of Islam in a theocracy of which the prophet and his successors were the divinely appointed rulers, — a theocracy outside of which all were infidels and beyond the pale of salvation, — was met by the Latin church with a similar belief in a theocracy in which Peter and his successors were the vicars of Christ. It may be regarded as one claim of the papacy to gratitude that it stood for a principle about which the crude sentiment of barbarous ages could rally, and thus prevent the surrender of the West to the religion of Mohammed. But it must also be remembered that so great a result was obtained by a corresponding sacrifice, and that Christianity approximated in its inmost principle to Islam. We have traced the process of deterioration in the Latin church, and more particularly in the theology of Augustine. In his idea of God as absolute and arbitrary will in which consists the only ground of right; in the depreciation of Christ, so that deism is the tacit assumption of the church on which its institutions rest; in his doctrine of election which differs in no essential particulars from the Mohammedan predestination; in his view of grace which becomes an act of the divine condescension, designed to exhibit chiefly the power and glory of God, and only incidentally considering the welfare of man;[1] in the

[1] "Der Begriff der Gnade bei Aug. ist noch nicht bestimmt als Liebe Gottes fixirt; sie ist vielmehr so gefasst, dass die Creatur ihr als Mittel dient, sich zu offenbaren. Es ist in dieser Vorstellung, dass ich so sage, der göttliche Egoismus noch nicht überwunden; Gott hat noch einen andern Zweck, wenn er den Menschen inspirirt, als den Menschen selbst zu vollenden; er inspirirt ihn nur, um sich durch ihn." — A. Dorner, *Augustinus. Sein theologisches System, und seine religionsphilosophische Anschauung*, p. 212.

"Mohammed deemed it a monstrous absurdity to suppose that the attributes of man gave him any peculiar claims on the consideration of God. But it was worse than an absurdity; it was blasphemy to suppose that man could claim any spiritual kinship with his Creator, that any particle of the divine essence had breathed into him." . . . "God is called the Merciful and the Compassionate, not because love is of the essence of His nature, but because, though all-powerful, He forbears to use His might for man's destruction." —*Islam Under the Arab,* by R. D. Osborn, quoted in Clarke's *Ten Great Religions,* ii. 379.

defiance of the reason and the subjugation of man under the divine omnipotence, — in such features as these do the Augustinian theology and the faith of Islam betray a fatal resemblance. Did we look to formal theology alone, the history of the church would remain inexplicable. But Christendom has never at any time quite lost its original birthright. Even in its darkest days and its lowest estate, the fact has never been forgotten that God had once visited the world in human form, that divine love had been manifested in the sacrifice upon Calvary. In that conviction, however much obscured or inadequately expressed, lay the difference between Christianity and Islam, and out of it has grown whatever is highest and most enduring in Christian civilization. The new world that was growing up in Western Europe had been taught, and believed sincerely, that the Bishop of Rome was the vicar of the absent Christ. So long as that belief prevailed, the papacy was supported by the sentiment of Western Christendom. When that belief died out, a new era in the world's history began.

THEOLOGY IN THE MIDDLE AGES.

Itaque lex pædagogus noster fuit in Christo. — GAL. iii. 24.

CHRONOLOGICAL TABLE.

A. D.
467-511. Clovis, King of the Franks.
500. [c.] Pseudo-Dionysius.
590-604. Gregory the Great, Pope.
680-755. Boniface, the Apostle of Germany.
785-818. The Adoptionist Controversy.
787. Seventh General Council approves image-worship.
800. Coronation of Charlemagne.
809. Acceptance of the *Filioque*.
816-840. Agobard, Archbishop of Lyons.
820-839. Claudius, Bishop of Turin.
831. Radbertus teaches transubstantiation.
840. [c.] Origin of the Forged-Decretals.
847-868. Controversy about predestination.
850. [c.] John Scotus Erigena.
858-867. Nicholas I., Pope.
1000. Expectation of the end of the world.
1033-1109. Anselm of Canterbury.
1073-1085. Gregory VII. (Hildebrand), Pope.
1079-1142. Abelard.
1091-1153. Bernard of Clairvaux.
1096-1291. Period of the Crusades.
1159-1164. Peter the Lombard, Bishop of Paris.
1170-1221. Dominic, Founder of the Dominican order
1182-1226. Francis d'Assisi.
1198-1216. Innocent the Great, Pope.
1209-1229. Crusade against the Albigenses.
1215. Twelfth General Council of the Latins.
1227-1274. Thomas Aquinas.
1232. Establishment of the Inquisition.
1265-1321. Dante Alighieri.
1265-1308. Duns Scotus.
1294-1303. Boniface VIII., Pope.

THEOLOGY IN THE MIDDLE AGES.

It has been the object of the preceding lectures to trace the characteristics of two distinct theologies. There were other theological movements in the early ages of the church, but they were relatively unimportant; the Jewish interpretation of Christianity, which may be seen in the Nazaritic and Ebionitic sects, had no enduring existence, and soon disappeared; Arianism, which had a kinship with the Hebrew or deistic phases of Christian thought, also disappeared, leaving no organized results as a monument of its influence. It was quite otherwise with what may be called the Greek and Latin theologies: they have been perpetuated in their essential characteristics in the two great divisions of Christendom known to-day as the Greek, or Holy Orthodox Church of the East; and the Latin, or Roman Catholic Church of the West. Before considering the mediæval development of Latin theological thought, which is the subject of the present lecture, let us review in a brief summary the differences on all essential points of the Greek and Latin theologies.[1]

[1] The general accuracy of this summary of the two theologies may be verified by consulting any of the doctrine histories, such as Neander, Hagenbach, or Baur. The Greek theology, it should be remembered, is distinct from the oriental tendency which prevailed in Asia Minor and elsewhere. Having been held in

The Greek theology was based upon that tradition or interpretation of the life and teaching of Christ which at a very early date had found its highest expression in the Fourth Gospel; while the Latin theology followed another tradition preserved by what are called the synoptical writers in the first three gospels. The fundamental principle of Greek theology, underlying every position which it assumed, was the doctrine of the divine immanence, — the presence of God in nature, in humanity, in the process of human history; in Latin thought may be everywhere discerned the working of another principle, sometimes known as Deism, according to which God is conceived as apart from the world, localized at a vast distance in the infinitude of space. By Greek thinkers the incarnation was regarded as the completion and the crown of a spiritual process in the history of man, dating from the creation; and by Latin writers as the remedy for a catastrophe, by which humanity had been severed from its affiliation with God. With the Greek, the emphasis was laid on the spiritual or essential Christ, who had always been present in human souls, who had become man in order that He might manifest the fullness of the Godhead bodily; with the Latin, the tendency was to magnify exclusively the historical Christ, who had come at a moment in time and then departed, leaving the world bereaved of His presence. Revela-

check for a time by Greek influence, its distinctive principle became more prominent after the age of Athanasius, when Greek theology entered upon the stage of decline. The oriental tendency showed itself more particularly in the doctrine of the sacraments, as in the case of Cyril of Jerusalem and even of Gregory of Nyssa, who represent in this respect the thought of Ignatius and Irenæus. A resumé of patristic teaching on the sacraments may be found in Norris, *Rudiments of Theology.*

SUMMARY OF THE TWO THEOLOGIES. 177

tion, according to Greek theology, was a continuous process, — a law of the spiritual creation, by which God was forever revealing Himself in and through the human reason; and reason itself was but the evidence in man of an immanent divine activity, of the light that lighteth every man that cometh into the world. While the revelation was continuous and in its scope included the whole discipline of life, there were great revealing epochs, such as the age of Hebrew prophets or Greek philosophers, and the work of these in turn was but fragmentary and incomplete compared with the life of Him who was God manifest in the flesh, — the incarnation of that divine reason which abides eternally in God. The tendency of Latin theology was to regard the reason as untrustworthy and dangerous; revelation was viewed as the definite and final communication of a message, a "deposit" in a book or rule of faith, to be guaranteed by tradition, or handed down as an heirloom from age to age.

It followed as a necessary sequence from the first principle of Greek theology, — the doctrine of the divine immanence, — that man should be viewed as having a constitutional kinship with Deity; by the image of God in man was understood an inalienable heritage, a spiritual or ethical birthright, which could not be forfeited. Deity and humanity were not alien the one to the other, and it was their constitutional relationship which made the incarnation not only possible but a necessary factor in the process of redemption. An opposite tendency was manifested in Latin thought; the tie which binds humanity to God was regarded as having been severed by Adam's fall. Only that part of humanity in whom the lost image of the Creator had been restored by a supernatural creative act could therefore be the recipients of redemption. With such a view of human nature the incarnation became a difficulty to the reason; and it is not surprising to find the mediæval theology developing a skepticism as to whether the incarnation was necessary, or if God might not have saved men in some other way. The Greeks held to the organic unity of mankind in Christ; the Latins recognized the principle of solidarity in Adam. With the one, redemption lay in evoking and confirming, by a spiritual education, the divine that is already in man; with the other, it consisted in an impartation of strength from without, through external channels. For the living presence in the soul of the spiritual Christ, the Latins substituted an inanimate thing which was designated in religious nomenclature as *grace*. The end of Christ's religion, as viewed by the Greeks, was the realizing of aspirations after a divine character, — the free imitation of God; as viewed by the Latins, it was obedience to an external law. Faith, in the Greek acceptation, was spiritual vision, — the insight of the soul into eternal realities; in the Latin, it was primarily assent to external authority.

The church, in its most essential aspect, was regarded by Greek theologians as the congregation of those who consciously acknowledged Christ as the way of righteousness and of life; the office of the clergy was a representative one; their authority came from the people, but they were also inspired by the Divine teacher to be the instructors and mouth-piece of those who constituted the body of Christ. In the Latin idea of the church, there was a tendency from the first to regard it as a divinely endowed, mysterious entity, distinct from the congregation, existing as a mediator between it and God. The church was practically identified with the hierarchical order, and the clergy held their office and prerogatives through a sanction away and apart from the people, — the delegates of a remote sovereign commissioned to rule in His name. The Greeks saw in the sacraments the symbols of the great verities of the Christian life, instructive monuments or witnesses to a divine presence and activity, whose traces were always and everywhere to be discerned. The Latins identified the symbols with the things signified, and with them the sacraments became external agencies, in the hands of the hierarchy, for communicating grace, the exclusive channels through which the divine life was imparted. In the comprehensiveness of the Greek estimate of Christ and His revelation, the salvation of which He is the author was not confined to those in union with the ecclesiastical organization, and His presence was seen working unconsciously in devout heathens in all ages; in the Latin scheme of redemption, salvability was not possible outside the communion of the visible organization; the whole body of heathens, without discrimination, as well as all infants dying without baptism, were inevitably lost forever to the vision and the presence of God. The Greeks thought of eternal life as consisting in that knowledge of God and of Christ which carried with it the harmonious development of the whole man in the way of truth and righteousness; the lack or rejection of this knowledge was death — the absence or negation of life. In the state of existence hereafter, the resurrection was conceived as the standing up again in the larger fullness of that immortal life which is in Christ. The Latin mind translated these conceptions into quantitative estimates: the resurrection was the revivifying of the identical particles of that body which had been laid in the grave and seen corruption; eternal life became unending happiness, and eternal death unending woe.[1]

The two theologies which we have contrasted do not stand to each other in the relation of the true to the false, but of the higher to the lower. The principle of historical continuity was not violated when Greek thought was translated into the theological idiom of the Latin mind. Latin Christianity was but the popularized version of Christian truth suited to the undeveloped capacity of the new races that were entering the empire, and alike adapted to the declining intellectual and spiritual forces of a people whose career of

---

[1] The "larger hope" for humanity which Clement and Origen asserted is nowhere denied by Athanasius; indeed, it was implied in his doctrine of the incarnation. The same view was entertained by Gregory of Nazianzus, and more emphatically by Gregory of Nyssa, — the one an intimate friend, and the other a brother, of Basil. It is found in the writings of Didymus, who was held in high repute in Alexandria, and was affirmed in the Antiochian school by Diodorus and Theodore of Mopsuestia, — a school of which Chrysostom was a pupil. In view of this harmony among the leading representatives of Greek theology, the language of Basil and Chrysostom may be regarded as dictated by the practical requirements of their work as great preachers and energetic administrators of large dioceses, rather than as theologians inquiring only after what is true. They may have acquiesced in an unfortunate admission of Origen's, of whom Basil was an earnest admirer, that it might be necessary to preach what one did not believe. Upon Chrysostom's position, see Neander, *Ch. Hist.*, iv. p. 442. Basil was also rebuking the presumption of those who abused the belief that punishment would have its limits. Cf. *Regulæ Brev. Tract, Interrog.* 267. See, also, Smith and Wace, *Dict. Chris. Biog.*, Art. Eschatology, for a careful summary of the opinion of the ancient church.

DETERIORATION OF GREEK THEOLOGY. 181

advance was over, and who were passing into the stage of senile weakness and decay. For the second childhood which was overtaking the old civilization, and for the first childhood in the history of the new, Greek theology, with its comprehensive range and its lofty spirituality, was unsuitable; even Origen had felt the inadequacy of the highest spiritual motives for those who were sinking into moral degeneracy with the growing barbarism, or for those who, in the first flush of physical vigor, were given over to bestiality and a brutal materialism. Under such circumstances it was a thing to be expected that Greek theology would show a tendency to Latinize, and the lower interpretation of spiritual truth be accepted in the place of the higher. Traces of such a deterioration may be seen in the Greek fathers of the fifth century; even in the latter part of the fourth century, such writers as Basil, the two Gregories, and Chrysostom, show a tendency to subordinate thought to rhetoric, and while true in the main to the spirit and method of Greek theology, are unconsciously affected by the waning light of the old Hellenic culture.

The age was over which had produced a Clement, an Origen, and an Athanasius; centuries were destined to roll away before the work which they had dropped could be resumed in their spirit and with their advantages at the point where they left it. Meantime no opening was offered to the Greek church, in the providence of God, by which its life might be quickened with the enthusiasm of missionary zeal. No mission devolved upon it to undertake the training of the new peoples, with whom, in the mystery of the divine purpose, lay the future of civilization. Closed in as the Eastern empire became by races inaccessible to Christian influences, the Eastern church was not only robbed of the larger part of its territory, but its spirit was benumbed and chilled, and it passed into that state of stagnant conservatism which has characterized its history to our own day. Tradition was substituted for free theological inquiry; scholastic refinements and adherence to formal orthodoxy were valued as of the highest moment. To make a mistake in the matter of dogma became to the Greek the one unpardonable sin. The anthropomorphism, against which its greatest theologians had struggled in the endeavor to maintain the divine existence as a purely spiritual one, became, through the blind and partisan efforts of the monkish orders, the popular conception of Deity. God was conceived as existing in human form, and with this belief came image worship, and the cultus which depends upon material agencies to feed the life of the immortal spirit. The writings of the pseudo-Dionysius (A. D. 500), who, following the later Neo-Platonists, put God at an infinite remove from man, filling up the chasm between them with a heavenly hierarchy of graded angelic existences, whose continuators in the church on earth were the hierarchy of bishops, priests, and deacons, — these writings were received, in the ignorance of the age, as having an apostolic origin, and became more influential than the fathers in moulding the opinion and practice of earnest and aspiring souls. The pious author of the *Celestial Hierarchy*, who had baptized under a Christian name the last expiring breath of paganism, had, like his Neo-Platonist teachers, declared it possible to attain the vision of God by throwing the soul into a trance through the well-known methods of oriental asceticism. It is interesting and touching, withal, to notice in the history of Greek mysticism so late as the fourteenth century, how a controversy arose on the point whether the light which the deluded monks, in their hallucinations, fancied surrounded their heads as a halo, was not the uncreated light which had also shone around the head of the Saviour upon Mount Tabor, — a feeble reminiscence of Greek theology in its better days with its postulate of revelation as light, — that light in which there was no darkness at all.

The Greek church still retains in its decayed and immobile condition the traces of its high descent. Despite its external resemblances to the Latin church, the ignorance of its clergy, or the superstitions and customs which repel the casual observer of its worship, there may still be seen in its standards and liturgies the ruling conceptions of those ancient masters of theology, Clement of Alexandria and Athanasius. In the high importance which it has always attached to preaching, in the ethical and homiletic tone of its liturgies, remaining substantially unchanged since their revision by Basil and Chrysostom, — liturgies which, to the practical mind of the West, seem interminably long, with a dreary waste of words, — in its attitude of doctrinal protest against the errors of Rome and of Geneva, there still speaks the voice of the most ancient, the most spiritual theology, as it existed in the days before its standard was lowered in the presence of an all pervading barbarism. The Greek church is as far removed from the spirit of Rome and of a Latinized Anglicanism on the one hand, as it is from the types of Protestant theology which, under the name of Calvinism, have perpetuated the spirit and the methods of Augustine, and to neither the one nor the other does it lend a willing ear. It still lies inactive, seemingly unconscious of the significance of later history, and may long continue to remain so. Its future is perhaps involved in the destinies of the vast empire which owns its allegiance; the fate of the Turk and the Mohammedan oppressor, when revealed, may be the signal for its awakening. No mission, as has been said, came to it as to its Latin neighbor to become the school-master to a new people with a high destiny; and yet, once in history, there came a great revival of the study of Hellenic literature, which, while attended by grave evils, especially in the home of the papacy, became among the northern nations the precursor of the Protestant Reformation. The study of Greek became from that time the basis of a *new learning* for Latin Christendom. Then it appeared that the Greek church had, during all of her apparent lifelessness, been assigned a providential role in history, — to preserve the ancient literature and hand it over when the new world was ready to receive it. In the consolation which Milton felt when he found himself debarred from the activities of life, there may be found the divine message to the apparently lifeless churches of the Orient, — they also serve who only stand and wait.

II.

The mission of the Latin or Roman Catholic church began when that of the Greek church had apparently ended. When the barbarian races overspread the Western Empire, overthrowing civilization and introducing everywhere the wildest disorder, there was one institution which was not overthrown, which not only resisted the shock, but girded itself anew to the formidable task of reducing the untamed mass of human ity to submission and order. The Latin church now began to reap the advantage of that labor of organization, which had been slowly elaborated for centuries, and, like a subtle net-work, had extended itself throughout the limits of the old society. The Roman church fell heir to the old Roman genius for conquest and discipline; the spirit of Roman law survived, and was perpetuated in ecclesiastical institutions. From the sixth to the ninth century the work of converting the new races to the recognition and obedience of the church went on with unabated and successful ardor, resembling nothing so much as that earlier process of conquest by which the city of Rome had made herself mistress of the nations. The races whom old Rome could never entirely vanquish became in course of time the submissive children of the Roman church, receiving from its hands the gifts which they had spurned at the hands of Roman warriors.

While the period of the early Middle Ages presents but little direct material for the history of theology, there may be traced in it the growth of sentiments which are charged with deep meaning for the future of humanity. Among these, the most prominent was a natural and spontaneous growth of reverence for the bishops of Rome. Up to the time of Gregory the Great (590–604) the papacy, although it had continued to make a persistent claim to the primacy of the church, had gained no acknowledgment of its author.ty in the churches of the East. But in the West, when the waves of the barbarian invasion began to subside, and the constructive instincts of men began to assert themselves, the opportunity had come for the Roman see, which had been long and patiently awaited. The papacy never appeared so fair, so attractive, as in the person of Gregory the Great, who stood, as it were, on the dividing line between two worlds, with the modest consciousness of a great destiny. Others might assume more pompous titles, as, for example, the patriarch of Constantinople, who called himself the "bishop of bishops," but Gregory was content, in the consciousness of an actual greatness, to be designated as the humblest of all, "the servant of the servants of God." The rise of the papacy in the new world was no usurpation; there was at first no eager grasping after power; the popes simply stood and received that which came to them as the willing offering of the people. In the confusion which everywhere prevailed there sprang up the desire for order, and as a prerequisite for order, some common centre of unity and authority. Where could such a centre be looked for except in Rome, whose bishops in the general depression of the age stood so high above their contemporaries? It seemed only natural in a world from which God stood at a distance, over which all His waves and storms had been breaking, that some one should have been appointed as His vicar or regent to stand in His place and act in His stead. The papacy, indeed, as men then began to regard it, was but the form which the conviction took among a rude people, of the truth that God had not abandoned the world to itself, and was present, in the person of His delegate, to order and control its affairs.

The idea of the church which Augustine had done so much to determine was now further developed, and gained a new significance from the force of external events. The church was viewed as an ark of deliverance, — a refuge from the dark and evil world. The

Augustinian idea, that only some of those within the church were predestinated to salvation, gradually disappeared in favor of the more comprehensive and genial view, that all the baptized were alike elected to a great opportunity. The church became more entirely than ever the mediator, the manifest bond of union and of reconciliation between God and man. In communion with the church, in obedience to the church, lay the principle of salvation and redemption.

Such was the aspect of the church to devout and timid souls, in an age of lawlessness and violence, when the great world had lost its attractiveness, and offered for the many no prospect of peace and security. As the conquests of the church progressed, and race after race were enrolled in its ranks by baptism, it became evident that it was the most potent of agencies for promoting the end most desired, — order and due submission to authority. A process was silently but surely operating, which, bringing the people under the control of the clergy, the clergy under the obedience of the bishops, and the bishops into due subjection to the earthly head of the church at Rome, was also consolidating the empire into one great family united by a common faith and hope. In this process the civil power lent its aid; force was employed to convert the peoples whose stubborn adherence to heathenism the moral influence of missionaries had failed to overcome; legislation was enacted by the state enforcing obedience to the church's decrees. What would have been the history of the church, if Charlemagne and his predecessors had not given their willing support to its policy, is a question concerning which it is idle to speculate. Those able rulers had also a policy of their own to support, and believed themselves to be strengthening the civil authority by an alliance with the Bishop of Rome. Such might have been the result had the external course of affairs been ordered differently than it was. It was made clear by the subsequent course of the history that the alliance with the church had not strengthened the state. When the vast empire of Charlemagne was broken into fragments, with a constant tendency to divide and subdivide, one thing became evident, that the Roman bishop was master of the situation; the state had become hopelessly divided, while the church was united under the rule of the pope; to all intents and purposes the state had been simply resolving itself into a church, — a theocracy, whose divine sovereign was the Bishop of Rome. The reverse had been taking place of what is seen in Christendom to-day, when the church is divided and the state is united, — a prophecy to the minds of some that the process is destined to go on, till the church grows into and becomes identified with the state.

The period known as the Early Middle Ages, extending from the beginning of the sixth century to the dismemberment of the empire of Charlemagne in the ninth century, is marked by many characteristics distinguishing it sharply from the age that followed. The supremacy of the pope, so far as it had been achieved, was chiefly of a moral kind, resting on the free recognition of the people, winning its way to such recognition because of its genuine services to the cause of morality and of order. This period is in some respects also analogous to the career of the Jewish church. Underneath its religious manifestations may be discerned the deistic conception of God as outside of the world in the distant heavens, while morality rested for its sanctions upon a belief in temporal rewards and punishments. But the connection of religion and morality was not a close one, and despite the efforts of the church there prevailed the idea, always seen in the initial stages of religious development, that God was pleased at His acknowledgment by men apart from the nature of the service rendered to Him, or that what was desired by them was to be obtained by asking. Even the missionaries themselves condescended to an argument, which had great weight with their heathen auditors, that the Christian God was stronger than the old deities, and disposed to aid by His powerful support those who accepted His allegiance or to thwart the schemes of those who rejected it. The argument told upon the barbarian races who were inclined to attribute to the weakness of their deities the disasters experienced in the long process of migration, and whose hold upon their worshipers had been further relaxed in consequence of the breaking up of the old local associations. Besides, as a matter of fact, victory did clearly seem to follow the acknowledgment of the Christian Deity. So reasoned the high-priest of heathenism in England, when Christianity was first presented for his acceptance, — the old gods had never done much for him, though he had been faithful in their service, and it might be expedient to make a change in the hope of better results. Clovis in an emergency prayed to the Christian God, and obtained a great victory. The Burgundians, who were among the earliest races to be converted, finding themselves at the mercy of the Huns, applied for baptism to the neighboring Christian bishop as a preservative against those sons of the demons.

In the dense ignorance that closed in around the Western empire, it is interesting to note that the traces of the old Hellenic culture have not entirely disappeared. The Irish-Scotch clergy alone seem to have maintained a knowledge of the Greek language and literature; and at a time when it was the universal belief that all outside the church were doomed to endless woe, it is curious to read of Irish monks proclaiming in Germany, to the great scandal of the Anglo-Saxon Boniface, the doctrine of a plurality of worlds and of the possible salvation of the heathen. The famous John Scotus Erigena in the ninth century holds the same relation to the world of letters that Charlemagne does to the slowly rising civilization, — both of them, as it were, men born out of due time, phenomena as striking as the sudden and inexplicable appearance of comets darting across the dark heavens. John Scotus was one of the very few with any knowledge of Greek. He had studied the works of Plato and of Origen to such advantage as to produce a system of religious philosophy of vast scope and profundity, the anticipation in all important aspects of the systems of our own day.[1] But John Scotus only confused and puzzled his age; he seemed to be orthodox, but in a fashion hardly available for practical

[1] "La théologie de Jean Scot, hérétière des plus grandes conceptions de l'Église d'Orient, ne convenait pas au Christianisme du moyen âge. Elle ouvrait à la pensée religieuse d'immense perspectives; elle répandait de hautes clartés sur les problèmes les plus difficiles de la métaphysique chrétienne; elle continuait les traditions de ces magnifiques génies, qui avaient élevé le Christianisme au sommet de la philosophie elle-même. Mais telle lumière était trop éclatante pour les faibles yeux de la Scholastique." — Vacherot, *Histoire de l'ecole d'Alexandrie,* iii. p. 81.

purposes; what could such an age as his do with a man who talked about evil as a negation, as having no real existence, or who defined predestination as the consciousness of achieving one's destiny. At a later time the justice which he failed to receive in his lifetime was meted out to him, and he was condemned as a heretic. His main contribution to Latin theology was his translation of the "Celestial Hierarchy" of Dionysius, hitherto a sealed book for want of knowledge of the Greek language. In the main the attitude of Gregory the Great toward learning was maintained throughout the early Middle Ages, — the pietism which regards all study that does not concern the salvation of the soul as useless and profane. Alcuin rebuked the too eager curiosity of Charlemagne to understand the secrets of the natural world; the study of nature and of the classics was regarded as dangerous and heathenish; attention was concentrated on the Bible and Latin ecclesiastical writers, among whom Augustine had the preëminence.

The theological controversies of the ninth century are significant as showing the drift of religious thought toward what became later the established authoritative teaching of the church, although none of them were conducted in a satisfactory way or brought to any definite conclusion by representative synodal action. The problem of the *filioque*, — whether the Holy Spirit proceeded from the Father alone, as the Greeks maintained, or from the Father and the Son, whatever may be its true speculative solution, was decided in favor of the latter hypothesis, and the filioque was added about the beginning of the ninth century to the Nicene Creed. It may be difficult to fathom the motives which have always made this conclusion most acceptable to the Latin mind, but there can be no doubt of the fact. One can readily see that with the generally received view of the church as an institution founded on earth by Christ, the government of which had been intrusted after His departure to the pope as His vicar, it would be incongruous to think of the Holy Spirit as a diffused spiritual activity not bound to the hierarchy or confined within the ecclesiastical organization, but proceeding from the Father alone, and therefore at liberty to act as the wind, where He listed. Such a view would undermine the received view of the nature of the church as a definite organization beyond the communion of which there was no salvation.

The adoptionist controversy which arose in Spain shows the influence of the prevalent Mohammedan faith in weakening the adherence of Catholic Christians to the doctrine of the incarnation. In the face of the vigorous proclamation of Islam, *Far be it from God that He should have a son*, the Spanish Christians were inclined to confine the real Sonship of Christ to His divine nature, and to regard His human nature as alien from God, and as brought into relation with him by adoption.[1] The church in the Frankish empire opposed the principle of adoption, but it is evident that on both sides of the controversy there was a disposition to lay the supreme stress on the divine element in Christ, while His humanity was becoming the mere shadow or reminiscence of the great reality of the God made man. The historical Christ had retreated to a distance by the side of the equally distant

[1] That the position known as *adoptionism* was only a natural inference from the decision of the sixth general council has been shown by Dorner, *Person of Christ*, b. ii. p. 252.

Father, and coming events were soon to transform Him into the cold, unpitying Judge who stood awaiting the close of this earthly dispensation, when humanity should be summoned to His dread tribunal.

It was in the ninth century that the doctrine of transubstantiation became for the first time the subject of formal discussion. In the ancient church from an early period, and chiefly by oriental writers in Asia Minor, a highly rhetorical language had been used on the subject of the Eucharist, which might seem to imply the belief in an actual transformation in the elements of bread and wine. The Greek theologians, as has been already said, interpreted the expressions, the *body* and the *blood* of Christ, as symbols or figures of a spiritual reality; and even the early Latin fathers, as Tertullian and Cyprian, vacillated in their utterances between the spiritual and material interpretation of the great Christian feast. Augustine had been obliged by his principle of predestination to hold the spiritual view, according to which the benefits of the sacraments were received only by the elect, while to all others they were but an empty sign. It certainly cannot be called a propitious moment in the ninth century for the clear and intelligent discussion of any theological topic, when the intellect of the new races was only just awakening to its first activity, when the few who bore the title of scholar were not only unacquainted with the history of theology, but were wholly untrained in the art of reasoning and the expression of thought. Under such circumstances it is remarkable how the common sense and robust spiritual nature of some of the most intelligent men of the age protested against the notion advanced by the monk Radbertus (831), that a miraculous change took place at the consecration of the elements. But Ratramnus (Bertram), John Scotus Erigena, Rabanus Maurus, and others could not remake their time; Radbertus had expressed the tendency of the church at large — the presence of Christ, His continuous incarnation in the world, was not in the activity of the reason or in the spiritual life of His followers, but in the sacrament of the altar, and even there it was not the spirit of Christ, but His body, that was offered in sacrifice and eaten by the people.

There was one other controversy (847–868) more bitter and of longer duration than the others. Gottschalk was a monk, the son of a Saxon count, who had been from infancy devoted by his parents to the monastic profession. Although of a deeply religious nature, he desired after reaching maturity to free himself from the shackles of monastic obligation, but when he made the attempt he found it to be impossible. Another power stood between him and God, making him realize that he was no longer free to follow independently the bent of his native disposition. Unable to escape the monastic thralldom he gave himself to a deeper study of Augustine, and advocated in an extreme form, and in a passionate way, the doctrines of predestination and reprobation. He became the type and forerunner of those who in later times would detach the Augustinian doctrine of election and grace from their close connection with the Latin institution of the church, as Augustine had held them, and find a larger liberty and higher manhood in depending upon God alone and directly, through the bond of His final decree. But meantime, as Gottschalk realized in a life of painful martyrdom, it was the church's decree and not God's which regulated the process of human salvation. Despite the prevailing reverence for Augustine, the doctrine of individual election by divine decree was abandoned by the most representative theologians for the election through baptism of an unconscious humanity to the discipline and the cultus of the church.

III.

The ninth century forms the culmination of the early Middle Ages. It was marked by the awakening of the human mind, a curiosity for knowledge, the rise of schools in which the rudiments of education were taught, and by a group of theologians who devoted themselves with great energy and vigor to the religious issues of the time. The papal see had been occupied by great men like Nicholas I. and Hadrian, who used their power during the political disturbances of the age in behalf of the higher interests of the church, and almost anticipated the sway of Hildebrand and his successors. But the results which had been so laboriously achieved in raising the new world out of barbarism suddenly disappeared in the latter part of the century, and two centuries rolled away before the work thus interrupted was again resumed on the same level. In the eleventh century, when the church emerges from the dark ages, and mediæval theology enters upon its second stage, it was no longer the same world that it had been. A mighty change had passed over the human spirit, which can be accounted for only by a divine Providence in human affairs mysteriously ordering external events in the interest of a spiritual development.

The early Middle Ages, taken as a whole, reveal a people that had not yet been brought into complete subjection to the church. It was characterized by a certain freedom and simplicity in the religious life. The image worship which the degenerate East had approved at a general council (789) was not acceptable to the healthier, manlier tone of the western mind, and had been rejected by the church in England and on the continent. There had been theologians like Agobard of Lyons, and Claudius of Turin, who had discerned the outlines of a purer Christianity with the clearness of vision of the reformers of the sixteenth century. The people, and even the clergy, do not seem to have stood greatly in awe of the pope's excommunications; such a thing as the papal ban or interdict was unknown; the property of the church had not been regarded as having a sacred, inalienable character, while the contributions demanded for its support needed civil legislation to enforce their payment. The common people showed no appreciation of a high moral ideal, no deep conviction of sin; on the contrary, the migration of the barbarians seemed to have had for its first effects the dissolution of morals in an extraordinary degree. If the course of external circumstances had not come to the aid of the church, it does not seem as though Europe would ever have bent its head to the yoke of the priesthood. What are called the "ages of faith" had not yet begun.

The causes of the change which came over the human spirit may be roughly traced to the profound as well as extensive social disturbances, caused by the second migration which went on in the ninth century. The Huns appeared with renewed numbers and energy, overrunning the Frankish empire as far as the sea before they returned; the Northmen came down upon the coast of France, and, sweeping south by sea, took possession of Italy; the Danes invaded and conquered England; the Saracens passed through the Mediterranean, and appeared even before the gates of Rome. In consequence of these movements, government and order grew weak and almost disappeared; monastic establishments were pillaged and burned; life and property became everywhere insecure. The terror bred by these events did not, indeed, undermine popular confidence in the stability of the natural order, though it may have given renewed vitality to the ancient conviction that the end of the world was near, when humanity would be summoned before the judgment seat of Christ. The shadow of a great dread fell upon Christendom, manifested in the deeper, more widespread realization of the horrors of the final judgment. Such was the divine method of revealing to men the sinfulness of sin, and rousing into activity the human conscience. The old idea that God was pledged, as it were, to protect His own people and to punish their enemies could thrive no longer after such a visitation at His hands. The attention of men was drawn away to a future world, where the sins which had been punished so terribly in this world would be followed by endless retribution, or where alone those who had served God faithfully would receive the reward which had been denied them here.

Under circumstances like these it did not require civil legislation to bring a terrified people into complete and even abject submission to the church and her offices. We read, on the eve of this dark period, of forged decretals, of pretended donations, and of stolen titles to honor and dignity; but it was not these which riveted the bands of ecclesiastical authority upon the people. It was rather the workings of the human conscience, — the feeling that there was something wrong, in man or in the world around him; that God was angry and was making His wrath felt in visible signs which could not be mistaken. It needed no longer urgent entreaty to induce the people to make offerings to God and His church of their worldly goods. Property had lost its value to those who were concerned about the safety of their souls. The church grew rich with the money and the lands that were so freely offered, and in return granted remission of sins through the confessional, and by the power of the priesthood kept the heavens open to human supplication in the stupendous mystery of the altar. When the tenth century had closed, and when hope again returned, as to the world after the deluge, the erection of great cathedrals began, — offerings to Heaven as for a great deliverance, in which were written the story of a people's experience. In their vast proportions, in the feeling of awe and the sense of the profound mystery of life which they inspired, — the mystery of the forest, with its chastened, solemn light, — in the dim hope for humanity revealed through the darkness by the twinkling candle before the consecrated host, in the columns, pinnacles, and spires, always pointing away from earth and upward to heaven, in an architecture thus calculated at once to enthrall the imagination and subdue the natural impulses, did the spirit of mediæval Christianity find its beautiful embodiment.

It was in the eleventh century, when external events had given one common tone and direction to Christian piety, when the popular belief found a satisfactory expression in the prevailing cultus, when asceticism was

ANSELM'S DOCTRINE OF ATONEMENT. 199

taking on an oriental severity, when the human mind sought a congenial field for the first exercise of its untrained powers in the effort to demonstrate the truth of the church's teaching, that Anselm arose, the first and among the greatest in the long line of scholastic theologians.

He was an Italian by birth, identified with the monastic revival of his time, and, when late in life he became archbishop of Canterbury, he devoted himself in an ultramontane spirit to the extremest claims of the papacy in its conflicts with the secular power. The merit of Anselm lay in the fact that, more than any one who came after him, he combined with his dialectic capacity the deep experience of an earnest Christian feeling. Hence he was successful in interpreting the deeper moods of the soul, and gave such a clear expression to the theory which underlay the religious tendencies of his age that he still remains their best exponent, whenever under similar circumstances they have reappeared in the church.

The doctrine of the atonement, with which his name remains associated, was elaborated in a treatise whose nominal object it was to demonstrate to the reason the necessity of the incarnation. But in elaborating this remarkable theory Anselm was in reality seeking for a bond of union between man and God which should satisfy the heart and conscience as well as the speculative demands of his intellect. According to Anselm's theory of the atonement, man owes a perfect obedience to the divine law; but no one has rendered this obedience, and so all men have fallen in debt, for sin is a debt, the failure to render what man owes to God. Divine justice dooms all men to endless punishment, since sin against an infinite being calls for infinite penalty. But if justice were executed the divine goodness would be thwarted, and the divine goodness cannot allow that all men should be endlessly lost. The divine wisdom therefore devises a plan whereby goodness can be manifested and yet justice satisfied. Man cannot pay the debt, and yet, if it is to be paid, it must be paid by man for it is man that has sinned. Only God can pay the debt; for only an infinite being can satisfy infinite justice, only God can satisfy God. The schism in the divine nature is healed by God becoming man and rendering a full satisfaction. The obedience of Christ as the God-man, even to suffering and death, possesses an infinite value, and is more than an equivalent for what the race would have suffered if punished forever, as the honor of God required. Thus the debt is paid, justice is satisfied, goodness is triumphant, and God can pardon sinners.

Upon this theory of Anselm, it may be remarked that it indicates an advance in theological thought, because it represents the action in humanity of a quickened conscience seeking for some firm ground on which to rest in its relation to God. In other respects, also, it marks an advance in formal theology as an effort to escape from that unchristian dualism which had been inclined to regard the death of Christ as in some sense a ransom paid to Satan, in order to withdraw mankind from his power. This view of a ransom paid to Satan was never, it should be said, the real doctrine of atonement in the ancient church. In Greek theology the incarnation in and of itself was the power which redeemed and regenerated humanity, — which reconciled man to God and God to man; in the death of Christ was seen the highest and most conclusive evidence of God's identification with the interests and the lot of humanity, the strongest proof of the divine love. But even in the ancient church when that vast transition of souls was taking place from the dreary under-world, as conceived by Jewish or pagan thought, upward to the abode of light and blessedness, there were vague and obscure allusions to a process by which Satan, the lord of the under-world, had lost his hold over spirits confined within his domain, through the power of the death and resurrection of Christ. For Christ Himself had, in obedience to the law of death, also been obliged to enter the under-world, and there by His preaching had made known to captive spirits His mission to them as well as to mankind, and when He rose again from the dead, He had won the right to empty Hades of all believers. Satan had for a moment held the Saviour in his grasp, and although he had been, as it were, outwitted by an event which he had not foreseen, — His resurrection again to life, — yet in that one moment in which he had held Christ in his power through His submission unto death, there had been an acquittal of his claims against humanity.

Such was the view which may have led to the insertion in the Apostles' Creed of the clause now so difficult to interpret: "He descended into hell." It remains there as a monument to a great historical process in human thought, — how through the belief in the universal mission of a Christ ascended into the heavens with God, the belief in an under-world passed away, yielding to the Christian heaven of perpetual light and ever-increasing growth in divine activities. In the Middle Ages, when the historical origin of the theory had long been forgotten, its residuum took the shape that the death of Christ had been a ransom paid to Satan for the deliverance of mankind from his power. Anselm took a great step forward when he combated such a view by declaring the ransom to have been paid to God, and for the schism or dualism of two hostile powers, Satan and God, substituted a dualism within the divine nature itself between justice and love. That the older view did not easily disappear is seen in the fact that it was reasserted in the following century by no less distinguished a personage than Bernard of Clairvaux, so far was he carried away by his opposition to the theological rationalism of his time.

It may be further remarked concerning this theory of Anselm that it reflects the local influences of the Middle Ages and of the legal attitude of the Latin mind. God is viewed as a distant and mighty suzerain, having an absolute claim on the obedience of his subjects, whose honor injured or diminished requires an awful reparation. No figure could have been chosen more expressive in the days of feudalism and of chivalry to bring home to the conscience the relation of God to man. In the conception of sin as the violation of an external law, was the only adequate representation of it to a people who were still in the condition of those to whom Moses had declared the commandments on Mount Sinai, amidst the awe-inspiring convulsions of the outward world, and who had not yet learned to regard the law as the expression of the divine character, written in the inward nature of man, — that alluring power in his constitution which attracts him onward in devoted love to the free imitation of God. The figure of sin as a debt had, indeed, been used by Christ Himself in the parable of the debtor; but there were some features in the Saviour's language which Anselm passed over in silence. What was the significance of the fact that the servant's lord had at first freely forgiven the whole debt because it was desired of him; and what was the reason that the debt came back upon the wicked servant after it had been once remitted? The Saviour when the parable had ended dropped the figure and came back again to the language of reality: "So also shall *my heavenly Father* do unto you, if ye from your heart forgive not every one his brother their trespasses." The real defect in Anselm's doctrine of the atonement is that he built upon the action or the fears of a diseased and guilty conscience in its sense of alienation from God, instead of the pure and free consciousness of Him who is the type of the normal man, who abode in undisturbed communion with the Father, and aims through the power of His living presence to bring all men into the same relation. The thought of Anselm was deficient also in another important respect, in not clearly exhibiting the process by which the individual man availed himself of the advantage springing from the payment of the debt. When in the later Protestant theologies Anselm's scheme of atonement, like Augustine's doctrine of predestination, was detached from its connection with the Latin idea of the church, the faith of the individual believer, or his assent to the transaction, became the means by which its benefits were appropriated. But Anselm made no such provision; the tendency of his thought was to hand over the result achieved by the death of Christ to the control or disposition of the church, and thus magnify the church as the real mediator between God and man.

Anselm had spoken of the suffering of Christ in its infinite character as constituting an equivalent for the endless punishment of mankind, but the later School-men thought to do greater honor to the death of Christ by regarding it as more than an equivalent, and as creating in addition a vast treasury of merit which, with the superfluous merit of the saints, was placed at the disposal of the church, and by it assigned at will to the credit of individual souls. Such was the foundation of the later doctrine of indulgences; it may seem but a parody of the gospel of Christ; it has appeared absurd and even grotesque to modern theologians; and yet in it can be discerned the gropings of the human mind in a crude way, and under great disadvantages, after that higher conception of the incarnation and of the solidarity of mankind in the Son of God, which has been presented as the leading principle in Greek theology. In the thought of Athanasius we see interpreted the struggles of mediæval scholasticism after the knowledge of Him who gave His body to the death for all, and thus paid the universal debt; in whom all mankind have died; who taking humanity up into Himself, and suffering in the flesh for all, bestowed salvation upon all; through whom humanity restored and deified is endowed henceforth in its own right with a divine, recuperative power.

IV.

Just as Greek theology, in the age of its decline, showed a tendency to Latinize, to fall away from the high interpretation of spiritual realities into literal and crude conceptions, so also does Latin theology, when it begins a career of fresh and independent activity in the later Middle Ages, show a tendency to Hellenize, to rise by processes of its own from the letter to the spirit, from the outward to the inward aspects of the revelation in Christ. Such a course is necessitated by the law of progress, which is the law of the life of humanity. It is impossible to stay the rising force of the human mind, or check the expression of the human consciousness divinely sown with the seeds of eternal truth, when the expanding germs press forward into the light. External repression may seem to hinder or even annihilate the process, but in reality deepens, intensifies, and strengthens it. In the long run, nothing can succeed against the truth, but for the truth.

The peculiar form which the intellectual activity of the Middle Ages assumed is known as Scholasticism, a name, however, which reveals nothing of the inner characteristics of a process which lasted for centuries before its task was demonstrated to have ended in failure, so far as its direct object was concerned, but which indirectly promoted in a powerful way the higher interests of humanity. Scholasticism originated in the schools, which were afterward developed into the great universities, and was therefore primarily an intellectual movement, as contrasted with monasticism, that other great institution of the Middle Ages, whose primary aim was the cultivation of piety. The real object, whether avowed or tacitly assumed, of this vast and long-continued intellectual process, was to adjust the theology of the church to the human consciousness; to show, if possible, by demonstration, that the dogmas and tenets, handed down by tradition from Augustine and his Latin predecessors, or modified since then by the practical necessities of the church, were in harmony with the reason of man, and were the absolute expression of divine truth. The movement did not begin in skepticism, but rested upon unquestioning assent to the church's teaching, so far as it was known or understood. The scholastic philosophers took it for granted, in the nature of things, that this demonstration could be reached, — the only question was as to the method. It need hardly be said that they were unaware that there had been an earlier interpretation of Christianity, made by a people in the full maturity of their intellectual powers, whose reason had been trained for ages by a philosophical culture of the highest order, and in possession of a language beautifully adapted as a perfect vehicle for the expression of the subtlest forms of human thought. They were not aware that this earlier interpretation of the Christian faith differed on every essential point from that which they had received from the hands of the Latin church. They did not know that Christianity, as it had been received in the West, was but a lower form of the truth adapted to a ruder apprehension; that it was a temporary expedient in the long range of human development; that the controlling principle in the development of theology, as they had received it, was its adaptation to the necessities of a hierarchical organization. To them the church, viewed as the Latin ecclesiastical organization, was divine, the possessor of absolute truth, to receive which, in unquestioning assent, was the highest duty of man. To bring such a system into accord with human reason, or the consciousness that is in man, necessitated its retranslating back into its higher and more ancient form, the passing at every point from the outward to the inward. But to succeed in such a process was to revolutionize theology — to change the conceptions of the being of God and his relation to the world, of the incarnation, of revelation, of the nature of man, of the origin of evil, of atonement, of the true cultus of the spirit, and of all that relates to the last things in human destiny. And yet of such a process the scholastic philosophy was the beginning, even though its results were mainly of a negative character. It lasted long enough to show that the highest reason could not defend or maintain the tenets of Latin theology; and in the course of its progress it revealed intimations of a higher attitude toward truth which could and did commend itself not only to the intellect but to the Christian heart.

The first step in such a process was the gradual revelation of the fact that the church itself was not meeting the needs of humanity. All through the twelfth century there went on a series of protests against the church and its teachings from almost every part of Christendom, some of them formidable in the extent of their influence, others of narrow proportions, all of them more or less disfigured by whimsical fantasies, by erroneous and even dangerous tendencies, and yet all of them connected by an inward principle indicating their organic relationship to human life, and all of them significant of the future that was to be. Such were the Cathari or Albigenses in France, the Sect of the Holy Spirit, the Petrobrusians, the Apostolical Brethren, and the Waldenses. These movements, however diverse in aspect, were yet alike in their aim to realize a closer relationship and communion between God and man, and to seek for God within the soul, rather than at a distance from it without; in their assertion of the in-dwelling presence of a Spirit who was no other than God Himself, of whom the human body was the abiding temple, and not merely the ecclesiastical edifice; in the emphasis attached to the morality of the Sermon on the Mount as concerning itself with the inward motives, and not exclusively, as the current morality taught in the confessional, with the outward act; in the opposition to rites, ceremonies, and ordinances as the means of conveying an external grace, or of infusing virtues into the soul from without; in the tendency to exalt poverty as a protest in behalf of the native worth and dignity of the human soul.

The age in which these movements originated (the twelfth century) was remarkable for its freedom as well as its range of intellectual activity. The freedom is accounted for by the circumstance that the attention of those in authority was called elsewhere. Absorbed as were the popes with struggles of a different character, there was little disposition or energy for watching the greater dangers that threatened the church from an unknown and hitherto unsuspected quarter. The church was dealing with kings, princes, and nobility; it was organizing great crusades; it was contending for the rights of the clergy against the secular power; and, above all, it had entered upon a life and death struggle with the German emperors, in which no less an issue was at stake than the civil supremacy of the papacy. The intellectual activity came by a law of its own in the life of peoples, but was greatly stimulated by the contact with Mohammedan culture and civilization, whether in Spain, or in the remoter East, where the crusades were carrying so large a part of the population. It was through Mohammedan mediation that the Latin church was becoming acquainted with Greek philosophy, a gift that could not be received directly from the elder church, because of the hostility that had long since resulted in a schism and sundered all ecclesiastical communion.

In this age of great freedom and incessant activity, when the larger world was first opening upon the vision of a hitherto secluded and quiet life, the most representative man was Abelard. He bears the same relation to formal theology that the new sects which are multiplying in Christendom sustain to the practical life of the church. His thought from beginning to end was in revolt against the accepted principles of Latin theology. He undermined the foundations of assent to authority, and it was his misfortune, not his fault, that he had not the power to substitute something better in its stead. The respective mottoes of Anselm and Abelard have often been put in contrast, as if they stood for diametrically opposite methods of inquiry, and yet both contain an element of truth. The motto of Anselm, " I believe in order that I may understand," — *Credo ut intelligam*,— was equivalent to saying that truth must have revealed its full influence in the life before it can be measured by the intellect. Abelard reversed the motto of Anselm, but in so doing, he had in view the formal definitions of a theology that had not originated in a living process of thought, but had been received by tradition on external authority, — a tradition which commanded a merely nominal assent, and which was maintained in the interest of ecclesiastical order. When his admiring disciples told him they did not understand the doctrine of the trinity, and that it seemed impossible to believe, unless they understood, Abelard assented to the principle, and undertook to explain the doctrine to their comprehension. In so doing, he was attempting a task to which he was unequal, and was further mistaken in supposing that he understood what he professed to explain, or that he had fathomed the truth which lay beneath the formula.[1] His situation was an anomalous one, where it was necessary that the mind should inquire and seek to understand, but where it must inevitably fall short of the reality until illumined by a fuller light. His attempt was not altogether a failure, though it might for a time create confusion of thought, and even lead to erroneous opinions. But it was something that he called attention to the doctrine as a great verity whose value would be enhanced by its full appreciation, rather than a mysterious formula, the investigation of which by the reason was in its nature irreverent.

The work of Abelard finds its real significance not so much in any immediate influence exercised upon his own age, as in the light thrown upon the workings of the mind — the prophetic disclosure of the road which future generations were to travel. In his treatise entitled, " Scito te Ipsum," the words of Socrates when he led the great innovation in Greek philosophy, it was his aim to show that sin lies in the motive or intention, and not in the outward act. The ultimate effect of this principle, had it been received, would have been to overthrow the whole mediæval system of the confessional with the abuses growing out of penances commutable into money payments at the discretion of the priest. The outward act was capable of being easily estimated or graduated on a financial scale, while to deal with subtle motives was a thing lying beyond the capacity of human confessors. But

---

[1] The tendency of his thought was toward Sabellianism. See Remusat, *Abélard, sa Vie, sa Philosophie, et sa Theologie*, ii. p. 303.

the confessional, based upon the view that sin was a transgression of an external law, with its arbitrary division of offenses into mortal or venial, was still destined to remain and manifest its tendency to degrade the tone of morality before it was rejected by an enlightened public opinion. The nature of Abelard's work, so far in advance of his age, was further seen in a treatise entitled "Sic et non," whose object was to show that church tradition, based as it was supposed upon the consensus of the ancient fathers, rested on an unstable foundation. The contradictions of the ancient writers when placed side by side were evidence that no such consensus existed, as had hitherto been taken for granted. Indeed, Abelard might have carried his contrast further if he had possessed the requisite knowledge of the materials at his disposition.

Although the twelfth century has been spoken of as an age of freedom, yet it was not a freedom which had been purchased by struggles and the martyrdom of blood. It was a premature thing, destined to disappear as suddenly as it had arisen. Even in the time of Abelard there were signs of the great ecclesiastical reaction which half a century later would reach its full dimensions. Bernard of Clairvaux (1091-1153) and others like minded were becoming alarmed at the rapid spread of heretical opinions, and at the seeming recklessness of those like Abelard who showed no respect for the sacred convictions of the church. Cause enough for alarm indeed existed. Within the memory of those still living Berengar had created a profound sensation by denying the reality of the miracle of the altar; Roscellin had speculated with such dangerous results about the trinity as to fall into tritheism, and his adherents still existed; Abelard and Gil-

212   THEOLOGY IN THE MIDDLE AGES.

bert de la Porree continued to exercise their dialectic upon the most sacred of mysteries; undisguised pantheism had appeared among the sect of the Free Spirit, and was spreading everywhere in the highest circles under the influence of Averrhoës' philosophy; an almost Manichæan dualism was taught among the Cathari; rites and ceremonies were being set at naught, the priesthood inveighed against, and, generally, a tendency was evident to break away from the authority and discipline of the church. It was also well known that the contagion of Abelard's influence had been felt by high dignitaries in close relationship to the Roman see.

The condemnation of Abelard, which was secured by the influence of the saintly Bernard of Clairvaux, was the first indication of the rising ecclesiastical reaction. It shows how ill-prepared was the age for the deadly conflict of truth against authority that Abelard retreated, at the most critical moment in his career, from his vantage-ground in the conscience, and appealed to the pope for his vindication. In one sense, it is true, there was deep meaning in the appeal; it was one of those tests applied to the papacy by which its inadequacy to its position was to be fully revealed to all thoughtful men. The principle of the reaction lay in the desire to maintain order and unity against the growing confusion which sprang from the unaccustomed use of the reason. When the popes were free to turn their attention to the dangers threatening the church from within, the work of subjugating the reason went on apace. Toward the close of the twelfth century the "Holy See" instituted a crusade for the complete annihilation of the Cathari; the work of destruction, as it went on, included all who dissented from received traditions and usages; no difference was made between the heretical sects, for their greatest guilt was common to them all — the assertion of the reason against authority; and all alike, Waldenses, Arnoldists, Petrobrusians, disciples of Amalric and Apostolic Brethren, vanished, or seemed to do so, before the invading hosts of the militant church. Stringent laws were enacted by which heresy could be detected and punished wherever it appeared, and of these, the bishops were appointed the executors. There were some who believed in the efficacy of preaching as a means of conversion from heresy; but a stronger, more quickly available engine was discovered in the inquisition, which was soon to be organized for the purpose of ferreting out heresy in its most secret recesses. In the year 1215, an imposing General Council assembled, which for the first time formally declared it to be the dogma of the church that the bread and wine in the Eucharist were miraculously transubstantiated into the body and blood of Christ. The leaders of the reaction were far-seeing men, aware that the growing reason was fed by the direct access to the Scriptures; and in order to extirpate heresy by the root, the influential Council of Toulouse in 1229 declared it a sin for the laity to be found in the possession of the Bible, or to read even the Psalter or the Breviary in the vernacular.[1]

[1] Labbé, *Concilia*, tom. xiii. p. 1239. "Ne laici habeant libros scripturæ, præter psalterium et Divinum officium ; at eos libros ne habeant in vulgari lingua."

V.

The severe measures taken for the repression of heresy may have had the effect of making the students of dialectics more cautious in their treatment of the dogmas of the church. The tendency to speculation had been so far checked that Mysticism seemed for a while to have taken its place, and contemplation to have been regarded as a better method than intellectual analysis for gaining an insight into the deeper things of the Christian faith. At this juncture of intellectual depression, it was a fortunate thing that Peter the Lombard was able to execute successfully the delicate task of interpreting the consciousness of the mediæval church, and to express in his "Book of Sentences" those opinions regarding Christian truth which were most in accordance with the mind of the age, and most in harmony with its ecclesiastical institutions. The "Book of Sentences" met with a wonderful success; it became the standard of orthodoxy, and was stamped with the formal approval of the church in the great council of 1215, the most important synod which had yet been held in the Latin church. It now became possible for those who wished to be orthodox to use their reason within the limits marked out by the church, without fear of transgressing those limits through ignorance of what the church intended to teach.

But although the church seemed to have been successful in banishing heresy, there still remained the unsettled question concerning the relation between reason and faith, out of which had grown the free thought and liberalism of the twelfth century. To adjudicate this issue, or to make some compromise with the human reason, was the task of theology in the thirteenth century, and until this was done the great ecclesiastical reaction was not complete. The theologian who accomplished this peculiar work for his age was Thomas Aquinas (1227–1274). In order to appreciate his peculiar place in the history of theology, it is necessary to glance for a moment at the inner history of Scholasticism from the time of Anselm.

The doctrine of "universals," as it is called, or the conflict between nominalism and realism, important as it was in the history of mediæval theology, should not be allowed to obscure another issue of deeper importance, — the transition which took place from Platonism to Aristotelianism as the basis of Latin theology.[1] The earlier Scholastic theologians had been Platonists. The impetus given by John Scotus Erigena to the thought of Plato was seen after a lapse of two centuries to be still working in the mind of Anselm, though he may have been primarily indebted for his knowledge of the Platonic philosophy to the encyclopædic works of Augustine, in which was contained sufficient information regarding it — which Augustine had fortunately not retracted — to enable an independent thinker to work out for himself its relation to Christian thought. The same was true of Abelard, whose knowledge of Greek philosophy was confined chiefly to Plato, and whose acquaintance with Aristotle extended only to his small treatise upon logic. The study of Plato in the Middle Ages seems to have been asso-

[1] Realism underlay the Greek theology, and was part of its inheritance from Plato, from whom also Augustine inherited it, transmitting it in a debased form to the mediæval church. The question in historical theology is, what is the true realism upon which the highest Christian thought is based.

ciated not only with an exalted estimate of the powers of the human reason, but to have led to a skepticism regarding the dogmas of the Latin church, — a result which was natural enough, inasmuch as Augustine had given shape to those dogmas only after his abandonment of philosophy in the interest of ecclesiastical authority. But there was still another result from this alliance between Scholasticism and Plato, — a modification in the conception of Deity which was so totally foreign to the prevailing Latin idea, that it was felt instinctively, especially in its grosser manifestations, to be utterly irreconcilable with the spirit and aim of Latin Christianity. The pantheism of the twelfth century as seen in Amalric of Bena, David of Dinanto, and Simon of Tournay, and in its popular forms among the "Brethren of the Free Spirit," may have been partly owing to a natural reaction from the growing importance attached by the church to the localization of Christ in the Eucharist. But this modification in the thought about God, which in its higher form was a return to the doctrine of the divine immanence, was also connected with the influence of Platonism; it appeared in John Scotus, and has been traced even in the speculations of Anselm.[1]

[1] It has often been remarked that the Scholastic realism was but a step removed from what is commonly called pantheism. Even Anselm's famous argument for the existence of God is not free from a suspicion of the same tendency. That the mind has a necessary idea of a perfect being, and that therefore such a being exists, was a method of proof accepted not only by Descartes, but by Spinoza and Malebranche. It was the opinion of Hegel also that with a slight modification, which would bring out more clearly the idea in Anselm's mind, this so-called *a-priori* demonstration of the existence of God was a strong statement of the truth that because God in-dwells in the reason, therefore the

TENDENCY OF PLATO TO RATIONALISM.

That the tendency of Platonism, rightly understood, was not toward the doctrine of the immanence of God is evident from the whole purpose of his philosophy. But the so-called Platonism of the Middle Ages was that religious interpretation of Plato's thought by the school of Alexandria which had attempted to reconcile his teaching with a certain leaven of Stoic influence. For this reason it was necessary that Scholastic theology should abandon Plato, if the cardinal tenet of Latin Christianity was to be maintained, — the doctrine of the transcendence of Deity and His isolation from the world. For this reason it turned by a true instinct to Aristotle, who like Plato believed in a Deity outside the frame-work of the universe, but unlike Plato had not been mixed up with religious speculations foreign to his system or obscuring its leading idea. There were other reasons, also, why Aristotle should have supplanted Plato in the affections of the School-men. The tendency of the study of Plato in every age of its revival, has been to what is called rationalism, — to a dissatisfaction with things as they are and a desire to attain some ideal vision of beauty and perfection, the type of which abides in its purity

necessary idea in the mind concerning God corresponds with the reality. See Remusat, *Saint Anselme*, p. 469. "Anselme est un Saint. Son orthodoxie ne fait pas question. Il est resté une autorité dans les écoles de théologie : et *pourtant nous avons trouvé dans ses écrits quelques traces de l'influence de la philosophie d'Alexandrie*. Nous voyons une influence analogue se continuer dans une partie du cartesianisme qui a donné prétexte à Spinoza, et le tout est venu aboutir aux éloges de Hegel et de M. de Schelling."

The great Scholastic theologians of the thirteenth century abandoned the *a-priori* method and adopted the *a-posteriori* as the only safe ground on which to maintain the existence of God.

in God. Aristotle on the other hand, whether justly or not, has always stood for that conservatism which maintains things as they are to be divine. To Platonic idealism, the world as it is is unsatisfactory, and Plato forever points away to a world where things correspond to the perfection of their original divine idea. Aristotle sought to redeem the world from the neglect into which such an attitude would lead, and the importance which he gave to the physical sciences is in reality the practical mark which distinguishes his philosophy from Plato. When such a tendency appeared in the Middle Ages, viz.: to combat an ideal rationalism in the interest of existing institutions, it would practically appear as the application of Aristotle to that which was most prominent in the consciousness of Christendom. The church was the one institution that seemed to belong to the eternal order of things. As it then existed, it had been existing for ages; its long continuance and power stamped it as the clear expression of the mind and will of God. For this reason, the alliance of Scholastic theology with Aristotle seemed to place the great ecclesiastical reaction of the thirteenth century upon a stable basis in philosophical thought.

And, still further, if there was to be any adjustment of the great issue between reason and faith, it was necessary that some authority should be placed over the reason, as there was already an authority for faith, — there must be a pope in philosophy as well as in theology. Hitherto, in the intellectual awakening of the twelfth century, the reason had seemed to flounder aimlessly about, producing as many differences of opinion as there were individual thinkers. Such divarication and confusion was in its very nature obnox ious to the spirit of Latin Christianity and defeated its essential aim. The church, therefore, set up a standard for the human reason, and henceforth the object of the Scholastic theology was not to reconcile its dogmas with reason, but with the Aristotelian philosophy. From the beginning of the thirteenth century, when the complete works of Aristotle were for the first time available in Latin translations, the Scholastic theologians[1] began their twofold line of commentaries, on Aristotle's philosophy and on Lombard's sentences. Thus the triumph which the church had celebrated over the hostile attacks of the reason was believed to be rendered secure by the great knights of theology, who rode forth in its defense invulnerable to every assault in the double armor with which they were invested.

This adoption of Aristotle as the ally of the Christian faith has been often regarded as one of those displays of an almost supernatural intuition by which the Latin church has been guided throughout its history. Certainly it was an expedient well calculated to meet the exigencies of the hour. But Aristotle concealed hidden dangers for the faith which were not seen at the time, or if they were it was thought they might be overcome. It is one among the many variations of Romanism, as it has sought to adapt itself to the changes which life always involves, that at first Aristotle was suspected of being the subtle cause of the pantheism which was so extensively diffused in the last half of the twelfth century.[2] His name, it was

[1] Alexander of Hales (ob. 1245) and Albert the Great (ob. 1280) were the first authorities for this combination.

[2] The physical and metaphysical writings of Aristotle were condemned at a synod held in Paris in the year 1209. Cf. Labbé, *Concilia*, tom. xiii. p. 805.

well known, was in great repute with the Mohammedans, and the tendency which he stimulated to cultivate the study of outward nature was thought to be almost as dangerous to the faith as the disposition to confound God with the world. From the time of Aristotle almost to the close of the Middle Ages nature remained a sealed book. There had come a revival for Plato in the early Christian centuries, but none for his successor. The world had lost its interest in the study of nature, and was preoccupied with spiritual and moral themes. Christian theology had held the field to itself from the time of Athanasius and Augustine, and no rival disputed its claims to be the one all-important, all-absorbing pursuit. Outward nature was not only rejected; it had fallen into contempt, as unworthy the attention of spiritual men. Like the human body, which the ascetics despised and maltreated, the outer world was a temporary prison house of the soul, originating out of nothing and destined to return to the non-existence from which it came. Just as fasting became a law of spiritual growth, and the nearer man could come to the condition of a disembodied spirit by denying the claims of the body to shelter, food, or clothing, the surer was his prospect of salvation; so also outward nature was believed to have no inner relationship to the human spirit; it was an evil thing, resting under the curse of God since Adam's fall. It was not in this world that the kingdom of God was to come, but in some other distant world, and the gaze of humanity was, like the cathedrals which symbolized its attitude, away from earth to heaven. From the time when Augustine fixed the dogma of original sin as the controlling principle in psychology as well as in theology, mankind stood

alone in its isolation, apart from nature on the one
hand, and apart from God on the other. In all this
there was a great purpose to be achieved in the divine economy. It was necessary that, through the
long-continued cultus of the immortal spirit as the exclusive object of human interest and attention, man
should come to the consciousness of himself and should
realize, as it had never been realized before, that he
was not a part of nature or identified wholly with its
life, but distinct from it as something higher and with
a higher destiny. The old nature religions, against
which Latin Christianity had been from the first a
sturdy protest, merged God in humanity and humanity in the life of nature. It had been the work of
the Latin church and hitherto its mission, to sharply
draw the lines between them; to carry God to a distance on the one hand, and as far as possible annihilate all communion with nature on the other.[1]

From the time of the introduction of Aristotle's
physical studies to the West, there had begun to be
manifested an interest in the outer world and its phenomena, which was the harbinger of an impending
revolution in the distant future. It was evident that
the mysterious relationship which man holds by a law
of the creation to the external world could no longer
be overlooked, nor could its study much longer be de-
ferred as a dangerous pursuit carried on by an unearthly compact with the spirit of darkness. The

---

[1] "In history the divine element lies hid; is missed at the
time, even by those who are its vehicle; and does not parade
itself in what they consciously design, but lurks in what they unconsciously execute. It comes forth at the end of the ages, —
the retrospect of many generations instead of the foresight of
one." — Martineau, *Studies of Christianity*, p. 292.

sentiment of distrust in regard to Aristotle's influence which at first prevailed was in some respects wiser, so far as the interests of Latin Christianity were concerned, than the second sober thought which placed him as sovereign over the reason. For the Latin church was still true to its original purpose, and had these two distinct objects to maintain as essential to its existence and the fulfillment of its mission — on the one hand to hold humanity distinct and separate from God, and on the other to insist upon a like separation between man and the world of outward nature.

The difficulty was to conjoin the two purposes with equal success. Monasticism or asceticism, which flourished under the first line of Scholastic theologians with whom Plato had been the authority, could not long continue to thrive under the sovereignty of Aristotle. The "spirit in the air" in the beginning of the thirteenth century was felt in the monastic ranks, and gave rise to two new orders, the Franciscan and the Dominican, which mark an epoch in the history of asceticism. Both orders showed a peculiar susceptibility to the changes which were taking place in the environment of human life. While they endeavored to intensify in their practice the ascetic principle, and to all outward appearance seemed to embody the spirit of the great ecclesiastical reaction, with whose triumph their rise coincides, yet they sustained a very different relation to the world from the orders of the Benedictine family of monks. The principle of seclusion was modified, or practically abandoned, which tied each monk to his domicile; Franciscans and Dominicans went forth into the larger world where they could not avoid the influences which were undermining the institutions of ascetism. Such were the dangers for which no mode of escape had been provided when Aristotle was approved by the church as the guide of the human reason. If the outer world should come to be regarded as sacred, and man were to be allowed to feel at home within it as the work of God which was very good — and to such a result the philosophy of Aristotle must tend — then it was all over, not only with monasticism and its ascetic observances, but the church itself, as an ark of deliverance from the miseries of this evil world, was likewise eventually doomed to succumb to some higher conception of the nature of Christian redemption.

The greatness of Thomas Aquinas as a theologian has been universally admitted, though the grounds upon which his distinction rests have not always been clearly discerned. While his sensitive spirit was susceptible to every living impulse that stirred his age, he saw with peculiar directness the dangers that threatened the church, and saw also, or thought he did, how the danger was to be averted. To him mainly it was owing that Aristotle assumed his sway over the reason, becoming in the sphere of the natural life a precursor of Christ, as John the Baptist had been in the sphere of the spiritual.

Aquinas also applied the corrective to that tendency in Aristotle's philosophy, which, if not checked, might lead to an exaggerated estimate of the importance of the physical sciences, — to the sanctity of the outer world as diminishing the sanctity of the church. To this end he drew his famous distinction between the kingdom of nature and the kingdom of grace,[1] a dis-

[1] This distinction between the kingdoms of nature and of grace had been first made by Albertus Magnus, of whom Aquinas was

tinction which he carried out in every direction and applied to every interest of human life. He accepted at once the fact of a kingdom of nature, and though he had not interrogated nature for himself, but had done so with Aristotle's eyes, yet he recognized and defined what he regarded as its proper sphere. It was a graded kingdom, with a hierarchy proceeding upwards from the lowest grades of life till it reached its crown and completion in man. But over against this kingdom, and above it, resting upon it indeed, as the spirit depends upon the body, towered the kingdom of grace, of which the church is the external embodiment. Like all his illustrious predecessors in Latin Christendom, he simply assumed the existence of the church as a hierarchy, which, proceeding upwards through the grades of clergy to the vicar of Christ on earth, found its continuation in angels and archangels, and its culmination in the throne of God. These two kingdoms of nature and grace are everywhere distinct from each other; the lower does not pass over into the higher, but is separated from it, as if it were simply its outer vestibule. The only door which opens from

---

the pupil. Cf. Ritter, *Die Christliche Philosophie*, p. 640. It belongs to Aquinas, in so far as he appropriated it, and because his reputation in the church eclipsed that of his teacher. Hauréau has remarked upon the relation between the two: "Les jugements de la postérité ne sont pas toujours équitables. Elle devait un éclatant hommage au génie de Saint Thomas, mais elle a manqué de justice lorsqu'elle a donné son nom á la doctrine de l'ecole dominicaine: cette doctrine est l'œuvre d'Albert-le-Grand. . . . Ayant donc protesté contre l'injure faite á la mémoire d'Albert-le-Grand, reconnaissons que Saint Thomas a considerablement développé le système de son maitre et l'a revêtu de cette forme solonelle, doctrinale, sous laquelle il est parvenu jusqu'á nous."— *De la Philosophie Scolastique*, ii. p. 104.

the lower into the higher is the sacrament of baptism, where the natural man, who has received a natural life at birth, receives a supernatural gift which constitutes his birth into the kingdom of grace. In the life of humanity, considered as belonging to these separate kingdoms, there was a twofold manifestation, represented by the secular affairs of the state or the empire on the one hand, with the emperor at its head, and by the church or sphere of spiritual things on the other hand, where reigns a higher potentate, — the pope as the vicar of Christ. There were the natural virtues capable of being acquired by unaided efforts, such as the natural man even in heathendom might possess, and which have their reward in conducing to a natural happiness; and there were the supernatural virtues infused into the soul by sacramental grace, which have also their reward in conducting to supernatural bliss. There was also a natural theology whose contents might be read or demonstrated by the natural reason, — such as the existence of God, the creation of the world, and the immortality of the soul. So much of a concession Aquinas was forced to make in deference to Aristotle or the well-known features of Mohammedan religion. But the natural reason could not discern, nor could it demonstrate to be true, the contents of a revealed or supernatural religion which must therefore be received on authority. This revealed theology includes the doctrines of the incarnation, the trinity, original sin, the sacraments, purgatory, the final judgment, and endless punishment. But because the contents of natural theology could have been discovered only by a few, they, too, are included within the revelation, in order to their more general diffusion. The scope, therefore, of revealed theology as a science becomes an all-comprehensive one, for it treats of God in all His relations, whether to the kingdom of nature by His power, or to the church by His grace.

Of such a system it is evident that if it should commend itself to the religious sentiment of the age, it would suppress any inordinate or unhealthy activity in the kingdom of nature which threatened the time-honored supremacy of the kingdom of grace. And, indeed, it did more for the church than all the repressive measures which had been devised to extirpate heresy. It was a view easily conceived as a whole, and, in all its bearings, it seemed rational and carried conviction to the religious mind. So strong is its rationality and cohesiveness when once its premises have been admitted, that it has ever since had a tendency to reappear among those who are leading the way in ecclesiastical reactions. It has the advantage also of opening up a field for the activity of the reason, so capacious that its boundaries are not immediately felt as a hindrance. For Aquinas assumed, as upon his principles he was justified in doing, that the revelation was not contrary to reason, but only above reason, as the kingdom of grace is above the kingdom of nature; and therefore if reason could allege objections against revealed religion, the reason also was competent to meet and overcome them. Thus was afforded a large scope for the dialectic activity of the School-men, without endangering the stability of dogmatic authority.

The basis of Latin theology, as it had existed from the time of Tertullian or Augustine, remained unchanged in the system of Aquinas. God conceived as outside of and remote from the world, communicating with nature by His power or with the church by His grace, was the primary assumption which regulated and bound together in harmony the tenets of his theology. That body of opinions which, from an early period, had been developed in the Latin church in order to maintain the economy of ecclesiastical administration, these he identified with the original divine revelation. The episcopate as the continuator of the apostolate, in which, by virtue of succession, inhered the gifts or *deposit* of truth and grace and authority, — a consolidated body which found in the pope, as the vicar of Christ, its head, mouth-piece, and bond of unity; human nature as essentially foreign to and incompatible with the divine; the incarnation as an arbitrary and mysterious arrangement for which it was conceivable some substitute might have been found; revelation as the communication of facts and doctrines, — a certain amount of information for which man has no inward aptitude in the reason, the acceptance of which on the authority of the episcopate or the church constitutes the merit of faith; the priesthood as intrusted with miraculous power through the grace of ordination, offering a veritable sacrifice which had power to take away sin, and therefore an indispensable mediator between God and man; salvation only through the grace that comes by sacraments; transubstantiation, purgatory, indulgences, by which the church on earth manifests its power over the unseen world and human destiny in the future, — these were the dogmas concerning the truth of which it is said that Aquinas never knew what it was to have a doubt, — dogmas which he fortified by a clearer and more positive enunciation.

The theology of Aquinas was the development, in

its full splendor and practical realization, of that which the Latin church had begun to dream of from its infancy. It marks the church in the hour of its completest triumph, when, after overcoming every other power, it made, or seemed to make, the conquest of the human reason. It holds the same relationship to religious thought and life in the Middle Ages that Innocent the Great sustained to the political and ecclesiastical institutions of his time, — it reflects the consciousness of Latin Christendom in the century that followed his reign, when, for nearly a hundred years, the papacy exercised an almost undisputed supremacy over Western Europe. As a system, it has become a part of the world's literature through Dante's imagination, and may be still read in the " Divine Comedy,"[1] as it appeared to a great poetic genius who lived and died within the inclosure of its thought.

But just as there were elements at work in the thirteenth century which were secretly weakening the foundations of papal authority, so that the humiliation of Boniface (1294–1303) by Philip the Fair of France was an event whose antecedents grew out of the very conditions which had seemed to secure papal autocracy, so there were elements also in the theology of Aquinas which were not altogether in harmony with the spirit of Latin Christianity, — rudiments, as it were, of a higher faith which could not be brought into subjection to the ruling idea of his formal system.

It is probable that the rivalry between the two great orders of mendicant monks stimulated Duns Scotus

[1] For the traces of Aquinas' theology in Dante, see Ozanam, *Dante et la Philosophie Catholique au 13ᵐᵉ Siècle*.

(1265-1308) in his effort to find the weak points in the position of the *Angelic Doctor*. For Aquinas had lent great renown to the Dominican order, as well as gained the gratitude of the whole church for the services he had rendered to the faith, while the Franciscans were as yet without a representative theologian. It is true, also, that the captious, hair-splitting tendency in the dialectics of the School-men received a great impetus from Duns Scotus, which tended to bring the whole method into ridicule. But however this may be, there is no reason for doubting his intellectual sincerity, although it may still remain an enigma by what common principle the various criticisms which he made upon the theology of Aquinas can be included in one consistent system of thought. Every great thinker has been followed by a Duns Scotus. Indeed, it is inevitable in the interest of freedom and of progress that the human mind should rebel against a system like that of Aquinas, which definitely fixed all things in heaven and earth without the need of any further inquiry, and stamped the whole result with the assumption of infallibility.

To the mind of Aquinas, theology was a comprehensive, universal science, embracing the whole range of human thought concerning God, humanity, and the world in a system of absolute truth. Duns Scotus, on the other hand, regarded theology as practical wisdom for the regulation of the life, dismissing its larger relationships as beyond the ken of human intelligence. The defect in Aquinas' attitude, to his view, was its exaggerated estimate of the importance of the human reason. Hence he reduced the contents of what Aquinas called natural theology; he admitted that the reason might attain to the idea of God, but the doctrines of the creation of the world out of nothing, and of the immortality of the soul, were beliefs that reason could not demonstrate, and must be relegated to the sphere of revealed religion. Aquinas had maintained, on the grounds of reason, that this was the best possible of worlds, but Duns Scotus disputed that the reason was entitled to make such an affirmation; all that could be said was, that it was such a world as it had pleased God to create. The doctrine of the atonement, as Anselm had stated it, and as the later Schoolmen generally received it, had to Duns Scotus no foundation in nature or in the fitness of things, — it was simply an arbitrary arrangement, the results to be accomplished by which, God might, had He willed, have attained in some other way. But while thus apparently disparaging the reason, and disowning any such authority as Aristotle for its standard, he was inclined to assert an inward kinship between the divine and the human, which resembles the fundamental postulate of Greek theology. Duns Scotus did not, therefore, lay the same emphasis upon the doctrine of grace, nor did he maintain the sharp distinction between the kingdoms of nature and of grace, but rather inclined to lessen the difference between the natural and the supernatural. Throughout his whole system, Aquinas had, as Duns Scotus thought, not only exaggerated the power of the reason, but he had lost sight of the high significance of the will, whether in God or man, or had so subordinated the will to the reason as to weaken its efficiency or destroy its creative activity.[1] Duns

[1] Le *volontarisme* de Duns Scot est à l'*intellectualisme* de Thomas (Aquinas) ce que le Kant de la *Critique de la raison pratique* sera au Kant de la *Critique de la raison pure*, et ce que le *panthéisme* de Schopenhauer sera au *panlogisme* de Hegel. Weber, *Histoire de la Philosophie Européenne*, p. 295.

Scotus affirmed the freedom of the will, as it is generally said, after a Pelagian fashion; he denied the doctrine of predestination, which Aquinas had taught with Augustine, and asserted that the highest virtue or merit in man lay in the obedience which he was freely able to render by the capacity of his nature. Such a system might seem to dispense with the necessity of the church, but Duns Scotus assigned to the church a higher prerogative than even Aquinas had done, if that were possible, for his denial of the claims of the reason tended to throw men back upon its absolute authority as the only recipient of a divine revelation.

These divergencies between the two master minds who stood at the close of the papal dispensation are sufficient to reveal that, despite the efforts of Aquinas to regulate the reason, and to adjust its relation to external authority, he had not succeeded. Differences like these in the two systems of theology, which from this time began to divide the allegiance of the schools, show the confusion into which mediæval thought had fallen, and from which it was powerless to extricate itself without revolutionizing the basis of Latin theology. The only point which Aquinas and Duns Scotus held in common was the authority of the church; and this was a bond which, while uniting them, was also the cause of the contradictions and confusions that marked their thought. Whatever they had succeeded in doing or failed to do, one thing had been rendered clear by their labors, — that Latin theology was dependent for its authority upon the Latin church, and must be subordinated to the end of maintaining its undiminished prestige.

The differences that have been enumerated between

the systems of Aquinas and Duns Scotus, however significant they are in themselves, or as permissible *variations* in Latin theology, gain a deeper significance when we trace them to their source in the conflicting ideas of God which were entertained by these two representative theologians.[1] In the theology of Aquinas, the will of God is viewed as the reflection of a divine character or reason, which is, as it were, the groundwork of the divine being. With Duns Scotus, there lies no character behind the divine will to which it conforms; the will of God is the ultimate factor in His existence, — an absolute, arbitrary, unconditioned will, which is the only ground of right. According to Aquinas, it is possible to regard righteousness or goodness as constituting the essence of Deity, and to view the divine will as the necessary expression of His moral nature. Hence, righteousness, as the human reason may discern it, becomes the law in accordance with which the universe is organized and directed. The action of the divine will does not create right, but is the expression of a righteousness that lies back of the will, to which the will must conform. All this is reversed in the thought of Duns Scotus. The will of God is the highest, divinest quality in God, the motive power of all that is, the only sanction which gives validity to the reason. God does not command what is good because it is good, but the good is such because He commands it.

[1] In the question discussed by Aquinas and Duns Scotus, — whether there was in God a divine essence to be distinguished from His attributes, — was raised one of the deepest and most fundamental issues in theology. A summary of the discussion is given in Morin, *Dictionnaire de Philosophie et de Théologie Scolastiques*, i. pp. 954 ff.

Theories like these may seem to have no connection with the experience of life or with our insight into the ways of God in the world. But history teaches that human convictions about the nature of God, however abstruse or speculative they may appear, do yet control the fate of races and of institutions. And of these two theories it may be said that they are charged with momentous consequences for civilization as well as religion. It is only when we look at them in their historical embodiment, as they have been lived out in human experience, that we are able to try them by more tangible tests than the dialectics of metaphysical subtlety.

The conception of God as maintained by Aquinas is substantially identical with Plato's "idea of the good"[1] which had passed from Plato as a ruling principle into Greek theology. In Aquinas, indeed, it appears but imperfectly developed, and does not have its full influence upon his thought, owing to the limitations of the Latin church and the tenets which he received on its authority. But the natural tendency of such a conviction, freely working itself out, is to elevate humanity by bringing it into closer relationship with God, by affirming in the human constitution the same essential relationship between the reason and the will, as it exists in God : it is a conviction which ennobles and consecrates the reason by regarding it as endowed with a constitutional capacity for the discern-

[1] "If it is the Idea of the Good which imparts to things their Being, to intelligence its capacity for knowledge, if it is called the source of all truth and beauty, the parent of light, the source of reality, it is not merely the end but the ground of all Being, efficient force, cause absolute."—Zeller, *Plato and the Old Academy*, p. 282.

ment of truth and righteousness; it emancipates the will by viewing it as predetermined, like the divine will, to execute the law of its being which is grounded in right. In the history of theology it marked a crisis when Augustine practically abandoned this conception of Deity, and fell back to the belief that God was absolute will whose decree alone makes righteousness, who reveals a system of regulative information which man must receive on external authority, who elects to salvation or condemns to endless misery by arbitrary determinations, to examine into or to question which is presumption and impiety. The outcome of this be-belief, in Augustine or in later Latin theology, may have been modified by a Christian influence from which they could not escape; but in Mohammedanism, where the principle is seen working out unchecked its natural consequences, it resulted in a complete divorce between God and humanity, it made the reason powerless, it robbed the conscience of any inward impulse, it reduced morality to a slavish fear, — a cringing obedience to omnipotent power; and the fatalism which it induced in religion when operating in the state deprived its civilization of those elements of enterprise and hope which make possible the stages of human progress.

Of these two ways of apprehending the being of God, that of Duns Scotus — that He is the unconditioned arbitrary will — is more in harmony with the spirit of Latin Christianity. This underlying belief may be traced in those ideas of the church as consisting in the episcopate, or of the revelation as a deposit intrusted to its charge, which were so fundamental that they had been the axioms of Latin Christianity from the time of Tertullian. The same belief is always and everywhere the principle of imperialism or despotism in church or state, — the principle which is invoked in the call for the "strong man" as he appears in history. When the Protestant Reformation brought great disasters to the Latin church in the sixteenth century, Ignatius Loyola led again an ecclesiastical revival, under the conviction that the church as it then existed, unreformed and unchanged, was the absolute expression of the divine will, and that to serve the church, by whatever methods, was to contribute to *the greater glory of God*. With this conviction Calvin arose, one might say that with it he seems to have been born — that God's will must at all hazards be made supreme. The existence and work of Loyola made Calvin not only necessary but indispensable for the nascent Protestantism. Both men were building upon the same foundation — the only difference was that Loyola said the divine will was expressed in the institution of the Latin church, while Calvin maintained that its only expression was to be found in Scripture. In the long and fierce duel between the followers of these two leaders, it is not strange that the theology of Aquinas in the Roman church, as well as the Lutheran type of theology in the Protestant churches, should have sunk into abeyance. The Jesuits have never had any great respect for Aquinas, but have always championed Duns Scotus as their favorite theologian;[1] the Calvinists also have regarded the Lutheran theology as a halting, half-hearted attitude, if not a compromise between truth and error.

[1] Most of the literature upon Duns Scotus belongs to the seventeenth century when the Jesuits were at the height of their activity. For a list of works then published cf. Franck, *Dictionnaire des Sciences Philosophiques*, ii. p. 169.

Once more in the history of Christianity, in our own age, an ecclesiastical reaction has been and still is in progress, which is based on the same principle that inspired Augustine or Loyola. To the mind of a writer like De Maistre, seeking to impose again on the modern world the authority of an infallible pope as the highest expression of the will of God, the theology of Aquinas, even though illustrated with the brilliancy of Bossuet's genius, seemed like shuffling, vacillating weakness. Carlyle, who at heart remained as he had been born, a sturdy Calvinist, presents in literature the spectacle of one who finds no institution that responds to his ideal; everywhere appears weakness, disorder, and confusion, accompanied with shallow talk about liberty; he bewails the absence of the "strong man" upon whose portrait in history he gazed with fascinated vision, whose coming he invoked as the one crying need of the time.

These illustrations may serve to show that what seem to be subtle theological distinctions are yet closely connected with the life and experience of men. The aim of the present occupant of the papal see to reinstate Aquinas in his former prestige, if it has any significance at all, indicates a purpose to overcome Jesuit influence, and to put the church, as far as is allowable, in harmony with the reason. For this purpose it may be that no better instrument could have been chosen than the revival of the study of Aquinas.[1]

---

[1] For a criticism on the significance and probable results of this modern attempt to revive the study of Aquinas' philosophy, see an article entitled Philosophy in the Roman Church, by Thomas Davidson, in *Fortnightly Review*, July, 1882. The author is right in maintaining that Aquinas is hopelessly out of sympathy with what is highest and best in modern thought. But it is not the

It even constitutes a ground of hope that the renewed interest in his writings and their deeper perusal may yet lead Latin theologians to discover, that while he represents a past when the Latin church was in the nooutide of its glory, he was also in some respects the prophet, though unconsciously to himself, of a larger and higher because more spiritual and more rational dispensation.[1]

system of Aquinas, but the inconsistencies and contradictions in his theology, which may render its renewed study a means of profit and of advance.

[1] The best works in English upon the Scholastic philosophy are Bishop Hampden's Bampton Lectures for 1832 — *The Scholastic Philosophy in its Relation to Christian Theology*; and Maurice, *Mediæval Philosophy*. Bishop Hampden traced clearly the prevalence of mediæval modes of thought and expression in the current Protestant theology, and in this lies the special value of his book. Other works which may be consulted are Haureau, *De la Philosophie Scolastique*; Rousselot, *Études sur la Philosophie dans le Moyen Age*; Kaulich, *Geschichte der Scholastischen Philosophie*; Stöckl, *Geschichte der Philosophie des Mittelalters*, — all of them dealing mainly with the relation of scholasticism to speculative thought. Ritter, *Die Christliche Philosophie*, is the best exposition of its relation to the progress of religious thought. The most elaborate treatise on the theological bearings of Scholasticism is Morin, *Dictionnaire de Philosophie et de Théologie Scolastiques*; but its labored and voluminous expositions lack an intellectual perspective. It professes to be a dictionary, but its object is to defend the Roman Catholic theology. Of its value there can be no doubt. Among the general histories of philosophy that of Ueberweg is the best.

THEOLOGY IN THE AGE OF THE REFORMATION.

Justificati ergo ex fide, pacem habeamus ad Deum per Dominum nostrum Jesum Christum. — ROM. v. 1.

CHRONOLOGICAL TABLE.

A. D.
- **1300.** [c.] Occam teaches nominalism at Paris.
- **1309-1377.** Papacy at Avignon.
- **1324-1384.** Wycliffe.
- **1329.** [c] Death of Eckart.
- **1348-1350.** Pestilence of the Black Death.
- **1361.** [c.] Tauler died.
- **1380-1471.** Thomas à Kempis.
- **1383.** Wycliffe's Translation of the Bible.
- **1415.** Martyrdom of Huss.
- **1440.** Discovery of the Art of Printing.
- **1453.** Fall of Constantinople.
- **1467-1536.** Erasmus.
- **1483-1546.** Martin Luther.
- **1484-1531.** Zwingle.
- **1491-1556.** Ignatius Loyola.
- **1497-1568.** Melancthon.
- **1498.** Savonarola died at the stake.
- **1509-1564.** Calvin.
- **1517.** Posting of the Theses.
- **1521.** Diet of Worms.
- **1529.** Discussion between Luther and Zwingle
- **1545.** Opening of the Council of Trent.
- **1553.** Servetus burnt at Geneva.

THEOLOGY IN THE AGE OF THE REFORMATION.

The period known as the Middle Ages reached its culmination in the thirteenth century. Up to that time, as it has been said, there was lurking in every movement the spirit of a Hildebrand; after it everything pointed to a Luther. For two centuries before the Reformation, the Latin church was slowly losing its hold upon the reason and the conscience of Christendom. When Luther appeared, he only declared the result which had been already accomplished. The decline of the Latin church as an institution implied the ultimate abandonment of that system of doctrine which is known as Latin Christianity. It had been from the first an economizing of the Christian revelation in the interest of an episcopal hierarchy, which had successfully claimed the right to teach and govern the world in the place of Christ. As a system of doctrines, it had been constructed in obedience to one test, — its fitness or utility for holding mankind in subjection to an external authority. When that authority was no longer needed, or could be no longer maintained, the system of doctrines which it had upheld might indeed long continue to survive through the conservative force of tradition, or through its lingering hold upon the imagination; but the time must come when it would appear as untrue to the divine revelation, as a hindrance to the growth of the human spirit.

The age before the Reformation reveals the Latin church in a state of hopeless decline. None of the peculiar institutions of the Middle Ages came any more to its help against the forces that were slowly but surely compassing its downfall. Monasticism put forth no more fresh outshoots full of life and vigor, as in the days of Hildebrand or Bernard or Innocent the Great. The old orders partook of the general decline which touched everything that the mediæval spirit had inspired. The corruptions that were bred within the cloister were an evidence that as an institution monasticism had outlived its usefulness, and was out of harmony with the larger life of the time. Scholasticism also, which in the days of Aquinas had turned back the tide of skepticism, could no longer avail itself of the compromise with the reason which the *Angelic Doctor* had proclaimed; it not only showed no energy in defending the church's teaching, but in order to save philosophy it proclaimed an absolute divorce between religion and speculative thought, leaving the church to defend itself as best it could without the aid of reason. Most of those who still bore the scholastic mantle settled down to the skeptical conclusion, that what was false in philosophy might yet be true in theology. At a time when the church most needed every support which could contribute to sustain its decaying strength, it was deserted by the reason. The reason which had been treated with distrust and suspicion, which the church had sought to humiliate as its vassal, was now taking its revenge.

As to the papacy, when in the fourteenth century it fled from Rome and took refuge in Avignon, it was seen as abandoning the rock from which it had been hewn, and the pit from which it was digged. It could then be contemplated as a thing apart from the mysterious source of its greatness, and the result was a blow at its prestige from which it never recovered. That the papacy could not be regarded as the source whence a new life might spring up for the regeneration of the church was evident from the papal conflicts with itself; it was becoming the heaviest burden which the church had to carry. It was only by proclaiming that there was a power in Christendom superior to the popes, and by which they could be punished or made amenable to law, that the hopes of reform continued for generations to be nourished.

If we ask for the causes which explain this apparently sudden decline of the papacy, and with it of the ascendency of the mediæval church, they are to be found in a reversal of that process which had accompanied its first appearance in history. The papacy rose at a time when men were unable or no longer free to think for themselves, when they had ceased to be competent to the task of self-government. Its career drew to a close when men were once more able to resume the office which in their weakness they had delegated to a priesthood, when they were once more free to think for themselves. The reason and conscience of humanity had outgrown the papacy, and refused to be held by its leading-strings. The tide which had been rising in the history of the popes, from the time of Leo the Great in the fifth century, had now begun to go out. The work of the popes was done, and He who had raised an institution so unwelcome in its first appearance, but so necessary, was now removing it or gently letting it down from its old supremacy.

No institutions which have played a large part in human history have lived in vain. Before they decline or disappear, they yield up to the larger life of humanity the secret of their success or influence. As history evolves its contents, and its seemingly unconscious purpose is disclosed, that which had appeared most untrue or antagonistic to the spirit of Christ's religion is seen to have subserved the progress of mankind.

The worship of relics, which was so prominent a feature in mediæval life, had, in the absence of literature or the want of ability to use it, ministered to the desire to get nearer to historic events and personages, or to realize more vividly their existence; it had stimulated pilgrimages to holy places, which had finally culminated in the great Crusades. The Crusades in turn changed the shape of society, broke down feudalism, and prepared the way for modern states; they enlarged the narrow horizon of Christendom by bringing it into contact with Mohammedan culture and civilization; they concentrated its gaze upon Christ, and intensified the consciousness of the Christian principle in contrast with that of Islam. Even by their failure to accomplish their direct aim — the wresting of the holy sepulchre from the hands of the infidel — they damaged irretrievably the prestige of the Latin church, for the popes had committed Christendom to the attempt, and could not evade the consequences which it entailed.

The worship of saints, which under one aspect was a disowning of the perfect humanity of Christ, and the substitution for it of lower ideals, was yet a testimony, in however debased a form, to the belief that humanity had been redeemed, — that in its inmost being it was affiliated with the divine nature; out of saint-worship had grown the miracle-plays, which were the germs of the modern drama; in the lives of the saints as they were read or commemorated, were the rude beginnings of the study of history as something deeper and more inward than a mere chronicle of events. The production of images was the preliminary step to Christian art, whose glory it was to have anticipated the long and arduous process of theological thought. The separation between humanity and Deity was overcome for the popular mind when artists, discarding conventional symbols like the halo, which had hitherto been considered necessary for representing the divine as distinct from the human, were content to see in perfect humanity the manifestation of God. In the tendency of painting to concentrate attention upon human personality, in its aim to reproduce upon the canvas the likeness of the inward spirit, may be seen a preparation for receiving the truth that in the human consciousness lies the reflection of a divine image.

The papacy had served the purpose of consolidating the different races of Europe into one great family, so that they could never again lose the sense of relationship; it had held men under subjection to an external law until they were able to hear a voice that spoke within; it had served as the conscience of the people at a time when otherwise they would have been mute under the oppression or brute force of the civil power.[1]

---

[1] "There is a spirit of community in the modern world which has always been regarded as the basis of its progressive improvements, whether in religion, politics, manners, social life, or literature. To bring about this community, it was necessary that the western nations should at one period constitute what may be

Monasticism had stood for the idea that human salvation was not a mechanical process by which the collective mass of humanity, within the communion of the church, was to be lifted by no effort of its own in the kingdom of heaven. It was a protest in behalf of the truth, which in the Middle Ages most needed to be emphasized, that salvation demands the activity of all the faculties of one's being. In this aspect monasticism was the assertion of the truth of individual responsibility. It declined as an institution because of the fearful perversion of which it had been guilty, — the abuse which it had heaped on things most divine, the neglect with which it treated a large range of human duties and relationships, whose right discharge is essential to the fullest salvation of man. But it did not decline till the truth which it had conserved, — the principle of individualism, — had been acknowledged as the basis of the coming reform.

To this same end Scholasticism contributed, in the change which it underwent from realism to nominalism in the fourteenth century. Whatever may be the speculative estimate of its value, nominalism was indispensable to the work of reform by the importance which it attaches to the processes of the thinking mind. Its tendency was to emancipate the reason from the yoke of authority, to disperse a host of false conceptions which embarrassed the mind in the search after truth, — especially to free the individual from bondage to a mysterious species in which his distinct existence was absorbed, to proclaim the man in his indi-

called a single politico-ecclesiastical state. But this also was to be no more than the phenomenon of a moment in the grand march of events."—Ranke, *Hist. of the Popes*, i. p. 25. (Bohn ed.)

vidual responsibility as the unit with which God dealt directly in His government of the world. Other influences were also combining to strengthen the same conviction. It had been one of the false assumptions of mediæval theology, that those in the communion of the church who had been regenerated by baptism constituted, as it were, a distinct species marked off by sharp lines from the larger circle of humanity, to which they only belonged by some lower tie. In its origin this belief had sprung from a strong desire on the part of men to realize their oneness through the church. The terrors of the "dark ages," as the tenth century has been designated, had consolidated a frightened people and made them feel that their strength lay in union. The Latin church, in its aspect as the outcome of this conviction, had offered the possibility of a collective salvation to the mass within its fold. But the world was no longer to the imagination what it had been in the days of Augustine or Hildebrand. Men were beginning to feel themselves at home within it as in a universe where God was dwelling; they no longer hesitated to explore its secrets or to travel till they reached its utmost bounds. As the times changed and the great outer world opened up its attractions to the eager gaze, the church as a secluded nursery for timid or despairing souls, under the guardianship of a vigilant hierarchy, must inevitably give way to the conception of a church which did not fear to trust an invisible head, in which each individual man stood in a personal relationship to an unseen but almighty Father.

All through the period which preceded the Reformation can be traced the reassertion of those divine elements in the life of humanity which, since the time of

Augustine, had been suppressed or subordinated in the interest of the church, — nature, the state or nation, the family and the individual. So vitally are all these connected with the environment of man as God intended it, that the revival of one seemed to carry with it the restoration of all to their true dignity. We have already seen how the introduction of Greek philosophy through the writings of Aristotle had created an impulse toward the study of nature. Following closely in its train came the development of the national consciousness. It was the proclamation of the sanctity of the state as an end in itself, in the regulation of whose affairs no external power had a right to interfere, which constituted the lever by which the papacy was overthrown. The popes never recovered from the humiliation of Boniface by Philip the Fair of France, in the beginning of the fourteenth century. The theory of the state in its relation to the church which Augustine had propounded, the realization of which by the great popes of the Middle Ages had made possible the retention of their supremacy over the civil power, could no longer be maintained in its ancient vigor, when men were convinced that the highest end of the nation was not merely to enforce by the might of its arm the legislation and policy of the church, but to consider its own well-being as its first and most sacred obligation. In the working out of this principle was involved the dismemberment of Christendom. It was not Luther who shattered a so-called Catholic unity into fragments, but the expansion of the national consciousness, whether in France, in Germany, or in England. This was the force which took from the church its temporal power, and by so doing initiated the process which was to restore it to its earlier and purer condition, when it was a pervasive spiritual influence, depending upon its advocacy of truth and the voluntary recognition of its disciples for maintaining and extending its influence.

Accompanying the growth of the national spirit was the development of the national languages as a vehicle for the expression of a people's thought. Nationalism, the use of the vernacular, and the desire for reform went hand in hand, whether in England or France, Germany or Italy. When the Latin language, which had been the sacred tongue into the mould of which the Christian revelation had been cast, was displaced by the vernacular, that repressive force was removed which had prevented the thoughts, the impulses, the longings of the people from finding a full and natural expression.[1] As we listen for the first fresh utterances of the people, as they found a voice in the rising national literatures, there is one tone which characterizes them all alike, — that of opposition to the hierarchy and the abuses which it was perpetuating.

The evangelical reformers and the mystics of the fourteenth and fifteenth centuries, great as were the differences that divided them, were alike in their sympathy with the rising nationalism, alike also in using the vernacular as the means for the expression of their

[1] "The language of the Roman people," says Heine, "can never belie its origin. It is a language of command for generals; a language of decree for administrators; an attorney language for usurers; a lapidary speech for the stone-hard Roman people. . . . Though Christianity with a true Christian patience tormented itself for more than a thousand years with the attempt to spiritualize this tongue, its efforts remained fruitless; and when John Tauler sought to fathom the awful abysses of thought and his heart overflowed with religious emotion he was impelled to speak German."

thought as well as for reaching the popular mind. Wycliffe was a statesman as well as a theologian, with a jealousy for his nation's honor; Huss, who followed him, was equally unable to separate his theological convictions from his politics; Savonarola was haunted by the vision of a perfect state, to the accomplishment of which in Florence he believed he had been divinely called. The mystic theology of Eckart, Tauler, and others was the first expression of the German consciousness, anticipating by centuries its maturer form in the systems, whether religious or philosophical, of our own age.

I.

Before treating of the differences that distinguish the two reformatory movements, known as the evangelical and the mystic, it is important to note the features which they possessed in common, by which both contributed to the revolution of the sixteenth century.

Evangelical and mystic reformers were united in rejecting the theory upon which the authority of the hierarchy reposed. Both had ceased to regard the church as a mysterious entity, existing apart from the congregation, or as possessing in this capacity a "deposit" of supernatural trusts. The abandonment of this belief carried with it also the rejection of the principle of sacramental grace. This, too, had been a peculiarly Latin growth, of which Augustine had laid the dogmatic basis in his doctrine of original sin. When God was thought of as at a distance, and mankind was believed, in consequence of the catastrophe of Adam's fall, to have lost all inward divine capacity, it had seemed necessary that man should be restored

THE RISE OF PREACHING.   251

and supported by influences infused into the soul from without. In Augustine's thought, redemption did not lie in the power of the incarnation, or in the personal influence of the present living Christ. To baptism and other sacramental channels was confided the operation of a quality which was known as grace, — a quality or force which, infused into the soul, would enable it to rise above the dominion of sin, and abide in union with its Creator.

So long as the sacramental theory prevailed, but little importance was assigned to preaching. In the Latin church, from the very earliest period, it had played a subordinate part; whereas, in the Greek church, not only had the sermon constituted an important element in the worship, but even the liturgies had taken on a homiletic cast. The absence of preaching is one of the striking features of the mediæval church. It cannot be accounted for altogether on the ground that the language of the people was not sufficiently developed for such a purpose. The sacramental theology dispenses with the need of preaching, for it professes to accomplish the end of preaching in another way. There were great preachers in the Middle Ages, but they rose in connection with the Crusades, when such a method was the only one of rousing the popular enthusiasm. Preaching, as a necessary and constituent part of religious culture, originated with the heretical sects of the twelfth century, such as the Cathari and the Waldenses. When its power was seen in diffusing heresy, the Dominicans seized upon it as equally effective for overcoming heresy. But even the Dominicans, though they never gave up the principle, were unequal to the task of coping with heretical oratory, and it is very significant that into their hands should have been intrusted the management of the inquisition. It really required the combination of the two means to suppress obnoxious thought.

Preaching, as a means of spiritual culture, presupposes a divine constitution of the soul, a human nature charged with divine possibilities. Its object is, by forcible exhortation, by attractive presentation and reiteration of the truth, to awaken the slumbering capacities of the soul into activity, to educate and strengthen that which is already divinely implanted in the germs, to evoke the divine that is in man, to feed the soul from within rather than from without. For such an end it was first used by the great mystics, Eckart and Tauler, in the pre-reformation age. Wycliffe maintained that preaching was the best work that a priest could do; better than praying or ministering the sacraments. He showed his sense of its value by organizing his band of preachers to go throughout the kingdom proclaiming the gospel as it was then read in its freshness and novelty in the newly translated Bible. The power of the new preaching produced a marvelous effect; the human soul responded to the spoken word as by an innate law of its being; all the pomp and splendor of the church and its ritual were as nothing compared with the fascination which the people felt under the spell of the preacher, whose heart, glowing with the truth, appealed to their own hearts with irrepressible power, interpreting to them the vague motives and longings of the soul. Preaching became from this time a factor in human development, and prepared the way for the Reformation. When the Reformation was accomplished, it took its rightful place in the newly constituted churches, becoming the sacrament, as it were, of the larger faith. Under its influence the confessional disappeared with its grace conveyed by priestly absolution; the preacher became the public confessor in the presence of the congregation; the declaration of absolution was ratified by the enlightened conscience of the people, as the voice of God speaking in human hearts.

When the principle of church authority, represented by the hierarchy as the *ecclesia docens,* was repudiated in the interest of reform, the appeal was taken by the evangelical reformers to the Bible as the word of God. Hitherto, in the long course of theological development, no attempt had been made to determine the relation of the Bible to the authority of the church. The voice of the church had been assumed as final in all matters relating to the faith, and a practical infallibility attributed to its decisions. When the evangelical reformers rejected the authority of the church, it became necessary to find another authority for the tenets of the Christian faith, to which all men could go alike in search of that absolute truth which God had communicated to men. When from the time of Wycliffe the church began to tend toward the form of a constitutional monarchy in contrast with the absolutism of the papacy, it became necessary that it should be governed in accordance with a clear and inviolable charter, instead of being subject to the arbitrary will of its former rulers. Wycliffe, and others like minded, while holding that the predestinated constituted the true though invisible church, were by no means disposed to sweep away the ecclesiastical organization, however they might have been inclined to dispense with the necessity of the pope, or been willing to make other changes in ecclesiastical and religious usages. But, whatever might be the form of its government, the church must have its charter to which all could appeal, to which, as to a standard and an ideal, the government, the discipline, and the ritual of the church must necessarily conform.

But the Bible now came to be regarded in a higher light than as a book for the people and a charter for the church. In the time of Wycliffe we stand on the eve of a long process, in which the Reformation is to be seen departing most widely from the whole method and spirit of the Middle Ages. When Thomas Aquinas first made the memorable distinction between natural and revealed theology, he made a contribution to theological thought which was destined to play a part of the highest magnitude in the future, — a distinction which would survive and retain its vitality when all else in his system would be neglected or forgotten. In making this distinction, Aquinas, however, did little more than call attention to two different directions which the human mind might follow. On the one hand, it might explore more thoroughly than had yet been done the real nature and contents of the Christian revelation, as given in Scripture, — for that was what mediæval theology had never done or dared to do ; or, on the other, it might investigate dispassionately, unhindered by prejudices or restraints of any kind, the nature and powers of the human reason, with reference to its capacity to originate or receive, to appreciate or criticise, a revelation. From the time of Wycliffe we can see in which direction Christian thought was moving. There was a deep conviction spreading like a contagion in all spiritual minds, that God had given to mankind a revelation in the Scriptures. To study and to know that revelation became the primary aim, the most pressing necessity ; and so late as the seventeenth century the mind of the church was still centred on the study of the Bible as an authoritative external revelation, before there came a change which demanded a rehearing of the claims of the human reason.

Wycliffe was impelled to the translation of the Scriptures into the vernacular by the profoundest tendencies of his age. Like the Jews at the restoration of their ancient city, as he fought with one hand the enemies of the truth, he was building with the other, when he set forth the Bible as the constitution and the charter of the true church against error and oppression, and called attention to the necessity of inquiring anew into the divine revelation by going to its source in the word of God. How his efforts to this end were regarded may be easily inferred from a representative criticism upon his work, made by a genuine pupil of the old school: "This Master Wycliffe," says Knighton, "translated into English, not an angelic tongue, the gospel that Christ committed to the clergy and doctors of the church, that they might administer it gently to laymen and infirm persons according to the requirements of the time and their individual wants and mental hunger. So by him it has become common and more open to laymen and women who know how to read than it usually is to clerks of good understanding with a fair amount of learning. And thus the gospel pearl is cast forth and trodden by swine! What used to be held dear by clerks and laymen is become as it were a common amusement to both; the gem of clerks is turned into the sport of laymen; and what was once a talent given from above to the clergy and doctors of the church is forever common to the laity." [1]

[1] Quoted in Gairdner, *Studies in English History*.

There were not wanting other critics who saw in the use made of Scripture by the evangelical reformers a perversion of its true purpose, and who, ecclesiastics though they were, uttered a protest in behalf of the reason, and of customs and usages, whose justification was to be found in reason, even if no authority could be found for them in the Bible. But the new day now dawning for humanity was one in which men were seeking to walk by what they believed to be the light of God alone. They were timid of any substitutes for Him, whether in papal vicars of Christ, or hierarchies, or in the reason which seemed to them identified with all the abuses of the past. They believed that God Himself had once actually spoken to the world, that His message of light and life to mankind had been recorded in a book, and that only one duty remained, — to regulate life and manners, worship and discipline, government in church or state, according to the revealed infallible letter of Scripture.

Mysticism, whether in its historical development or in its abstract character as a religious movement, is best understood by placing it in comparison with the ruling aim of the Latin church. That the church not only tolerated it in some of its forms, but even sanctioned it, does not indicate that mysticism was in harmony with the predominant purpose of Latin Christianity. Just as there was a rationalism, whether that of Anselm or Aquinas, or even a skepticism, like that of Duns Scotus or Occam, which could adjust itself to the principle of church authority, so there were phases of mysticism which have not only existed undisturbed in the Latin church, but have been regarded with complacency, and even with approval.

The historical source from which mysticism in the

Middle Ages drew its inspiration was the writings of the pseudo-Dionysius, popularly regarded as Dionysius the Areopagite, who had been converted under St. Paul's preaching at Athens. It was one of the numerous offenses of Abelard against the judgment of the church, that he had questioned the identity of the author of the "Celestial Hierarchy" with the Dionysius who was the patron saint of Paris. What the effect would have been upon Latin theology had it been known that Dionysius wrote in the latter part of the fifth century, and was not entitled to apostolic authority, would be a curious subject of inquiry. For from the time when his books were first translated into Latin in the ninth century, they were regarded as having the highest sanction; even a theologian like Aquinas was indebted to them for elements in his thought which accorded imperfectly with the general tenor of his theology. It is even possible that the tendency to pantheism, against which the School-men were always struggling, might have been eliminated earlier and more easily if it had not been believed that Dionysius spoke to the church with the authority of an associate of the apostles.[1]

[1] The writings of Dionysius are given in vols. iii. and iv. of Migne's *Patrologia*, as if belonging to the age of the Apostolic Fathers; and the late Archbishop of Paris demonstrated anew that the author was Dionysius the Areopagite,—evidence that the Roman Catholic church, as represented in France, still clings to the old tradition. These writings have been translated into German and French, but there is no complete English translation. Colet, the famous Dean of St. Paul's in the time of Erasmus, translated parts of the *Celestial Hierarchy*, of which a new edition has recently been published. For a fuller account of Dionysius, see Ritter, *Die Christliche Philosophie*, pp. 385–390; Vacherot, *Histoire de l'école d'Alexandrie*, iii. pp. 37, ff; Herzog-Plitt, *Real-Encyklopädie*, Art. Dionysius; Maurice, *Hist. of Philosophy*; Vaughan, *Hours with the Mystics*.

Viewed in its largest relations the system of Dionysius was a combination of Neo-Platonic philosophy with the leading characteristics of Latin Christianity. As that philosophy had already been used as an agent for reviving the various forms of heathenism, it is not strange that when Christianity had triumphed and become the religion of the Roman state, Neo-Platonism should seek an alliance with the church through those lower characteristics which, though they had received their original development in the West, had become the common property of Christendom. The hierarchy and the sacraments were the two features of the church which presented themselves to the mind of the pseudo-Dionysius as most easily harmonizing with the Neo-Platonic method of uniting the divine and the human. To this end he increased the number of the sacraments to six, attaching to them a supernatural potency, and emphasized the orders of bishops, priests, and deacons as corresponding to the lower orders of demons in the Neo-Platonic scale of emanations, and as means through which the soul took its first steps toward union with Deity. Above the earthly hierarchy rose the heavenly, where angels and seraphim, each in its threefold order, carried on the process of mediating between humanity and the distant Deity. A system like this, which glorified the human institution by incorporating it as an integral part of a divine unearthly order, throwing around the church's rites a resplendent lustre of supernatural color, could not but win for itself an almost universal acceptance.[1] But despite its easy and apparently

[1] Maximus, the Confessor, in his exposition of the system of Dionysius, modified it in one important respect. Dionysius had made the vision of God attainable in this life; Maximus post-

THE SPIRIT OF THE PSEUDO-DIONYSIUS. 259

natural affiliation with Latin Christianity, the system of Dionysius was only Neo-Platonic heathenism in a debased form, and its author had done little more than baptize with a Christian nomenclature the various grades of personal agency which in the heathen view stretched themselves across the vast abyss that separated humanity from God.[1]

It is not, however, in the form of Dionysius' thought, but in its spirit, that we must seek for the cause which made him in the Middle Ages the source of mysticism. While the aim of the Latin church was to hold God and humanity apart, — to maintain their separation as the foundation of the only true cultus for the human spirit, — the object of Dionysius was to bring them together in the closest relationship. In this respect he was still perpetuating, although in a degraded form, the purpose of the earlier Neo-Platonism, and not only so, but there was speaking through him the spirit of the early Greek theology. If he seemed to make unduly prominent the hierarchy and ritual ordi-

poned the vision to another world and the distant future. A change like this put Dionysius in closer accord with the spirit of Latin Christianity. See Ritter, p. 392, and Vacherot, iii. p. 38.

[1] Le faux Denys semble un néoplatonicien des derniers temps, qui, en passant au Christianisme, a gardé, comme avait déjà fait Synesius, ses doctrines philosophiques, en les fondant habilement avec les principes de sa nouvelle croyance. La distinction des trois méthodes, rationelle, symbolique, et mystique, pour parvenir à Dieu, est empruntée à Proclus, ainsi que la théorie de l'extase ; la doctrine de la *Hiérarchie Céleste* n'est que la théorie des *Ordres divins* assez heureusement adaptée à la théologie chrétienne ; le traité de la Hierarchée ecclésiastique rappelle la description du culte païen restauré par le néoplatonisme. La théologie du faux Denys n'est pas même un mélange des idées alexandrines et chrétiennes ; sous des formules et des noms empruntes au Christianisme, le fond en est tout néoplatonicien. Vacherot, iii. p. 37.

nances of the church, it was always as a means to a higher end. That end was never allowed to fade from the view, or the means to the end usurp its place as a home in which the soul might rest. Hence the study of Dionysius' writings by vigorous and independent minds must put them on a track which diverged from the road which the church was traveling, leading them back again to higher conceptions of God and of man, and of their mutual relations, than those which the Latin church had inherited from Augustine. The hierarchy and the ritual were relegated to a subordinate sphere, as the lower rounds of the ladder are left behind in mounting the higher.

It is unnecessary to do more than refer to the mysticism of the twelfth century, which is known as the French or Romanic, to distinguish it from the later German school. It was connected chiefly with the monastery of St. Victor near Paris, although its mood was shared by Bernard of Clairvaux, and in the following century it found a distinguished representative in Bonaventura, the *Seraphic Doctor* of the schools. While it drew its inspiration from Dionysius, it differed from the later German mysticism in the absence of an intellectual or speculative temper, owing partly to the disfavor into which the exercise of the intellect had fallen through the condemnation of Abelard. In the place of the reason as the faculty which apprehends the divine, the French mystics were inclined to believe in some special faculty of the soul to which was vouchsafed, under certain conditions, the immediate intuition of God. This school of mysticism was also wanting in the ethical tone which pervades the thought of Eckart and Tauler; its tendency was to conceive of God as if a physical essence; it sought in the emotions for the evidence of the union of the soul with God; its language in describing the ecstatic sweetness of the divine communion assumed a passionate and sensuous tone.

It was left to the German mystics of the fourteenth and fifteenth centuries to assert for the first time in the history of Latin theology a higher and truer conception of God. They did not constitute a sect in the church; they were simply independent thinkers with a kindred aim; there were diversities in their method, and variations in the results of their thought, but they were agreed in declaring that God dwells in the innermost recesses of the spirit, that there is in the natural constitution of man a divine element, that to find God or to grow in the knowledge of God is to be accomplished by looking within, and not to extraneous infusions from without. The scholastic theologians were always on their guard against pantheism, checking or modifying the free expression of their thought for fear of confounding God with the world. But the mystics had no such fear, for in their conception of God righteousness was conjoined as essential with the divine love; with such an idea of God it was not possible to identify Him in a pantheistic fashion with the life of nature or of humanity. Hence they asserted the divine immanence without fear or qualification. "God (says Eckart) is alike near in all creatures. I have a power in my soul which enables me to perceive God; I am as certain as that I live that nothing is so near to me as God. He is nearer to me than I am to myself. It is a part of His very essence that He should be nigh and present to me. God is in all things and places alike, and is ever ready to give Himself to us in so far as we are able to receive Him;

he knows God aright who sees Him in all things."[1] This doctrine of the divine immanence as held alike by all the German mystics, Tauler, Suso, or Ruysbroek, involved the correlate truth that human nature, in which God can dwell so intimately, must be in its inmost essence akin to the divine nature. The two natures can no longer be conceived as foreign to each other; the one is the image of the other. The capacity for God is not, as Augustine and Aquinas had conceived it, a thing of which man is destitute by creation in consequence of Adam's fall, and therefore a supernatural gift infused into the soul at baptism; the divine in man is the very essence of his soul. That which, according to Aquinas, is a superadded quality not to be found in the kingdom of nature, is with Eckart the inmost principle of man's being as it exists by nature; the supernatural becomes with him that which in the highest sense is the most truly natural. The kingdom of God does not stand apart from man's constitution by nature under the rule of an external hierarchy; it is a kingdom manifested within the soul: he who knows and perceives how nigh God's kingdom is may say, "Truly the Lord is in this place and I knew it not." The doctrine of the incarnation, which in Latin theology had been an incomprehensible, mysterious fact, before which man humiliated himself in awe, became the central point in mystic theology, as showing how closely God and

---

[1] A sermon of Eckart which contains his most distinctive belief is given among Tauler's sermons (Second Sunday in Advent), translated by Miss Winkworth. See, also, Dorner, *Person of Christ*, b. ii. pp. 1-50, for a discussion of German mysticism in the pre-reformation age, and Schmidt, *Les Mystiques du 14ᵉ Siècle*.

man could come together, how Deity had assimilated to itself in Christ that which in its essence was congruous with the divine. The relationship was so close between God and man, that in Eckart's thought humanity was as necessary to Deity as Deity to humanity. The incarnation reveals God as love, and love as God. The essence of Deity is not physical, but moral or spiritual, and the object of this union of God with man is that man also may develop his personality in love, according to the law of the divine existence.

The German mystics did not aim to lose themselves in ecstatic emotion, or to gain merely some sensuous impression of a vision of the divine. Tauler, who was the great preacher of his age, sought to impress his hearers with the idea of righteousness as indispensable to knowing God and realizing the divine nearness. The position of the mystics seemed open to the objection, that if God's presence is a reality in the soul and in the world, everything may be left to the divine activity in accomplishing human salvation, while man may remain merely passive in the process. But to this Eckart's answer would be that man's blessedness does not consist in this, that God is in him and so close to him, but in his perceiving God's presence and thus knowing and loving Him. Only he who knows in this sense will feel that God's kingdom is nigh at hand. Knowledge, as Eckart uses the expression, carries with it the obedience of the whole nature. In this sense Plato had used the term, and the early Greek theologians, when they said that sin lay in ignorance; or to speak after a higher authority, *This is life eternal, to know Thee the true God, and Jesus Christ Whom Thou hast sent.* In the language of Eckart: "God is ever ready but we are very unready; God is nigh to us but we are far from Him; God is within, we are without; God is at home, we are strangers. God leadeth the righteous by a narrow path till they come unto a wide and open place; that is unto the true freedom of that spirit which has become one spirit with God."

The German mystics when compared with the evangelical reformers are seen to have had a different motive and aim. They had little interest in proclaiming the revelation of the book; they were occupied with that which God revealed in the inner life of the soul. There lay the real revelation, compared with which the other was a thing without, powerless to help as are all external agencies. The ground of certitude with them lay not in the outward letter of the record, but in the attestation of the spirit within. They took little part therefore in the effort to change the form or structure of the church; they had little of that spirit of combativeness or antagonism which would lead them to any open revolt; they were content with the old organization so long as they were free to put their own more spiritual interpretation upon its cultus. The order to which they belonged, the "Friends of God," had no political aim; its object was to develop true religion in the soul, and to bind together for that object all men of a kindred spirit. But while they seem inactive compared with a Wycliffe, they did in some respects a greater, more positive work than the evangelical reformers, although with the latter lay the more immediate future. The one class was preparing the way for the overthrow of the hierarchy, and at the same time presenting a substitute that would still hold man in subjection to an external authority; the mystics developed a principle, which, when its full significance should be discerned in later ages, would appear as the foundation of a more spiritual, more comprehensive theology than the Latin church had ever known in all her history. The voice of Eckart is not merely the echo of an Athanasius pleading for the truth of the divine immanence. It is an utterance from the fresh consciousness of a new race which hitherto, under the tutelage of Latin discipline, had not come to itself or recognized its true descent. But the day was as yet far off when the church would be prepared to receive the message with which he was commissioned.

German mysticism was not a vague reverie with no practical purpose in view. The labors of Tauler, who was a pupil of Eckart and adopted his speculative philosophy, are an evidence that it had a mission for men in the midst of trouble and desolation. Tauler was not only the great preacher of his time, but he put his Christianity to a practical test in Strasbourg when the pestilence known as the black death was carrying off its victims by thousands. At a moment when the city lay under the papal interdict in consequence of its political affiliations, he defied the authority of the church in order to minister to the sick and dying. The fraternity known as the "Friends of God,"— a beautiful designation, summing up in a word the whole spirit and aim of German mysticism in accordance with the saying of Christ, *Henceforth I call you not servants but friends*,— this order, which owned Eckart as its founder and guide, was widely spread in the southwestern part of Germany; it included a large number of laity in its fold, and its object was not only the cultivation of religion among its members, but a spirit of helpfulness to others. A similar organization arose in the Netherlands, — the Brethren of the Common Life, — which undertook the training of the younger clergy, and was a powerful agent for the cultivation of spiritual religion. To this order belonged Thomas à Kempis, whose "Imitation of Christ," it is said, has had a larger circulation than any other book except the Bible; akin to it in spirit, was a little treatise called "German Theology," which Luther republished, and to which he acknowledged his deep indebtedness. The spirit of mysticism had extended also into the Dominican and other orders, and was still surviving in the sixteenth century. In Staupitz, the provincial of the Augustinians, whose spiritual relations to Luther prepared the way for his conversion, we have the outward connecting link between it and the German reformation.

But although the Reformation could not have taken place without the preparatory labors of the mystics, yet there were deficiencies in the theology of Eckart, of Tauler, or of Thomas à Kempis, which made impossible for them the work which Luther accomplished. They had reverted to the essential principles of an earlier theology, overleaping, as it were, with one bound the intervening ages which separated them from Athanasius and other kindred spirits of the ancient church. They talked like the Stoics and the Neo-Platonists of the purification of the soul in order to spiritual contemplation or to the union of the soul with God. But they were oblivious to the principle of historical continuity; they did not take into account the influence of the training of the Latin church through long ages, and how the basis of that training had been laid in the doctrine of original sin with the guilt which it assumed for every man at birth, or the fearful consequences which that primordial crime was thought to have entailed here and hereafter in separating humanity from the source of its life. Whether the Augustinian dogma of original sin was true or false, it had entered into the fibre of mediæval religion, and could not be eliminated by a mere negation. Any readjustment in theology must now take it into consideration as if it were a part of the divine order, and, even supposing it to be true, still find a principle by which God and humanity could be reunited in an organic relationship. It was here that Luther diverged from the track of German mysticism. Because he started from the attitude of the people as they had been educated by the church, he was able to make a successful protest against the abuses of his age; he was powerful to restore again the simple faith of Christ's religion. While the mystics had been preaching the purification of the soul as the way to the union with God, the church was selling pardons or indulgences for sin, which never would have been bought so eagerly if there had not been a demand for them on the part of the people. To overcome so gigantic a perversion of the spirit of Christianity was a task for which the mystics were unsuited by their distance from the popular mind.

There were other deficiencies also in German mysticism. In its idea of human nature there still lingered a relic of the Latin tradition, that it was an evil thing to be repressed or subdued. It talked of renunciation rather than consecration. In the "Imitation of Christ" there still breathed the close, unhealthy air of the cloister. The full imitation of Christ implied directions of human aspiration and endeavor which did not enter into the thought of Thomas à Kempis. There was yet a longer preliminary work to be done before theology and the Christian life could revert to their true ground in Christ, in whom and by whom and for whom are all things.

II.

The evangelical reformers prepared the way for revolt from church authority. Wycliffe, Huss, Savonarola, and others, while differing from each other in the extent to which they carried their opposition to mediæval doctrines, were alike in one respect, — they had emancipated themselves from the Latin idea that the church was identical with the hierarchy. That idea, the traces of which go back almost to the time when Christianity was planted in Rome, the development of which is found in Latin writers, as Clement of Rome, Tertullian, Irenæus, Cyprian, and Augustine, — the idea of the solidarity of the episcopate holding by tactual succession from the apostolate, to which as a body had been intrusted the graces and powers for the salvation of man, together with the "deposit" of the faith, whose purity it guaranteed by its continuous existence, — that idea of the church which by a natural and necessary process had developed a pope as the representative of Christian unity and power, was the first feature of Latin Christianity which yielded to the solvent influence of the growing intellect and conscience. That which had been the first to rise was the first to succumb, and its fall was equivalent to freeing the human mind from the yoke of external authority.

The great reformers before the Reformation had made the issue clear to all the world. Although Wycliffe had been allowed to die quietly in his bed, yet at the command of Pope Martin V. his grave had been opened, his bones had been burned, and the ashes thrown into the little river that flows by Lutterworth. In the quaint words of Thomas Fuller, that river "took them into the Severn, Severn into the narrow seas, they into the main ocean, and thus the ashes of Wycliffe are the emblems of the doctrine which is now dispersed all the world over." [1]

Huss had been condemned to death in 1414, at the Council of Constance, for heresy, — a heresy which lay not so much in the denial of special doctrines as in his unwillingness to disown the conviction of conscience at the bidding of external authority. The issue was plain, and the wayfaring man could read it, that Huss stood for the sacred majesty of conscience, undaunted in the presence of the most imposing assemblage that the church could muster. His condemnation was meant as a declaration of the principle that the conscience had no rights against the hierarchy. In the answer of Savonarola from the stake, when the bishop who preached the customary sermon declared him cut off from the church militant and the church triumphant, was the same issue repeated, — "No, not from the church triumphant; you cannot cut me off from that."

To all outward appearance the Latin church stood strong as ever at the opening of the sixteenth century. There was no sign of the catastrophe which was to

---

[1] It has been generally supposed that Huss, although indebted to Wycliffe, was by no means a blind disciple of the English reformer. How entirely the Bohemian movement was the after-effect of Wycliffe's labors, and how closely Huss had accepted his teaching, is shown by Lechler, *Johann von Wiclif und die Vorgeschichte der Reformation*, ii. pp. 233–270.

dismember Christendom, the popes revealed no consciousness that their prestige had been weakened, and walked smiling to their downfall. In reality all things were hollow with decay; the mediæval age was over, the preparation for a new age was already accomplished, and the world was waiting for him who should lead out the people from the house of bondage. When Luther burned the pope's bull in 1520, he took the bold step toward a revolution which set free one half of Christendom from papal subjection. When at the Diet of Worms, in 1521, he declared that he could not retract his writings at the bidding of any external authority, unless shown that he was wrong, he affirmed the supremacy of the human conscience as the highest earthly court of appeal; and so firm did he stand in this conviction that he dared to invoke God to set His seal to the truth which His servant proclaimed. As one contemplates Luther at the council hall in Worms, an insignificant monk, a man of the people standing before the highest potentates of church and state, with his life depending upon the answer he made to his judges, the mind travels back to a similar scene when Abelard also stood before his judges, a man whose intellect was clear, but whose moral nature had been hurt by the sins of his earlier life. Between the two men whose attitude was so similar, between the appeal of the one to the pope, and the other to the conscience, lay the distance of nearly four hundred years, — so long had it taken for God to educate a race to understand and to maintain its high prerogative.

The events of the sixteenth century have been too often regarded as constituting a break in history. But to the eye of thought reviewing the course of history the continuity remains unbroken. Luther was but the child of the ages preceding; the Protestant revolution was the natural and orderly sequence of a long course of preparation. It was indispensable indeed for a time that men should regard the Reformation as breaking with the past, in order that they might estimate more deeply the meaning of the truth which had been revealed to them, and secure its firmer establishment. So, also, in the ancient church, there had appeared a violent antagonism to Judaism, and to heathen art, which served the purpose of making more clear and emphatic the vital difference between Christianity and other religions. In the turmoil of an age of transition it is not always given to the leaders to discern the route by which they have been led. Luther entered upon the inheritance of Wycliffe and of Huss, and still further was he indebted to the spirit of German mysticism. But his greatness was also peculiarly his own. He was not so much a theologian as a man who afforded in his own rich nature, unveiled so completely before his age, the materials for theology. His life was a type of humanity for his own and succeeding ages. He lived through the religious experience of the mediæval dispensation before he came to his knowledge of a higher birthright. Viewed from the standing point of a formal theology, he is full of inconsistencies and contradictions, and even dangerous errors. But regarded simply as a man with his rich endowment of human instincts and yearnings, to which he gave the freest, most unguarded expression, he was in himself a revelation of the human consciousness in its freshness and simplicity, with which a complete theology must come to terms. It is because the explosive utterances of his vigorous, tumultuous nature have been weighed as if they were carefully formed dogmatic statements, that Luther has been so often misunderstood by Protestant as well as by Roman Catholic writers.

It is a popular mistake to regard the Reformation as having for its main object the correction of abuses which had grown up in the church. While some justify the work of Luther by exposing these abuses in detail, others have tried to show that the abuses were not so great as had been supposed, or that some things which the reformers regarded as such were in reality customs which are consonant with reason or with piety; and still a third class, defending the Latin church against the assaults of Protestantism, have boldly affirmed that there were no abuses whatever in the sixteenth century which called for protest or reform, — that the movement of Luther from beginning to end was the work of an evil will setting itself against divine authority.

Luther, it is true, began his work as a reformer by opposition to the principle and the practice of indulgences, in which he saw not only a perversion of the gospel of Christ, but the source of a vicious influence injurious to ordinary morality. The doctrine of indulgences as taught by Lombard or Aquinas may differ from the belief regarding their operation which was preached by a Tetzel, and received by the people in the sixteenth century. But the fact cannot be obscured that indulgences were then regarded at Rome by those high in authority as the best available means of replenishing the papal treasury, whose resources, as it was alleged, were heavily taxed in building St. Peter's cathedral, or in carrying on the war with the Turks. The Latin church, as a matter of fact, saw no objection then, and indeed has never yet been able to see any, why people should not be made to pay for spiritual privileges, or, if they value God's pardon, why they should not be called upon to express their sense of its value in some such tangible form as money. The practice of selling indulgences by which were remitted the penalties of sin, whether enacted by God or the church, — for the two were practically identified, — grew out of the disposition to guard zealously the "deposit" intrusted to the hierarchy. From such a point of view, there was reason to fear that if people were not called upon to pay for God's pardon, they would not attach to it any exalted importance.

Luther saw from a very early stage in his career as a reformer, that it was not against abuses in themselves alone that he was waging his warfare, but against the principle from which they flowed, — the Latin idea of the church, by which was maintained and justified what the enlightened conscience of Christendom was beginning to regard with abhorrence and contempt. In his "Address to the German Nobility," written in the year 1520, only three years after the posting of the theses, he had come to see that the root of all that was obnoxious in the traditional Christianity was the assumption that the church consisted primarily in the hierarchy or episcopate, and as such was commissioned to teach and rule the world. In the "Address to the German Nobility" we have at last the direct and final answer to Tertullian and Irenæus, Cyprian and Augustine.[1] The church does not consist in the episcopate. No privileges, no "deposit," no trusts are assigned by God to the bishops which do

[1] *An kaiserliche Majestät und den christl. Adel deutscher Nation*, in Luther's *Sammtliche Schriften* ed. Walch, x.

not also belong by right to every Christian man. Ordination is but a human arrangement, by which the divine prerogatives lodged in the church as the congregation of faithful men are delegated to a few to exercise in the name and by the authority of all. If a small number of Christians were to find themselves in a desert without a regularly ordained priest, and with no means of obtaining one, it would be only the exercise of their divine and natural right if they were to set apart one of their number for the office. Such an one would just as truly preach and absolve and administer the sacraments as if he had been consecrated by all the bishops in Christendom. Between laymen and clergy there is no other difference than that of function or office; the highest dignity which can be conferred on man is common to both, — that of belonging to the body of Christ, and being every one members one of another.

But Luther could not so successfully have attacked and overthrown the mediæval conception of the church had he not grasped with singular strength and clearness another principle, namely, that there is no inherent and essential difference between religious and what are called secular things.[1] The dualism which the mediæval church had inherited from ancient Latin fathers, which had even found expression in the decisions of general councils, sharply distinguishing between the divine and the human as incompatible with each other, was also at last met by a principle which, in proportion as its significance was apprehended, would reverse the thought of ages. The belief that the divine and the human were foreign to each other had led to distinctions between clergy and people, be-

[1] *Werke,* ed. Walch, x. pp. 302, 303.

tween church and state, between nature and grace, and had been the underlying sentiment which supported the aspiration of the popes to set themselves above kings and princes. Luther taught that the secular power was divine, and directly ordained by God without papal mediation; that civil or secular functions do not differ in kind from those called religious; that even a shoemaker, a blacksmith, or a peasant, were alike set apart with bishops and priests to a calling that was sacred, inasmuch as all kinds of service minister to the well-being of the community and knit together the members of the one body in a closer communion and fellowship.

And still another principle, closely connected with the preceding, was set forth by Luther before he proceeded to enumerate to the German nobility the abuses which stood in need of correction.[1] He calls it one of the walls by which the church had intrenched itself apart from the Christian community that the Bible had been regarded as a "deposit" in the hands of the episcopate or hierarchy, and that to it alone, or speaking through its mouth-piece, the papacy, belonged the right of determining what was the meaning of the divine revelation. If, as Luther argued, the laity were on an equality with the clergy, then it must be also admitted that they have the faith, the spirit, and the mind of Christ, and are entitled to interpret the Scriptures for themselves. It was of them that it had been said, *they should be all taught of God;* to them Christ had referred when He said, *Neither pray I for these alone, but for them also which shall believe on me through their word.* Such was the original idea in Luther's mind of what was afterwards designated

[1] *Werke,* ed. Walch, x. p. 309.

as private judgment — the affirmation of the Christian consciousness as the basis of certitude for Christian belief. From a historical point of view it may be regarded as the first emphatic protest coming from the heart of the church against the argument of Tertullian in his "Prescription of Heretics," or of Irenæus appealing to a tradition of whose purity the episcopate was the guarantee, or of Augustine asserting against human reason the divine prerogatives of the episcopal office to teach infallible truth.[1]

But the assertion of great principles like these, far reaching as they are in the full extent of their application, does not constitute Luther's most distinctive work as a religious reformer. His title to greatness as a spiritual hero rests upon his proclamation of the doctrine of justification by faith, or, in other words, his readjustment, first for himself, and then for others, of

[1] The most characteristic of the thoughts and beliefs in which, according to Bunsen, all the reformers of the sixteenth century agreed, are summed up by him in the five following propositions : —
1. "The congregation in the full sense of the word, the whole company of faithful people, and not the clergy alone, constitute the church.
2. "The whole church as thus defined is the deposit of man's consciousness of God in the public worship of Him.
3. "The collective community in its national capacity ought to represent a people of God.
4. "There is no difference between spiritual or religious acts and secular acts.
5. "A personal faith is the condition of inward peace with God. But this personal faith necessarily involves free convictions, and therefore free inquiry and free speculation on the results thereof, though carried on under a sense of responsibility to God ; and this again presupposes freedom of conscience and thought." — *God in History*, vol. iii. pp. 199–201.

the conception of man's relation to God. In the conflicts of his inner life, — the bitter struggles through which he passed before he attained that for which his soul was hungering, — he stands for humanity itself as it had been left by the tutelage of the Latin church; made to feel his need of Christ, but not having yet known Him after the spirit; stricken with a sense of sin and guilt, laboring under the consciousness of separation from God, and yet demanding an absolute assurance of His pardon and reconciliation with Him in the inmost depth of his being beyond the possibility of uncertainty or doubt. His experience in the monastery at Erfurt, where he put to the test the mediæval method of asceticism, confession, and penance, failed to bring him the conviction of forgiveness. Indeed, this was not its intention or aim. The Latin church did not profess to impart certitude of salvation to her children. It preferred to retain them in a condition of hope which would stimulate to activity, but the certainty of their acceptance with God could not be known till life was over. When the church was girding itself to its distinctive task in the beginning of the Middle Ages, Pope Gregory the Great had replied to a correspondent who demanded the assurance that her sins were forgiven, that such assurance was difficult and unprofitable.[1] In uncertainty and self-distrust the soul should remain as its normal attitude till the end of life revealed the final result. The idea of probation, as thus defined, became the ruling principle of the church, and had been known in Latin theology as the *conjectura moralis*. As a principle it was not out of harmony with the mediæval practice of asceticism, by which the soul might increase the

[1] Neander, *Church History*, v p. 200.

probability, but not secure the certainty, of its salvation.[1]

After this confidence, however, Luther was struggling in his earlier years, and the attainment of the principle by which it was gained constituted his conversion. In his later life, when he saw more clearly the nature of the struggle through which he had passed, he described the process in unmistakable terms. He then recognized that his thought about God had undergone a change. When he first read the words of St. Paul, so he tells us, as given in the Latin Vulgate, *the justice of God is revealed in Him*, —*justitia Dei in eo revelatur*, — he hated the expression because he misunderstood its meaning. "I said to myself: 'Is it not then enough that wretched sinners, already eternally damned for original sin, should

[1] How firmly the mediæval church was wedded to this view of the Christian life was shown anew at the Council of Trent, where, in opposition to the Lutheran doctrine of justification by faith, a decree was put forth condemning the "vain confidence of heretics." Sess. vi. c. 9. "No one can know with a certainty of faith which cannot be subject to mistake, that he has obtained the grace of God." Neither Augustine, Luther, nor Calvin, held the doctrine of probation. Indeed, it may be said that the doctrine of justification, as Luther propounded it, involving as it did the *fiducia* or certainty of acceptance with God, was a protest against probation. The idea of probation is clearly incompatible with the Calvinistic doctrine of election. The retrogression from Calvinism, as its founder proclaimed it, to the mediæval idea of life as a probation, was recorded at the famous Westminster Assembly in the seventeenth century. Cf. Sir William Hamilton, *Discussions on Philosophy and Literature*, pp. 505 ff. In his essay on Luther, Canon Mozley has selected this point for his strongest animadversion. Luther, in his view, made his great mistake in not being willing to walk in the subdued and uncertain twilight in which the mediæval church retained humanity; he attempted a flight beyond the reach of man in this world.

be overwhelmed with so many calamities by the decrees of the Decalogue, but God must further add misery to misery by His gospel, menacing us even there with His justice and His anger?' It was thus the trouble of my conscience carried me away, and I always came back to the same passage. At last I perceived that the justice of God is that whereby with the blessing of God the just man lives, that is to say, faith. . . . Thereupon I felt as if born again, and it seemed to me as though heaven's gates stood full open, and that I was joyfully entering therein."[1] In other words, the "justice" of the Latin Vulgate when understood as righteousness became the most attractive thing that the soul could know; it constituted the bond between man and God, that man by the insight of faith was able to read the inmost nature of God revealed in Christ, and to find in the divine nature that which the human nature was struggling with all its powers to attain.

But the gospel, according to Luther's new reading of it, contained a still more marvelous truth. Although man was a sinner, and fell infinitely below the divine ideal of his destiny, yet such was the goodness of God, that those who through faith in Christ as manifesting God's righteousness had come to love and to follow Him, were in God's sight already sharers in Christ's deified humanity, they stood before God not merely clothed in the feeble and meagre righteousness which they could call their own, but in the glory of Christ's righteousness imputed to them. So long as a man looked away from himself to Christ and His righteousness, he was not only in the way to making that righteousness his own, but he already shone with

[1] Michelet, *Mémoires de Luther. Écrits par lui-même*, i. p. 26.

the reflected righteousness of Christ, in virtue of the mysterious oneness which unites Christ to all believers. And this was only an endeavor to regain the truth which Clement of Alexandria and Athanasius had asserted when they spoke of humanity as having been deified in Christ, and of an actual redemption already accomplished in which all men shared by their constitutional relation to the head of the race.

Such was Luther's doctrine of justification by faith. He arrived at his conviction by processes which have now become unfamiliar, and the language which he used often serves to conceal his thought from the modern inquirer. It was his misfortune that he studied St. Paul's Epistle to the Romans too much under the guidance of Augustine's commentary, instead of reading the gospel as it is condensed in one brief illustration given by Christ Himself in the story of the Prodigal Son. What Luther was trying to express, what flashes out in his occasional remarks interspersed amid his technical language, was nothing else than the principle contained in that most complete, most beautiful of all the parables of Christ. The story of the prodigal reveals how man in all his sinfulness and degradation and guilt is yet received into the divine favor, and treated as though he were a son that had never wandered from the father's house. But when Luther used the phrase "justification by faith," he was borrowing a figure of speech from St. Paul, by which the great apostle sought to convey to the legal mind of the Roman people how it was possible that a guilty person might be acquitted at the bar of infinite justice. The Latin mind naturally fastened upon an illustration so apt, and the word "justification" became, like "grace," one of the current phrases of Latin theology. Instead of a figure of speech, an adaptation of language for a special end, it was made the cornerstone of a system of theology by the successors of Luther, and its very significance perverted and lost in the effort to follow out the figure to its logical results.

But with Luther the reality was greater than the now almost obsolete language in which it was clothed would seem to convey. The doctrine of justification by faith implied that man stood to infinite Deity in the closest and most endearing relationship. It carried with it the positive assurance, the certainty (*fiducia*) of ultimate salvation from sin to holiness. Every man by the power of a true faith could henceforth know himself as a son of God, and the intimacy of true sonship gave rise in the soul to an experience of blessedness and peace which the storms of doubt could not weaken or destroy. The Romanists wished to add works to faith as the instrument of justification, but that would have changed the whole complexion of the truth, and brought back again the error which Luther was resisting. It was justification by faith only, just as the prodigal was received into divine favor by the faith which led him to arise and go to his father. In the strength of this mighty conviction Luther stood with a majesty unsurpassed, confronting the world that had been, and that which was to be. It made no difference to him that he stood alone, opposed by all the sacred traditions of Latin Christendom running so far back in the past that they seemed coeval with Christianity itself. He stood before his age with the uplifted open Bible, and the truth which he there read so corresponded with the life within him, that it made no difference if, as he said, a thousand Augustines, or a thousand Cyprians, or a thousand councils were against him. In such a spectacle as this we read a testimony to the divinely endowed consciousness of human nature which has no equal in history. Compared with this testimony to the reality of the life of God in the soul, the contradictions, the inconsistencies, the mistakes of Luther weigh as a feather in the balance.

The sixteenth century was a period of intellectual confusion. When a great revolution is in process of accomplishment there is little room for calm, dispassionate examination of intellectual formulas. No philosophers arose after the decline of scholasticism in the fifteenth century, until the reformation period was over. The turmoil was unfavorable to the interest of scholarship, of which Erasmus stood as the representative. To look for an intelligent criticism of the doctrines of the Latin church at the hands of Luther or any of the reformers, is to seek for the impossible. In retaining some or rejecting others they were governed by impulses and instincts which were often healthy and true, while at the same time they were still to a large extent unconsciously under the influence of that tradition which they professed to discard as having no authority in the light of Scripture.

With this qualification, it becomes an interesting task to review the opinions of Luther. He rejected the Latin idea of the church, and fell back upon the earlier and higher view, that it was composed of the body of Christian believers. The form of ecclesiastical organization which ministered to the spiritual welfare was a matter of indifference, so long as it met the need of holding men together in Christian communion and fellowship. The sanction of the clergy lay in no gift communicated by an external authority, but was derived from the body to which it ministered as its representative. The episcopate had been so involved in the Latin theory of the hierarchy, that it seems to have been spontaneously dropped without discussion as an unnecessary excrescence out of harmony with the new order. At a later time, when the signs of a reaction against the Reformation were evident, and when the reformers themselves were growing timid in the presence of the increasing disorder, there were expressed some regrets that so much concession had been made to the democratic principle in the church, and that the episcopate had not been retained as an efficient means of centralizing authority. But even the temporizing Melancthon was careful to specify that it should be regarded, if restored, as a thing of human origin, or, according to the mediæval distinction, *jure humano*, not *jure divino*.[1] With regard to priestly powers in what had been called the sacrament of penance, Luther attached importance to the declaration of absolution, but thought the confession or enumeration of special sins unnecessary and even injurious. But the power to make the declaration of God's absolution belonged as a right to every Chris-

[1] For a list of passages bearing upon this point see Gieseler, *Eccles. Hist.*, iv. p. 529. The words of Melancthon are, — *Utinam, utinam possim non quidem dominationem confirmare, sed administrationem restituere Episcoporum.* "It is evident," says the Memorial of the Wittenberg and other divines to the Diet at Smalcald, 1540, "that the churches need to be visited by those high in office, else the churches will not be long honored, and pastors will be evil treated in villages." There would have been no difficulty in securing bishops, or what is called the "succession," had the sentiment of the church or the policy of the princes been in favor of their restoration.

tian man, in virtue of the universal priesthood of believers, and its exercise by the ministry was a matter of human administration.[1]

A peculiar interest attaches to Luther's treatment of Scripture, because underlying it may be discerned a grasp of a larger view of the nature and method of divine revelation than was afterwards held by the common consent of the reformed churches. He seems indeed to have united in a living combination the apparently contradictory positions of the evangelical reformers and the mystics: with the one he upholds Scripture as an external and absolute authority, the very Word of God, the charter and constitution of the church; and with the other he exalts the divine consciousness in man as that by which Scripture is known and judged to be from God. The Bible is divine because it is the mirror in which is reflected the experience of humanity in its highest exaltation, under the influence of a divine Spirit. No amount of hostile criticism could shake a man's faith in Scripture whose reverence for it was based on such a foundation. In this way may be explained Luther's extraordinary freedom in criticising the contents of the Bible, a freedom and boldness which was a source of mortification to his successors, which they endeavored to cover over and forget.

The following specimens of Luther's biblical criticism, were their source unknown, would appear to some like the destructive attacks of modern rationalists. In regard to the Pentateuch, Luther thought it a matter of indifference whether or not it was written by Moses. The Book of Kings he spoke of as excellent, — a hundred times better than the Chronicles.

[1] Gieseler, *ibid.* p. 540.

Jeremiah, as a prophet, was much inferior to Isaiah. None of the discourses of the prophets were regularly committed to writing at the time, but were collected subsequently by their disciples and hearers, and thus the complete collection was formed. In the Gospel of St. Luke the Saviour's passion is best described; but the Gospel of St. John is the true, pure gospel, the chief of the gospels, because it contains the greatest portion of Christ's sayings; it is far preferable to the other gospels, "the unique, tender, true, main gospel." Even the Epistles of St. Paul are higher in authority than the Gospels of St. Matthew, St. Mark, and St. Luke, for they deal with faith in Christ and how it justifies, while the latter are mainly occupied with His works and miracles. In a word, St. John's Gospel with St. Paul's Epistles, especially those to the Romans, Galatians, and Ephesians, and also the first Epistles of St. John and St. Peter, these contain and teach all that it is necessary to know, even if one were never to see any other books. Luther did not regard the Epistle to the Hebrews, nor that of St. James, to be of apostolic origin, and the latter he characterized as an epistle of straw, with no trace of the gospel in it. He estimated very lightly the Epistle of St. Jude, and thought it was a copy of the Second Epistle of St. Peter. He could detect no trace in the Book of Revelation of its having been inspired by the Holy Ghost. The causes which led him to reject it from the canon were its visions, whose obscurity was in contrast with the clearness of a genuine revelation; many of the church fathers had long ago rejected it; Christ is not presented there as it was the duty of an apostle to recognize and teach Him.[1] In harmony

[1] Luther's biblical criticisms are found in the various prefaces

also with Luther's attitude towards Scripture was his estimate of miracles. They had, to his mind, a very subordinate value as evidence of the truth of Christ's teaching. "External miracles," he said, "are the apples and nuts which God gave to the childish world as playthings; we no longer have need of them."

Luther is not to be regarded as a constructive, systematic theologian; no ruling idea gives symmetry and completeness to his thought; in many of his positions he retained the old scholastic phraseology. He did not combat the doctrine of original sin, which, as interpreted by Augustine, had colored the entire teaching and cultus of the Latin church. In the prominence which he gives to the agency of the devil may be seen the expression of his desire to relieve Deity of all responsibility for human evil; but he makes no effort to define the relationship of Satan to God in any formal way. It must be admitted, also, that Luther denied, in extreme and even violent language, the freedom of the human will, in order to assert the activity of God and man's absolute dependence upon Him. Erasmus, who was carried away by no overpowering impulse, selected this point as the weak spot for an attack upon Luther's position. But there was an element in this denial of human liberty, made alike by all the reformers, which Erasmus did not appreciate, — an element which grew out of the very situation of reform. In order to snatch men from the servitude of the church it was necessary

to his commentaries on the books of Scripture, *Werke*, ed. Walch; also in his *Table-Talk*, translated by Hazlitt, and in the fuller edition of the *Tischreden*, by Bindseil. Compare, also, Michelet and Hagenbach's *History of the Reformation*.

to bring them into bondage to God; the denial of human liberty meant the profound conviction that God Himself was acting and speaking in His human agents, that they were under the spell of an Almighty Spirit which they were powerless to resist. The concession of human liberty, as in the Latin church, had carried with it subjection to the power of an earthly priesthood; to assert the absolute subjection of the will to God was to bring men into that servitude which is perfect freedom.

III.

The Reformation in Switzerland was independent of the movement led by Luther; it began earlier, it followed a leader widely different in character from the hero of Germany, it originated from another impetus than that which impelled Germany to revolt, it was based on a different principle and reached in theology a different result. While Luther and Zwingle were both indebted to the influence of mysticism, yet that which can be traced only as latent in Luther's mind, or may be implied but is not clearly stated in the doctrine of justification by faith, — the idea of the divine immanence, — was the fundamental principle with Zwingle, giving unity and consistency to his life as well as to his theology. Luther was roused to indignation by the practice of indulgences, in which he saw exposed for sale the free forgiveness of God; Zwingle was moved to action by the crowd who came to worship the miracle-working Madonna at Einsiedeln. The one was seeking to find a true basis for the distinctively religious life, the other for a principle that would harmonize man on all sides of his nature and in all departments of his activity with a divine purpose in the creation.

The idea of Deity in Zwingle's thought is that of a being whose indwelling life constitutes the essence and the reality of all things, who is not only infinite wisdom but infinite love. The creation had its origin in the divine love; humanity was called into existence that it might rejoice in God; all the grades and ranges of existence are so many revelations of the divine existence which operates in and through them.[1] The divine action in the world is immediate, and even miracles, as they are called, are not abrupt and sudden interpositions, but fall within the lines of uniform and all-pervading law. To Zwingle's mind the whole aspect of the world was in the highest sense miraculous, and ordinary phenomena were more divine than events which merely strike the imagination because of their extraordinary or rare character.[2]. Man is born with the capacity to know and to possess God. His spirit, by its very nature, goes out to God. But it is not by and in himself, as a being distinct from God, that man can rise either to the knowledge of God or the true knowledge of himself. Hence revelation becomes part of the organic process of things — a living, actual, present process, whose results are not exclusively re-

---

[1] Numen enim ut a se ipso est, ita non est quicquam quod a se ipso et non ab illo sit. Esse igitur rerum universarum esse numinis est. Ut non sit frivola ea Philosophorum sententia, qui dixerunt, omnia unum esse ; si recte modo illos capiamus, videlicet ita ut omnium esse numinis sit esse, et ab illo cunctis tribuatur es sustineatur. Quo fit ut ab illo nihil possit negligi. Quum enim omnia ex illo et in illo sint, iam nihil aut ex illo aut in illo esse poterit, quod ab illo aut ignoretur aut contemnatur ; vetant enim sapientia et bonitas. — *De prov. Dei, Op.*, iv. 139.

[2] *Op.*, iv. 129.

corded in Scripture. In one sense the Bible is the word of God, but in a higher sense the word of God is a personal force stirring within the soul, speaking with supreme authority, and constituting the standard by which the written letter of the book is to be criticised and judged.[1] Hence Zwingle, more than others among the reformers, recognized the traces of historic growth in the different parts of Scripture. Luther's principle, that the Bible is essentially the mirror of devout experience, misled him more than once into grave errors. Zwingle approaches the book with no anxiety about reconciling discrepancies. He expects to find there things which belong to a lower as well as a higher stage of spiritual development. But the word of God has spoken not only in the Bible, but always and everywhere, wherever there is any knowledge of that which is good and true. Heathen writers, like Plato and Pliny and Seneca, have uttered the truth under the inspiration of the revealing word.

The law of God as revealed in Scripture or elsewhere is not a series of arbitrary, external statutes, but reveals the inmost divine nature, and the basis, therefore, of human morality lies in the inward sentiments which determine action. The widest divergence in Zwingle's views from the traditional opinions still retained in the reformed church is seen in his view of sin. He denied the doctrine of original sin as set forth by Augustine, maintaining a position similar to that of the Greek Fathers, Chrysostom and Theodore of Mopsuestia, that misery but not guilt attaches to man in consequence of the fall. Zwingle also makes an effort to define more precisely the nature of sin, seeing in it a principle of disharmony which a divine in-

[1] *De vera et falsa religione, Op.*, iii. 130, 288 ; also *Op.*, iv. 85, 95.

dwelling presence is working to overcome, rather than a successful revolt against the divine purpose. Sin is even necessary as part of an educating process by which man comes to know and follow the right, just as justice could not be appreciated without the experience of injustice, or good be fully measured without a sense of evil.[1] Hence sin is best described as a state of death in which man is unconscious of God and lives only to himself. The law of God does not excite to sin, but it reveals sin and shows how great is the barrier it has raised between the soul and God. Christ comes to remove this barrier, which prevents God and the soul from flowing together like two streams in a common life. Zwingle's thought with reference to this aspect of the Saviour's work does not differ substantially from that of Luther. Christ delivers man from the sense of condemnation by revealing not only the divine justice and horror of sin, but also the divine mercy and love. If Zwingle does not seem to lay stress upon justification by faith, it is not because he underrates its importance; it is everywhere assumed as true without need of discussion; that which Zwingle dwells upon is the divine character to be built up in those who have made the beginning in the Christian life. Faith, hope, and love are three qualities not to be separated in Christian experience — the three constituents of the divine life in man, which from first to last is inspired and perfected by the indwelling infinite Spirit.

Zwingle seems to have shocked the religious sentiments of the German reformers not only by his clear denial of the Latin view of original sin, but by his conception of the salvability of the heathen, and his

[1] *Op.*, iv. 109.

doctrine of the sacraments. In regard to the former he expressed himself in a memorable passage in the confession of his faith, sent shortly before his death to the French king. "In the company of the redeemed," he said, "you will then see Hercules, Theseus, Socrates, Aristides, Antigonus, Numa, Camillus, the Catos, and the Scipios. In a word, not one good man, one holy spirit, one faithful soul, whom you will not then behold with God."[1] The Latin idea, that there was no salvation outside of the church, lingered on with the reformers long after they had rejected the view that the church was identical with any one organization. At a later time Bossuet selected this passage for severe animadversion in his "Variations of Protestantism," oblivious of the fact that Justin Martyr, an approved saint of the early church, and so recognized in the Latin calendar, had expressed himself in similar terms.

The controversy with Luther about the sacrament of the Lord's Supper was one of the painful incidents in the Reformation, if for no other reason, because Luther appears in the affair so far below his true self. It was a case where the disputants failed to understand each other, because neither fully understood himself. Zwingle made the sacrament a memorial of the death of Christ, and found in it as such a spiritual efficacy; to Luther's mind this seemed to empty the sacrament of its significance; he preferred to regard it as charged with a divine presence, as containing the actual body and blood of Christ. But Zwingle had no necessity for confining to the eucharist a beneficent presence with which the world was full, whose secret shrine was in every faithful heart. If Zwingle seemed to rob the sacrament of a real presence of Christ,

[1] *Fidei Christianæ Expositio, Op.,* iv. 65.

Luther seemed to rob the world itself of such a presence, just as the Latin church had done when she lost the idea of the immanence of Christ in humanity, and made the sacraments channels for the conveyance of grace from His remote abode. The controversy illustrates the inevitable confusion of thought in the age of the Reformation, but it also shows how Zwingle had revolutionized theology from its basis, while Luther remained divided in his allegiance between two systems, one of which claimed the devotion of his life, while the other held him bound by the sacred associations of religious sentiment. So long as Luther did not formally recognize the immanence of the essential Christ as the redeeming force in human life, there was a want in his thought, which his doctrine of the eucharist was an attempt to supply. It was creditable to Zwingle that he still wished to maintain Christian fellowship with Luther, despite their difference of opinion. It was characteristic of Luther, that although the hour was full of danger, he would make no compromise of his convictions for the sake of advantage. The words of Luther to Zwingle when the discussion was over, "You have a different spirit than we," — *Ihr habt einen andern Geist denn wir*, — were true in a deeper sense than either of the antagonists were aware.[1]

It would seem as if the great ecclesiastical reaction,

[1] Wilson, *Bampton Lectures*, 1851, on the *Communion of Saints*, points out the bearings of Zwingle's theology on the deeper problems of the Christian life and its relation to Christian psychology; Spörri, *Zwingli-Studien*, traces his theological views to one common principle, — that the material symbol is inadequate to the expression of spiritual ideas and relationships. Dorner, *Hist. of Prot. Theol.*, compares Zwingle with Luther and Calvin, and expounds these three distinct types of theology to which the Reformation gave birth.

led by the followers of Loyola, might have been rendered powerless to injure the work of the Reformation could the views of Zwingle have been generally received. But he was so far in advance of his age that his teaching produced no immediate influence. It remains only as a monument to the workings of the Christian mind at a rare moment when it shone forth in all the richness of its native endowment, in a creative epoch when its powers were stimulated and exalted as if by special communion with its divine source in God, when for a time there was no restraint upon its action in thought or utterance. Zwingle was not merely misunderstood; he was hardly understood at all, or, so far as his meaning was comprehended, it was regarded with distrust, if not with derision. Under happier circumstances than those which followed the Reformation, his death upon the battle-field of Cappel might have seemed a bright example of martyrdom for the truth; as it was, it appeared rather as a gloomy warning, — a penalty for mixing up his religious profession with the political affairs of the state. Zwingle made little or no distinction between the church and the state; his ideal was the commonwealth in which the Christian was sunk in the citizen, after the model of that higher state of which it is written that *our citizenship is in heaven.* He lived long enough to see that his dream was not soon to be realized. In his last years, he fell back for support and comfort upon that higher view of the Christian revelation which regards it as finding its natural expression in the human reason; he consoled himself with the vision of the divine reason, the word of God, which speaks always and everywhere to human souls, — the only pledge for the fulfillment of the Christian anticipation, — that the kingdoms of this world shall become the kingdom of our Lord and of His Christ.

IV.

In considering the influence of Calvin upon theology, it is important to remember that he was French as to his nationality. The character of his mind is not that of the Germanic races, whether in Germany or England. He had the tendency of his nation to adhere relentlessly to abstract principles; he made no allowance for the utterance of the consciousness in man, sacrificing without a struggle that large part of our nature, where spirit and sentiment appear in a living combination. It is certainly interesting to note how the French influence, which was destined to dominate the literature, the art, and the morals of both Germany and England during the seventeenth century and on into the eighteenth before it was thrown off, should have been anticipated in theology by Calvin in the sixteenth century, and that French theology should have maintained an ascendency in Protestant Christendom for two centuries before Germany shook herself free from foreign control.

Calvin was born in 1509, the interval of a generation elapsing between the commencement of his work and that of Luther and Zwingle. When he appeared as a reformer, the first glow of enthusiasm and zeal which characterized the earlier generation had begun to die away, and in its place had come timidity and distrust, a tendency to compromise truth in the interest of quiet and order. There was no longer the disposition to seek for truth at all hazards, or to put faith in that which was true as that which must conduce to

EVILS ATTENDING THE REFORMATION. 295

the highest well-being of society. Melancthon, who best represents this mood of the Reformation, was a timid, or, as Luther said, a pusillanimous spirit, capable of seeing two sides of a question, or enough to weaken his allegiance to truth, but not capable of seeing all around and through it. With him it was not so much what was true as what would be useful in maintaining social and ecclesiastical order. His compliance was so great that there seemed no limit to the concessions he was inclined to make to this end. Even the doctrine of justification by faith he thought might be modified so as to include works, in order to avoid the abuses to which it was exposed; it was better to allow man a little freedom than to make him altogether dependent upon God's action; there might be no harm in restoring the old cultus, with its rich and tender associations.[1] Luther stood firm to the truth as it had been revealed to him. But his last days were full of sadness; he seemed to lose hope for the world, and at times longed to be delivered from the impending evil. The fearful strain which he had undergone in leading the revolt from the papacy may have been too much for his constitution. The situation was indeed a trying one. As in the case of Moses when he led the Israelites out of Egypt, the crossing of the sea was a light task, because of the spiritual exhilaration attendant upon the consciousness of a Divine presence; but the real trial came afterwards when the people had no fixed home, no laws with the sacred associa-

---

[1] Although Melancthon fills a considerable place in the theology of the sixteenth and seventeenth centuries, he has no special interest or importance for the larger process of theological development, and is therefore omitted in this account of theology in the age of the Reformation.

tions of ages, when the customs which bind a people together had not yet grown up.

It had been one of the inevitable effects of the Reformation that it caused a profound unsettlement of the human mind, even in those by whose faith it had been accomplished. Speculation about the foundations of religion or morality or human government is always attended with danger; the great mass of men take these things for granted, and any event which leads them to think that the institutions of life are not as divinely fixed as the everlasting hills, is sure to precipitate in its train the wildest disorder. The Protestant Reformation had served, as it were, to discover "the foundations of the round world." As men glanced at the process by which the order of things had grown up and been maintained, it seemed as though anything might be changed, as though the hour had come for the reconstruction of society as well as the church. Communism and polygamy were preached as the basis of a new civilization; so-called prophets traveled about proclaiming themselves in possession of new revelations, throwing discredit upon adherence to the Bible as a vile servility to the letter. Under such circumstances, the claims of order became more pressing than inquiry after truth. No one ever misread his age more than Servetus when he took for granted that the reformers were engaged in a process of free theological investigation, and would welcome the aid of any who could throw a new light upon the interpretations of old doctrines. Calvin stood for order and discipline as the primary requisites of his time. He became the founder of a church whose value as an ally in promoting these ends was recognized far and wide, — an organization which rivaled the church of Rome in its discipline as well as in its power of adaptation to different nationalities. Its cosmopolitan character, in comparison with the organization of the church in England or in Germany, is seen in the fact that it became the ecclesiastical polity of Scotland and the Netherlands, of the Puritans in England, the Huguenots in France, of a large part of Germany, as well as Switzerland where it originated.

Calvin held that the church consisted of the elect, and like all the reformers asserted the invisible aspect of a body which could only be known to God. But he was far more interested in the visible church than in the invisible, and devoted a large part of his "Institutes" to delineating its constitution and its discipline. That feature of discipline, as it is called, which the Church of England did not retain, which the Lutheran church also dropped, assumed in the church organized by Calvin a prominence as marked as it had possessed in the old ecclesiastical order. But it was retained at the expense of sacrificing the idea which Luther and Zwingle and others had maintained — that the clergy were the representatives of the congregation and gained the sanction of their office from the approval and choice of the body. Neither Luther nor Zwingle had attached importance to ordination as conveying any gift from a source away and apart from the people. But in Calvin's system, as in the mediæval, the clergy are the delegates of a remote sovereign, separate from the people, endowed by the Holy Spirit with the gifts and the powers of their high office. In other words, Calvin retained substantially the Latin idea of the church with some necessary modifications, intending that the reformed clergy should take the place of the Latin hierarchy, with supreme authority over the congregation. The duty of the state, in its relation to the church, as in the Middle Ages, was to sustain the action of the clergy by the sword.

Calvin's system of church organization and discipline may be studied apart from his peculiar theology. In the seventeenth century in England, under the régime of Cromwell, the Independents or Congregationalists discarded the former for a more democratic constitution, while still retaining his system of doctrine. His labors as an ecclesiastical administrator were not so enduring as his work as a theologian. In this direction he so impressed himself upon Protestant Christendom that his influence still lives, even in ecclesiastical circles which believe themselves emancipated from any traces of his spirit.

Calvin's theology is drawn, or professes to be drawn, exclusively from Scripture. The Bible, as he defined and understood it, is the corner-stone of his system. He had no respect for Luther's view of Scripture as the mirror of the religious experience of humanity, nor for Zwingle's view of a "word of God" in the soul by which man judges the value of the written word. He denied the position of the Latin church, that the Bible was given and attested by the authority of the hierarchy, or the continuous existence of the episcopate. According to Calvin, God reveals Himself to man through the book by the power of the Holy Spirit. Man was incapable of knowing himself or knowing God, except by this revelation. Revelation, as given in the book, is a communication from God to man, supernaturally imparted, apart from the action of the consciousness or reason; Calvin speaks at times of the human writer as an amanuensis only of the Spirit. He does not, therefore, presume to criticise the canon or its formation; the Bible is received as one whole, as it has come down through the ages. There is no other revelation except that which God made to the Jewish people through the Old Testament, and to the Christian world through the New. God may have given light enough to the heathen to secure their condemnation, but that is all.[1] The revelation which God makes of Himself in the Bible may not disclose to us the inmost character of Deity; there is in reason no ground for believing that it does so; God only reveals what He designs that man should know and practice. The God who is thus revealed is a being outside of the frame-work of the universe, who called the world into existence by the power of His will. Calvin positively rejected the doctrine of the divine immanence. When he spoke of that "dog of a Lucretius" who mingles God and nature, he may have also had Zwingle in his mind. In order to separate more completely between God and man, he interposed ranks of mediators, the ministers of the divine will in nature, or in the process of redemption, — angels as ministers of the good, and demons as instruments of evil. Satan is the supreme agent in the hand of God for accomplishing evil; it is he that secures the punishment of the reprobate and disciplines the elect. According to the prologue of the Book of Job which Calvin read as veritable history, Satan has a knowledge of the mind of God, and though an evil spirit, he never thwarts, but always fulfills, the divine purpose. Why there should be evil in the world it is as presumptuous to inquire as why there should be a world at all, but there is no evil which does not redound to the glory of God. The fate

[1] *Institutes*, ii. c. 2.

of Adam was not an unforeseen catastrophe; it had been decreed by God before the creation. He also decreed that Adam's sin and guilt should be imputed to his entire posterity. All men were born under the divine condemnation, not merely because they had inherited the effects of Adam's transgression, but because God willed that Adam's guilt should be also theirs. He elects a few of the human race to salvation, and the vast majority He leaves to the condemnation which by their sins they deserve.[1] He does not make them sin in order to merit the condemnation which He has decreed, but He simply withholds His grace so that they cannot but sin. Those who are elect are not so in virtue of any goodness of disposition which God foresees, but simply by the act of His sovereign, arbitrary will. Upon the elect He confers greater benefits than upon Adam before his fall, for He endows them with the gift of perseverance which insures the fulfillment of their destiny; even their transgressions and failures minister to their humility, and thus secure the perfecting of their character.

With reference to the doctrines of the trinity, the incarnation, and the two natures in Christ, Calvin does not differ from the statements of Latin or mediæval

[1] Calvin admits that all this may seem horrible, but it is just, because it is God that has decreed it. *Institutes*, iii. c. 23 (7). It is a common mistake to represent Calvin as attributing the decree of reprobation to the divine anger. Calvin does not think that God is ever angry; he speaks like a modern rationalist of the *accommodation* of Scripture, in this respect, to our weakness: "Though God declares that He is angry with the wicked, we ought not to imagine that there is any emotion in Him, but ought rather to consider this mode of speech *accommodated to our sense*, God appearing to us like one inflamed and irritated whenever He exercises judgment." — *Institutes*, i. c. 22.

theologians, except in relying on the authority of Scripture for their confirmation in place of tradition or the authority of the church. He was unacquainted with the history of their dogmatic development in the ancient church, nor had he attempted its study would he have found it a congenial one. He accepts, like the other reformers, the mediæval idea of an atonement, as Anselm had given it expression; he sees in the offering of Christ a provision for escape from the consequences of sin, but he modifies the view of Anselm in one important respect, — he looks upon the sufferings and death of Christ as a veritable punishment in which the Saviour bore vicariously the wrath and condemnation of God. To this end he is inclined to magnify the intensity and horror of Christ's anguish upon the cross, and His descent into hell was viewed as necessary for the completeness of his vicarious punishment. The doctrine of the atonement became in the following period a subject of discussion and controversy as it had not been in the age of the Reformation, and it then received a more exact statement; but in all its later modifications the doctrine still bore the stamp of Calvin's mind rather than of Anselm's, and as such has come down to our own day.[1]

[1] *Instit.*, ii. c. 15. Upon this view of the atonement it has been correctly remarked: "For three centuries it has been the popular view in England, though not without protest. Grotius's early work against Socinus (*de Satisfactione Christi*) helped to fix it in our theology, even Hammond, Outram, and Bishop Pearson embracing it ; and so largely has it been adopted, that it has come to be viewed as the orthodox view of the English church, although it has no place in our prayer-book, and although even those who adopt it (as Dr. Shedd, in his *History of Doctrine*) are fain to acknowledge that it has never received the stamp of Catholic truth." — Norris, *Rudiments of Theology*, p. 267.

The vista of future ages in the world to come, as Calvin saw and described it, is clear and definite. The earthly life of Christ he regarded as the period of His humiliation, when His divine glory was concealed behind a veil. When He rose from the dead He departed to distant realms to sit down at the right hand of God. His mediatorial kingdom then commenced, and will continue until the elect are gathered in. For these He died and rose again; His merits are imputed to them by divine decree; they are sheltered by His intercessions at the throne of God; they partake of His life, and are progressively sanctified till they are called away into His presence. He is to come again to judge the world, and then will be made manifest the divine glory; His mediatorial kingdom will then come to an end; He will return back again into the bosom of the Father, as He existed before the foundation of the world; the period of humiliation will be over, and the veil which now covers the face of His glory will be done away.

In some respects the system of Calvin not merely repeats but exaggerates the leading ideas of Latin Christianity. In no Latin writer is found such a determined purpose to reject the immanence of Deity and assert His transcendence and His isolation from the world. In his conception of God, as absolute arbitrary will, he surpasses Duns Scotus; he rivals Mohammedanism by a doctrine of decrees that subdues the creature into fatalistic submission to necessity. The separation between God and humanity is emphasized as it has never been before, for Calvin insists, dogmatically and formally, upon that which had been, to a large extent, hitherto, an unconscious though controlling sentiment. And yet there were features also about this theology which show some advance over Latin Christianity, — it contained elements which prepared the way for future developments. Although Calvin aimed by his doctrine of the church to restore the ascendency of the clergy over the conscience of the people, yet the action of this principle was modified by the force of his doctrine of an individual election, which obliged men to contemplate themselves as forever standing face to face with the sovereign majesty of God. The effect of this conviction was necessarily to destroy every tyranny, whether in church or state; to break down all human mediators which professed to control human destiny, and thus to minister in reality to human freedom. The importance which Calvin attached to the sanctification of the elect made the cultivation of righteousness and the obedience of the moral law stand forth more clearly as the end of all true living. He has also the merit of drawing attention to the life of Christ, and not solely His birth, His death and resurrection, and of bringing into greater prominence the perfect righteousness which made an element in His offering to God. In his treatment of the life of Christ he was the pioneer of modern efforts to reconstruct, in more complete and scientific form, the contents of the gospel narratives. He was the first theologian, since the days of Greek theology, to bring out the spirit that was in Christ. While he admits the miraculous birth of the son of Mary, yet it was not to the virgin mother that Christ owed anything of the purity or sanctity of His nature, but to this, that God directly endowed Him with all the fullness of spiritual wealth.[1] Hence he struck intelligently at that lower conception of the incarnation so prominent

---

[1] *Institutes*, ii. cc. 13, 14.

in the Latin church, whose tendency was to deify the mother of Christ as the source whence the Saviour drew His human purity or excellence. His sharp distinction between the elect and the non-elect contributed to destroy that almost Egyptian cultus of the dead, which in the later Middle Ages had absorbed so much of the prayers, the wealth, the energies of the living. The assertion of the absolute supremacy of the divine will destroyed all lingering fondness for images of every kind; it concentrated the worship of man exclusively upon God.

Such was the system which carried with it the immediate future in the history of Protestantism. It professed in every part and smallest detail to reflect faithfully the teaching of Scripture; in reality it only rested for its confirmation upon a misreading of St. Paul's Epistle to the Romans, and was then applied to all Scripture as a measuring-rod. But when such a system had once taken possession of the mind it was not difficult to read the Bible in the light of it, and indeed it was impossible not to do so, especially when ingenious treatment of special passages was capable of bringing them into harmony with the preconceived assumptions of the reader. And the system of Calvin had, strange as it may now seem, a wondrous fascination for the generations that followed him. It was voluntarily adopted to a large extent, even in the Lutheran and Anglican churches. It was, so to speak, the spirit in the air. It had a genuine mission to accomplish for humanity, and not until its mission was over would its real weakness be apparent. Then it would be seen that it rested upon assumptions which Calvin had been unwilling to analyze, and that at its basis lurked the spirit of what is called modern skepticism.

CONFLICT OF THE TRADITIONAL THEOLOGY WITH REASON.

Hoc primum intelligentes quod omnis prophetia Scripturæ propria interpretatione non fit.
Non enim voluntate humana allata est aliquando prophetia; sed Spiritu sancto inspirati locuti sunt sancti Dei homines. — 2 PET. i. 20, 21.

CHRONOLOGICAL TABLE.

A. D.
- **1436.** Raymund of Sabunde taught at Toulouse.
- **1553-1600.** Richard Hooker.
- **1555-1621.** Arndt, a German Mystic.
- **1558-1603.** Reign of Queen Elizabeth.
- **1559.** Beginning of Puritan dissent.
- **1571.** Robert Browne, the first Independent.
- **1576-1624.** Jacob Böhme
- **1593-1632.** George Herbert.
- **1599-1658.** Oliver Cromwell.
- **1604-1610.** Bancroft, Archbishop of Canterbury.
- **1608-1675.** John Milton.
- **1617-1688.** Cudworth, the philosopher.
- **1618-1648.** Thirty Years' War.
- **1620.** Landing of the Pilgrim Fathers.
- **1623-1662.** Blaise Pascal.
- **1627-1696.** Michael Molinos.
- **1628-1688.** John Bunyan.
- **1630-1694.** Archbishop Tillotson.
- **1632-1704.** Locke, the philosopher.
- **1633.** First Congregation of Baptists.
- **1635-1705.** Spener, Father of German Pietism.
- **1642-1717.** Madam Guion.
- **1642-1727.** Sir Isaac Newton.
- **1646.** George Fox begins to preach.
- **1649-1660.** Age of the Commonwealth.
- **1660.** Restoration of Charles II.
- **1688.** The English Revolution.
- **1689.** Act of Toleration passed.
- **1692-1752.** Bishop Butler.
- **1694-1778.** Voltaire.
- **1703-1791.** John Wesley.
- **1711-1776.** Hume, the philosopher.
- **1729-1781.** Lessing.
- **1745.** Swedenborg in his religious career.

CONFLICT OF THE TRADITIONAL THEOLOGY WITH REASON.

There were elements of hope and of progress in the attitude of the reformers of the sixteenth century which were not fulfilled in the age that followed. In the prevailing theology of the seventeenth century there was no divergence in principle from the scholastic theology of the Middle Ages. Indeed, it seems as though the aim of the leaders of thought was to return as near to the spirit of Latin Christianity as was possible without actually passing the line that divided the hostile communions.

The thought about God which always underlies and controls all other thought, remained unchanged. Deity continued to human vision as a sovereign will enthroned at an immeasurable distance from man. God and man were regarded as alien to each other, in their inmost being; the characteristic of fallen humanity was not only incapacity for the divine, but even an active hatred and enmity for God. The incarnation resolved itself into a scheme or plan of salvation, by which the schism in the divine nature between justice and love might be overcome, and God be free to pardon man and to receive the chosen few into His favor. The nature of this scheme was revealed in the Bible. Man had no inward power in the reason to appreciate its fitness; the glory of revelation lay in its confounding the mind and humiliating it in abject submission to that which had been arbitrarily revealed. Revelation was a matter of the past; God had once spoken finally and for all in the book — the oracle that had been miraculously communicated and preserved. The Bible took as it were the place of the living Christ; its very letter was deified; in it alone was thought to lie the power of imparting life and salvation. The kingdom of God that was to be was viewed as rising in another world than this. Here all was darkness and misery, saving the revelation that God vouchsafed to make to those whom in His inscrutable purpose it might be His will to save. The outer world still lay under the curse of the divine displeasure, serving to conceal rather than make known its divine Creator; it had been called into existence out of nothing and was destined to relapse again into its original nothingness. Despite Luther's teaching of justification by faith and the inward assurance that it implied, or Calvin's doctrine of predestination, which was also an effort to overcome the uncertainty about salvation, the *conjectura moralis* of the Middle Ages came back again in more distressing form. It took the shape of the doctrine of probation, according to which each individual man, in his loneliness and isolation, is awaiting the final day of judgment, when the outcome of his career shall be disclosed. On the issue of this probation it depended whether man should be ultimately admitted in the distant future to the presence of God, or be forever banished from the society of the redeemed. The motives to obedience were found in external sanctions — the endless bliss which awaited the saved, the endless woe which awaited the lost. Salvation was not construed ethically but physically, as an escape from the horrors attending the divine condemnation. Be cause salvation was not primarily an ethical process, it followed that other considerations than righteousness and conduct modified the issue of human probation. To think rightly became of the highest importance; orthodoxy in belief was capable of covering a multitude of sins; to give one's assent to the scheme of salvation was the first step toward acceptance with God. It will always remain one of the curiosities of theological literature, that Lutheran divines should not only have maintained that right belief might exist in those who are wholly unregenerate, but that carelessness of life did not necessarily diminish the preacher's power to convey to others the salvation of God.

Such were the leading features of the formal theology of the seventeenth century. Its development was attended by bitter controversies and angry recriminations, which hurt the spiritual life of the newly organized churches. When orthodoxy of opinion assumed such indispensable importance, it was inevitable that any deviation from the traditional system of Scripture interpretation should be opposed with a corresponding hatred. And yet the system had a side which commended it to many of the noblest men of the age. It did assert in an age of great political confusion and low moral ideals the absolute supremacy of God, the fact that He did rule this world, however mysterious and incomprehensible might be His will. For those who could believe themselves within the charmed circle where operated the divine grace there was comfort and peace. Like the Mohammedan mosque which outwardly bristles with a threatening aspect, there was within a beautiful inclosure which was like the garden of God. As a system of theology, it possessed a charm for the imagination, as may be seen in the great epic poem of "Paradise Lost." Milton did for the theology of his age what Dante had done for the theology of Thomas Aquinas. He translated it into poetry, he remoulded it into a beautiful theosophy, which long held men in thralldom to that against which their hearts revolted. More than the Bible itself, more than all the theologians combined, has Milton's imagination identified the thought of the seventeenth century with divine revelation; it created a picture which the world having once seen could never forget.

In the immortal work of Bunyan, "The Pilgrim's Progress," the same theology was reproduced in attractive guise for the needs of the humblest Christian. Despite the fact that Christ is only to be reached when the pilgrim's journey is over — when the dark river which separates man from God has been safely crossed; or that only angelic or other intermediaries aid the traveler on his way; or that there is no recognition of the dearest and closest relationships of life compared with the celestial selfishness that inspires the desire for salvation; despite the fact that the Christian life is not regarded as preëminently one of charities and of doing good to others in the name of Christ, the work of Bunyan will always be regarded with pride and tenderness not only as one of the masterpieces of Christian literature, but as a rare and beautiful picture of Christian experience whose fidelity to human nature will prevent it from ever becoming antiquated.

The theology of the seventeenth century on its practical side is exemplified, better, perhaps, than anywhere else, in the career of Oliver Cromwell. In him may be seen its genuine fruits, — the hardness and severity, even the cruelty which he systematically manifested for the accomplishment of his ends, the narrow range of the intellect, the confusion of his own ambition with the divine will, and yet withal the inspired hero, who wrought in the consciousness of a God-appointed mission, who humiliated himself only before God and never before man, and to whom the English people are largely indebted for that liberty which has made them foremost among the peoples of the world. The same religious characteristics that are found in Cromwell, and the leaders of the civil war, are seen also in those who led resistance in the Netherlands against the tyranny of Spain, and above all in the Pilgrim fathers who consecrated to God the new world in the West. These were the practical results which attested the power of a living belief in God, — that He was calling men to the execution of His will, to the making of that will dominant in human society.

So long as external events called out the heroic side of human nature, so long as the reformed churches were engaged in a struggle to maintain their existence against the machinations of Rome, the Calvinistic theology preserved an inward life, notwithstanding its grave defects. The human heart to some extent unconsciously supplemented its deficiencies, while the wants, the necessities which it failed to recognize, were such as required another age with other conditions of life in order to their full appreciation. Then the system would appear in its emptiness and hollow formality, and men would realize that, if they were to retain their belief in God, they must find some deeper, more organic relationship, as the basis of the divine communion with humanity.

Even in the age when it was at its best, one can read the painful skepticism which it engendered in the writings of Pascal. As a Jansenist, devoted to the spirit and letter of the Augustinian theology in opposition to the Jesuits, he may also be taken as the most illustrious representative of Calvinism on its intellectual side. The "Thoughts" of Pascal reveal the tortures of a soul, which, in its search for God, can find no ground which satisfies the reason, and falls back in a spirit akin to despair upon a supposed revelation which defies the reason. To such a mind, the principle of Tertullian affords the only rationale of belief, — to accept the impossible because it is impossible; to find the evidence of truth in its absurdity. The attitude of Pascal is a thorough-going agnosticism [1] which sees no evidence of the being or goodness of God in the nature of things, or the constitution of the soul; his faith rests upon a precarious foundation which the intellect refuses to examine. How could a man have any well-founded confidence in the reality of a divine life in the soul who could write: "All nature,

[1] "Il serait difficile aujourd'hui, après la démonstration victorieuse de M. Cousin, de nier que dans Pascal se rencontrent à chaque page des traits qui trahissent un absolu scepticisme. Il attaque la philosophie dans ses sources psychologiques en niant la légitimité de tous nos moyens de connaître ; il ébranle la morale et la religion naturelle en niant la justice et en n'admettant que la force ; il ébranle la théologie elle-même en justifiant l'athéisme comme une marque de force d'esprit, en substituant aux démonstrations philosophiques de l'existence de Dieu la fameuse preuve tirée du calcul des probabilités qu'il venait d'inventer, jouant Dieu à croix ou pile. Il n'est pas moins sceptique sur les affections que sur les idées, et il a écrit cette phrase odieuse, que Hobbes ne désavouerait pas ; 'Les hommes se haissent naturellement les uns les autres."'— Janet, *Les Maitres de la Pensée Moderne*, p. 249.

both within and without us most manifestly declares a God withdrawn from us;" or again: "The appearance of things indicates neither the total abandonment, nor the manifest presence, of the Divinity, but the presence of a God that hideth Himself."[1] "The strange secrecy impenetrable to the view of man, into which God has retired, is an impressive lesson to teach us to withdraw into solitude far from human observation. He remained concealed under the veil of nature which hides Him from us until the incarnation, and when it was necessary that He should appear, He was more fully concealed under the garb of humanity."[2] How could one long continue to believe in a divine revelation who could assert that out of all the world God revealed Himself only to the Jews, and that all other religions, except the Christian, are notoriously false.[3] The interest attaching to Pascal lies in the fact that he endeavored to square his religious experience with a formal theology which he accepted as revealed truth. Other men, not organized like him, might hold their theology somewhat loosely, living by convictions which were larger than their thought. Pascal was bent on subduing his nature, his heart, and conscience within

---

[1] *Pensées*, ed. par Louandre, c. xxi. 2.

[2] *Lettres à Mademoiselle de Roannez; Pensées*, ed. Louandre, p. 427.

[3] *Pensées*, p. 266. Also the following passages: "L'homme n'est donc que déguisement, que mensonge et hypocrisie, et en soi-même et à l'égard des autres." p. 141. "Dieu étant ainsi caché toute religion qui ne dit pas que Dieu est caché n'est pas véritable; et toute religion qui n'en rend pas la raison, n'est pas instruisante. La nôtre fait tout cela: *Vere tu es Deus absconditus.*" (A favorite text with Pascal.) p. 240. "L'abandon de Dieu paraît dans les Païens; la protection de Dieu paraît dans les Juifs." p. 321.

the hard and narrow limits of a revived Augustinianism.[1] A distant Deity, an absent Saviour; humanity utterly depraved and worthless, life full of vanity and misery; a dim revelation of a hidden God arbitrarily communicated from without, and full of difficulty, to which no inward voice of the soul responds in divine confirmation, — a revelation to be received, if at all, on the authority of the book; the heavy burden of an individual probation or responsibility before God, not lightened by the sense of solidarity or of the fellowship within the church, as the old mediæval theology presented it, — such are the thoughts of Pascal, full of the deepest sadness, of an unutterable melancholy.

[1] There is a suggestive contrast between the religious experience of Pascal and of George Herbert. The latter shared in the new life which was stirring in the Church of England, when it broke away in the early part of the seventeenth century from the Calvinistic theology. Herbert, while still retaining the dogmas of a Latinized Christianity, could rise as a poet above the trammels of his theology; he had escaped, also, from the depressing influence of an individual solitary probation, into the joyous sense of a Christian fellowship which was under the dominion of a law of love. Traces of the struggle against the limitations of his churchmanship are apparent in his writings. But the beautiful lines entitled the "Elixir" show how at times the spirit triumphed, and how grand and complete the triumph was. They reflect an experience to which Pascal seems to have been a stranger. They imply a redeemed world where man through his kinship with Deity possesses, as it were, a magic spell by which the commonest things may be transmuted into divine. All that was highest in the theology of Luther and Zwingle was working as a leaven in the heart of Herbert beneath the external aspect of a representative priest of the Anglican school.

But one can never dwell upon the deficiency in Pascal's theology or religious life without deep reluctance, after knowing of the physical tortures which he must have suffered from malformation of the brain. For the details upon the results of an autopsy made upon his body, cf. Louandre, p. 74.

I.

In Pascal may be seen a typical illustration, however exaggerated, of the religious experience generated by a conscientious adherence to the Augustinian or Calvinistic theology. It is not surprising to discover by its side the assertion of a larger, freer life, the unconscious life of the larger world moving apart from the church, with elements of health and truth, with a sense of joy and triumph which cannot be seen within the ecclesiastical confines. A Spenser, a Raleigh, a Shakespeare, are the best representations in some respects of the fullness and wealth of that promise which the Reformation in its maturity did not seem to have reaped. Lord Bacon was at the same time withdrawing from the sphere of ecclesiastical prerogative the rising science of nature which was to absorb the intellect and energy of coming generations. It still remains doubtful whether he spoke in earnest faith when he put revelation and the church on the one side, and the natural sciences on the other, as two distinct departments of life which had no connection with each other. In the one, reason was to be discarded; in the other, it was made the only guide. The spirit of enterprise and healthy activity which had been stimulated by the discoveries of navigation, especially the opening of the new world in the west, does not seem to have affected the ecclesiastical atmosphere. The absence of the missionary spirit in the Protestant communities is a fact of deep significance. The church was experiencing the gloom which came from the realization that the bridegroom was absent. The sense of melancholy which arose when the disciples felt themselves bereaved by the death of the Master must remain the characteristic of the church's life until the higher truth should be experienced, that He had risen from the grave, and that His life has become the immanent spirit of life in a redeemed, regenerated world.

But the best intellect of the age had not broken with the church in the seventeenth century, nor had the line of real progress and historical continuity been even temporarily sundered. In some respects the Roman Catholic church, especially in France, appeared to greater advantage than Protestantism, as in a certain freedom and largeness of spiritual apprehension. The old organization was renewing its youth.[1] The many converts it received, repelled by the coldness and severity of the reformed faith, seemed to point to the failure of the revolt which owned Luther as its leader. The Jesuits were trading successfully in the weaknesses of human nature, and the ease with which they relaxed all moral considerations would have made them more dangerous than they were had not the heart of humanity been sound at the core. But Protestantism remained true, in theory at least, to that which God had actually accomplished by the hands of the great reformers. In rejecting monasticism it had asserted, more forcibly than it knew, that the world was redeemed and sacred, that life in the world as God made it was better and higher than in a cloistered world of man's construc-

[1] The seventeenth century was an age of missions for the Roman church. The relative inactivity of Protestantism was owing to causes beyond its control; among others to an inherent weakness in its theological attitude which was not overcome till the close of the eighteenth century. But the development of North America under Protestant auspices must be regarded as part of a spiritual history.

tion; in discarding the theory of sacramental grace it was preparing for the larger sacrament of life itself, with all its events and circumstances ordered for the education of man; in the importance attached to preaching lay a means of educing the divine elements in the constitution of the soul, whose fruits must appear when the training was complete; in the attention concentrated upon Scripture it was in reality bringing the consciousness of man into contact with the highest expression of the human consciousness as revealed in saints, prophets, and apostles, and especially in Him in whom the consciousness of a perfected humanity found its absolute and perfect utterance. The importance attached to individual salvation, as against the collective salvation through the medium of the church, although lacking important qualifications, and resting upon a false conception of God, was the one grand truth which was never obscured, in whose train must inevitably follow a higher reverence for the spirit in man, in all its manifestations, — in the reason, the moral nature, and the inward sphere of the affections.

But the formal Protestantism of the seventeenth century, as represented in its orthodox systems of theology, contained within itself the seeds of its ultimate dissolution. Hardly had it been established when the protests arose, and continued to increase in extent and duration, — the protests of humanity against being shut out from the presence of God. The mystics again appear, as they had done under somewhat similar circumstances in the age that followed the great system-makers of the thirteenth century. The Lutheran church gave birth to Arndt, who endeavored, in a popular treatise called "True Christianity," to show what the apostle means when he says, "I live, yet not I, but Christ liveth in me."[1] Jacob Böhme took for a motto these words; — "Our salvation is the life of Jesus Christ within us." Of the books which he had written, he said, "I have written not from human teaching or knowledge gained from books, but from my own book, which was opened within me." The Quietists in France, represented by Madam Guion and Fénelon, taught that God was to be served for Himself alone, and not for the sake of external rewards and punishments; that the end of religion was to find Christ living within the soul. The Quakers in England declared the existence of an "inner light" in every man whereby God was constantly revealing Himself, a divine light, by which is discerned the meaning and the truth of the outward revelation given in the book. Molinos, the Spaniard, attached little importance to outward ritual compared with the silent inward communion of the soul with God.[2] The

---

[1] Arndt's *True Christianity* is divided into four books : 1. The Book of Scripture, to show the way of the spiritual life, and that Adam ought to die and Christ to gain the ascendant in the heart more and more daily. 2. The Book of Life, directing the Christian to rejoice in sufferings, and to endure persecutions after Christ's example. 3. The Book of Conscience, wherein the Christian is taught to recognize the kingdom of God within his own heart. 4. The Book of Nature, that all creation leads men to the knowledge of their Creator.

[2] I have not thought it necessary to call attention to the defects and mischievous results attendant upon all these movements known as mystic, especially as they were not illustrated upon a large scale. Their historical interest lies in the common protest they all made against the fundamental principles of Augustinianism, whether in its Latin or its Protestant forms. That they were all guilty, more or less, of confusing their fancies with a divine light must be admitted. But this was just the trouble also with Augustine and with Calvin.

Pietists, in Germany, sought to restore Luther's conception of the Bible, as the mirror of religious experience, the object of whose study was to deepen the life of Christ in the soul rather than to extract isolated proof-texts to confirm a system of theology. These and similar utterances are not interesting merely as opinions; they illustrate the workings of the human consciousness in its relation to God; they bear an impressive testimony to the truth that a religion can never be imposed from without, or become authoritative, unless it be the expression of that spirit in man upon which God has stamped the impress of His own nature.

There were other lines of divine activity where humanity was struggling to realize its high calling in the face of obstacles which could only be overcome by a fierce and stubborn resistance. Hitherto the church had been indifferent to that liberty which is the rightful heritage not of a few, but of all men in virtue of their creation in the image of God. Hildebrand had talked of the liberty of the church, but he had meant only the emancipation of the clergy from secular control, in order to their more complete subjection to the authority of Rome. The hierarchy of the Middle Ages was a graded system by which the clergy represented the bishop, the bishops represented the pope, and the pope represented God. When Luther asserted the rights of the individual conscience against all external authority, he had given the principle which did away with all artificial castes, whether in church or state, — a principle by which, as it were, every man became a pope, standing in immediate relation to God, owning no other or higher allegiance than the will of God should sanction. But a long time must necessarily elapse between the declaration of a principle and its realization. The struggle in the seventeenth century for civil and religious freedom was wrapped up as in a germ in Luther's attitude, and ever since the course of history has witnessed one continuous effort to secure in increasing measure the liberty which is the rightful heritage of man.

Luther himself was well aware that such a liberty could only come to those who were prepared to receive it. At first he had been inclined to a more democratic constitution of the church than he afterwards approved. The church at Hesse, where the first rough draft of the changed ecclesiastical order was made, had been a purely democratic one, in which the people were to rule, and the popular voice was to administer discipline. But this organization did not commend itself to Luther's judgment when he became more impressed with the prevailing popular ignorance. He saw, also, that in the aristocratic organization of German society, the nobility and the princes would never submit to be controlled in religious matters by the voice of the people. Hence the final organization of the church in Germany followed the social order; princes became the superintendents or bishops over the clergy and people, forming, together with their body of advisers, a sort of ecclesiastical oligarchy. The constitution of the Lutheran church thus assumed a sort of hap-hazard, accidental character, dictated by the emergencies in which it arose. The organization, on the other hand, of the Reformed or Calvinistic churches was based upon what was believed to be a divine order revealed in Scripture. In the place of the ancient hierarchy, which was abolished, the ecclesiastical administration was intrusted to the body of the clergy, elders or presbyters, who ruled like the hierarchy, not in the name of the people, but in virtue of a power and commission with which they were intrusted by God. Such a scheme was identical in principle with that of the Latin church, differing from it only in appearance, or in so far as it was modified by circumstances which the church could not control.

The reformation in England was conducted on a method of its own, which differs widely in principle from either of those just mentioned. Its peculiarity lay in the fact that it was essentially a lay movement originating with the King and Parliament rather than with the clergy. Convocation led in no reform, nor had it any disposition to do so; the bishops and clergy accepted and ratified what Parliament dictated. It was the laity and not the clergy who led the Church of England in the great revolution of the sixteenth century by which the authority of the Bishop of Rome was declared no longer binding. With a king whose authority was practically absolute, and a submissive clergy who accepted his decree, whether voluntarily or not, there was no necessity and indeed no moral possibility of abolishing the old ecclesiastical order. The Church of England continued in possession of the church property, the bishops remained in their respective sees, and the outward aspect of the church was substantially unchanged by the revolution which had deposed its ancient sovereign the Bishop of Rome. In such a method of reform, there were great advantages; but it also involved great dangers. The Church of England, by retaining so much of the old ecclesiastical order and ritual, also retained and bore witness to the historical continuity of the church, as an external institution, through all the vicissitudes of time. In the reformed churches there was a tendency to undervalue this principle; they appeared rather as "new" churches, with a "new" order and a "new" faith, while the Church of England appeared as an orderly growth, with its roots in the historic consciousness of humanity. But there was danger, also, that the old spirit of mediæval religion would linger about its accustomed haunts, and when the opportunity offered reënter and take possession.

The theory of the church which underlay the English reformation — the tacitly accepted, working theory, whether avowed or not, was not the old Latin idea that the church lay in the hierarchy. In all the changes that took place, there was implied an organic relationship to the state; the king was regarded as directly and primarily the anointed of God; the church was simply the whole nation in its religious aspect, for whose well being the king was as directly responsible as for its civil order and prosperity. The worst that is usually said against such a theory is that it is Erastian, whatever that may mean. Cranmer regarded the bishops as holding their jurisdiction from the king, and on the accession of Edward VI. took out a new commission of authority. This theory prevailed through the long reign of Elizabeth before it yielded to another conception of the church and a different view of the relations of church and state. But the older view, Erastianism, if it must be so known, has given to the Church of England its peculiar charm and its most distinctive merit.

The Church of England produced no great theologian and followed no one special type of theology. It represented in the age of the Reformation the large *communis sensus* of the people, so far as they were educated to speak for themselves. The influence of Luther and of Calvin is apparent in the articles of religion, but it nowhere appears as bondage to the *ipse dixit* of a man. Justification by faith only is clearly set forth with no evasive qualification. The doctrine of predestination is admitted, but a caution is given against its abuse. The highest reverence is expressed for Scripture; yet there is no worship of the letter; it was enough to declare that "it contains all things necessary to salvation." Tradition is rejected as an absolute authority, when it is affirmed that the creeds are to be received because they have the warrant of Holy Scripture, not because they are given on the authority of the church. And yet tradition is regarded as having a value which forbids it from being entirely thrown aside, in that the old ritual is not discarded but modified, or when it is asserted that the government of the church is in accordance with ancient custom. The definition of the church has the true Protestant ring, when it is affirmed to be the "congregation of faithful men," and not the mysterious impersonation of Latin Christianity. The large practical wisdom of the reformers is seen in the absolute rejection of that which the reason has demonstrated false, such as image-worship, purgatory, and transubstantiation, and a cautious tone prevails where there is room for difference of opinion. In one respect, and that the most significant of all, the Church of England assumed a position which no other communion had dared or been willing to take. It not only does not assert its own infallibility, but it declares that other churches have erred in matters pertaining to the faith — a position from which the only inference is that it does not claim for itself the infallibility which it has denied to them. The clergy are called upon to be faithful to their conscience, and to teach nothing as requisite for salvation in which their private judgment of Scripture does not concur; nor is any provision made for the exigency of their conscience leading them in opposition to what may be at any time the prevailing interpretation of the church's standards. The predominant tendency in its standards is to throw the clergy back upon their conscience as enlightened by the word of God.

Such an attitude may appear to the dogmatist or to the skeptic as essentially weak and unworthy; but to the eye of faith, which acknowledges an infinite Spirit of truth, pledged to lead humanity into an ever-increasing knowledge of the truth, it is the highest, sublimest attitude that a church can assume. And the Church of England has been true, in the main, to the idea which was implanted in its constitution in the plastic moment of its rebirth; it has remained open to all the tides of thought and spiritual life which have swept over the nation; it has been able to retain in its fold those whom no other form of organized Christianity could tolerate.

The power of the Church of England lay not so much in its formal theology as in its liturgy. The Prayer-Book was placed in the hands of the people, as an educating, elevating influence, whose intention was to raise the laity to a sense of their equality with the clergy, as participants in the spiritual priesthood of all Christians. "There have been few things," says a recent writer, "which have affected the character of the modern English more than the liturgy." "The Prayer-Book," said Dean Milman, "is the best model of pure, fervent, single devotion as it were, and concentration of all the orisons which have been uttered in the name of Christ since the first days of the gospel; that liturgy which is the great example of pure vernacular English, familiar yet always unvulgar; of which but few words and phrases have become obsolete, which has an indwelling music, which enthralls and never palls upon the ear, with the full living expression of every great Christian truth, yet rarely hardening into stern dogmatism, satisfying every need and awakening and answering every Christian emotion, entering into the heart, and, as it were, welling forth again from the heart, the full and general voice of the congregation, yet the peculiar utterance of each single worshiper." "In many respects," said Macaulay, "it was well for the Church of England that in an age of exuberant zeal her principal founders were mere politicians. To this circumstance she owes her moderate articles, her decent ceremonies, her noble and pathetic liturgy. Her worship is not disfigured by mummery, yet she has preserved, in a far higher degree than have her Protestant sisters, that art of striking the senses and filling the imagination in which the Catholic church so eminently excels."

The Church of England retained the threefold order of bishops, priests, and deacons, as it was to be found by reading Scripture and ancient authors, but a change was made in that order which completely transformed its character. From the time when Tertullian wrote his "Prescription of Heretics" the belief had begun to prevail in the Latin church that to the bishops had been intrusted the guardianship of the Christian revelation; that to them alone had been primarily committed the "deposit" of faith, whose integrity they guaranteed in a continuous line of descent through the ages. Hence had originated the bishop's vow at his consecration to "defend the faith and to banish and drive away from the church all erroneous and strange doctrine contrary to God's word." The Church of England at the Reformation showed its sense of the change which had come over Christendom by intrusting to the presbyter the same guardianship as had hitherto devolved alone on the bishop, requiring from him at his ordination the same identical vow.[1] By this simple change the clergy ceased to be mere creatures of the bishop, representing the bishop in their respective parishes, as had been, and still is, their position in the Latin church; they became the spiritual representatives of the congregation, charged with the responsibility of inquiring for themselves into the nature of the Christian revelation, and of presenting to the people that only which they believed had the sure warrant of Holy Scripture. Thus the Church of England had secured, without discarding the episcopate, that which the reformed churches of the continent had only been able to secure by the abolition of the ancient order.

[1] "I call this," says Bishop Hampden, "a very remarkable injunction of the Service for the Ordination of Priests; because, in no other church is the like commission given to any other but to the highest order of the ministry, the bishops of the church exclusively. Neither in the Greek forms of ordination, nor in the Roman Pontifical, do we find any such charge given to the ministers of the inferior orders, but only to the bishops. All that is exacted of the priest and the deacon, according to the formularies of the Greek and Roman churches, is the promise of obedience to the bishops; an absolute and summary power being vested in the bishop to restrain and censure them at his discretion." *Memorials of Bishop Hampden*, p. 196.

II.

When the church was established, under Queen Elizabeth, in the shape which it still substantially retains, it was confronted by another theory of the church and the ministry, which was plainly irreconcilable with its own. The Puritans, or, as they were afterwards known, the Presbyterians, had derived from Calvin the principle that the clergy held a divine commission directly from God to teach a system of authoritative doctrine, and in God's name to rule and administer discipline in the congregation. From such a point of view the order of the Church of England was plainly opposed to Scripture, in which discipline no longer existed, where authority was vested in the sovereign, or in a body like Parliament, of which the great majority were laymen. The inevitable conflict was precipitated by the Act of Uniformity put forth by Parliament in 1559, which made the use of the Book of Common Prayer binding upon the clergy and the people throughout the kingdom. Whatever the bishops may have thought regarding their own prerogative, there is no doubt of the fact that Queen Elizabeth regarded them as convenient servants of the crown, for enforcing its will throughout their jurisdictions. The Puritan or Presbyterian clergy, who were not yet separated as a body from the communion of the church, resisted the law which commanded the use of the Prayer-Book, and soon passed from the stage of hostility to the petty details of ritual, to a denial of the authority of bishops to enforce its use; the episcopate was denounced as a "man-made" institution, having no sanction in Scripture; and gradually the feeling arose that it was a Christian duty to separate from their communion. When the state entered into the struggle, and bishops and sovereign endeavored to enforce uniformity and to suppress the obnoxious dissidents, the Puritans entered the third stage of the controversy and resisted the arbitrary policy of the crown. Thus was precipitated the civil war, which led to the temporary establishment of the commonwealth under the protectorate of Cromwell, and the momentary ascendency of Presbyterianism.

The controversy about church authority is interesting because it concealed deeper issues than the combatants on either side acknowledged. Before speaking of the ultimate consequences which flowed from it, the positions assumed on either side deserve a brief consideration. Hooker, the greatest intellect whom the Church of England had then produced, and who died as the seventeenth century was opening, had taken the ground, in the first five books of his "Church Polity," that the organization of the church was not to be deduced from Scripture, but was a thing to be judged and regulated by common sense, and convenience. Even if it were not found in the Bible, it was no less divine, because all established order was divine, having its basis in the very bosom of God, from whom all law acquired its sacred and binding character. Even if the order of bishops was a "man-made" institution, as the Puritans alleged, and its origin and growth could be traced in the early church, coming out of an antecedent order of some other kind, yet, as Hooker reasoned, that did not impugn its divineness, provided it was convenient for the maintenance of the well-being of the church.[1] But such a lofty and comprehen-

[1] Or, in the words of Matthew Arnold, "Hooker's great work against the impugners of the order and discipline of the Church

sive conception of the true nature of church government did not commend itself either to the bishops or the Puritan clergy. The Church of England had insensibly imbibed the Puritan view that Scripture contained an authoritative revelation not only of a system of doctrine, but of church government as well. Moreover, it was not in the nature of bishops, when their order was attacked as a "man-made" institution, not to resent the charge.[1] From this time we hear again the familiar refrain in Bancroft, Andrews, Laud, and others, of that doctrine of apostolic succession, which had been elaborated in the Latin church under Tertullian, Irenæus, and Cyprian.

of England was written (and this is too indistinctly seized by many who read it), not because Episcopalianism is essential, but because its impugners maintained that Presbyterianism is essential and that Episcopalianism is sinful." *Culture and Anarchy*, p. xxxvii. See, also, Hunt, *Relig. Thought in England*, i. pp. 57, 58. The following passage from Hooker would seem to be sufficient to put all doubt upon this point to an end :—

"Which divisions and contentions might have easily been prevented, if the orders which each church did think fit and convenient for itself had not so peremptorily been established under high commanding form, which tendered them unto the people as things everlastingly required by the law of that Lord of Hosts against whose statutes there is no exception to be taken. For by this it came to pass that one church could not but condemn another of disobedience to the will of Christ." Keble's ed. p. 161.

[1] The "Preface" to the Ordinal is conceived in the spirit of Cranmer and Hooker rather than in that of Bancroft and Laud. It affirms it to be evident from the study of Scripture and ancient authors that there have always been these three orders in the church, and that their maintenance, so strictly preserved, testifies to their importance — a general statement which commands assent on the ground of its apparent truth. But this is a very different thing from saying that Scripture contains a definite form of church government which is unalterably binding by divine command, that it is a part of the revelation which Christ came to bring, and that to dissent from it is of the nature of sin.

The hostility of the leaders of the Church of England to the Puritans led them also to dislike that system of doctrine which, under the name of Calvinism, had been accepted to a large extent in the church during the sixteenth century, which had been taught at its great universities and held by its great divines.[1] There grew up in consequence a system of theology in the Church of England widely remote from that which the reformers had accepted, the details of which are so familiar that it is only necessary to allude to them. The church became again practically identified with the episcopate — a personification as it were of Deity Himself, a mysterious entity intrusted with the divine gifts necessary for human salvation; the sacraments became the channels of grace; baptism secured the remission of original sin, and implanted in the soul a principle of life, which was nourished in the Eucharist; the bishops conveyed to the clergy, by a tactual process, the power to administer the sacraments with validity. The ritual became more ornate, a tendency appeared to restore the confessional and the custom of praying for the dead, tradition resumed its old authority, and the church claimed to be the custodian and interpreter of Scripture. While all this was a return to the spirit of Latin Christianity, yet there were also elements in what is known as High Anglicanism, which may be interpreted as a desire to restore neglected truths which Puritanism had discarded. In the doctrine of baptismal regeneration, as asserted by seventeenth century divines, as well as in other fea-

---

[1] Calvin's *Institutes* had been used as a text-book at Oxford and Cambridge in the sixteenth century. Archbishop Whitgift had endeavored to get the Thirty-Nine Articles amended so as to include the distinctive points of the Calvinistic theology.

tures of the system, we may discern an effort, however blind, to escape from the arbitrary principle of election as taught by the Puritans, by resting the Christian life upon a larger basis in some universal law. The reverence for antiquity was the expression of the feeling that all truth must have its roots in the consciousness of the past. The importance assigned to the principle of salvation through the church, instead of by individual effort, may be viewed as a desire to regain the sense of the solidarity or collective life of the human family in opposition to the individualism which, by making men stand alone in solitary isolation, threatened to disintegrate the sacred fellowship of humanity.

But whatever interpretation we may claim as the under-current of a movement, which on its face was a feeble imitation of mediæval Christianity, the important fact remains to emphasize that in England in the seventeenth century two systems confronted each other, each calling itself divine, each claiming for its clergy a divine appointment and sanction, each declaring the other false and untrue to the word of God. As time went on, there grew up a third movement known as Independency or Congregationalism, which denounced Presbyterianism as unscriptural, and demanded for the laity a place in the government of the church. The Independents not only deduced from the Bible a still different form of church government from any hitherto taught, but they took a further step toward dissolving the larger fellowship of Christendom by declaring the entire and absolute independence of the local body of believers. It remained for the movement known as the Baptist, which followed on the heels of Independency, to finally dispel the larger vision of a redeemed humanity in which even unconscious children participated, and of which infant baptism might be regarded as an expressive symbol. The Baptists were only more consistent interpreters of Calvin's theology than their predecessors. So long as the incarnation was resolved into an arrangement for saving from the consequences of sin, or for securing the salvation of the elect, the baptism of children was an unintelligible performance; it was pointing to another and higher interpretation of the incarnation of which no trace is discerned in the Puritan theology — the actual redemption of all mankind. The number of sects received one further addition by the appearance of the Quakers, who also drew from Scripture the tenet that a regularly constituted and educated ministry was unnecessary, and even an injury to the well-being of a true church. The hireling clergy, as they were called, were only an obstacle in the way of the inner revelation of the spirit. The churches, to the mind of the Quakers, had all alike missed the true reading of Scripture in adherence to outward worship and visible sacraments.

It is an interesting question why in England differing religious opinions should have been embodied in hostile organizations, when in Germany they rarely led to separation from the Lutheran communion. It was owing in a great measure to the attitude of the Tudor sovereigns in enforcing their will upon the nation, a policy which the Stuart dynasty endeavored to follow out when the age would no longer endure it. But the fullest answer to such an inquiry must admit an ulterior element in the problem, — that God had chosen England as the theatre in which the development of human freedom should be exhibited for the benefit of the larger world. The moral of the Puritan struggle against the authority of the Church of England does not lie, as some fondly think, in the confusion and enmities which arise when ecclesiastical uniformity is broken down. The confusion may be only the sign of a deeper life. The evils of the sectarian spirit, the divisions and subdivisions of religious parties, undoubtedly weakened the true church idea, which aims at the largest, most comprehensive human fellowship as the truest expression of the one common spirit that indwells in humanity.[1] But little as the actors in the great struggle might discern its full significance, it can now be seen that the confusions eventually ministered to a higher order. The rigid, invincible exclusiveness of hostile sects became the indispensable condition for obtaining religious toleration. It was for civil and religious freedom that the English people had been blindly striving through all the confused and complicated struggles of the seventeenth century. When the principle of religious toleration had been acknowledged, the confusions and

[1] How great these evils were is shown by the contemporaneous testimony of witnesses who themselves contributed largely to the confusions of their time. "We are a people," said Cromwell, "that have been unhinged these twelve years; as if scattering and division and confusion came upon us like things that we desired, these which are the greatest plagues that God ordinarily lays upon nations for sin." Milton, in the latter years of his life, is described as attending no place of public worship; "he was above the sects and loathed their mutual jarrings." Bunyan, who was a Baptist, said, "I would be and hope I am a Christian. But as for those factious titles of Ana-Baptists, Independents, Presbyterians, and the like, I conclude that they came neither from Jerusalem nor Antioch, but rather from hell and Babylon. For they naturally tend to divisions: You may know them by their fruits."—Quoted from Curteis's *Bampton Lectures*, p. 227.

the enmities subsided, and England entered into the serene and placid atmosphere of the eighteenth century.

III.

The eighteenth century occupies a large and important place in the history of Christian thought. The traditional theology, as it had been developed in the Latin church, as it had descended unchanged in its fundamental aspects to the Protestant theologians of the seventeenth century, was now compelled to enter into conflict with the human reason. Once before, in the time of Abelard, a similar process had been summarily arrested by the power of the church; but no power now existed which could hinder its progress. The movement which defied the traditional theology may be said to date from the English Revolution in 1688, when religious toleration was granted to the dissenting sects. In the course of its development every dogma of the church was assaulted, whether in its Latin or its Protestant form. How far we still are from a common understanding in regard to the work of the eighteenth century is shown by the divergent estimates of its significance in our own day: to some it appears as if inspired by an evil agency for the destruction of the truth; to others, a necessary part in a divine process by which God was taking away the old that he might establish the new.

Before speaking of the movement known as deism, or rationalism, it is necessary to revert once more, even at the risk of repetition, to the place in history which is occupied by the seventeenth century. It is here that the clew is apt to be lost by the student of religious thought. The political history of the period which follows the Reformation has been thoroughly and impartially explored; but in the history of theology there still exists confusion, owing for the most part to the continued rivalry of the sects which then took their rise, which still nourish the prejudices of that remote epoch as part of a sacred heritage. Even now, there are those to whom the names of Charles I. or of Archbishop Laud are dear as martyrs for the truth, with whom the name of Baxter is a laughing-stock, and the memory of Cromwell is execrated. Churchmen cannot forget or forgive, much less explain, the mortal insult to the establishment in the civil war; Presbyterians and their Puritan sympathizers are still painfully affected when they recall the Act of Uniformity of 1662, with the sufferings it entailed upon their ancestors.

The difficulty in tracing the line of progress in theological thought through this age of confusion is owing also to the fact that theology seems to have gone backward, reverting again to those principles of Latin Christianity which the Reformation had discarded. The influence of Zwingle ceased to be felt after the rise of Calvin. In the Lutheran systems of theology of the seventeenth century one can scarcely hear the voice of Luther. His doctrine of justification by faith was so changed as hardly to be recognized; his freedom in the use of Scripture gave way to a bondage to the letter which put the Bible in the place of Christ; the rights of private judgment were usurped by a traditional method of biblical interpretation. In England the comprehensive spirit and lofty ethical tone of the reformers, such as Cranmer, Jewell, or Hooker, yielded in the next age to the contracted vision and narrow ecclesiastical policy of men like Bancroft,

Andrews, or Laud. Calvinism alone continued to thrive in its native purity, whether on the continent or in England.

The cause of this theological retrogression must be sought in the great Catholic reaction which was led by the Jesuits. Even before the death of Luther it had become apparent that the immediate result of the Reformation had been to put two armies in the field which must prepare for battle. The old church, after awakening from the lethargy in which the Reformation found it, determined upon the effort to regain what it had lost. The wars in the Netherlands, the Thirty Years' War in Germany, the papal intrigues against the throne in England, have their counterpart in the theological controversies of the seventeenth century. When the Jesuits arose, declaring that the maligned church of the Middle Ages, with all its abuses and corruptions, with its services and ritual, and offices of every kind, was consecrated by the will of God, — that to touch any, even the least of these, for the purpose of reform, was to raise one's hand against God; when, in the strength of this conviction, they went forth everywhere to restore the old order, regarding every means as justifiable which conduced to such a meritorious end, it was necessary that Protestantism should step down from the heights it had occupied in a great creative epoch, and gird itself for the conflict with a deadly foe by borrowing its armor.

It is here that Calvinism finds its place in the philosophy of history. Its merit lay in its ability to resist Jesuitism on its own ground. It did not hesitate to identify Calvin's opinions with the divine will. In this respect its audacity may be equalled, but is not surpassed, by the disciples of Loyola. Calvinism was the fighting mood of the Reformation. It deserves admiration and praise for what it accomplished, as do the sovereigns of England, Henry VIII. and Queen Elizabeth, for their devotion to the principle of absolute government, or the Stuarts and High Anglicans for their assertion of divine right, which did much to save the national independence against the intrigues of Rome.

The theological entrenchment which was built up in the emergency of the conflict with Rome, and chiefly under the inspiration of Calvin, was the authority of Scripture as a communication from God, miraculously given and preserved, to whose teaching reason and tradition must bow, — an authority supreme in all that related to the doctrine, the worship, and the discipline of the church. To have held with Luther, that Scripture was to be tested by the inward experience, or with Zwingle, that there was an inner word of God in the human reason, by which the word of God, as given in the book, was to be judged, — positions like these were thought to be of little avail in the controversy with Rome. To have allowed the reason to examine or criticise the contents of the Bible would have been to weaken its authority.[1] Its very style and letter had been dictated by the Holy Spirit to men who acted as only mechanical amanuenses; no human element had been permitted to participate in

---

[1] The Duchess of Ferrara had intimated to Calvin that the higher spirit of the New Testament condemned such acts, recorded in the old dispensation, as the execration of his enemies by David. But Calvin answered that to take such liberties with Scripture would undermine its authority. Henry, *Leben Calvin's*, i. 452.

the communication of so divine a message. The Bible was as distinct in kind, and separated from all other books, as God is distinct and separate from the world.

So far as the controversy with Rome was concerned, it must be admitted that the Protestant position was a strong one. Transubstantiation, the additional sacraments, image-worship, the cultus of Mary and of the saints, purgatory, prayers for the dead, the papacy and the hierarchy, — for none of these could there be found any support in Scripture. Admitting, as Rome did, the premise of its opponents that the Bible was "a book of which God was the author," it was continually tempted away from its own stronghold in tradition, and was worsted in the encounter whenever it sought refuge in Scripture. But when the war with Rome was over, the situation changed. A new era began, in which it might have been possible to take up the line of advance where it had been dropped in the sixteenth century, had it not been necessary first to get rid of the false attitude which Protestantism had assumed under the leadership of Calvin, and which long continued to embarrass the progress of Christian thought.

It is customary to-day, now that Calvinism is spoken of as something from which we have been emancipated, to drop a pious tear to its memory or to eulogize the services which it has rendered to humanity. But it is not quite so clear that these eulogies are deserved. The service which it rendered cannot be traced altogether to its theology as its inspiring source; the evil which it has done is all its own. Had not the system of Calvin, like that of the mediæval church, possessed some features of a common Christianity which still exerted their influence, despite the restrictions with which they were bound, or had it not as a system been engrafted upon a people whom God had chosen, with whom lay the future of the world, whose native instincts and powers were still in the freshness and hopefulness of youth, far from the period when decline and decay would assimilate them to the exhausted races of history, — had it not been for conditions like these, Calvinism, like Mohammedanism, might have been an incubus too heavy to be thrown off, and have dragged humanity down to a lower plane where liberty and progress would have seemed like the baseless fabric of a dream. It was not the influence of Calvinism which has given the modern world its superiority. It is quite as legitimate to believe, that, because so large a part of Protestant Christendom refused to accept it, the world is what it is to-day.

The deistic movement did not appear until after its essential principle had been reached by leading divines in the age of the English Revolution.[1] Even during the period of the commonwealth, there were not wanting those like Chillingworth, Jeremy Taylor, or Hales, who had seen that the Bible was not to be identified with any one definite system of doctrines, the acceptance of which was a necessary condition of salvation. The internal conflicts of Protestant sects which were attended with so much bitterness and scurrility, the hatreds generated by theological differences, the growing complications of the theological method, all tended

[1] Lord Herbert of Cherbury, who lived in the first half of the seventeenth century, is sometimes mentioned as the first deist. But he stood by himself, and his thought grew out of other conditions than those which originated the later movement.

to impress men with the conviction that peace and security could only be attained by adopting some other standard in theology than the appeal to Scripture. It was impossible any longer to fall back upon the authority of the church, as Anglican divines had sought to do in the early part of the century. Church authority had fallen into discredit with its failure to overcome Puritanism, as well as by its inability to restrict that liberty of thought which was leading to the rejection of all external authority in religion. If the church had not been able to prevent the evil by its appeal to antiquity, how could it be expected to cure it? There was only one ground to take, if religion was to be saved from the inroads of the invading skepticism, and that was to assert the supremacy of the reason.

The Cambridge school of Platonists, which flourished in the latter half of the seventeenth century, and whose disciples belonged for the most part to the Church of England, were agreed in proclaiming the reason as having a divine quality. "Scripture faith," said Cudworth, "is not a mere believing of historical things and upon artificial arguments or testimonies only, but a certain higher and diviner power in the soul that peculiarly correspondeth with Deity."[1] Whichcote believed that there was no incongruity between the grace of God and the use of the reason. Rationality had a divine foundation. "The spirit in man is the candle of the Lord, lighted by God, and lighting man to God." To go against reason, therefore, was to go against God, for reason was the very voice of Deity. The Bible was not the only or even the first discovery to man of his duty. It only gathered and repeated and

[1] Preface to *Intellectual System of the Universe*.

reinforced the principles of truth scattered through all of God's creation.¹ Another member of the same school, John Smith, saw in revelation "the free influx of the divine mind upon our minds and understandings."² In his book on the "Light of Nature," Culverwell, a Puritan divine, asserted the supreme authority of the reason in matters of religion; to blaspheme the reason "is to reproach Heaven itself, to dishonor the God of reason, and to question the beauty of His image."³ Archbishop Tillotson, the great preacher of his age, whose popularity enabled him, as it were, to set the fashion in theology, affirmed that every doctrine before it could be received must be "judged by its accordance with those ideas of the divine character which are implanted in man by nature."⁴

The importance attached to the religion of nature is the most prominent characteristic of formal theology in the eighteenth century. In any attempt to trace the development of Christian thought, the profoundest significance must be attributed to the fact that natural theology should have taken the place of revealed religion, as the one absorbing subject of human interest and inquiry. In a change like this there was implied a revolution at the very basis of Christian theology. The extent of the change, which the transition reveals, may be seen by reverting to the time when Thomas Aquinas first made the memorable distinction between natural and revealed religion. He had made the distinction in the interest of re-

¹ Whichcote's Aphorisms, quoted in Tulloch, *Rational Theology in the Church of England*, vol. ii. p. 100.
² Discourse v. c. 3.
³ Tulloch, ii. p. 416.
⁴ *Sermons*, vol. iii. p. 485.

vealed religion, either for the purpose of carrying out his analogy between the kingdoms of nature and of grace, or in order to get rid of speculative difficulties which had been raised by the progress of heresy. But in the thirteenth century no practical importance was assigned to the distinction. Natural religion had been passed over as unworthy of the notice of those to whom a revealed theology had been intrusted. In the eighteenth century the situation was reversed : revealed religion was sinking into abeyance or neglect, while the religion of nature commanded an almost exclusive attention.

But the transition was not a sudden one. The preparation for it had been going on within the human consciousness, in obscure and devious ways, from the time when Latin theology had emphasized the separation of humanity from God on the one hand, or from nature on the other.[1] In the ready acceptance of the miraculous, which was a characteristic of popular Christianity from an early date, may be seen the traces of a surviving though latent belief in some organic relationship between man and his environment. The marvels and wonderful legends of the Middle Ages were the substitute for science. The taste for the miraculous points to a view of nature which sees in it the

[1] "There is also a considerable difference between the Greek and Latin Fathers in respect of their estimate of nature and its service to theology. Largely imbued with the genial spirit, as well as employing the language of ancient Greece, the Fathers of the Alexandrian school regarded nature with somewhat of that comprehensive and tender sympathy which distinguished the most nature-loving people of antiquity. Among these nature seems partly relieved from her ancillary position, and is awarded her own merits independently of theology." — Owen, *Evenings with the Skeptics*, ii. p. 437.

reflection of the human spirit, as if it contained a response to humanity in its deeper moods or in the crises of its career. In the marvelous effects which were wrought by relics and dead men's bones, in the recuperative power that lurked in the touch of a holy man, in the inanimate images that winked or bowed in response to prayers, — in the belief in these was an unconscious testimony to the truth that the material world stands in close relation to the experience and aspirations of the human spirit. We may read the same unconscious testimony in Gothic architecture, as if, when the Teutonic people first gave expression to the spiritual life that stirred within them, they were inspired by the ancient religion of nature with its cultus developed in the native forests of Germany, before Christianity had reached them. Now and then, at rare intervals, we hear voices in the Middle Ages like those of Bernard of Clairvaux or Francis of Assisi, which tell of an intimate relationship between man and nature, although the bond that unites them is still concealed. Bernard speaks almost in a modern strain of his delight in nature; "You will find something," so he writes, "far greater in the woods than you will in books. Trees and stones will teach you that which you will never learn from masters." In the exquisite sites selected for their monasteries, as in England by the Cistercian and Carthusian monks, it has been thought may be read the growing inclination for communion with nature, for which the heart hungered, while its study was condemned as fatal to the well-being of the soul.

After the study of nature had begun, under the influence of Aristotle, its progress was slow, owing to the prejudice it encountered from the accepted principle that nature was not only subordinate to revelation, but that the law of nature had been abrogated in the kingdom of the supernatural. But though the interest in religious questions was still supreme, although the Reformation diverted attention for a while from all other issues, the conviction was secretly cherished that the study of nature was closely connected with theology. Raymund of Sabunde [1] may be called the first clear herald of the truth that God's revelation of Himself in the outer world or in the nature of man is the foundation upon which rests all certitude in religious knowledge. The spirit of the German reformation tended in the same direction.[2] If the appreciation of nature finds no expression in the theologians who succeeded Luther and Zwingle, yet with

---

[1] On Raymund of Sabunde or Sabieude, see Owen, *Evenings with the Skeptics*, c. xi.

"The Book of Nature has always occupied a more or less subordinate position in all the great religions of the world. Buddhism despises nature and tramples it under foot; Judaism, in its later phases, has recognized it, but by no means admits it to a footing of equality; Mohammedanism ignores it; Christianity has for the most part patronized it as a corroborative but altogether subsidiary proof of its own truth. Raymund of Sabieude is the first Christian writer who not only vindicates the right of the Book of Nature to an equality with Holy Writ, but who asserts the superiority in many respects of the former over the latter. According to Raymund, the Bible is only true so far as its utterances agree with and are confirmed by the higher testimony of nature." Vol. ii. p. 448.

[2] As compared with Luther and Zwingle, Calvin was indifferent to nature. Although living for so many years at Geneva, he made no allusion in his letters, says his biographer, to the wonderful beauty by which he was surrounded.

On the place which nature holds in Milton's poetry, cf. De Laprade, *Le Sentiment de la Nature chez les Modernes*, pp. 240-250.

the German mystics of the seventeenth century, who more truly represent them than those who clung to the letter of their teaching, there is a vital connection between the spiritual life in man and the external world. Through their contact with nature they had been aided in reaching a closer relationship to God than they could gain from the received theology. Jacob Böhme was accustomed to see all things " environed with a divine light;" in the outward world was reflected to his vision an inner spiritual world; through the contemplation of nature, the mind of man rose to an insight into the inmost essence and glory of God.[1] It is a curious fact that Arndt, one of the most practical and spiritual of German mystics, should have been suspected of tampering with alchemy, or of making gold by the use of the philosopher's stone. It is also a circumstance of no slight importance, that almost contemporaneous with the mysticism that demanded a closer alliance between nature and humanity should have been the appearance of landscape painting, as an especial branch of art, in which nature was presented for the first time for its own sake, and not as the setting for some historical subject or human drama.[2] The mystic and the artist

[1] For the influence of Böhme upon Sir Isaac Newton, see an interesting note in Overton, *Life and Opinions of the Rev. William Law*, p. 189. According to Law, "Sir Isaac ploughed with Behmen's heifer."

[2] "Durant tout le moyen age, la figure humaine avait seule paru digne d'occuper l'art humain. Qu' était ce que le paysage dans les fresques du treizième et du quatorzième siècle ? Il n'existait pas, les peintres semblaient ne pas avoir regardé la face de la terre maudite. Michel-Ange lui-même meprisait tout ce qui n'est pas de l' homme. C'est contre ce point de vue de l'Église que s'élève Leonard de Vinci, dans son Traité de la

were like sensitive barometers foretelling subtle changes in the spiritual atmosphere.

By the opening of the eighteenth century the results achieved in the study of nature had begun to be apparent. The discoveries of Galileo, of Kepler, of Harvey, of Leibnitz, and Newton had illustrated the principle that the outward world is organized and governed in accordance with uniform law. The inference was a natural and inevitable one, that, if Deity revealed Himself in nature, He had also revealed Himself in the constitution of man, — that in a religion according to nature must be sought the principles which should guide human conduct and the basis of certitude in the knowledge of God. In religion, as in science, a silent revolution had taken place, modifying the conception of God, which lay at the basis of the Calvinistic theology. The notion of Deity as absolute will, unconditioned by a law of righteousness to which it must conform, yielded to the conviction that the divine will is subordinated to a law which constitutes the ground of the divine nature ; or, in the words of Bishop Butler, " I have argued upon the principles of the fatalists, which I do not believe, and have omitted a thing of the utmost importance, which I do believe, — the moral fitness and unfitness of actions, prior to all will whatever, which I apprehend as certainly to determine the divine conduct as speculative truth and falsehood necessarily determine the divine judgment." [1]

peinture ; relevant de sa déchéance l'univers visible, il replace 'homme au sein de toutes les formes de la creation." — Quinet, *Les Révolutions d'Italie*, c. 8.

[1] *Analogy*, part ii. c. 8.

IV.

The religion of nature, as it was generally understood in the eighteenth century, included, as its primary tenets, the existence of God, the immortality of the soul, the necessity of virtue, and a future state of rewards and punishments. The great advantage of the religion of nature, which commended it to all alike, whether deists or their opponents, was its simplicity, as contrasted with the intricacies of revealed theology; its universality, as compared with the divergent and contradictory teaching of hostile sects; its unalterableness, as built upon the eternal and uniform laws of nature. It was a religion peculiarly fitted to meet the skepticism and the decline of morality which set in with the restoration of Charles II. However the decline in morality is to be explained, whether, as was generally thought, it was a reaction from the enforced puritanical severity of the times of the commonwealth, or whether it was owing to the contagion of French example, it constituted a serious circumstance, challenging the attention of the church. To produce a moral transformation now came to be regarded as the end of religion — a view which was congenial to the practical bias of the age.

As to the tenets of revealed religion there was a general disposition to leave them in abeyance. It is hard to resist the doubt that, even before the seventeenth century closed, those who best represented the leading tendencies of the time had felt that the foundations, on which the traditional theology rested, had been shaken, — that it was no longer possible to justify their retention on the grounds either of reason or of practical utility. But to pass them quietly by was impossible. The deists insisted on raising the question of the relation between natural and revealed theology.

Toland, the author of a treatise entitled "Christianity not Mysterious," which was published in 1696, may be said to have opened the deistic controversy.[1] A man of impulsive temperament, he was led to speak out what many others were thinking. There was scarcely a point in the long controversy with the deists which he was not the first to raise. His book produced an excitement only to be compared, in the history of religious thought, with Luther's posting of the theses. His object, he said, was to defend Christianity, to which end he had prayed that God would vouchsafe His grace. It was his fundamental principle that religion must be reasonable and intelligible. Reason was above the authority of the fathers or of general councils. As there can be no infallible interpreter of Scripture in the past, it is by reason that the Bible must be examined and interpreted. It was a mistake to assert the authority of Scripture before examining

[1] Mr. Hunt, in his *History of Religious Thought*, does not class Toland among the deists. Nor does the term "deist" apply accurately to some other writers who are generally so designated. The word is now used to indicate a certain conception of the Deity, such as the Jewish or Mohammedan, which makes impossible the idea of the trinity. Hence it has lost its applicability to one like Toland, who leaned toward pantheism. The German distinction between the Illuminati and the Rationalists, if applied to the movement in England, would include Toland in the former class. Illuminism was the application of the principle, that the moral consciousness in man is divinely inspired, to any department of human thought or interest, whether education or society, literature or art. Rationalism was the effort to reconstruct religion upon the same principle by seeking for it in the Bible. The English deists, properly so called, did not labor with the Bible as did their German brethren.

its contents, as it was also the fault of Protestants that they had taken for granted that its teaching was to be identified with the tenets of the sects. He combated the principle that we should receive what we do not understand, or that there were mysteries in Scripture which, while above reason, were not contrary to reason. Reason was the only ground of certainty. Whatever has been revealed, has been revealed through reason. Revelation is essentially an unveiling of that which had not been understood. A mystery in religion is something that has now been made clear which before was not clear. In one sense, to be sure, all things are mysterious, — even a blade of grass or any object in the outer world whose essence we do not know. But we do not speak of these as mysterious. So in religion, while the essence of God is unknown, His character and attributes are revealed. No Christian doctrine can be properly called a mystery. All things in religion, as in nature, speak to the reason. There is nothing in the gospel contrary to reason or above reason. The notion that things might be above reason and yet not contrary to it was a distinction without a difference — a theological subterfuge or evasion.

The natural inference from Toland's position would have been that God revealed Himself in and through the human reason. But the inference which was drawn was that he denied the existence or the necessity of a revelation. On this point, while agreeing in first principles, the Christian apologists divided from those who were to be known as deists. Among the opponents of deism, as it was now understood, there was a general concurrence in maintaining that natural religion required for its efficiency to be supplemented by a revelation. Christianity furnished additional motives to the practice of virtue, as in the announcement of the doctrine of endless rewards and punishments which the natural reason could not have discovered, or in the clearer assertion of the doctrine of immortality by the resurrection of Christ from the dead. It was indeed hinted by some that such traditional tenets as original sin, the atonement, and the sacraments still held a place in revelation; but it was done in the way of apology, as if there might be points of view where they did not appear as altogether irrational or useless. The stress of the controversy did not turn upon questions like these.

In reply to these strictures upon natural religion the deists maintained that natural religion was not only clear, certain, and unalterable, but that it was sufficient, without any addition or confirmation. Tindal, who published his book called "Christianity as Old as the Creation," in 1730, represents this advanced stage of the controversy. He summed up the arguments in behalf of the sufficiency of natural religion by boldly declaring that Christianity was identical with the religion of nature. In order to think rightly concerning God, it was necessary to hold that He should, from the first, have given men an adequate knowledge of Himself, and of those elemental truths by the obedience to which they might become acceptable to Him. As much as this He must have done, and more than this He could not have done. If the law of nature is perfect, it can receive no additions; or if it was so imperfect at the beginning as to need alterations, it argued a want of wisdom in the divine lawgiver who promulgated it. "The law of nature is absolutely perfect, it has the highest internal excellence, the greatest plainness, simplicity, unanimity, universality, antiquity, and eternity. It does not depend upon the uncertain meaning of words and phrases in dead languages, much less upon types, metaphors, allegories, parables, or on the skill or honesty of weak or designing transcribers (not to mention translators) for many ages together, but on the immutable relation of things always visible to the whole world."

As the controversy went on, two distinct lines of procedure against deism were adopted. According to the first of these, objections began to be made to the law of nature, that it was not so perfect, so clear, so universal as its advocates supposed. Even before Bishop Butler appeared it had been often suggested that if there were difficulties in revealed religion there were also enigmas in the religion of nature. It was shown that nature had its dark side, that it was full of mysteries to faith, that the evil in the world, on the whole, predominated over the good. The pessimistic rôle now assumed by the advocates of revelation forced the deists to assert, as Leibnitz had already been doing, that this was a perfect world after all, the best possible of worlds, that the good more than counterbalanced the evil, that the evil only appeared to be such, and was in reality the good in disguise, or, in the words of Pope:—

> "Respecting man, whatever wrong we call
> May, must be right as relative to all.
> Discord is harmony not understood;
> All partial evil universal good."

But in order to maintain the universal good, or "the right relative to all," it was necessary to subordinate the individual, or to count out his interests and experience as non-essential to the well-being of the whole.

It is here that we touch the point where deism entered upon its rapid decline as a proposed substitute for Christianity. While there was a profound truth in deism which the age did not grasp, and yet only by the full acceptance of which could Christianity be upheld as a divine revelation essential to man, there was also a fatal lack in its premises, the influence of which began to be disclosed when Shaftesbury and Bolingbroke took up the movement at this point and proceeded to carry it on to its necessary conclusion. If divine Providence was revealed only in a care for the general well-being, and did not extend to the individual; if God was manifested only in general laws, whose operation might call for the sacrifice of the individual, there must be, according to the current reasoning of the time, an end to personal or churchly religion. Prayer, whether in private or in the congregation, must come to be regarded as a vain and empty performance. With the depreciation of the value of the individual soul in the sight of God there would follow a weakening of the belief in personal immortality. When the doctrine of immortality had disappeared, morality would inevitably decline to a cold, prudential estimate of duty. And, finally, God Himself would be no longer necessary, His existence would become an enigma, — a burden from which men would be happier if they were free. Such was the process by which the deism of Shaftesbury was resolved into the atheism of Hume, to whom the whole subject was an inexplicable mystery.

There was another line of procedure against deism besides this negative method of finding defects in the law of nature. If Christianity was identical with natural religion, how was the Bible to be accounted for, with its vast preparation, as if for some supernatural disclosure? Why should evangelists and apostles have sealed their teaching with their blood, if Christ had not come upon some supernatural delegation to the world? The miracles which had been wrought by Christ and His apostles were surely the evidence that God had interposed in the affairs of the world, either in order to communicate truth, which the human reason could not have discovered, or to confirm and give additional sanctions to the law of nature.

Upon this point there was complete accord among the opponents of deism; the signs of a revelation were the miraculous exhibition of God's power in external nature. The deists would be content only with internal evidence drawn from the fitness of things or the testimony of the reason. They saw no necessity for an interposition which, in its very nature, was opposed to a government of the world by law. It has been often said that the philosopher, John Locke, laid the foundations of the deistic movement. But Locke was not a deist, and it was upon his views of the human understanding that the Christian apologists rested in combating deism. He distrusted the whole matter of internal evidence. He rejected the theory of innate ideas, as Descartes had held it, because it lacked clearness; under its cover the old confusion might return about the nature of the mind from which he was seeking an escape. In his book on the "Reasonableness of Christianity," published in 1695, he maintained that Christianity might be reduced to one single tenet, that Christ was the Messiah, whose advent was foretold by prophets, the truth of whose divine mission had been attested by miracles. Beyond that position the orthodox theology of the eighteenth century did not go.

The assault upon this position was opened by Collins in his "Discourse of the Grounds and Reasons of the Christian Religion." In this work he took up one line of the evidences for the Messiahship of Christ — that drawn from the prophecies of the Old Testament. To his mind it was a clear case that the prophecies which were supposed to refer to Christ had a relation only to contemporary events, that none of them had been literally fulfilled, that it was only by the use of the allegorical method of interpretation that any allusion could be found in them to the being whom the Christians claimed as Messiah. This attack upon prophecy was followed by Woolston's effort to demolish the evidence drawn from miracles. His scurrilous and even blasphemous method in treating the subject must not be allowed to diminish the importance of his constructive attempt to show that the significance of the miracles lay in the moral or spiritual truth which they were designed to convey — an application, as he proved, which had been made by the ancient fathers. Neither of these treatises possessed any scientific value. Collins's scholarship was defective, and it was generally believed that Woolston was insane. A much more significant work in reference to miracles was Middleton's "Free Inquiry into the Miraculous Powers which are supposed to have existed in the Christian Church through several successive Ages." The inquiry where and on what grounds the line was to be drawn between the miracles of the early ages of Christianity and the ecclesiastical miracles of later ages raised another and more important question as to the nature of all historical evidence.

We are thus led to the great controversy, which, after the lapse of more than a hundred years, still goes on with unabated ardor about the genuineness and authenticity of the books of Scripture. The contributions to this controversy in its early stages, by English writers, have only an historical interest. The answers of the apologists to the attacks of the deists met the demands of the hour, it may be, but they did not touch the deeper principles involved in questions of historical criticism. These lay beyond the vision of the eighteenth century. As to the deists, while they anticipated at times the modern lines of biblical criticism, they were too much under the influence of deep-seated prejudices and antagonisms to read the Bible any longer in a right spirit. They had rejected the popular theology as it had been moulded under Calvin's influence, and they saw, or thought they saw, too much in the Scriptures that sustained it. The Calvinistic system, with a Jewish conception of Deity at its basis, had made the Old Testament necessarily a favorite with the Puritan churches. It is this which explains the antipathy in every writer among the deists for Judaism and its history. Nor could any amount of historical evidence reconcile them to the theological or dogmatic view of the miracles of the New Testament. Any hypothesis or alternative, however rash or absurd, was welcome to them, if by it they could embarrass their adversaries. They assumed such attitudes as would make the study of history impossible; and indeed for history itself they felt somewhat the same contempt as they did for the ancient records of revealed religion. They grew distrustful of all transmitted written documents. They could more easily believe in the willful perversions of transcribers or the mistakes of translators, or in forgeries, of which, as in the case of "Eikon Basilike," they had seen a recent illustration. If a great part of the English people, including its scholars and clergy, could be thus imposed upon by a bare-faced forgery in the seventeenth century, why should not similar attempts have been perpetrated with success in the early ages, when men were even more uncritical and there were fewer opportunities for detecting imposition. It was harder to accept an obnoxious theology, which their reason and moral nature condemned, than it was to admit that evangelists and apostles had been falsifiers, dupes, or impostors. But such gross charges against the apostles shocked the Christian common sense of the people, and enabled the apologists and evidence-writers to win an easy victory. It was easy to show that the apostles could not have been forgers or impostors or dupes, and upon this line of evidence the adversaries of the deists continued to ring the changes until the century closed.[1]

[1] Among the more important works in recent years bearing upon the history of deism may be mentioned: Lechler, *Geschichte des Englischen Deismus*; Pattison, *Tendencies of Religious Thought in England from 1688 to 1750*; Hunt, *Religious Thought in England*; Stephen, *History of English Thought*; Abbey and Overton, *English Church in the Eighteenth Century*; Lanfrey, *L'Église et les Philosophes au 18me Siècle*. Mr. Stephen has not been content to enumerate merely the tenets of the different deistic writers, but he has undertaken to trace the inner significance of the movement as a whole. Many of the distinctions which he has made are valuable. But his range of vision is too short. He belongs to that school of theological critics who find it confusing to have meanings assigned to theological terms different from those which they carried in the seventeenth century, and who denounce the modern tendency to see in the old language a higher meaning as an evasive if not dishonest process. At the expense, however, of removing from such critics a convenient target, which they have acquired great skill in hitting, it must be maintained that the theologians of the Calvinistic era had no prescriptive

When the deistic movement had exhausted itself in England, as was the case before the middle of the eighteenth century, it was taken up in France, and thence passed into Germany. England was the country that led Europe in this mighty effort to reconstruct religion and theology upon some other basis than that which Augustine or Calvin had assumed. Voltaire, with his keen vision, watched the process as it went on in England, and drew his own conclusion. Rousseau adopted the principles of the religion of nature, disseminating them in France by writings whose popularity has never been surpassed. A new school of French philosophy and ethics arose, combining the teaching of Locke with that of the later deists. In France, more than in England, there was reason for suspecting lawgivers, kings, and priests of creating and upholding systems for their own advantage. The Latin church was more obnoxious to the illuminated reason and conscience than the modified form which it had assumed in the Protestant sects. The French Revolution, in its relation to theology, was only a more violent and disastrous effort than the English Revolution had been, to get rid of the notion of God

right to fix forever the use of terms in theology, and that the modern tendency is in reality older, as well as possessed of a higher authority, than that which it aims to supersede. On the history of rationalism in Germany, cf. Hagenbach, *History of the Church in the Eighteenth and Nineteenth Centuries* (translated by Hurst); Kahnis, *Internal History of German Protestantism;* Hurst, *History of Rationalism;* Amand Saintes, *Histoire Critique du Rationalisme en Allemagne;* Tholuck, *Abriss einer Geschichte der Umwälzung, welche seit* 1750, *auf dem Gebiete der Theologie in Deutschland stattgefunden hat.* Dr. Pusey's *Historical Inquiry* into the cause of German infidelity is valuable, although retracted by the author.

which made Him the absolute will, as Augustine or Loyola or Calvin had conceived Him, whose will, not being grounded in a prior righteousness which the reason of man could discern, had become a shelter for worse abuses and tyrannies, whether ecclesiastical or civil, than had ever been recorded in human history.

The ideal of human government, as it had been discerned under the influence of natural theology, was a government according to constitutional law to which the will of princes must be subordinated, just as God was the constitutional ruler of the world, subjecting His will to the eternal law of right. Upon this truth was founded the American Republic, whose indebtedness to the principles of the English deists may be read in the opening sentences of the "Declaration of Independence," which justify the revolt from foreign rule by appealing to the "laws of nature" and the "God of nature."

The movement which is known as "Illuminism" in Germany was essentially the English deism, however modified by passing under the influence of French thought, or colored by the enthusiasm and subjectivity of the German people.[1] As in England and France,

---

[1] In this brief sketch of religious thought in the eighteenth century I have confined myself to England, because the field is a more familiar one, as also because the extent of the subject makes it necessary to select some one particular country in which to trace the operation of principles that were felt everywhere in Christendom. It was England also that gave the impetus to the revolt from the traditional theology. It is the more important to call attention to this fact because there has long been a disposition to saddle Germany with the responsibility of rationalism. On the direct influence of English deism in Germany, see Lechler, p. 447.

it carried with it the rejection, in root and branch, of
the Latin theology. It was attended by much that
was puerile and absurd, by an exaggerated senti-
mentalism peculiarily offensive to the English mind;
but in Lessing, its chief representative, was a man of
whom his country has never seen reason to be ashamed,
whose fame is part of the world's heritage, who, coming
forth from the bosom of a Lutheran parsonage, has
conferred upon theology, no less than upon literature,
the highest obligation. Illuminism, like deism, as a
definite movement, or school of thought, had no enduring existence ; but the influence which it exerted
indirectly in Germany was vast. Without it we
should not have had Herder or Jacobi or Jean Paul,
or, in a word, the modern German literature, or the
modern school of German philosophy. But influences
of another and higher kind had combined with its
essential principles before Schleiermacher appeared
as the herald of a new epoch in theology. On the
rationalism with which it was associated (*rational-
ismus vulgaris*) it is unnecessary to dwell. It was
simply an effort to make the Bible conform to the
tenets of deism, as they were generally accepted, by
eliminating from Scripture, or explaining away in
various methods whatever was obnoxious or contradictory. Such an attempt must end in Germany, as
it had done so far as it was attempted in England, in
utter and inglorious failure. But in its failure, with
all the negative results attending it, it had yet accomplished one manifest result of the highest value,
— it had shown that the Bible could no longer be
regarded as a miraculous book, whose composition
and interpretation violated the laws of the human
reason. The Bible could no longer be regarded as

a storehouse from which to collate proof-texts in defense of foregone conclusions. It had been demonstrated that reason and the individuality of the different writers entered into its composition, that it reflected the local historical influences of the various times at which its books had been written. Discrepancies had been discovered, to reconcile which was too much for human ingenuity. The effect of the discovery that the human element entered so largely into what had been supposed to be a purely divine communication was, at first, to destroy faith in the authority of the Bible as the record of a revelation from God. But when this point had been reached, the Christian mind of Germany was ready to return to what had been one of the first principles of Greek theology, — that the divine and the human are not foreign or alien to each other; that if God speaks to man it must be through the reason or the consciousness which is in man; that human reason is the reflection of a divine reason; that humanity, by its constitution, participates in the eternal Wisdom which became incarnate in Christ.

It is not by turning again to the voluminous treatises written in defense of Christianity that we shall best learn the place of deism in the history of Christian thought. Such works, as Butler's "Analogy," Lardner's "Credibility of the Gospel History," Sherlock's "Trial of the Witnesses," Chandler's "Defense of Christianity," or Paley's "Evidences," no doubt served a valuable purpose in the immediate exigencies of the time. But the circumstance which calls for explanation is this — that the leading writers of the age, including the apologists, should have become so indifferent to the doctrines of Christianity in their traditional form, as to make it difficult to draw a line between them and the deists. They were not only indifferent, they seem to have lost the clew to dogmatic Christianity altogether. Doctrinal preaching almost ceased in the churches. Such doctrines as the trinity, incarnation, and atonement, whatever might be their meaning or value, it was taken for granted were above the popular comprehension, and had no connection with the practical duties of life.[1] Such a position was equivalent to their rejection or denial. The apologists had found it hard to say in what respects Christianity supplemented the religion of nature. Even Bishop Butler was more of a moralist than a theologian. After so many centuries of Christian training it had become a matter of uncertainty as to what Christianity really was.

The subtle cause which explains the situation may be discerned, though it may not be easy to trace its workings. The assertion that the foundation of religion lies in the moral consciousness was a silent challenge to the Augustinian doctrine of original sin. The doctrine to which Augustine had attached supreme importance, which had led him to disown the authority of the reason and the freedom of the will, which had reduced man, as it were, to a mere animal until he had been regenerated by an outward grace imparted in baptism, which had suggested the idea of election, together with the condemnation of the whole heathen world, which had separated humanity from God, which had made revelation impossible except by arbitrary agencies external to reason, which had reduced revelation itself to a mystery, and had put men

[1] Abbey and Overton, *English Church in the Eighteenth Century*, ii. p. 41.

at the mercy of the priesthood and the church, — this doctrine which Calvin had again enforced in Protestant theology, practically ceased to be believed in the eighteenth century. The result of its rejection is more manifest than is the application to theology of the principle which supplanted it. It is this which accounts for the negative character of the work of the deists or for their influence upon their Christian opponents. They attacked a system of doctrine which was not built upon the reason or the moral consciousness. Neither the Augustinian nor the Calvinistic theology professed to respect the reason, — they simply defied it as an unruly thing to be brought into subjection to the divine will. Calvinism, with its doctrine of total depravity, is at the furthest possible remove from the conviction that in the moral nature lies the test of certitude in religious truth. Hence it was not so much that the traditional theology was attacked, as that it simply succumbed, in the presence of a truth which it had no power to withstand.

The principle that in the moral consciousness lies the foundation of religious truth had been clearly apprehended and set forth by the Cambridge Platonists, by Archbishop Tillotson, and others; it had been taken up by the deists; it had been accepted by their opponents. But as a principle in theology it must eventually conduce to higher results than those which attended it in the last century. Its inevitable tendency was to bring back the belief, which underlay the ancient Greek theology, that God and humanity were connected by an organic tie, that God indwelt in His creation, that the revelation through the reason or the moral nature was the manifestation of present Deity. Of truths like these we may trace the unconscious workings in the deistic controversy, but they do not appear on the surface of its thought. Indeed, they only led to contradiction and confusion, serving rather to embarrass than to aid the combatants. The old idea which had descended through Latin Christianity to Calvinism, that God was at a distance from the world, could not be easily overcome. It had become so firmly rooted in the imagination that it must long continue to hamper the reason and the conscience. In the deistic controversy, so far as only the interests of formal theology were involved, it was this view of God which was assumed by both parties alike. Men reasoned of God as if He were a mechanician in the distant heavens. On the comparison of the watch and the watchmaker the whole discussion hinged. The deists thought that the world would go of itself as the handiwork of an almighty and all-wise Creator without the need of special interpositions in order to the better regulation of its affairs. To suppose the necessity of miraculous interference was to imply that the work of the creation had been imperfectly ordered at the first, — it was to reflect upon the wisdom and the power of God. To the Christian apologists, miracles were the credentials of a divine teacher; to deny their possibility was to give up the Bible as the record of a revelation. Approaching the subject from this point of view, although agreeing with the premises of their opponent, they were obliged to maintain that there were cases which called for an interposition, — that a revelation could not be given without a miraculous interference with the laws of nature.

The effect of this conception of Deity as a sort of colossal man, who acts upon the world from a distance by His power, is farther apparent in those doctrines which were still nominally retained, though they had ceased to be of vital importance to the religious consciousness. The idea of such a Deity becoming incarnate in Christ was an impossibility to the reason. The doctrine of the trinity seemed a palpable absurdity, whose origin, if it were worth tracing, would be found in the corruption of Christianity by heathen philosophy. The tendency to Arianism is apparent through the whole of the eighteenth century. That Christ was a supernatural being, who had come to the world as a delegate from the distant Deity, had been the only view possible to Milton's imagination; it had commended itself to Newton; it lurked under Locke's conception of Christ as the Messiah sent from God; it had been openly avowed by Dr. Clarke; nor could Waterland's defense of the Christian doctrine of the trinity avail to check the tendency to acquiesce quietly in a belief like this, which accorded so naturally with the ruling idea in theology. With the deists, even Arianism was unnecessary as a theory of the person of Christ. As there had been no special message, there was no necessity for a supernatural messenger.

The doctrine of the atonement, in its Anselmic or Calvinistic form, had also ceased to be held or preached by those who had come under the peculiar influence of the age. That God would pardon sin upon condition of repentance was one of the tenets of the deists. The reason for the decline of belief in what was essentially a Latin dogma may be more readily seen by referring to its origin in the time of Anselm. It had then been offered as explaining the meaning of the incarnation. To Anselm's mind, the inquiry, why God had become man, had suggested an answer, which was the echo from the heart of the age in which he lived. But if men were unconsciously under the influence of a doubt whether God had indeed become man, such a theory of the atonement with its complications to the reason as well as to the moral nature, must pass into abeyance as having no practical or theoretical significance, even if it were not openly rejected. So far as the apologists, who were the theologians of the time, felt the necessity for answering Anselm's inquiry, they subordinated the death of Christ to His resurrection, by which the natural intimations of the immortality of the soul had been confirmed.

In an age when the final appeal was taken to the reason and the moral consciousness, it might have been expected that the doctrine of endless punishment would have been more obnoxious than it seems to have been.[1] It was one of the charges against Archbishop Tillotson, that he had made hell precarious by his admission that God had a dispensing power from His threats and penalties. Tindal, in his "Christianity as old as the Creation," had maintained that the object of all punishment was disciplinary. That a disposition already existed, in the earlier part of the eighteenth century, to reject the doctrine may be also inferred from the treatment of the subject by Bishop Butler. If it was not openly impugned to any great extent, it was owing, in part, to the practical view which was then generally taken, that religion was preëminently useful as a sort of police-force for keeping society in order. Hence it was asserted by the apologists that morality

---

[1] Cf. on this subject, Abbey and Overton. vol. .. pp. 308–318. "If by the majority the doctrine in point was practically shelved, it was everywhere passively accepted as the only orthodox faith, and all who ventured to question it were at once set down as far advanced in ways of deism or worse." p. 312.

needed stronger sanctions and motives than natural religion could discover, and that endless punishment constituted one of the distinguishing features of revealed theology. It is a profound remark of the late Isaac Taylor that the hand of God in the great evangelical awakening of the last century is seen in this, — "that it took place at the very verge of that period when the ancient belief as to future punishment was still entire."[1]

In a history of the Christian life or of Christian institutions, the "great awakening" under Wesley and Whitefield would assume the highest prominence. In a history of Christian thought, its place though important is only incidental. What its relation has been to the intellectual life of the church an attempt will be made to determine in the following lecture. It must suffice to say, in concluding this sketch of the conflict between the traditional theology and the reason, that the results of the struggle were unsatisfactory and disappointing. Theology suffered from the divorce between the intellect and a living Christian experience. Religion, in the first half of the eighteenth century, was practically identified with ethical culture, and so it continued to be throughout the century, except among the few who were stirred by the appeals of Wesley and Whitefield. The devotion, the zeal, and enthusiasm of an inward spiritual life were rarely exhibited, and were even discouraged as leading to mischief. The age was still suffering from the over-zeal, the heated passions, the misguided enthusiasms, which characterized the times of the commonwealth. When things are separated, which should go together, the result must be

[1] *Wesley and Methodism*, p. 154.

disastrous. Theology tended to assume a cold, intellectual tone, as though it were merely an affair of the head, while in the revival under Wesley or in the Evangelical party in the Church of England, we sadly miss that intellectual element which lends dignity and strength to religion, which saves it from degenerating into superstition. Could the rationalism of the last century have been united with the mysticism which was struggling for recognition, the God of the deists would not have become a mere impersonation of general laws.

But such is not the law of human progress. Movements must first differentiate themselves from all that would obscure their significance, in order that the peculiar truth which each is divinely appointed to reveal may be plainly and distinctly seen. It was not the fault of the deists, it was their misfortune, that while destroying the old they could not replace it with something better. They rejected what was called revealed theology as not in harmony with the reason; they were mistaken in supposing that the theology which they scorned was the only form which Christian thought could assume. They made impossible the old interpretation of the Bible which had perverted its meaning, which had destroyed its true significance as the "word of God," by a forced conventional treatment of its letter. They were unable to show how it should be interpreted, so as to restore it once more to its true supremacy over the free spirit. But whatever their failures, we may be thankful to them for what they did, in breaking down all tyrannies over the human mind, whether of Scripture or of the church. As we review their work we can see how to them is owing that later theology has been able to build upon surer foundations. In emphasizing the laws of nature, in their assertion that true religion was like the laws of nature, simple, certain, uniform, and unalterable, grounded in the constitution of man, they were preparing the way for a return to the truth which underlay the ancient Greek theology, — that the incarnation of the Son of God was also intimately connected with the laws of God as they are revealed in outward nature, that His manifestation in the flesh was part of an immutable, eternal process.

Yet while the instinct was a true one, which led the deists to reject a religion based upon miracles, in so far as it seemed to imply a God outside the "reign of law," who was planning schemes and revising His work, interposing in human affairs in order to guard against emergencies, who could only attest His interest in man by signs and wonders, while we may admit the reasonableness of their protest against an anthropomorphism which degraded the nature of God — yet it is also important to do justice to the opponents of deism, the once famous Christian apologists whom we have been led too often to decry. They too were bearing witness in their own way to another truth, equally indispensable with that which the deists proclaimed. They stood for the importance and necessity of the idea of revelation. In the presence of much that was calculated to disturb or weaken their faith, they clung to the conviction that God had actually spoken to man in some direct, immediate way through Christ, however He might also have spoken through the law engraved upon the heart.

How to unite these truths held in separation and hostility in the last century,[1] how to bring revelation

[1] There were others in the eighteenth century who gained a

within the sphere of law and to lift up law to the higher level of divine revelation, has been the problem of what we call our modern theology — a problem, however, whose solution had been already grasped in its essential principle by Clement, by Origen, and by Athanasius, when they proclaimed a Deity indwelling in outward nature, but more especially in humanity, and above all in Christ.

fuller view of the relation of God to the external world than the English deists. Such were in Germany, Lavater and Stilling, and more especially Oetinger, to whom is attributed the profound remark that the end of the ways of God is corporeity. Cf. Dorner, *Hist. Prot. Theol.*, ii. pp. 234–240. Oetinger anticipated most that was true in the interesting visions of Swedenborg. The Swedish seer endeavored to combine in his system what he rightly regarded as the two revelations, that in nature and that given in the Bible. But his idea of the process of revelation, as recorded in the Scriptures, rose no higher than the then current theory of verbal inspiration. In order, however, even on this theory, to make the Bible serve his purpose, he was obliged to omit from the canon of Scripture many of the most valuable books, while he also exaggerated the importance of others, for example, the Book of Revelation, about whose genuineness and authenticity there have always been grave doubts in the church. Swedenborg was profoundly read in the study of nature, as he was also profoundly ignorant of the history of Christian theology, which is the history of the consciousness of man under the guidance of divine revelation. He, therefore, saw no other way of introducing to the world the truth, which, in common with others, had dawned upon his mind, than by smuggling it into the Bible by means of allegorical interpretation, the key to which he seems to have sincerely believed had been imparted to him in some external supernatural way. The sect sometimes called after his name still survives as a monument to a movement in the last century which was summarily interrupted by the great ecclesiastical reaction in our own age.

RENAISSANCE OF THEOLOGY IN THE NINETEENTH CENTURY.

Ergo jam non estis hospites et advenæ, sed estis cives sanctorum et domestici Dei. — EPH. ii. 19.

CHRONOLOGICAL TABLE.

A. D.
- 1632–1677. Benedict Spinoza.
- 1686–1761. William Law.
- 1700–1760. Zinzendorf, Founder of the Moravians.
- 1703–1791. John Wesley.
- 1714–1770. George Whitefield.
- 1724–1804. Immanuel Kant.
- 1725–1807. John Newton of Olney.
- 1726. The Wesleys and Whitefield at Oxford.
- 1741. Separation between Wesley and Whitefield.
- 1747–1821. Thomas Scott, the Commentator.
- 1749–1833. Goethe.
- 1753–1821. Count Joseph de Maistre.
- 1759–1827. William Blake, artist and poet.
- 1759–1836. Charles Simeon of Cambridge.
- 1768–1834. Schleiermacher.
- 1770–1831. Hegel.
- 1770–1850. William Wordsworth.
- 1772–1834. Samuel Taylor Coleridge.
- 1775–1851. Turner, the landscape painter.
- 1775–1854. Schelling.
- 1789. Beginning of the French Revolution.
- 1790–1866. Keble, author of the "Christian Year."
- 1800–1882. Dr. Pusey.
- 1805–1872. F. D. Maurice.
- 1814–1863. F. W. Faber.
- 1833. Beginning of the Tractarian Movement.
- 1835. Publication of Strauss's "Leben Jesu."
- 1845. Newman received into the Church of Rome.
- 1858. Mansel's Bampton Lectures
- 1870. The Pope declared infallible.

RENAISSANCE OF THEOLOGY IN THE NINETEENTH CENTURY.

I.

It is a familiar truth that all great changes which have revolutionized society have proceeded from the people. The thoughts which may have been anticipated by philosophers must take shape as popular sentiments before they become active forces for the amelioration of human interests. It was so in the beginning of Christianity, when the teaching of Christ, the loftiest spiritual truth that has ever been uttered, met with its first response, not in the upper classes of society as they are called, but among the outcast and the lowly; when not many mighty, not many noble, were called, but when God chose the weak things of the world, and base things, and even things that were not, as His agency for overcoming the mighty and for bringing to naught the things that were. The principle of Descartes, that all true knowledge must begin with doubt, which when once enunciated could not be forgotten, received its application as a working principle in the history of the church during the eighteenth century, when a general suspicion was everywhere current that the church, the priesthood, the traditional dogmas, and even the received Christianity, were an imposition of designing men, which must be utterly destroyed if true religion were to rise and flourish. The principle of the philosopher Kant, that in the consciousness of man lay the certification and authority of all truth, may seem as a metaphysical principle to be far removed from the popular apprehension. And yet to an idea like this, powerful enough to become an agency by which humanity was to be moved through the whole range of its activities, the people were responding in ways, it may be, that were vulgar or extravagant, but which yet attest how the speculative process of the highest thought may be corroborated by the inward moods and necessities of the soul.

The transition from the last century to our own age may be sought among the leaders of thought, such as Lessing or Goethe or Kant, or we may seek it among the uneducated, uncritical followers of Wesley and Whitefield and Zinzendorf. Under the influence of Spinoza, Lessing disowned the prevailing theological conception of a God outside of the world who could attest His existence only by so-called supernatural evidences, such as signs and miracles. Kant demonstrated that such a deity was impossible to the reason, rejecting any external authority which upheld His existence, whether of the church or of the Bible; only in the reconstructive process which is based upon the inward convictions of the soul can God, as Kant declared, be sought and found. Upon the same basis, whether consciously or not, stood the ranting Methodists and Evangelicals in England, the Pietists or Moravians in Germany. Their religious faith and life, their very existence, is in striking contrast with the temper of an age which regarded God as immovably fixed at a distance from the world, which inclined to deny a special Providence, or the value or significance of prayer, which regarded the church and its ordinances as a sort of superfluous clothing with which the human spirit had been overlaid by an ambitious priesthood. What the age was discarding the disciples of Wesley and Whitefield were accepting with a new zeal and enthusiasm which England had not seen for a century. But they no longer accepted the faith on the old authority, however they might think or profess to do so. It came to them with a new authentication which they found in the feelings.

We have become so familiar with the idea of conversion as the characteristic of much of the popular Christianity of our own day, that we realize with difficulty that it was presented as a new truth in the last century, — a thing so obnoxious to the common sense of the age that it seemed to defy all dignity and decency in religion. It is not easy to recall the prevailing tone of thought which explains why the doctrine of conversion was so obnoxious. One reason of its offensiveness lay in that which constituted its peculiar charm to those who had experienced it, — that God came into direct contact with the soul. It was this conviction which underlay the great evangelical awakening, and that marks the movement as distinct in its kind from every other in history. It controverted the deistic conception of God, not by the reason, but by the experience. It declared that every man might be conscious of the action of Deity in the recesses of the spirit. It rested the reality of the religious life in sensations and emotions which were regarded as bearing witness to the presence of God.

The doctrine of conversion, as it was preached by Wesley and Whitefield, has another interest in the history of religious thought besides the change which it indicates in the conception of Deity. It passed out of the narrow sphere in which it was first proclaimed among the Methodist or evangelical societies; it invaded, to some extent, the Church of England; it was accepted by Presbyterians, Congregationalists, and Baptists. It gave homogeneousness to the sects which date their birth in the seventeenth century, thus binding together in a common method bodies which had originated in antagonism to each other. It illustrates how when God is believed to be in immediate, and, as it were, tactual relationship with the soul, there is no longer any inclination for priesthoods and sacramental agencies which usurp His place. As the idea extended that God Himself works the great change in man by which he is turned from sin to holiness, the last relics of the system of sacramental grace vanished from the popular mind.

Another distinctive feature of the evangelical awakening, whether in England, Germany, or America, was its social character. It did what the church was not doing, — it bound men closely together in groups or societies, making them feel their close relationship to each other, by making them realize their relationship to God. Such was the origin of the Methodist movement in its germ at Oxford, — a band of men associating themselves for a religious purpose. It was here that the evangelical movement began to correct the disintegrating tendencies of the age. Wherever it spread it carried with it the spirit of coterie. The charm of the movement, in its earlier days in the Church of England, was the bond which united its adherents as in some mystic brotherhood. As in the ancient church, the scorn and contempt which they encountered only served to deepen the ties which bound its members together. Such may be called the first practical step toward dispelling the illusion that society was based upon some selfish contract, by which a check was put upon those natural tendencies of men which would otherwise tend to their destruction. The idea of the church was reappearing in its original beauty and simplicity, as a form of association growing out of the very necessities of the religious life, — a prophecy of a regenerated society which has its being in God.

It is useless to look to the evangelical movement, in any of its forms, for any theologian who directly advanced the progress of Christian thought. The study of the evangelical theology is only interesting as showing what were the truths in the formal theology which appealed most strongly to the emotional moods. Methodists and Evangelicals were children of the feelings. In what they accepted or rejected they were guided by instinct, not by reason. As we examine the tenets to which they attached the highest importance, we can see that the motive which imparts to them their significance is the bearing they have upon the central truth of conversion. If they took up again the discredited doctrine of original sin, holding to it with surprising energy and tenacity, it was not so much, with Augustine or Calvin, as the cornerstone of a system of theology, but because it magnified, by contrast, the value of that work of redemption of which they were conscious as the work of God in the soul, — a transformation which no human effort could accomplish. If the divinity of Christ became to them as an essential truth in the presence of an Arianizing tendency which hung like an atmosphere over the age, lowering the tone of Christian piety, it was because they felt it to be indispensable to their religious life, not because they had reasoned out its necessity or saw its speculative value in a system of theology. They returned to the Bible with an unqualified devotion, because they found in its teaching that which corresponded to their experience or met the deepest wants of the soul. They did not stop to reason about prayer, or how a special Providence could be reconciled with general laws; they prayed because they found in prayer the vital principle of religion. In a word, it was a theology reposing upon the feelings as the only sure foundation when every other support had given way.

The evangelical movement has been thus briefly referred to because it constitutes the transition to Schleiermacher, the representative theologian of the nineteenth century. Before dismissing it, attention should be called to the principle which divided the Evangelicals into two distinct schools, and which has also made itself felt in the later history of theology. The separation between Wesley and Whitefield involved a point of primary importance. Wesley rejected the Augustinian or Calvinistic idea, that the will had lost its freedom through Adam's fall, — a tenet which Whitefield retained. While with both conversion was a change sudden, revolutionary, and complete, with the one it was regarded as a process for which man might prepare the way, with the other it was necessary to wait until God chose to act. But while the assertion of Wesley, that the will was free, might seem to be an advance in theology — a rejection of the Augustinian dogma of original sin, yet it does not appear that Wesley grounded his belief in a truer intellectual conception of the nature of God or of His relation to man. It is a characteristic of Wesley, as a religious reformer, that he is disclosed to us in his earlier life as undertaking anew the search after God. How to find God, and how to adjust one's relationship to Him, under the consciousness of sin, are the uppermost questions in his mind. The one man of the age who, above all others, may be said to have lived and to have had his being consciously in God, was William Law, a non-juring clergyman of the Church of England. To him Wesley turned for assistance, but came away disappointed. When, at last, he had reached a principle which seemed to solve his difficulty, he reproached Law with not being a Christian, nor understanding the true meaning of the work of Christ. Wesley had accepted as the fundamental principle in religion that which Law intelligently and determinately rejected. He had found peace with God through belief in a doctrine of the atonement such as Anselm or as Calvin had taught it. The doctrine came to him through the Moravians, and while essentially the old Latin doctrine in its spirit, it had assumed a grossness of form and statement which makes Anselm's view seem lofty by comparison. The effect of this belief in Wesley's theology was to give an almost exclusive prominence to the person and work of Christ. As with the Moravians, Christ takes the supreme place in Christian experience, while, if one may so speak, God is relegated to the background, as if a being from whom Christ had come to deliver us. Thus an element had entered again into the popular theology which affiliated it with the predominant characteristic of mediæval religion, and which also explains the ease with which the transition has been so often made from the Protestant faith to the acceptance of Romanism.

With the evangelical school in the Church of England, while a similar importance was attached to the doctrine of atonement, yet the Calvinistic influence which it perpetuated prevented it from seeking to escape from God. There was, on the contrary, a tendency to degrade the idea of Deity by too familiar association in the experience of conversion. The element of awe and of mystery, which enters so vitally into a true relationship with Deity, was in danger of disappearing, unless some corrective could be found which evangelical theology was unable to supply. The defect of the evangelical movement, as a whole, and in all its phases, was the narrowness of its range. It limited too much the sphere of the feelings in religion. It had no interest in art or science, in philosophy or in intellectual culture. It had a tendency to disclaim all human learning as corrupting to the simplicity of faith. It stood so near the old deism, from which it was reacting, that it failed to catch the profound truth which it contained, — that religion was included in the realm of universal law. There was something irregular, if not spasmodic or fitful, in the ideas of revival and conversion. There still lurked beneath them the principle of election, even though Wesley intended to reject it. The conception of a redeemed humanity, whose solidarity was in Christ, was still a truth waiting for recognition. Without the evangelical awakening, the restoration of a higher theology would not have been possible. Its great service was in illustrating the profound reality of the religious life. Its defect was its want of an intellectual tone and a more ethical aim. For the lack of these it failed to retain its grasp upon the advancing life of Christendom. Its methods became distasteful to a more enlightened sentiment. It was unable to meet the skepticism of an age which had seen the exposure of the unreasonableness of the formal theology of Protestantism when traced to its foundation.

II.

The spirit of the evangelical movement, as it was represented in Germany by the Moravians, formed an important element in the training of Schleiermacher for his great work as the regenerator of theology. In this respect, with his ardent devotion to the person of Christ gained in the schools of Moravian piety, he stands in striking contrast with the religious temper of his age. It was in the closing year of the eighteenth century that he stood up before the German people to advocate personal religion as a relationship to God grounded in the deepest instincts of human nature. Religion is not a system of dogmas addressed to the intellect, it is not a ritual, neither is it a collection of precepts enjoined upon the will. It is the essential primitive action of the human soul, a feeling or sentiment innate in man which unites him with God and with the universal order of things, — it springs from the constitutional endowment of humanity in God's own image. Religion may be developed by reflection and by a process of external training; it may act upon all other departments of human interest, and even come to include in its sphere the intellectual or moral sciences; but primarily it is not these, — it resolves itself into a simple feeling of dependence upon God.

In thus basing religion upon the feelings, which possess, as it were, a certain cognitive power, whose perceptions it may be the work of the intellect to interpret, Schleiermacher was returning to the principle of the ancient Greek theology, before the true relationship of man to God had been misrepresented by the Augustinian dogma of original sin. His idea of the feeling as the basis of religion implied, however, much more than the superficial life of the emotions, or that sensuous mood into which Moravian or evangelical piety had a tendency to degenerate. It included the deeper instincts and yearnings of the soul, as they were seen not merely in the individual man or the local transitory phases of some particular age, but as they were illustrated in the experience of humanity through all its history. At a time when the old intellectual conceptions of God and of the world had lost their meaning, when as yet they had not been replaced by larger conceptions which would meet the demands of the growing reason, what other mode of procedure remained than to revert to the original endowment of human nature as it might be read in history, or in the individual consciousness, — to those intimations within the soul however dim or shadowy,—

"Which, be they what they may,
Are yet the fountain light of all our day,
Are yet the master light of all our seeing."

In his idea that religion is based upon the feeling and consists in the consciousness of a personal relation to Christ, Schleiermacher was reflecting the immediate influence of his Moravian training. But other elements than the somewhat narrow pietism of the evangelical movement had entered into the composition of his theology. There converged in his mind, as if it had been a focus for the preceding ages, the scattered rays of truth, which had been illuminating individuals here and there in the long course of human progress. Into his thought concerning God there had entered the influence of Spinoza, of whom he had remarked in his famous " Discourses on Religion : " —

" The sublime spirit of the world penetrated him ; the infinite was his beginning and his end ; the universal his only and eternal love ; living in holy innocence and profound humility, he contemplated himself in the eternal world, and saw that he too was for the world a mirror worthy of love : he was full of religion and full of the holy spirit."

In Schleiermacher we have also, for the first time since the days of Greek theology, a representative theologian of the highest intellectual capacity, who had drunk deeply at the springs of Greek philosophy and culture. The habit of devotion to the classics among the students of the last century brought forth a positive result in the deeper insight into the workings of the Hellenic spirit. Upon Schleiermacher the study of Plato had produced its inevitable effect, releasing him from intellectual servitude, enlarging his mental horizon, stimulating the critical faculty, imparting the desire for the truth at any hazards, the love for all that was highest and best, the conviction that the world when rightly viewed was resplendent with the glory of God. He remained in full possession of the truth contained in German illuminism, after what was weak or foolish in its tentative applications had been eliminated. He had followed the new philosophy of Schelling, who, in his search after God in the history of nature and of humanity, had traced the profound analogy between the laws of matter and the laws of thought; who no longer regarded nature as under the sway of a blind fatality, but as penetrated with a divine intelligence, slumbering unconsciously till it came to the knowledge of itself in man; who saw that humanity, although free, was still under the dominion of law; that the spiritual life which had been engrafted upon an organic basis in nature reproduced its movement in completer form and upon a vaster scale. He rejoiced in the German awakening, of which Lessing had been a pioneer, whose results were seen in the rejection of foreign influence, in the rise of a distinctively German literature in which all that was most truly characteristic of the German people found an untrammeled expression. He had drawn from France, in the earlier years of the French Revolution, an enthusiasm for the idea of humanity, — an idea which, before Europe had been startled by the wild excesses that marked the struggle for its realization, had caused a thrill of wonderful expectation as of some great and unexampled good that was coming to man. He was in the first flush of his manhood at a time when, in the words of the poet who has caught so exquisitely the mood of the hour, —

"Bliss was it in that dawn to be alive,
But to be young was very heaven."

Influences like these were unknown to Latin theology as well as repugnant to its spirit. The same is true, also, of Protestant theology so far as it had inherited from Calvin a similar tendency and aim. Their introduction as ruling principles in modern religious thought marks a quiet revolution which has modified the traditional theology at every point, — a revolution, compared with which that of the sixteenth century was insignificant. As we review the leading features of the theology, which has been gradually extending its reception in the church, from the time of Schleiermacher, it appears in every essential aspect as a reproduction of what Greek theologians had taught, when the influence of Christ was yet fresh in the world, when the Christian intellect was quickened as if by a supernatural impulse, when, as yet, the teaching of Christ had not been modified or economized, reduced or disowned by the interests of ecclesiastics claiming authority to teach and govern the world in His name.

To trace this revolution as it has been silently wrought in so many noble minds, — to follow the struggles by which one after another of the leaders of the modern church have attained a higher and more comprehensive conception of the religion of Christ, — interesting as such a task would be, it is impossible to undertake it here. We must be content to note the process in a single mind. For this purpose Schleiermacher may be taken as a representative man, who being dead yet speaketh; whose insight was so true and so far-reaching, that as a religious thinker he is still in advance of many who feel and acknowledge his influence.

While there were deficiencies in his conception of God, to which allusion will be made hereafter, the statement needs no qualification that the theology of Schleiermacher is affected throughout by the conviction that God indwells in the world. His belief in a divine presence in the world and in man was deep and vivid. Against the cold idea of deism, he asserted a living spiritual presence, a God who is with us and in us, who is allied to humanity by an organic relationship. The result of this conviction of the immanence of God implied the restoration to a supreme place in his theology of the spiritual or essential Christ, who is above the conditions of time or space. As in Greek theology, or in every school of mystical thought, whether mediæval or Protestant, it is no longer the Christ after the flesh, but after the spirit, who occupies the central throne in Christian thought and experience. Christ was the incarnation of the divine consciousness as it exists in its fullness in God. To think of Him exclusively as one who had come upon a mission to the world from the distances of space, and then departed, was to miss the idea of One who stands by an eternal law of God-head in intimate and continuous relationship with the human spirit. That He was now set down at the right hand of the Father did not mean that, His work being accomplished, He had retired from the world, passively awaiting the end of the dispensation. To be seated at the right hand of immanent Deity, is to be in the thick of the conflict which humanity is waging with sin and evil, it is to be forever here in our midst, the inspiration of all strength and courage, the source of hope and faith, the pledge of ultimate victory. It is through contact with the personal Christ that sin is overcome; it is by entering with Him and through Him into the divine life, that man attains union and reconciliation with God.

Schleiermacher contradicted the inmost principle of the mediæval or Calvinistic theologies, when he declared that in the earthly life of Christ there was to be seen the glorious exhibition of manifested Deity. Calvin had regarded the life of Christ in this world as the humiliation of the Son of God, in which the divine glory was concealed as it were behind a veil, while His glorification, when the universe should behold Him in the fullness of divine exaltation, was reserved to some period in the future when this world should have been swept away. Because Schleiermacher had also risen above the dualism of Latin theology which made the human and the divine alien to each other, the incarnation appeared once more as it had in Greek theology, — the actual manifestation of God in the human, the entrance of the divine into humanity itself, so that Jesus of Nazareth became the revelation of God in His absolute glory. From the time when Augustine wrote his "City of God," the sentiment prevailed in Christendom that the divine kingdom, for whose advent we pray, was to come in some other world in the remote future. In this world the Christian must always remain a pilgrim and stranger, journeying through darkness and danger to the celestial hearthstone. The veil has been upon the face of man and not upon the face of Christ. When Schleiermacher discerned, as by a revelation, in the humble existence of the prophet of Nazareth the unveiled glory of the infinite God, the thought of ages was reversed. This world was seen as if lit up with the light of God: man was introduced even here to the fellowship of saints and angels, to the intimate converse of the only-begotten Son of God with the Father. Or, in the words of an apostle: "Now therefore ye are no more strangers and pilgrims, but fellow-citizens with the saints and of the household of God."

Another principle which Schleiermacher regarded in its larger relationships and restated from a higher point of view was the doctrine of election. The Latin church had called itself Catholic, but its catholicity had been limited by the epithet Roman. In reality it had not aspired to do more than to build up a Latin family: it had been committed to the principle, from the hour of its birth, that part of the human race and not the whole was destined for salvation. Calvinism had only emphasized in a different way that which constitutes the motive of ecclesiasticism in all its forms. So far as the principle is concerned it makes little difference whether it is an election by baptism through the church, or an election of the individual by special decree. The genesis of this belief in election has been already traced in the history of Latin theology to the negation of the truths which constitute the essential features of Christianity. As those truths began to reappear in their pristine strength and beauty in the eighteenth century, the belief in election tended to grow weak and to yield to some higher conviction. To the ideas that religion is included in the sphere of law, that God is the constitutional ruler of the world, responsible to the infinite righteousness which is the charter of the divine activity, that humanity has a common life, and is endowed with native rights which every human government must respect, that God must rule the world for the good of all, and not in the interest of a few, — to these truths, Schleiermacher added the conviction that humanity as a whole had been redeemed in Christ, that grace, no less than law, was the dispensation under which all men everywhere were living. The idea of election in some form will always continue to prevail, as it always has done. To Greeks and to Romans, no less than to the Jews, election was the principle by which they lived. But Schleiermacher gave a different answer to the question, What end was the election intended to serve? He distinguished between the predestination of all men to salvation as the end of their being, and the election which in this world and within the limits of time is able to save only a few in order that all may eventually attain to the same result. Election may still seem an arbitrary principle, but it is necessary in the ordering of this present world. It is a provisional arrangement by which the few are called for the ultimate benefit of the many, not merely to secure their individual salvation. From such a point of view, the belief in election with its wonderful tenacity points to a divine inspiration as its source, which has led nations and institutions and individuals to make their calling and election sure.

Not only the principle of election, but the doctrine of life as a probation, was transformed into a higher and more comprehensive truth by the idea, of which Schleiermacher saw the full bearings, that human life was essentially an educational process, for which no limits could be assigned through conditions of time or place here or hereafter. To Lessing belongs the credit, in his treatise on "The Education of the Human Race," of having first restored a truth, of which it may be said that it solves more problems in theology, as well as in practical life, than any other view which has been suggested. It is to history, and to religion more especially, what the doctrine of evolution, of which it is the anticipation in its highest form, has been to science. That it should have lain dormant from the time of Clement of Alexandria, by whom it received so full an elaboration as a prominent truth in theology, is a suggestive commentary on the intervening ages of history. The belief that humanity as a whole, as well as each individual man, are in this world to begin an education under the tutelage of a divine instructor, lends sacredness to human life under all its manifestations, in every period of its development. Election is therefore an incident of a universal process. Probation also is a necessary accompaniment of a moral history, but its results at any one stage of progress cannot be measured except by the eye of Him who sees things in the perspective of infinity, who as the Teacher of humanity has at His command the resources of omnipotent and omniscient love. The idea of the divine education of the race is also, as it were, the complement to the truth which Kant affirmed so strongly, that the human consciousness is the only authority for the verification of truth. But the reason or consciousness in man is educed by a divine training; the original forces of the soul are trained and enlarged by a process in which converge the course of external nature and all the events of human history. The reason grows from age to age. The reason of the individual can be no standard for the truth until he has lived in the experience of humanity, discerning, however dimly, some measure of the arc which spans the progress of the whole. Into this experience Schleiermacher had entered more deeply than any theologian who had preceded him. Living in the universal reason, he could no longer be hampered by the restricted opinion of Augustinian theology, which had confined all direct revelation to the Jewish people until the coming of Christ. He saw that Christianity was as closely connected with paganism as with Judaism; that, so far as its inner character was concerned, there was no more affinity with it in Judaism than in the higher forms of heathen thought.

Schleiermacher also gave a new definition of the supernatural, which, if accepted, disposed entirely of the questions which had been debated between the rationalists and their opponents. He did not regard miracles as the mark of a divine revelation, nor was it by them that the truth of Christianity is confirmed. He agreed with the deists or rationalists in so regarding the nature of the divine activity in the world, that interpositions or interferences were incongruous or impossible. The sphere of the supernatural includes the whole life of the spirit in man, in so far as it is higher than the life of nature. Christianity, as a revelation or in history, belongs wholly to the region of the supernatural, as do also all of God's relations with the human conscience. But the supernatural as well as the natural falls within the realm of eternal immutable law. While Christianity and the results it produces are supernatural in the truest sense, as belonging to a higher sphere than the natural life of man, yet from another point of view the supernatural is also most truly natural, for it represents the eternal nature of things in the kingdom of the spirit, — it follows a law which is the expression of the inmost mind of God. Hence there is no distinction between natural and revealed religion, though there may be grades in the process of divine revelation. Christianity is revealed, but because it corresponds to the needs and aspirations of man as a spiritual being, it is also a natural religion. The human spirit cannot be divorced from its relationship with God. Since God indwells in humanity, the mind of man is in necessary and continuous contact with an infinite spirit, by whose inspiration alone he is led to know and receive the truth. The reason or consciousness is divinely gifted with the power to read what God imparts. It is as vain as it is irrational to attempt to draw the line between the human reason acting by itself and a divine reason which imparts a revelation. To do so is to separate things that are allied by an inner principle of fitness, to regard man as separated from, or independent of, the action of God.

When such a principle is applied to Scripture, it redeems it from the misinterpretations and abuses which have obscured its meaning. The Bible is the record of God's revelation of Himself in the human consciousness, — a revelation addressed to man through human channels, through reason, through experience, through all the events and discipline of life. It finds, therefore, in the reason or consciousness the confirmation of its truth. The authority of the Bible lies in the appeal which it makes to the reason. Even in its highest utterances, where it reflects the consciousness of Him who was in the fullest sense God immanent in humanity, it still rests for its attestation upon the consciousness in man which is made in the image of God. And this consciousness in man, it is necessary to repeat it, to which is referred the divine revelation as the only authority capable of attesting its truth and preserving it inviolate, is bound in eternal ties to an infinite spirit whose work it is to educate it to its task. It is a consciousness in which lie imbedded the germs of a vast process. It is not an isolated or individual thing. It exists necessarily in relationships: on the one hand with God who is its author, and on the other with humanity. It involves in its highest, completest action the idea of humanity as a corporate whole.

From this point of view is easily seen the derivation of the principles of modern biblical criticism. If the Bible is the record of a progressive revelation, it must contain much in its earlier portions which is superseded, or even contradicted, by the later and higher truth. The deists had been repelled from Scripture because it appeared to sanction what seemed to them irreconcilable with their reason or conscience. They could make no allowances for the imperfections, the half-truths, the unlovely distortions which confronted them in what was claimed to be an inspired, infallible book. But while they were urging the application to religion of immutable law, they were ignorant of the all-inclusive law which runs through human existence, that all things grow from rude beginnings. To the modern mind the Bible would be incomplete, unfit to be the text-book of religion, if it did not include the traces of childhood's faith as well as the matured experience of the perfect man. To look beneath the surface of much that is repugnant to the ideas of a later age, for the presence of the same humanity that speaks in ourselves, bearing witness to its relationship with God, to follow the growth of the conscience as under a divine tuition it rises to more adequate conceptions of God and man, — it is this principle in modern criticism which has given a higher sanctity to Scripture, and imparted to its study a more fruitful interest.

But Schleiermacher did not stop here. He applied the same principle in the criticism of the New Testament. Although evangelists and apostles spake as they were moved by the Holy Ghost, it does not follow that the attribute of infallibility pertains to all their utterances. They were expressing, in accordance with their different temperaments and habits of training, the influence upon their minds of the revelation in Christ, as it was given to them to read it. It is not necessary to reconcile their utterances in some artificial way, to interpret St. Paul in harmony with St. Peter or St. James, or to make any one assertion the standard to which all must bend. The true object of biblical criticism is to ascertain exactly what they thought, and, if possible, why their thought should have taken the shape it did. The different types of Christian teaching in the New Testament point to differing mental and religious attitudes, to differing degrees in the power of apprehending the truth of Christ, or differing points of view in coming to its study. This variety in the interpretation of Christian truth is, in Schleiermacher's opinion, one of the most valuable features of the New Testament, too valuable to be explained away. It further points to the comprehensiveness and true catholicity of the church in its early days. It shows that Christian fellowship does not depend upon agreement in the intellectual apprehension of the truth, but rather upon love and devotion to the personal Christ.

Schleiermacher spoke not only of a religious consciousness in man, whose primary characteristic was the feeling of dependence upon God, but also of what he called the Christian consciousness, — the product of specifically Christian influences during the ages of the church. The fact of a Christ, His teaching, and the events of His life, had entered into history, becoming inwrought, as it were, into the consciousness, as if an essential part of its furniture. For this reason the history of the church became the continuation of a revealing process, in which the action of God, as the indwelling spirit, perpetuated and developed the work of Christ. Wherever the human mind was seen seeking to understand or explain the teaching it had received from Christ, there also the traces of an infinite spirit might be discerned struggling to overcome human errors and infirmities, or enforcing some neglected aspect of Christian truth. A view like this redeemed the study of history from the perversions which, like the Bible, it had suffered from those who claimed it as their own. As in the one case the nature and method of divine revelation, in all its breadth and grandeur, had been sacrificed to the exigencies of what was called the "analogy of faith," so Christian history had been interpreted in accordance with ecclesiastical analogies, whether Latin or Calvinistic or Anglican. It was a wonderful moment in the church's life, when, under the inspiration of Schleiermacher's example, Germany turned away from empty disputes between rationalists and supra-rationalists to study the records of Christian history, with the single purpose of following the Christian principle as it evolved itself in the human consciousness.

It was a feature in Schleiermacher's thought, which commended him to Roman Catholic as well as Lutheran theologians, that he attached the highest importance to the church and its institutions. The effort to escape from the tyranny of the Latin church over the intellect and the conscience had necessarily bred a disposition to regard organized Christianity as a matter of secondary importance. With this tendency the spirit of individualism was in harmony. The doctrine of election, when detached from the ecclesiastical organization with which Augustine had associated it, had led men to feel that salvation was altogether a private or personal affair. The same consequence resulted from the doctrine of probation. In its mediæval interpretation, after Gregory the Great had substituted it as the true theory of life in place of predestination, it was still a process within the church. In the modified Calvinism of the seventeenth century, when probation again displaced election, it was practically presented as a view of life to which the church was not essential; each man was to be saved in his solitariness and isolation; the fellowship of men, desirable as it might be for other reasons, had no necessary organic relationship to the accomplishment of individual destiny. When men had rejected the mediæval idea of the church, which claimed for the clergy peculiar gifts and powers of grace held in trust for the laity, it was not easy to say exactly what purpose the church served in the economy of religion. The deists and rationalists, more particularly, had reached the conclusion that it was an incumbrance and not a help, an antiquated relic of a superstitious age.

Schleiermacher asserted the importance of the church, as vitally related to the well-being of men, with a vigor and directness which even an adherent of the old order might welcome. It is true that the church, as he conceived it, was no longer the hierarchy, or an institution holding a deposit of grace, which might be thought of as separate from the people. He agreed with Wycliffe, with Luther, with Hooker, that it is the congregation of faithful men. But to the church, as thus defined, he assigned the highest significance, making it essential to the realization of human redemption. Salvation, instead of being exclusively an individual process, is accomplished only through the fellowship of the church. The principle of association enters into the religion of Christ as a necessary factor. The Spirit which saves men is a spirit of holy fellowship, seeking to unite them more closely together. It is a spirit of love, and not of selfishness or division. Man is most highly exalted and honored by his membership in a common humanity, of which Christ is the head. It is in his relationship to the race of mankind that he has been redeemed. In the church, as the congregation of faithful men, there is the conscious knowledge of the work of Christ; it is the pledge of a regenerated society to be realized in the future, the picture and the model after which is slowly fashioning itself the kingdom of God in the world. To the church, in this higher conception of its nature, is committed the work, under the Holy Spirit, of educating humanity, by preserving and extending the Christian consciousness till the prayer of Christ is fulfilled. To this end its organization is important; its positive institutions possess a sacred and binding character, — they are essential to the well-being of an external society which proposes to itself no less an end than the conversion of the world to Christ.

The theology of Schleiermacher, if it had been presented to the world under different auspices, or in some other period of the church's history, might have left no impression and been soon forgotten. It shows the change which has come over the church, that such has not been its fate. It is a theology which has grown out of the conditions of modern thought. As truly as Augustine represented his age, and therefore profoundly affected the fortunes of the church, so Schleiermacher still utters the truth to which all that is highest in modern Christianity continues to respond. The spiritual forces which combined to form his thought at the opening of the century have none of them lost their power; as time has gone on they have rather gained in intensity and extended their action more widely. Wherever their influence has been felt, or the influence of any one of them, there has followed, as by a necessary law of human thought, the inclination to pronounce the conclusions which he was the first to draw. His name is held in honor in Germany as that of one from whom dates a "new era in the history of theology." The great German theologians who have come after him have been his disciples. Directly or indirectly his influence has been telling upon every student of religious truth in this country and in England. Even the traditional theology of the Latin church has caught something from his inspiration by which it has been enabled to present its tenets in a fairer light, and to give a more rational account of its origin and place in history.[1]

In other ages Schleiermacher might have passed for a mystic. It is among the changes which his influence has helped to accomplish that what has been called mysticism has at last been legitimatized in the church. Mysticism was indeed but the Latin name for the Greek theology, which had become so unfamiliar that those who, ever and anon, had caught something of its spirit seemed to their contemporaries to be speaking in an unknown tongue. Even Athanasius would have been called a mystic had he lived in the Middle Ages, or in the seventeenth century, when principles so diverse from his own were the axioms of Christian thought. The modern church has given birth to none who are specially designated as mystics, because the essential principle of mysticism has entered as a ruling idea into advancing inquiry in theology.

[1] Among the best known of the German theologians who have acknowledged the influence of Schleiermacher are Neander, Nitzsch, Lücke, Olshausen, Ullman, Julius Müller, Dorner, De Wette, Gieseler, Twesten, etc. Among Roman Catholics, Möhler adopted Schleiermacher's idea of development, applying it as a method of explaining the contents of tradition, in place of the old method of urging the "secret discipline." In this respect even Cardinal Newman must plead guilty of having come under German influences.

As the positive convictions of Schleiermacher, which have wrought the revolution in modern religious thought, are identical with the principles professed by Clement of Alexandria in the second century, so also his negations were the negations of Greek theology. He resisted the spirit and the results of rationalism, so far as they were antagonistic to the interests of genuine Christianity; but he accepted what the last century was almost unanimous in affirming, — that the tenets of Latin theology had no ground in the reason. To him, as to the deists, such beliefs as the total corruption of human nature by Adam's fall, or the expiation of sin by the blood of Christ shed as in a literal sacrifice of the old Jewish dispensation, or the endless punishment of the wicked, were repugnant, — he found them, as he said, neither in the gospel nor in his heart. So also with the doctrine of the trinity, as it had been expounded by Latin theologians. The current conception of personality, when applied to Deity, seemed to him inadequate, as though it limited the nature of God. While he denied the divine personality, in its popular acceptation, and his thought of God in this respect remained vague and unsatisfactory, yet his denial was a preliminary step toward a vaster, more spiritual conception of the nature of Deity. In this respect also he was a type of his age, prophesying by his failures that an hour was coming again in the history of religious thought when the mind would concentrate its energies, as in the ancient church, upon the idea of God. For the same reason that the ordinary idea of personality seemed inapplicable to God, the popular notion of immortality seemed unworthy of belief. That man should simply continue to exist forever in his independence and separateness from God appeared to him as unreasonable as it was undesirable. For immortality, as meaning merely an endless existence, he found no warrant in the instincts of the soul. But to gain an immortal life in God, to lose the individual existence in order to find it again in God in fuller measure, this was the only goal worth placing before humanity, the only view which would emancipate religion from sordid and selfish considerations.

III.

However inadequate may have been Schleiermacher's expression of the larger conception of Deity which he aimed to reach, such a conception was none the less the motive which inspired every attitude of his thought. The doctrine of the immanence of Deity gives to his theology the vast expansion of its range, its profound suggestiveness, its lofty spirituality. A certain tone of exhilaration marks his language, as though the paradisiacal conditions of human life had been restored, as though God were making all things new. As if he breathed the air of a redeemed world redolent with the presence of Deity, in whom he now lived and moved and had his being, as truly as he should do hereafter, he broke forth in those remarkable words which recall the spiritual enthusiasm of his great predecessor in the ancient church: —

"Unenfeebled will I bring my spirit down to life's closing period: never shall the genial courage of life desert me; what gladdens me now shall gladden me ever; my imagination shall continue lively, and my will unbroken, and nothing shall force from my hand the magic key which opens the mysterious gates of the upper world, and the fire of love within me shall never be extinguished. I will not look upon the dreaded weakness of age; I pledge myself to supreme contempt of every toil which does not concern the true end of my existence, and I vow to remain forever young. . . . The spirit which impels man forward shall never fail me, and the longing which is never satisfied with what has been, but ever goes forth to meet the new, shall still be mine. The glory I shall seek is to know that my aim is infinite, and yet never to pause in my course. . . . I shall never think myself old until my work is done, and that work will not be done while I know and will what I ought. . . . To the end of life I am determined to grow stronger and livelier by every act, and more vital through every self-improvement. . . . When the light of my eyes shall fade, and the gray hairs shall sprinkle my blonde locks, my spirit shall still smile. No event shall have power to disturb my heart; the pulse of my inner life shall remain fresh while life endures." [1]

The poet Goethe had felt, like Schleiermacher, the influence of Spinoza, experiencing a profound disturbance in the depths of his being as he received the idea of indwelling God. When applied to nature, it

[1] Hagenbach, *History of the Church in the Eighteenth and Nineteenth Centuries* (Amer. trans.), vol. ii. p. 330.

"In contradistinction, therefore, to the older people, the new people are called young, having learned the new blessings; and we have the exuberance of life's morning prime in this youth which knows no old age, in which we are always growing to maturity in intelligence, are always young, always mild, always new; for those must necessarily be new who have become partakers of the new Word. And that which participates in eternity is wont to be assimilated to the incorruptible; so that to us appertains the designation of the age of childhood, a life-long spring-time, because the truth that is in us, and our habits saturated with the truth, cannot be touched by old age."— *Clement Alex.*, Pædag., i. c. 5.

revealed to him the outer world instinct with a divine life; as he expresses it in "Faust," "the living garment of the Deity." The precocious child who corresponded with him was revealing his spell upon her sensitive imagination, as she wrote, "When I stand all alone at night in open nature, I feel as though it were a spirit and begged redemption of me. Often have I had the sensation, as if nature, in wailing sadness, entreated something of me, so that not to understand what she longed cut through my very heart." In one of his shorter poems Goethe has given an almost dogmatic form to his belief in the immanence of God:—

> "No! such a God my worship may not win
> Who lets the world about His finger spin
> A thing extern: my God must rule within,
> And whom I own for Father, God, Creator,
> Hold nature in Himself, Himself in nature;
> And in His kindly arms embraced, the whole
> Doth live and move by His pervading soul."[1]

Coleridge was to England, both in theology and literature, what Schleiermacher and Goethe were to Germany. The same antecedent influences had entered into his being. Growing up under the traditions of the eighteenth century he had undergone a revolution in his spirit, as he yielded to the magic power which was transforming the age. He read Plato in the light of his Alexandrian commentators; he studied Kant,

[1] "Was wär' ein Gott, der nur von aussen stiesse
Im Kreis das All am Finger laufen liesse!
Ihm ziemt's, die Welt im Innern zu bewegen,
Natur in Sich, Sich in Natur zu hegen,
So dass was in Ihm lebt und webt und ist,
Nie Seine Kraft, nie Seinen Geist vermisst."
From verses entitled *Gott und Welt*.

and more especially Schelling; he also was thrilled by the prospect of a great future for humanity, of which the French Revolution had seemed to him a foretaste; he bent before Spinoza, receiving the full significance of his thought, and yet discerning more clearly than Schleiermacher had done wherein lay the deficiency of the doctrine of the "one substance." It has been said of him, that taking up a volume of Spinoza he kissed the portrait of his face, and said, "This book is a gospel to me;" but he immediately added, "His philosophy is nevertheless false." The weakness of Spinoza's teaching, he went on to affirm, lay in his beginning with an "it is" instead of the "I am." In his desultory poems, where the truth of the divine immanence is seen inspiring his thought, he reveals also the process in his mind accompanying its reception, as though such a belief were unbecoming to weak and sinful man; as if a lower flight were better suited to humanity in its present stage of existence. There are passages, however, in Coleridge's poetry which assert this conviction in language so unqualified that if we did not know how deep and unshaken was his adherence to the personality of God, we might think them the utterances of undisguised pantheism, confounding God with his creation:—

> "'T is the sublime of man,
> Our noontide majesty, to know ourselves
> Parts and proportions of one wondrous whole.
> This fraternizes man, this constitutes
> Our charities and bearings. But 't is God
> Diffused through all that doth make all one whole;
> This the worst superstition, him except
> Aught to desire, Supreme Reality."

Or again, speaking of nature in its relation to God:—

> "And what if all animated nature
> Be but organic harps diversely framed,
> That tremble into thought, as o'er them sweeps
> Plastic and vast one intellectual breeze,
> At once the soul of each, and God of all?"

The true idea of immortality is finely expressed in language that would meet the demand of Schleiermacher's aspiration: —

> "Lovely was the death
> Of Him whose life was love. Holy with power
> He, on the thought-benighted sceptic, beamed
> Manifest Godhead, melting into day
> What floating mists of dark idolatry
> Broke and misshaped the Omnipresent Sire;
> And first by Fear uncharmed the drowsed soul
> Till of its nobler nature it 'gan feel
> Dim recollections; and then soared to Hope,
> Strong to believe whate'er of mystic good
> Th' Eternal dooms for his immortal sons.
> From Hope and firmer Faith to perfect Love
> Attracted and absorbed; and center'd there
> God only to behold, and know, and feel,
> Till, by exclusive consciousness of God,
> All self-annihilated, it shall make
> God its identity; God all in all!
> We and our Father one!"

The spirit of Wordsworth's poetry bears witness to his consciousness of the larger revelation which God was vouchsafing to his age. In its light he saw humanity clothed with a new dignity: even the lowliest and most common things were invested with a sacred charm, because all things were viewed as if in God: —

> "I have felt
> A presence that disturbs me with the joy
> Of elevated thoughts; a sense sublime
> Of something far more deeply interfused,

> Whose dwelling is the light of setting suns,
> And the round ocean and the living air,
> And the blue sky and in the mind of man:
> A motion and a spirit, that impels
> All thinking things, all objects of all thought,
> And rolls through all things."

Even Shelley, who has been set down as an atheist for rejecting, in somewhat contemptuous language, the deism which the popular religious mind had not outgrown, illustrates the working of some deeper, more comprehensive idea of God at the basis of the aspirations, the struggles, the confusions, and the discontent which marked his inner life. "His subtle intellect," says his biographer, "delighted in the thought that behind the universal mind, behind even the life of its life, which he calls spirit, there was some more recondite principle, some more essential substance, the nature of which we cannot imagine or find a name for."

The same influence which was remoulding religious thought and inspiring a fresh literature appears also in art, whose affiliation with theology is of no accidental kind.[1] The founder of a new school arose in Turner, whose greatness lay in his power to represent nature as it appeared after passing through the

[1] "We shall find," says Ruskin, "that the love of nature, wherever it has existed, has been a faithful and sacred element of human feeling; that is to say, supposing all the circumstances otherwise the same with respect to two individuals, the one who loves nature most will always be found to have more capacity for *faith* in God than the other." The devotion to nature, he further remarks, "will be found to bring with it such a sense of the presence and power of the Great Spirit as no mere reasoning can either induce or controvert." "It becomes the channel of certain sacred truths which by no other means can be conveyed."— *Frondes Agrestes*, sect. viii. 62.

medium of the human spirit. The principle of the spiritual interpretation of nature in art, through the power of the human imagination in reading its hidden meaning, was seen by William Blake, to whom religion and artistic insight were identical, though his statement of the principle may seem exaggerated or fanciful: —

"I assert for myself that I do not behold the outward creation, and that to me it is hindrance and not action. What! it will be questioned, 'when the sun rises do you not see a round disc of fire, somewhat like a guinea?' Oh, no! no! I see an innumerable company of the heavenly host, crying Holy, Holy, Holy is the Lord God Almighty. I question not my corporal eye any more than I would question a window concerning a sight. I look through it, and not with it."

It has been a fortunate coincidence that modern science should have been attended by such a companion as modern art, to prevent it from degenerating to a merely physical basis, apart from God and from its inner relations to the human spirit. But science also has contributed to illustrate and enforce the belief that God indwells in His creation. The acknowledgment of its indebtedness to science for the confirmation of this truth is a duty which theology has been slow in rendering. The mystics of the last century were hovering in thought about a mystery contained in nature which had some close connection with the religious life. The mystery was no other than the divine immanence in nature as revealed in the forces whose activity is everywhere governed by eternal, immutable law. Hitherto, in the popular conception of the Middle Ages, as well as under the influence of Calvin's theology, the great processes of nature were believed to be carried on from without by angelic mediators, to each of whom was assigned his special office. It would have been a poor substitute for so beautiful and poetic a belief, if the laws of nature had been shown to be necessary forces apart from God. But when Deity is revealed as immanent in the life of nature, it implies a sense of nearer and closer relationship to God than the angelic host in all its beauty and splendor could ever convey. To have God Himself is the highest reach and aspiration of the soul.

IV.

The influence of any great reformer like Schleiermacher, who opens up a new era in the history of religious thought, may be traced in those who are unprepared to receive the truth which he announces as well as in those who embrace it or carry on its development. To the former it will seem a source only of confusion and disintegration. To the large majority with whom the idea of a personal God was associated with the deistic notion of His separation from the world, all efforts to reach a larger conception of His personality, or to view Him as indwelling in nature and in humanity, seemed to savor either of pantheism or atheism. Such a Deity as Schleiermacher worshiped was to them no God at all. They were lost in a wilderness of vague negations when they attempted to follow the tendencies of modern thought. It seemed as though all definite truth was slipping from their grasp. They could not distinguish between the destructive spirit of the old rationalism and the constructive mood of the new era.

The impulse given by Schleiermacher to biblical

criticism was leading to results which to the minds of many made all revelation seem impossible. They could understand how revelation could be imparted in a book, which had been preserved by ecclesiastical guardians or by some miraculous agency, but they could not see how the revelation of God to man was a continuous process through the reason, through experience, through the courses of history, or through the events and discipline of life. The free handling of Scripture, although in a devout spirit, was to them an endangering of its integrity as the word of God. What was to be the end of it all, what would remain of the Bible, if every man was to be at liberty to select or reject, according to his own judgment, what was true or false? If certain books were to be set aside as having no place in the Canon, who could say by what principle others should be retained? If certain accounts were to be regarded as poetical or allegorical, which had been always thought to be the statements of sober facts, who could tell where romance ended and reality began? If it were once allowed that there were mistakes in Scripture, or irreconcilable discrepancies, if it were admitted that narratives had been exaggerated or colored by the individuality of the writers, or that certain books had been written in the interest of some tendency of opinion, what guarantee had any one of the truth of a divine revelation?

The idea that reason was divine, or that humanity emancipated from the old superstitions was entering upon a higher stage in its career, or that liberty was the inalienable possession of all men, — truths like these which had been identified with the French Revolution, and were believed to have sanctioned its excesses, did not commend themselves to statesmen and ecclesiastics who still imagined that the conduct of the world had been committed to their charge. It had been one of the indirect results of Schleiermacher's influence that he had stimulated a revival of the old ecclesiasticism as well as a higher view of the nature and functions of the church. Even before the reaction began, men were getting tired of the confusion and of the freedom which seemed to mean only license, and were turning again with longing eyes to the "ages of faith" when the church held men in due subjection to authority. The Middle Ages seen by the light shed upon them by the modern study of their history were not as repulsive as an ultra-Protestantism had painted them. To restore the church to its old supremacy seemed to be the one duty of the hour in view of the dangerous tendencies which the democratic principle was encouraging. The treatment which the Roman Catholic church had received in the French Revolution, as well as at the hands of Napoleon, was awakening everywhere a sympathy for the old ecclesiastical order. The French writer, De Maistre, in whom was concentrated, in its most virulent form, the spirit of the rising reaction, denounced the French Revolution and the principles which led to it, as the work of Satan let loose upon the world. To his mind the democratic idea was essentially false in all its manifestations; the Pope was the only saviour of society from impending dissolution. The Jesuit order which had been dissolved by Pope Clement XIV., in the latter part of the eighteenth century, was reconstituted in 1814 by Pius VII.; attention was again directed to the inquisition and the "index of prohibited books," as means for suppressing within the church all knowledge and inquiry not favorable to the dignity and prerogatives of the Roman see. Statesmen united with ecclesiastics in the endeavor to restore and support the church as the best bulwark of society against the destructive tendencies of democratic reform, as well as the no less fatal tendencies of liberalism in theology.

The ecclesiastical reaction was precipitated in England by the movement of a liberal government toward a reform of the church. Already the idea had taken root in the minds of those who were to be its leaders, that the church was too sacred to be touched by the hands of the secular authority. To arouse among the English people a deeper sense of the sanctity of the ecclesiastical organization was one object of the agitation which owned Newman as its leading spirit. But to Newman's mind liberalism in theology was the worst enemy which the church had to encounter,— the source of every other evil which afflicted it. The object of the movement known as Tractarianism, Newman confesses in his "Apologia," was "to hurl back the aggressive force of the human intellect." In order to overcome liberalism, he set himself to restore the idea of the church as it had appeared to the Latin fathers in the early centuries.[1] The first doctrine which he attempted to revive was the "Apostolical Succession," as it had been held by Tertullian, Irenæus, and Cyprian. To the bishops, according to this idea, had been committed the "deposit" of the faith, and at their hands the church must continue to receive it. Tradition must take the place of free inves-

[1] A glance at the *Tracts for the Times* is sufficient to show that it was Latin fathers almost exclusively who received attention from the Tractarian School.

tigation as the sole authority for the truth. Newman felt that the Bible was an unsafe book unless interpreted by the Fathers. He rejected the idea that God revealed Himself through the consciousness of man, or that the human reason was an evidence of the indwelling of a divine reason. "If I looked," so he said, " into a mirror and did not see my face, I should have the sort of feeling which actually comes upon me when I look into this living, busy world, and see no reflection of its Creator. The sight of the world is nothing else than the prophet's scroll, full of lamentation, mourning, and woe." God and humanity to his mind were alien to each other, — the human race was implicated in some terrible aboriginal calamity. " The tendency of the human reason is toward a simple unbelief in matters of religion. No truth, however sacred, can stand against it in the long run." To the discoveries of modern science, that the powers which control the life of nature are immanent in nature, Newman was indifferent. God was separated from nature as from humanity. It was angels who conducted as mediators the processes of the external world ; or in his own exquisite language, whose beauty might make one oblivious to the higher truth : "Every breath of air and ray of light and heat, every beautiful prospect is, as it were, the skirts of their garments, the waving of the robes of those whose faces see God." [1]

[1] One of the worst evils which has been wrought by the ecclesiastical reaction in the nineteenth century has been the breach between religion and science. Their relation in the last century has not only not been retained, but has given way to an actual hostility, the fault of which lies mainly at the door of the church : "Le théologien compromet les augustes vérités dont il est le dépositaire dans une lutte impossible avec des vérités moins

From such a position there followed naturally a return to Latin theology in all its details. Starting from the same premises as the Latin fathers of the second century, Newman lived over again in his experience the course of Latin history. It became gradually more evident that there was nothing in Latin Christianity which was repugnant to his mind. The sacraments appeared again as the conduits of grace; the soul was fed from without by supernatural influences lodged in the episcopate, and conveyed to the people through a priesthood receiving its divine consecration in the sacrament of ordination. He made one last effort to harmonize the Latin theology with the Articles of the Church of England, before he recognized where his logic was driving him, and, in the customary phrase of ecclesiastical circles, transferred his adherence to the Latin obedience. His life has been a parable to his age. Side by side with men who had attained a higher view, he pursued his re-

hautes, mais plus saisissantes et plus palpables. La science physique s'est ainsi constituée en dehors de la religion ; par cela même elle est devenue impie. La science est coupable d'avoir accepté cet exil qui l'eloignait du monde moral ; elle aurait dû forcer les portes du sanctuaire par ses supplications. La théologie n'aurait pu lui refuser place au banquet spirituel. N'y vient-elle pas apporter pour écot mille vérités sublimes qui rendent la Providence plus manifeste, tout un aspect de l'infini, et comme une part de Dieu lui-même retrouvé dans la Nature ! Osons le dire, la faute première est a la théologie ; elle a précédé la science, elle est son ancêtre logique et sa mère dans l'ordre des temps ; elle aurait dû l'élever dans son sein, et la nourrir de son lait, elle l'a repoussée de l'Eglise comme une autre Agar, elle l'a rejetée dans le désert du matérialisme et les nombreuses tribus engendrées d'Ismaël s'élèvent contre la postérité légitime d'Abraham." — De Laprade, *La Nature avant le Christianisme*, p. xcvii.

actionary way; what to them was as light, to him was as darkness; he began with skepticism and ended by disowning that which was most divine.

There were other elements [1] in the Tractarian movement than that which was represented by Newman, though he must always remain its most logical and consistent exponent. The Latin infusion was not so strong in either Pusey or Keble. Pusey, indeed, believed in asserting ecclesiastical tradition as the main defense against what he took to be the skepticism of modern thought. As with Newman, what to others appeared as a divine revelation was to his mind a dangerous infidelity. A recent writer has said of him, that "his religious seriousness was the condition

[1] The current of the Tractarian movement received accessions from various minor tributaries. There gravitated naturally toward it, "the martyrs of disgust," as they have been so aptly called, who were repelled by what seemed to them the vulgar familiarity with God which was found in the evangelical school, whether in the Church of England or among the Non-conformists. Here, also, at the root of the disaffection, may be traced a certain " blind desire" to realize in God some deeper, more mysterious relationship than found expression in the type of piety represented by Newton, Scott, or Simeon. Witness the language of the saintly Faber, who, like others, disowned with a bitter contempt his evangelical antecedents: "The dreadful facility of turning to God inculcated there (in the evangelical school) throws such a complete mist over the face of the sacraments that it perverts and distorts all my views of the symmetry of the scheme of Redemption. It seems as if I could never get free from the entanglements of that base theology. However, it is in such difficulties as these that I find the doctrine of the Church such an inestimable privilege. There I cease to be an individual. I seem to fall into my own place quietly, and without disturbance; and the noiseless path of childlike obedience, slow as my progress must be, here a little and there a little, offers a calm and peaceful progress of spiritual growth." — Faber's *Life and Letters*, p. 72.

of one who not only believed, but was penetrated in his whole being with the belief, that God *had made a communication to men.*"[1] Such also was the profound conviction of Latin theologians from the time of Tertullian. It might have been said of Dr. Pusey's great contemporary, the late Mr. Maurice, that he was only asserting another phase of belief among those Catholic fathers whom the Tractarians neglected, when he proclaimed that God had never ceased to make a communication to men; that now, as always, He revealed Himself, by the law of His being, in the reason, the conscience, the experience of humanity. To neither Pusey nor Keble was it given to read this law of the divine life, in the order of nature or in the courses of history. And yet they, and others like them, were aspiring for a higher truth than they could find in the current belief of Protestant Christendom.

The Church of England, as an institution, had hitherto been unmoved by the influences that created the evangelical awakening of the last century. If a new life was to enter the Church of England, it must come in some other way. The popular belief that

[1] Rev. E. F. Talbot, Warden of Keble College, in *Fortnightly Review*, March, 1884. He also remarks : " There was a passage in the Canon concerning preachers, passed in the very synod which imposed the thirty-nine articles, which was a kind of *locus classicus* with the Tractarians, and which ran, 'Let them teach nothing in sermons . . . except what is agreeable to the doctrine of the Old and New Testaments, or what Catholic fathers and ancient Bishops have gathered from the same doctrine.' " That there might be any divergence of a decided and important character among the " Catholic fathers" which affected every tenet of the received theology, was a fact not taken into consideration.

God acted in an irregular, spasmodic manner, as in revivals, by occasional effusions of grace, was repugnant to those who had unconsciously come under the influence of the modern principle, — that the spiritual life is part of an eternal order, and not at the mercy of the transient moods of the soul. The doctrines of apostolical succession, of baptismal regeneration, and of sacramental grace, seemed to the minds of the leaders in the Tractarian movement to be expressive of a divine order, — a divine supply to human needs, granted in no fitful way, but as regular in its action as the laws in accordance with which planets move. From another, and that a higher point of view, these doctrines were but symbols of an order which included not only the elect in the Church of England, or its supposed branches, but also all humanity, — the law that God is always and everywhere seeking to impart Himself to human souls, employing to this end all the events and circumstances of life. Because the Anglican leaders were still hampered by Augustinian or Calvinistic notions of election, they were blind to the larger scope of the law of the spiritual life ; they were forced to contradict their own principle, and to hold that, in the case of the vast number of Protestant Christians who could not depend upon the apostolical succession, God was obliged to act in irregular ways. Their view of the divine life was too narrow in its range ; it shut out more than it included ; it implied, when closely examined, irrationality and confusion. And yet with all its defects it marks an advance ; it shows how the spirit of the age acts even upon those who set themselves to resist it.

Of the Tractarian movement it may be further remarked that, in its theory of the church, there was a desire to escape from that national conception of the Church of England which isolated it from the larger outlying life of Christendom. The leaders of the movement separated sharply between those bodies who had the so-called apostolic succession and those who had not; but they sought to overcome the effects of the principle which cut them off from fellowship with their Protestant brethren, by tying more closely to the older historic churches, in which the succession had been preserved. For the purposes of their theory it made no difference that their advances toward fellowship with the Greek and Latin churches were coldly, or even contemptuously met.[1] It was something still

[1] How the Tractarian idea of the church, which was only the old Latin idea rehabilitated, was received by the Greek church, has been shown in W. Palmer's *Visit to the Russian Church*, lately edited by Cardinal Newman. In the Preface, the editor sums up the result of this labored effort to get the Russo-Greek church to commit itself to an unwelcome theory: "Some of their highest prelates and officials go out of their way to deny altogether, or at least to ignore the catholicity, as recognized in the creed, as if their time-honored communion was but a revival of the ancient Donatists. They say virtually, even if not expressly, we know nothing about unity, nothing about catholicity; it is no term of ours," etc. But let one of these high officials speak for himself: "It (the church) seems to me like a great sphere revolving round the sun. All the different churches and sects are attracted to the same centre and revolve around the same centre, but at different distances; the church which is simply true orthodox and catholic, *i. e.*, the Eastern, being the nearest, and being joined to it by a more close and legitimate connection; but of the rest, some are further off, some nearer, without there being any distinct separation or difference in kind." p. 271. M. Sidonsky, a professor of philosophy, remarked, "Nothing has forced us hitherto to consider the question of the definition of the Visible Church. When our circumstances require it, it will no doubt be examined." p. 250. Mr. Palmer seems to have gone to Russia with the impression that its church

to be able to feel, in accordance with the notion that now began to prevail, that the church was divided into three great branches, — the Greek, the Roman, and the Anglican, although by some dark and mysterious dispensation all fellowship between them was suspended.

The Church of England was reviving its spiritual life by a law of its own constitution. As a church, it had not forgotten its historic existence, running back through the ages. It resisted the efforts of hostile sects to make it become like one of them, a product of the Reformation. Everywhere were visible the landmarks that pointed to an ancient lineage. Its cathedrals, its churches, its ritual, its order, were the product of a piety long antecedent to the revolution by which it had been severed from its fellowship with Rome. It was easy for the leaders of the Tractarian movement to accept the principle that the continuity of the divine action upon humanity through the church had never been broken. Instead of that feeling which had prevailed in the eighteenth century, that the life of the church before the Reformation was a thing to be discarded as a memory of shame and degradation, there spread the conviction that the church's record in history might be recalled with a sense of pride and triumph. In the historic life of the church lay the evidence that God had never left the world to itself; that the life of Christ had been somehow perpetuated in the life of the ecclesiastical organization.

This was, indeed, the same truth which Schleier-

already accepted the Latin idea of catholicity, and with the purpose to induce it also to accept and act upon the Anglican modification, known as the branch theory, — that the Catholic church was Greek, Roman, and Anglican.

macher had proclaimed, whose reception in Germany was leading to a revolution in the methods of studying the church's history. But the Tractarians held it with limitations which weakened or perverted its true significance. They were unable, for this reason, to discriminate between that which was transient or provisional and that which was permanent. They confined themselves mainly to a study of Latin theology or the revival of a Latin ritual, oblivious to a higher theology with a better lineage than that which descended through Latin Christendom. Like every great principle which is seized with rapture by the imagination and imperfectly apprehended by the reason, the doctrine of historical continuity was so presented as to lead the church in a false direction. There arose a contempt for Protestantism in all its forms, for its theology, and for its methods of cultivating the religious life. Men talked of the historical continuity of the Church of England, but there was one ugly fact in its history which they wished might be blotted out, — that it had been implicated in the disgraceful, so-called, reforms of the sixteenth century. There was a continuity in the life of Christendom, but they could not conceive it as including a Luther, a Zwingle, or a Calvin. Hence the tendency to Latinize the Church of England, to make it a mere satellite of the Church of Rome, which had been the unconscious purpose of Newman in the days of his greatest influence, still continued to operate, carrying back to the fold of Rome hundreds of its clergy and thousands of its laity.

The presentation of the principle of historical continuity, as apprehended by Newman or Pusey or Keble, was indeed absurd and self-contradictory. To talk of the continuous incarnation of Christ in the world as dependent upon "apostolic succession," or the communication of the life of God to the soul, as involved in the validity of sacraments administered by those who have been episcopally ordained, carries with it its own condemnation. As one takes a look at things as they are, its falsity is manifest enough without any serious refutation. But obsolete beliefs like these revived in the nineteenth century may yet have served a different purpose or led in a different direction than when first announced by Tertullian or Cyprian. The drift of the age and its counter-currents must be taken into consideration as forces which modify all statements of truth. Such beliefs may even tend to reflect the larger spirit which dominates the time when they reappear; they may be efforts even to give it expression, taking this shape as the most convenient clothing in which to present themselves to the popular mind. Some living truth may be incased in a mouldering husk which is unsightly and repulsive, — a great reality be implied beneath a teaching which, in its literal form, seems like a grotesque caricature of Christ's religion. The idea of apostolical succession may be interpreted as a testimony of the human conscience to the belief that God is a God of order and not of confusion. Its preservation in the church for eighteen centuries — admitting the fact for the sake of the argument — may testify to the vitality of ecclesiastical institutions as surviving through all the changes of society, the dissolution and fall of empires, through calamities so great that they threaten to wipe away all traces of civilization. The emphasis laid upon the exact form in which the sacraments are to be administered, while concealing, or even distorting, their significance, may be a testimony to the truth that the spiritual life is part of an eternal order based upon a law which knows no exception; that the relationship of man to God is an immutable fact, not dependent upon the passing phases of depression or exhilaration which mark the emotions. Whatever men may have thought or still think of the sacraments, however materialistic or superstitious the notions which obscure their meaning, they still remain to all in the ages of illumination or the ages of darkness, whether men can read or are too illiterate to do so, they remain the two great symbols, the two instructive monuments of Christianity, pointing to an actual relationship with God. Baptism is the witness to a divine power which purifies from sin; the Lord's Supper testifies to the incarnate Word as forever giving Himself to the soul, to the communication of the divine life to the human spirit, the eternal reason to human thought.

The Tractarian school refused to read the lesson which the French Revolution so impressively taught. Its leaders distrusted the instincts of humanity; they feared the reason as a dangerous possession; they sought to restore the priesthood as it ruled in the ages when men could not think for themselves, as it had impersonated the conscience when the conscience could find no other utterance. The overthrow of the Roman Catholic church in France might have shown them that if humanity is to receive the teaching of Christ, it must be because there is an inward aptitude for its reception, not because it is imparted on some external authority. Here lay the weakness of the Anglican revival in the hour of its birth, that it dared not trust the divine constitution of man. There was no recognition of the truth that the incarnation was the light of the eternal reason addressing itself to the reason in man as akin to its own essential nature. It was this distrust which vitiated its scholarship and the value of its patristic learning.[1] It showed no love of truth for its own sake. The study of the past was undertaken in order to confirm a foregone and erroneous conclusion. History was written on the principle which throws out pamphlets in a time of confusion with their special pleading for some partisan purpose.

The skepticism which lurked beneath the Augustinian and Calvinistic theologies is also to be seen in the Tractarian movement. It is implied in its very attitude of disowning the reason, of seeking refuge in some remote, obscure principle of external authority which the reason is forbidden to examine. The Tractarian reaction may be said to have culminated as a movement in thought, when Professor Mansel, in his Bamp-

---

[1] "The Tractarian movement," says Tulloch, "was in no sense a scientific movement. It threw no light on theological or scientific difficulties. It travestied rather than studied church history, and instead of seeking to explain its great epochs, it made a mere polemical quarry of them for the support of foregone conclusions. It scouted the idea of new light; its pride was to reproduce old traditions and 'Catholic' dogmas. It not only held no key to the great movements of Christian thought in the past, but it blundered over the simplest of them, as Cardinal Newman did so notably in the history of the Arians of the fourth century. What may be said to be now a commonplace in all historical inquiry, that every great epoch in the formation of opinion is the product of all the forces operating in the preceding time, and therefore so far justified in the very fact of its existence, — that it is a living growth in short, and not a mechanical manipulation of parties, — was never realized by them. They took their stand on an imaginary platform of their own, which they identified with Christian antiquity."

ton Lectures on the "Limits of Religious Thought," attempted to defend on a philosophical basis the skeptical principle that God was the unknown and the unknowable. In the name of orthodoxy he boldly avowed what has since been designated as Agnosticism. In theology, as in philosophy, the difficulties which beset the human mind in its effort to find out God were to his mind insoluble. Since even to think of God implied irreconcilable contradictions in the very nature of thought, religion must rest upon some other authority than the reason. The true attitude of reason toward things divine is that of simple acquiescence in what purports to be an authoritative revelation. Like Calvin, whom in his formal theology he so closely followed, he maintained that revelation is a purely regulative affair. Whether God has revealed to us His inmost nature we have no means of knowing. He has imparted what He wills that man should receive. Mr. Mansel accepted the methods of Kant in demonstrating that such a Deity as the popular mind had been taught to receive was impossible to the reason. Of the two alternatives, that of retaining the lower conception of God in defiance of the reason, or of rising to a higher conception in harmony with the reason, he chose the former, falling back upon some supposed external authority for its support. He rejected the intuitional theology, as he called it, asserting the necessity for traditional dogmas which the higher development of the conscience had outgrown, because they seemed to him, without inquiry into their origin or meaning, to form a part of that authoritative revelation which man was bound to receive even in defiance of his reason. The controversy which took place between him and Mr. Maurice, in which the latter called attention to the question, "What is revelation," is perhaps the most significant one in the whole history of the church since Athanasius stood up to resist the Arians on a similar, if not the same identical issue.

The ecclesiastical reaction which was led by Newman in England was felt throughout all Christendom. The same desire "to hurl back the aggressive forces of the human intellect," was manifested in the church of Rome, in the Lutheran and Reformed churches, whether on the continent, in England, or America, wherever Christian thought was still resting on its old basis. Tractarianism, Romanticism, Ritualism, Millenarianism, all the theologies of fear and despair arose to contest the larger truth. It is now fifty years since Newman arose with his "fierce thoughts against a liberalism that was invading the church." Two generations of men have passed away while the conflict has been going on between the advocates of a higher theology and a larger faith, and those who were bent on maintaining Christianity as it had been handed down in Latin tradition. With the third generation, as Isaac Taylor was fond of remarking, there comes a change of outlook.

As we review the history of the ecclesiastical reaction, which now shows signs of having spent its force, it is safe to say that the crusade against the human reason, in which Newman was a leading representative, has not been successful. The free investigation which he deprecated in dread of its tendencies and results has been carried on with unabated ardor. If there is danger from its activity, it is because the flood of light may bewilder us, which has been thrown upon the Bible, upon the history of the church, upon the ways of God in revealing Himself to the human spirit. The time is ripe for quiet reflection upon the results which have been achieved. What the age now demands is the enforcement of the principles for which the reason has been furnishing the materials in superabundant measure. The effort to repress the reason has come too late in the world's history to attain success. The tide of things is setting more and more strongly against ecclesiastical obscurantism. Even reactions against the reason are lifted up into a higher sphere, and serve the cause of God against their will. We owe another debt to Newman and to Mansel, than those we generally acknowledge. The one has shown in a typical way, which has had no such illustration since the conversion of Augustine, how distrust of the reason must logically end in acknowledging an infallible pope; the other in his chivalric attempt to defend the traditional dogmas or to overcome the Germanism, as he called it, which was infecting the church, could accomplish his purpose only by cutting away the foundations on which the possibility of a revelation rests. These instances teach us anew that modern Christianity is committed to progress and growth in the knowledge of God and of His revelation. If it is dangerous to advance, it is only more dangerous to retreat. The human reason at last is free, and is increasingly realizing what freedom means. Christianity must now trust, as indeed it is trusting, to its own merits for its vindication to the reason. It must stand or fall as it can show itself to be true.

The term reaction, when applied to the movement we have been considering, may mean that there are neglected aspects of truth which need to be reasserted. A reaction is, as it were, a check applied to the wheels of progress lest it go too rapidly for the good of all. In every reaction there is a backward look, as if before the church committed itself to a great advance, it were necessary to take a careful survey of the past, in order that nothing which is true should be left behind. The church, like the world, possesses a conservative spirit, requiring that every step forward be carefully tested, offering an opposition, which, despite its blindness or irrationalism, serves the cause of truth by becoming its foe. It has been among the advantages of the reaction of the nineteenth century, that it has served to preserve a home for those who were not prepared for the advance. It has done also a great service to the cause of theology by keeping before us the life of the past in such a vivid and living way that all that was true and enduring in the ages that are gone is still before our eyes to be read and interpreted. In this way it has also clarified our vision by revealing the concrete evils that obstruct the reception of the larger thought. It has illustrated impressively the truth which Schleiermacher taught, that the church as the fellowship of men under the consciousness of a relationship to God is essential to human salvation in its truest sense. It has again borne witness by the revival of Christian activities, that such a church alive to its social obligations is the strongest evidence of the incarnation of Christ.

V.

The representative process of the nineteenth century in its spiritual history has been the transition from the deistic conception of a God outside of the universe to the Christian idea of God as indwelling in His creation. It has been a process illustrated in the mental history of every religious thinker who has been seeking for a larger and truer theology. It is a process which may be studied in its various degrees of completeness. With some it has been so imperfectly apprehended as to lead to merely negative results. They have rejected the traditional view of Deity which has been so long identified with Latin or with Protestant theology, but they have assumed that, in the nature of the case, there could be nothing to take its place. They have professed themselves atheists, rejoicing to believe that there is no God, or have called themselves agnostics, maintaining that if there be a God He cannot be known. They have sought for substitutes for the discarded belief, such as the worship of humanity, thinking to find in it an ideal worthy of their highest devotion. Others still, after struggling to reduce to some intelligible objective form the vague intuitions, as they deem them, by which they have obtained glimpses of a higher truth, have renounced it all as unprofitable and vain, falling back to the old idea, despite the protest of the reason, in order to obtain a "definite faith" by which they may live and train their children. We hear impressive voices warning us of the danger of advance or sounding the note of retreat.[1] As the century draws toward its close, which

[1] The following may be taken as a representative utterance: "Quand il est bien établi que Dieu n'est pas immanent, mêlé au

opened with a boundless prospect whose beauty thrilled the soul, the intellectual confusion seems to have increased rather than abated, — a state of things from which the ecclesiastical reaction continues to profit.

There must be some hidden weakness or defect in what we call our modern theology which accounts for what seems to many its failure to make good the place of what has been rejected. The intellectual confusion is no sign, it is true, of failure; it may be also viewed as the necessary condition of progress. But it is not a state of things whose permanence is desirable. It certainly becomes us to labor for its removal.

It is by reverting again to Schleiermacher's attitude in theology that we may discover one source of the weakness which embarrasses our progress. He grounded religion in the feelings, or the deep instincts and sentiments of our nature. He used his great dialectic power within certain limits to interpret the feelings in the language of the intellect. But he paused at the idea of God; Deity he maintained was incomprehensible, except through the feeling; only through the pious affection could the Infinite and the Eternal one be known.[1] His idea of God remained

---

monde, tout péril de malentendu grave est écarté. . . . Revenous à ces simples expressions de la vieille métaphysique, pour désigner Dieu: la première Cause, l'Être des êtres, en y ajoutant l'attribut qui détermine le mieux son rapport avec le monde, l'intelligence." — Caro, *L'Idée de Dieu*, pp. 386, 387.

[1] It is common to hear Schleiermacher, as also Coleridge, Hegel, and others, spoken of as pantheists. The term, however, has never been defined. It was generated in the deistic atmosphere of the last century, and was applied to those who dissented from the mechanical notion of God as the distant architect of the universe. It seems also to have been regarded, and quite naturally, as equivalent to atheistical. Bayle, for example, charges

in consequence incomplete and unsatisfactory; it may have met a certain transitory demand when the mind was escaping from a notion of personality which limited the Divine being after some inferior anthropomorphic conception; but it was no final resting-place for the heart or the reason. The thought about God must control all other thought. If our idea of Him be so vague or imperfect that it can find no expression in language, or if the attempt to find some approximate expression is forbidden as undertaking the impossible, then uncertainty and vacillation will be apt to attach to all the results of religious inquiry. The appeal to the feelings, as that consciousness in man by which all truth is attested, may be the necessary beginning of a great era in religious history, but to stop with the feelings is to disown another part of our nature which imperatively demands that it shall not be sacrificed.[1]

Spinoza with having introduced, not pantheism, but atheism, into theology. The term seems to have been first used by Toland, who applied it to himself. It is a word still associated in the minds of many with the opprobrium of a deistic antipathy, but it is also used in another and a higher sense. What its future destiny may be is still uncertain. See article Pantheismus, in Herzog, *Real-Encyklopädie*.

[1] A recent writer, speaking of what is called the "New Theology," remarks: "But the new theology will not be wise above what is written. The fundamental facts of revealed religion are received in their simplicity. Theories about the application of the facts to the spiritual needs of men are not formulated. Thus, we are agreed upon the truth that 'God was in Christ reconciling the world unto himself;' but we do not attempt to unravel the interior workings of the divine nature, that clothes the man of Nazareth with the habiliments of the superhuman. In like manner, the doctrine of the trinity is accepted for its practical worth, as a revelation of the many-sidedness of God; while all endeavors to define the doctrine, on the basis of tri-personality, are abandoned to those ingenious persons who are

The appeal to the feelings or instincts is made in order to gather fresh materials for the use of the reason. Even if the mind fail to do justice to the whole content of the consciousness of humanity, as it is disclosed in history, it is still bound to make the effort, and to continue to repeat it, notwithstanding successive failures.

It has been said that the nineteenth century resembles more closely the age that gave birth to Greek theology than any intervening age in history. The comparison holds true in some respects to which attention should be emphatically called. Schleiermacher closely resembled, both in his general attitude as well as in the principles he set forth, Clement of Alexandria, the great founder of Greek theology. But the age of Clement was succeeded by that of Origen and Athanasius, when new conditions required that just that which Clement had left undetermined should be definitely expressed if the truth of the incarnation was to be retained as the one all-important, all-inclusive idea which gave unity to human thought, or made the history of mankind intelligible. Schleiermacher, in consequence of the deficiency of his thought regarding God, illustrated again the process of thought in the

fond of enigmas." What is it that is *written*, unless it be upon the human reason, which is an integral part of our spiritual nature? Why should we not, if we are made in God's own image, attempt to unravel the interior workings of the divine nature? If we have abandoned the traditional misconception of the trinity, why must we be forbidden to define the doctrine in some truer formula? Is the use of reason in religion to be confined to those ingenious persons who are fond of enigmas? And what difference is there in principle between such an attitude in theology and that of the Roman Catholic church which disowns the reason as dangerous?

ancient church in his disposition to adopt what was called Sabellianism,[1] of which it may be sufficient to say that its tendency was to destroy the historic reality of the life of Christ, and thus eventually to return, like Arianism, to the deistic conception of God.

But, in another respect, the resemblance between our own age and the early church is a striking one. Once more in history we are confronted by the same problem with which the Greek fathers were occupied, and in substantially the same form. Like the Greek philosophers of the Neo-Platonic school, they aimed to reconcile the idea of the divine immanence, which had been the groundwork of all their culture, with the idea which was then invading the sphere of thought as well as of religion, that God was outside of the world, existing in solitude and passivity apart from the creation. The process of reconciliation between these two conceptions of Deity, neither of which would give way to the other, was begun by Origen and completed by Athanasius in the doctrine of the trinity, according to which transcendent Deity, as the eternal Father, the mysterious background or abyss of all existence, is united by a holy and infinite Spirit with immanent Deity — the eternal Son by whom and for whom all things were made and in whom all things consist, who in the fullness of time became flesh and dwelt amongst us, the glory of the invisible Father, full of grace and truth. The problem is the same for us, but we approach it in history in our own way. Then the idea of immanent Deity was already beginning to fade out of the consciousness; now it is slowly returning after centuries of abeyance. We bring with us a conviction of the divine transcendence which has been the basis

---

[1] See *ante*, p. 76.

of thought and experience through so many generations, both in Latin and Protestant Christendom, that to escape from it is impossible, and we seek to reconcile with it the conviction of the immanence of God, which is enforced upon us by the deeper, utterances of the consciousness, by all that is highest in the researches of modern life, whether in history, in science, in art, in philosophy, or in religion.

Hegel was Schleiermacher's successor in the order of thought, although contemporaneous with him in the order of time. He was the continuator in the modern church of the mystic succession to whose representatives John Scotus, Eckart, and Böhme, he acknowledged his relationship. But his system goes back for its fundamental principle to Origen and Athanasius. The statement of Hegel may differ in form from that of ancient Greek theology, but it is the same thing in its essential principle. His idea of Deity going forth out of Himself in order to return again in a self-conscious process through the mediation of the spirit is not essentially different from Origen's doctrine of the "eternal generation of the Son," upon which Athanasius stood when he announced the Christian formula of the trinity. If, according to the belief to which the church is committed, God exists in the triune distinction of Father, Son, and Holy Ghost, then this distinction must underlie all thought or experience of His presence and operations in the world. It was characteristic of the Latin theology that it formally accepted the doctrine of the trinity, and then reasoned about God on an Arian or deistic basis, as if the trinity were a sort of accidental attachment to His essence, to be used for a *Deus ex machina* as occasion demanded. The same was true of Calvin and his successors. The clear vision of the eighteenth century rejected such a trinity, which seemed to have no organic relationship to the outer world or to the life of man. Hegel stands for the restoration of the Athanasian or Nicene formula, as having its ground in the reason, which is also the vehicle of revelation, — as the one essential truth in philosophy or in theology, without which we are unable to elicit the meaning of nature or the course of human history.[1]

[1] The history of theology in England, so far as it has been influenced by Coleridge and by Maurice who was his disciple, has been guided by the principle of Hegel rather than that of Schleiermacher. Coleridge in his early life, while still under the influence of eighteenth century traditions, became a Unitarian minister. But acquaintance with Schelling's philosophy, which is akin in its theological bearings to Hegelianism, led him to see the larger relationships of the trinity to human reason as well as human life, so that a doctrine which had seemed to him irrational or absurd from the stand-point of deism, became of vital importance in his maturer thought. In this respect Coleridge has been followed by Maurice, the greatest of modern English theologians. He, too, fought his way through the representative struggle of the age, — from deism to the Christian idea of God. The application of the doctrine of the trinity to the spiritual needs of man, or as the clew to the interpretation of human history, may be said to constitute the substance of Maurice's theology. More than any other modern theologian was he in accord with the fundamental principle of Hegel. It is this which explains his obscurity to those not yet emancipated from deistic notions, or who regard the trinity as an attachment to the idea of God, to which justice has been done in acknowledging it as a Catholic tradition. It is strange that Maurice should have given so little attention to the one man whose philosophical thought he reproduced in its practical and religious bearings.

The life of Maurice, lately published, brings out one fact of considerable importance, namely, that he thought English theology must always remain different from German, because it started

It is sometimes said that Hegel has been discredited in his own country, that his philosophy has been shattered into fragments.[1] It may be that the details of the system as expounded by the master must undergo revision. It may be that a further preliminary process is necessary before the full significance of his principles can be generally discerned. There is still much to be done in fields which Hegel did not exhaust before an intelligent assent or denial can be given to his generalizations. He lived in an age when the materials were collecting for a great ecclesiastical reaction, the spirit of which was also affecting other departments of inquiry than theology. It may be for these

from a different principle and followed a different method. Cf. i. p. 253. "Bunsen's book on the Church of the future taught me clearly what I had suspected before, that every earnest German must begin with the Spirit, that he may come to learn something of the Father and the Son. I am as certain as I can be of anything, that our process is the opposite one, that we must begin from the Father in order that we may know something of the Son and of the Spirit." See, also, ii. p. 468. "We (English and Germans) must be to a considerable extent unintelligible to each, because we start from exactly opposite points; we, naturally, from that which is above us and speaks to us; they, naturally, from that which is within them and which seeks for some object above itself. . . . I am most anxious to assert the worth of our English position, to prove that truth must look down upon us, if we would look up to it; that Truth must be a person seeking us, if we are to seek him." But this distinction may be said to also mark the difference between Schleiermacher and Hegel.

[1] "For any one whose view is not limited by words or superficial appearances, it is not difficult to see that, in the scientific life of Germany as of other countries, there is no greater power at present than Hegelianism, especially in all that relates to metaphysics and ethics, to the philosophy of history and of religion." — Professor Caird, in his *Sketch of Hegel.*

among other reasons that the religious thought of the age seems to have halted for a moment as if realizing the mighty change which the full acceptance of the Christian doctrine of the trinity involves. A great position like this is not taken without many defeats and many successive assaults on the citadels of tradition and prejudice. In this respect history teaches us the lesson of the patience of hope.

The effort of Hegel to find in the trinity the comprehensive formula which explains the phenomena of nature and the course of human history, has been followed by what has seemed the most destructive attack upon the verities of the Christian faith in the annals of Christianity. The criticism of the last century appears like trifling compared with the attempt of Strauss to reduce to a myth the facts of the gospel history. The author of this famous theory claimed to be applying the teaching of Hegel more fully and consistently when he practically denied the historic reality of the events relating to the life of Christ, making Christ Himself only an ideal creature of the human imagination. It was fortunate, if we may so speak, in a world where God is present as the one controlling force in the evolution of history, that the attack of Strauss should have coincided with the ecclesiastical revival whose object it was to reassert with a new vigor the historic personality of Christ, calling attention anew to the history of the church as the best evidence of its reality. But dangerous as the attack may seem, there is a point of view from which it may be regarded as a hopeful sign for the future of theology. It shows that the age has become conscious of the antagonism, the deepest, the most significant that is involved in the true apprehension of Christianity.

We have already seen [1] how the Latin church, when it began its independent career, lost the vision of the spiritual, essential Christ in its effort to know Christ after the flesh or to realize His earthly existence through a more vivid portrayal of His earthly environment. He who was the light that lighteth every man that cometh into the world, or as Greek theologians, Justin, Clement, Origen, and Athanasius had expressed it, the Eternal reason in whom humanity participated in virtue of its constitution, by whom the world in every age had been enlightened, by whom even Socrates was a Christian, as Justin had said, though but in part, — this conception of the higher spiritual Christ, the Latin church had sacrificed in order to emphasize and make its own the historical fact of an incarnation. It is not strange, therefore, that when Christ after the spirit had been once more apprehended in the fullness of His relationship to humanity, Christ after the flesh should have seemed like a limitation which hindered the appreciation of His true character. It is not strange that to Strauss and others, the events recorded in the narrative of His life should have appeared as so many efforts to express in tangible forms the idea of a being who was beyond and above the limitations of humanity. It may even have been necessary that for a moment in the church's history men should have refused, like St. Paul, to know Christ any more after the flesh, in order that they might discern more clearly the spiritual relationship by which Christ in man, and no longer outside of him, becomes the transforming power of a new creation. The work of Strauss has shown the Christian world the antagonism in its clearest form between the

[1] See *ante*, pp. 141, 142.

two ways of regarding Christ which have been represented in the Greek theology on the one hand and in the Latin on the other. As the Latin church has shown by its history and its influence on modern thought, that if Christ be not known after the spirit, the incarnation possesses no inner necessary meaning in the history of redemption, so Strauss has demonstrated that if the fact of an historical incarnation in the person of Jesus be denied, it is impossible to retain as a great objective truth the spiritual, essential Christ indwelling in humanity. The higher conception of Christ's person evaporates into thin air, it becomes like the baseless fabric of a vision which cannot be disentangled from other dreams, if the fact be doubted or denied of the historic manifestation in Jesus of the fullness of the eternal God-head. The reconciliation of the two attitudes must be sought in the church in its higher aspects, as the congregation of faithful men called out from the world to bear witness to an historic influence as well as created by it. It must be sought further, in the more definite rejection of that pernicious dualism which has separated nature and humanity from God, as though it were beneath the divine dignity and greatness that the Eternal should unite Himself in close organic relationship with man. It is a reconciliation that is possible because it was once achieved in the theology of a people who stood facing the oriental and occidental worlds, who combined the subtle speculative power of the one with the practical bent and capacity of the other. It is a reconciliation that must be accomplished in the heart and intellect of the church before Christianity can address itself with something of its old power to the great world of the Orient, which has so long been waiting for the solution of the problems which have pressed heavily upon its spirit. To this end, it is a mark of progress that the issue should be clearly perceived.[1]

In concluding this sketch of the history of Christian thought, we are leaving it on the threshold of a larger future. Modern theology in its essential principle has risen above the negations of Latin Christianity, whether in its Augustinian or Calvinistic form. Things that have been separated in order to the more distinct realization of each are coming together in a comprehensive unity. Whatever may be the difficulties that await adjustment, and they are many, it is a great step in advance that we have regained our confidence in human reason as participating in Eternal wisdom. Back of all the theories and imperfect explanations of religious truth there stands a silent judge, the heart of that humanity which is larger than individual thought. Such a judge is quietly recording the infallible verdict against all that is untrue, or approving all that is genuine and final in the results of sincere inquiry. When the confusion that surrounds all efforts to reach the higher truth is gradually cleared away, the judgment will be manifest and wisdom will be justified of all her children. Christian

---

[1] Substantially the same issue raised by Strauss had been anticipated among the Quakers in the movement led by Hicks (1827), who pushed to an extreme the doctrine of the inner light, denying all positive Christianity.

Among the many replies made to Strauss, the most valuable was given by the late lamented Dr. Dorner, in his truly great work on the *Person of Christ*, whose object is to trace the course of Christian thought which takes its rise in an historic personage.

theology has regained at last the point where it was left by the master minds of the ancient church. Latin Christianity is seen as a parenthesis in the larger record of the life of Christendom. The factors of a true theology are now in our possession as they have never been before in all the church's history, — God, humanity, and nature, bound together in indissoluble relationship. The preparation begins to be approximately complete for undertaking the result which theology aims to achieve, and which it alone can achieve, — a science which shall embrace all knowledge, because it sees all things in God. Even now the church holds the key to the situation as the collective body of those who live in the consciousness of a relationship to God in Christ, through the indwelling of an infinite Spirit. Some facts there are which speak louder than any words. The interest in foreign missions which characterizes the church to-day, bears witness to the deep-seated conviction that the incarnate Christ stands in organic relationship to humanity. Notwithstanding the differences that divide the Christian world, it constitutes a ground of hope that the Catholic church, as a whole, has never committed itself to any theory of its existence which can prevent the congregation of faithful men from expanding itself into the fuller life of a redeemed humanity, where the communion of men shall become the communion of saints, and God shall have fulfilled the meaning and the promise of the incarnation.

INDEX.

ABBOT, EZRA, 30 note.
Abélard, a seeker for freedom, 209; contrasted with Anselm, 209; view of sin, 210; "*Sic et non*," 211; condemned through the influence of Bernard, 212.
Adam and the fall of man, in Augustine's theology, 157, 177 *f*; in Calvin's system, 300.
Adoptionist controversy, 192 *f*.
Agnosticism, 421 *f*, 426.
Alexandrian Christianity, its freedom of thought, 33; its catholicity, 34 *f*; the problems given it to solve, 36 *ff*.
Ambrose, influence on Augustine, 147.
Anselm, his earnest Christian feeling, 199; his doctrine of the atonement, 9 *f*, 199 *ff*; its legal character, 202 *ff*; "*credo ut intelligam*," 209; his ultramontane spirit, 199.
Antioch, theology of, 135 *ff*.
"Apostles' Creed," a protest against the Gnostic heresies, 111 *ff*.
Apostolic Fathers give us little positive information, 23–25.
Apostolic succession, spiritual rather than tactual (Clement), 60 *f*; the dogma outlined by Ignatius, 102; enunciated by Cyprian, 107 *ff*; formulated by Irenæus, 116 *f*; magnified by Tertullian, 117–120; revived in the Church of England, 329, 410; true interpretation of the idea, 419 *f*.
Apuleius revives polytheism, 100.
Aquinas, an exponent of Aristotle, 223; distinguishes between the kingdoms of nature and grace, 223 *ff*; other features of his system, 226 *ff*; the criticism of Duns Scotus, 228–232; conflicting ideas of God and the divine will, 232 *ff*; modern revival of Aquinas, 236 *ff*.
Arianism. See *Arius*.
Aristotle combats Plato's idea of the external world, 44; Plato and Aristotle compared, 217 *f*; significance of the adoption of Aristotle by the Schoolmen, 218–223.
Arius, the mistakes of his early training, 85; taught to regard the relation of God and man as an artificial alliance, 85; the oriental idea of God, a transcendent deity, and the incarnation inconceivable, 86; Arianism a reversion to Jewish deism, but inferior to it or to Mohammedanism, 87; revived in the 18th century, 364.
Arndt, a Protestant mystic, 317 *f*, 318 note, 345.
Arnold, Matthew, on Hooker, 328 note.
Art and religion, the Cathedrals, 198; images, 245; William Blake, 406.
Asceticism, Clement of Alexandria condemns false asceticism, 64 *f*; first appeared in oriental sects, 86; in Arianism, 86; in Montanism, 106 *f*; its principle, 220; change in its history, 222 *f*.
Athanasius, an ecclesiastical hero, 77; stood not only "*contra mundum*," but also "*contra ecclesiam*," 77; by birth, education, and culture a thorough Greek, 78; adopts a new method of controversy with the Greeks, 78 *f*; asserts the divine immanence, 79 *ff*, the solidarity of the human race in Christ, 82, and the incarnation, 83 *f*; defends the Christian doctrine of Father, Son, and Holy Spirit against Arius, 89 *ff*; his lasting influence in the church, 429–432.
Atonement, the doctrine not formulated in Clement, 51, 56 *f*; Athanasius' teaching, 82 *f*; Anselm's famous doctrine, a ransom paid to God, not to Satan, 199 *ff*; criticism of Anselm's theory, 200 *ff*; Luther's doctrine of justification by faith, 276 *ff*; Calvin's theory, 301 *f*; the deistic position, 364 *f*.
Augustine, the importance of his conversion, 143; a prophet to the Roman world, 144; at first a Manichæan, 145; skepticism, 146; influence of Ambrose, 147; "Confessions," 144 *f*, 148; opportunity for a career in the church, 147; his earlier theology, the immanence of God, 6 *f*, 148 *f*; the authority of the church, 149–156; controversies, 150 *f*, 153 *f*, 156; transcendence of God, 151; argues like a lawyer, 152; doctrine of original sin, 157 *ff*; predestination, 159 *f*; grace, 162 *ff*; sacraments, 163; endless punishment, 164 *f*; purgatory, 166 *ff*; opposition to Augustine,

160 ff; estimate of Augustine's work, 168-172; faulty view of Christ, 157 f; Augustine made possible the career of the Latin church, 4 f, 413 f, 169 ff; the great mistakes of his system reproduced in Calvinism, 11-17, 361 f; his teaching seen in Tractarianism, 421 f.
Authority, a refuge from uncertainty and skepticism, 3; not appealed to by Clement, 60; growth in the Latin church, 104; Augustine's view, 149 f; church authority repudiated by the evangelical reformers, 253; human consciousness the ultimate source of authority, 14, 17, 26, 302.
Baptism, not essential to salvation (Clement), 62 f; becomes a magical rite in the Latin church, 126; restores the image of God (Augustine), 159 f; infant baptism, 160 and note, 331 f; admits to the kingdom of grace (Aquinas), 225; its true witness, 420.
Baptismal regeneration, 159 f, 163 note, 330 f.
Baptists, narrow conception of the incarnation and of redemption, 331 f.
Baur criticised, 10 f; quoted, 163 note.
Bernard of Clairvaux, 202, 211 f.
Bible, placed above the church by Clement, 59, 62; must be interpreted by the church (Tertullian), 118; forbidden to the laity, 213; substituted for tradition by Wycliffe, 253 ff; Luther's free use, 284 f; Zwingle, 289; Calvin, 298 f; Scripture takes the place of the living Christ, 308, 335; verbal inspiration, 337 f; authenticity, 354 ff; human element in, 359 f; deistic view, 367; Schleiermacher, 392; modern biblical criticism, 393 f, 407 f; Newman, 411.
Bishops, the Roman theory, 107, 118 f; exalted by Constantine as state agents, 130, 132; rivalry of, 133; power of, 147. See *Episcopacy*.
Böhme, 318, 345 and note, 431.
Buddhism, view of sin, 13; consciousness of evil, 43; reflected in Gnosticism, 110.
Bunsen, 276 note, 433 note.
Bunyan, defects and beauties of "Pilgrim's Progress," 310; denounced sectarianism, 333 note.
Butler, Bp., 346, 351, 360 f, 365.

Caird, on Hegelianism, 433 note.
Calvin, the divine will, 235; order and discipline, 294 ff; church and elect, 297; Bible, 298 f; the fall, 299 f; atonement, 301; God as arbitrary will, 302 f; merits and errors of his system, too large an inheritance from Latin Christianity, 302 ff, 338 ff, 361 ff; church government, 320 f; Calvinism and Church of England, 330 f; Calvinism vs. Jesuitism, 336 ff; unconscious influence of Calvinism, 2.
Cambridge Platonists, 340 f, 362.
Carlyle at heart a Calvinist, 236.
Cathedral building, 198.
Catholic (*i. e.*, universal) church, the embodiment of humanity in its ideal aspect, 27; Greek and Roman conceptions contrasted, 104 f. See *Church, Latin church, Roman Catholic Church*.
Catholic faith, so-called, 8, 414 note.
Catholic reaction, 336.
Celibacy, inferior to marriage (Clement), 65.
Charlemagne, 187 f.
Christ, the spiritual, essential Christ, 26, 29 f, 141 f, 176; the Eternal Wisdom, 32; foretold by Greek thought (Clement), 39 f; the indwelling God, 46 f; the divine teacher, 51 f; personal presence of, 63; second coming, 66 f; head of the race, 82 f; the church's life the true witness to the Christ, 84; the incarnation of the divine consciousness (Schleiermacher), 385 ff, 394 f; Hegel, 431; the reconciliation of the historical and essential Christ, 435-438.
Christ, wrong conceptions of, Arius, 85 f; exaltation of Mary, 141 f; absent from the world (Augustine), 155 ff, 176, 192 f; Calvin, 302; deism, 364 f; Wesley, 379; Strauss, 434 ff.
Christian consciousness, or reason, 14, 17, 26; Schleiermacher, 392, 394 f.
Christianity to be distinguished from a Latinized Christianity, 8; a universal religion, 27, 35.
Christological controversies, 137-143, 192 f.
Chrysostom, 180 note.
Church, large view of Clement, 61 f; Ignatius, 102; Roman conception, 102 f; outside it no salvation, Cyprian, Augustine, 150, 152 f; Greek theology, 178 f; Latin theology, 186 ff; Luther, 273 f; other reformers, 276 note; Calvin, 297 f; Church of England, 323 f; Schleiermacher, 395 ff; Tractarian theory, 415 f, note; the church and the individual, 77.
Church and state, in Augustine's day, 147; in the Middle Ages, 187 f; at the Reformation, 248; Luther, 274 f; Zwingle, 293; in England, 321 f.
Clement of Alexandria, the father of Greek theology, 38; vindicates the alliance of Greek philosophy and Christian theology, 39-42; immanence of God, 42-46; Christ the indwelling God, 46-49; man, 49 f; education, 51 ff; redemption, 55 f; faith, 57 f; Scripture, 59 f; heresy, 60 f; church, 61 f; sacraments, 62 ff;

opposition to asceticism, 64; immortality, 66 f, 167; his influence, 68 f, 183, 399, 429, 435; bibliography, 38 note.
Clementine recognitions, 101.
Coleridge, 141, 402 ff, 432 note.
Collins attacks the old interpretation of prophecy, 354.
Confessional, its views of sin, 210 f.
Congregationalism, 298, 331 f.
Conscience, supremacy of, 270.
Constantine and the church, 129 f.
Continuity of Christian thought, 5; Greek and Christian, 25, 29, 39 f; Greek and Latin, 180 f; not broken at the Reformation, 270 f; in the Church of England, 321 f, 417; misapprehension of the principle, 418 f; true significance, 419 f.
Conversion a new thought in the 18th century, 375 f.
Councils, general, 92, 130, 139 f.
Credo ut intelligam, 209.
Cromwell, his mission, 310 f.
Crusades, influence of, 244.
Cudworth, 340.
Culverwell, 341.
Cyril, 139, 140 note, 154 note, 175 note.
Cyprian, enunciates "Apostolical Succession," 107; view of the church, 107 f; life a probation, 124 f; a "Protestant" at heart, 127 f.

Dante reflects Aquinas' system, 228.
Deism, Jewish, 40, 86 f; in Latin church, 176; in England, 339, 347–356; in France and Germany, 357 ff; its significance, 360 f, 366 ff; bibliography, 356 note.
De Maistre, upholds papacy, 236; denounces French Revolution, 409.
"Deposit" theory of truth, 150, 177, 227; Luther, 273 f; Newman, 410, 413 f.
De Rossi, 168 note.
Descartes, 353, 373.
"Descent into hell," its true significance, 201 f.
Devil. See *Satan*.
"Diognetus, Epistle to," a philosophical apprehension of Christianity, 24–27.
Dionysius. See *Pseudo-Dionysius*.
Discipline, church, Calvin, 296 f; lacking in Church of England, 327.
Donatists, 151 ff.
Dorner, 9, 139 note, 171 note, 292 note, 437 note.
Dualism in the Latin church, 143; opposed by Luther, 274; still to be avoided, 436.
Duns Scotus, a minute critic of Aquinas, 229 ff.

Ebionism, 55, 84 f.
Ecclesiasticism, early rise in the Latin church, 103 f, 117, 120.

Eckart, his mysticism, 261, 431; God's immanence, 261 ff.
Education and redemption (Clement), 51–55; Schleiermacher, Lessing, 389.
Election, Augustine, 158; Calvin, 300; Rome, 387; Schleiermacher, 389 f; in Church of England, 415.
Endless punishment, the Koran, 12; Tertullian, 121 f; Cyprian, 124 f; Augustine, 164–168; deism, 365 f.
England, Church of, the reformation a lay movement, 321; Episcopacy, 321 f; ritual, 321 f; theology, 322 f; definition of the church, 323 f; liturgy, 324 f; clergy, 325; the Puritans, 327 f, 331 ff, Hooker, 328; apostolic succession, 329; Calvinism, 330; High Auglicanism, 330 f, 335 f; deism, 339 f, 348 ff; reason, 340 f; apologists, 360 ff; Methodism, 376 ff; Evangelicism, 380; Coleridge, 402 ff; Tractarian movement, 410 ff; historic continuity, 417 ff; reaction and progress, 423 ff.
Episcopacy, Ignatius, 102; Cyprian, 107; Rome, 108 f; Constantine, 130, 132; rejected by Lutheran Church, 282 f; in Church of England, 325 f. See *Bishops*.
Erastianism, an indefinite term, 322.
Eschatology, Clement, 66 f; Schleiermacher, 386 f, 399. See *Endless punishment*, *Eternal life*.
Eternal generation of the Son, Origen, 74 f; Hegel, 431.
Eternal life, 66 ff, 179, 386 f, 399 f, 404.
Eucharist, 63. See *Lord's Supper*.
Evangelical movement, 374 ff, 380 f.

Faber, F. W., 413 note.
Faith, Clement, 57 f, 178; justification by faith, 276–281.
Fall of man. See *Adam*.
Fasting, true (Clement), 64 f.
Fatalism, Gnostic, 50 note.
Fear as a motive to right conduct, Clement, 52 f; Cyprian, 124 ff; Evangelical revival, 365 f.
Feeling, Schleiermacher, 381 ff, 427 ff.
"Filioque," 191 f.
Fourth Gospel, Baur, 11 note.
Freedom, civil and religious, 319 ff, in England, 332 f.
Freedom of will. See *Will*.
French Revolution, a protest against God as absolute will, 357 f, 384, 408 f, 420 f.
"Friends of God," 265.

Gieseler, 9, 140 note, 165 note, 283 note.
Gnosticism, 55 f, 110 ff.
God, different ideas of, 1–3; Greek, 2, 176 ff; Latin, 3 f, 176 ff; Plato's "Timæus," 31, 43, 217 f; Justin, 31 f; Stoicism, 44; Clement, 45, 55 f; Origen, 73 f; Athanasius, 79 ff,

442   INDEX.

89; Arius, 85 *ff*; trinity, 89 *ff*; Augustine, 148 *f*, 155 *f*; Mohammed, 170 *ff*; Anselm, 202 *f*; Pantheism, 216 and note; Aristotle, 217 *ff*; Aquinas and Scotus, 232 *ff*; the will of God, Jesuitism and Calvin, 234 *ff*; mysticism, 261 *ff*; Luther, 278 *ff*; Zwingle, 288 *f*; Calvin, 299 *f*, 302 *f*; post-Reformation theology, 307 *f*; Pascal, 312 *f*; Cambridge Platonists, 340 *f*; deism, 347 *ff*, 363 *f*, 368 *f*; Schleiermacher, 385 *ff*, 400; Goethe, 401; Coleridge, 402 *ff*; agnosticism, 421 *f*; recent theology, 426 *f*.
Goethe, 401 *f*.
Gottschalk and freedom, 194.
Grace, a Latin substitute for the immanent God or indwelling Christ, 16 *f*, 162, 178, 250 *f*; kingdom of grace (Aquinas), 223 *ff*.
Greek church, 175, 181 *ff*, 416 note.
Greek philosophy, 2, 29 *ff*; a preparation for Christianity, 39 *ff*.
Greek theology, 2; had but one dogma, the incarnation, 14; summary, 176-182; modern return to, 360, 362, 368 *f*, 382 *ff*. See *Latin theology*.
Gregory of Nazianzus, 68, 160, 180.
Gregory of Nyssa, 40, 68, 160, 176, 180.
Gregory the Great, 170, 185 *f*, 277, 395.

Hampden, Bp., quoted, 326 note.
Heathen, salvation of, 29 *f*, 291.
Hegel, 216 note, 431, 432 note; his influence to-day, 433 note.
Heine, quoted, 249 note.
Herbert, George, 314 note.
Herbert, Lord, 339 note.
Heresy, at Alexandria, 35 *f*; Clement's wise treatment of, 60 *f*; Rome, 114; spread in 12th century, 211 *f*.
Higher criticism, 392, 407 *f*.
Hildebrand, 319.
Historical evidence, 354 *ff*, 434 *ff*.
Holy Spirit, Origen, 74 *ff*; Athanasius, 90, 92 *f*; Montanism, 105 *ff*; Rome, 107; *filioque*, 191 *f*; Schleiermacher, 396 *f*; Hegel, 431; Maurice, 432 note.
Ὁμοούσιος, 91 *f*.
Hooker, 328 and note.
Humanity, revival of idea, 384.
Huss, 269 and note.

Ignatius, 102.
Ignorance and sin, 50.
Illuminism, 348 note, 358 *ff*.
"Imitation of Christ," 266 *f*.
Immanence of God, 1 *f*, 6 *f*, 45, 55 *f*, 73 *f*, 79 *ff*, 176, 292, 385, 406, 426. See *Transcendence*.
Immortality. See *Eternal life*.
Incarnation, "Epistle to Diognetus," 26; Clement, 47; is the atonement, 57; Origen, 73 *f*; Athanasius, 81 *f*, 89 *f*; Augustine, earlier view, 6; not essential to Augustine's system, 158; nor to Aquinas', 227; deism,

368; evangelicism, 377 *f*; Schleiermacher, 385 *f*; Greek and Latin conceptions compared, 176, 435 *f*; the essence of the Christian faith, 20.
Independency, 298, 331 *f*.
Individualism, 246 *f*.
Indulgences, 204, 272 *f*.
Infallibility, disclaimed by Church of England, 323 *f*; of Scripture not held by Luther, 284 *ff*; Zwingle, 289; Schleiermacher, 392 *f*; asserted by Calvin and other reformers, 256, 298 *f*, 335 *ff*.
Infidelity, 8. See *Skepticism*.
Inspiration of Scripture, 59. See *Infallibility, Bible*.
Intermediate state, 166 *ff*.
Irenæus and tradition, 115 *f*.

Janet, quoted, 312 note.
Jesuits, the divine will supreme, 235; declared reform unnecessary, 336 *f*; methods, 316; order revised, 409.
Joubert's "Pensées," quoted, 16 note.
Judaism, its superstitions and culture foreign to Christianity, 26 *f*, 32 *f*; its legalism, 32; deism, 87 *f*.
Judgment, the, a continuous process, 53 *f*, 67.
Justice and love, 56; righteousness, 279.
Justification by faith, 276-281; the figure of speech obscured, 280 *f*.
Justin Martyr, a philosophic theologian, 27-33, 291, 435.

Kant, 374, 390, 422.
Keble, 413 *f*, 418.
Kempis, à, 266 *f*.
Kingdom of God, 387.
Knowledge and faith, 57 *f*, 209, 389. See *Reason*.

Laprade, De, 344 note, 411 note.
"Larger hope," 180 note.
Latin church, inheritance from pagan Rome, 99 *ff*; natural drift to externals, 100 *f*; its ideal, authority, and order, 100-120, 187, 243; conversion of the nations, 184 *ff*; decline, 241 *ff*; its catholicity limited by the epithet Roman, 387. See *Papacy, Roman Catholic Church*.
Latin theology, based on Augustinianism, 157 *f*; scholasticism, 205 *ff*; rejected by Luther, 273 *ff*; survives in Calvinism, 302 *f*, 307; revived in Church of England, 412; contrasted with Greek theology, 1-20, 156, 175-181, 435-438.
Laud, 329, 335.
Law, William, 379.
Law of God not an external code, 48 *f*.
Legalism, in Christianity, 19 *f*; Justin, 32 *f*; Augustine, 169; Anselm, 202; in Calvinism, 307 *f*; in Tractarianism, 415, 418 *f*.

INDEX 443

Leo the Great, 4, 140 note.
Lessing, 359, 384, 389.
Locke, 353.
Logos, the, or Word, 29, 48, 83 *f.*
Lombard, Peter, 214.
Lord's Supper, 63, 126, 193, 213; its true significance, 420. See *Mass.*
Love and justice, 56 *f.*
Loyola, 235 *f.*
Luther, affirms the supremacy of the conscience, 270; not so much a theologian as a man, 271; indulgences and abuses, 272 *f*; abandons dualism, 274; view of church, 274, 282, 319 *f*; Bible, 275; justification by faith, 276–281; biblical criticism, 284 *f*; denies freedom of will, 286; controversy with Zwingle, 291 *f*; last days, 295.

Macaulay on Church of England, 325.
Maine's "Ancient Law," 50 note.
Man, in God's image, 48 *f*; akin to deity, 57; has been redeemed, 82.
Manichæanism, 50 note, 145 *f*, 153.
Mansel and agnosticism, 421 *f.*
Marcion, 54.
Marcus Aurelius, 44, 69, 99.
Marriage, honored by Clement, 65.
Martineau, 116 note, 221 note.
Mary, exaltation of, 141 *f*, 303.
Mass, doctrine of the, 126, 193, 213. See *Lord's Supper.*
Maurice, view of sin, 13; revelation, 414, 422; the trinity, 432 note.
Melanchthon, a compromiser, 295.
Mendicant orders, 222 *f.*
Methodism, 366 *f*, 374 *ff.*
Middle Ages, characterized, 184–191, 195-198; study of, revived, 409.
Middleton on Miracles, 354.
Milman on the Prayer-Book, 324.
Milton, reflected current theology, 310; denounced sectarianism, 333 note.
Miracles as evidence, 353 *f*, 390 *f.*
Missionary spirit, in 17th century, 315 *f*; significance to-day, 438.
Mohammedanism, 12; foreshadowed, 84 *f*, 87 *f*; *vs.* Augustinianism, 170 *f*; influence in Spain, 192.
Monasticism, the assertion of individual responsibility, 246; love of nature, 343; decline of, 242.
Montanism a protest against ecclesiasticism, 105 *ff*, 120, 127.
Morality, decline of, in 4th century, 133 *f*; of the Middle Ages, 242; of the Restoration, 347.
Moravians, 374, 379, 381 *f.*
"Mother of God," a "dangerously deceptive epithet," 141.
Mozley, J. B., quoted, 149 note, 278 note.
Mysticism, a substitute for speculative thought, 214; in the Latin church, 256-260; German mystics, 261-267;

Protestant mysticism, 317 *f*; Quietists, 318; and theology, 398.
Nationalism, rise of, 248 *f*; influence on the Reformation, 320 *f.*
Natural and revealed religion, a false distinction, not found in Clement, 47; emphasized by Aquinas, 223 *ff*, 341 *f*; rejected by Schleiermacher, 391.
Nature, study of, revived at the close of the Middle Ages, 220; love of, 343, 405 note; modern natural science, 346; mystery of, 351.
Neale, the Eastern Liturgies, 10 note.
Neander, 9, 38 note.
Nectarius and Sisinnius, 136 note.
Neo-Platonism, 45; Origen, 72; decline, 135, 182, 258.
"New Theology" anticipated by the Greek theology, 17 *ff.*
Newman, 3 *f*, 161 note, 398 note, 410 *ff*, 421 note, 423 *f.*
Nicene Creed, 91 *f*, 131.
Nineteenth century compared to the second, 34 *f*, 429 *f.*
Nominalism, 215, 246 *f.*
Norris, 176 note; quoted, 301 note.

Oetinger, 369 note.
Optimism, of the Greek theologians, 113; of deism, 351.
Origen, his great reputation and influence, 70 *f*; Neo-Platonism, 72; "the eternal generation of the Son," 74; trinity, 75, 431. (See the preface to the first edition.)
Original sin, foundation of Augustinianism, 157; denied by Zwingle, 289; Calvin, 299 *f.*
Owen, quoted, 342 note, 344 note.

Palmer, William, visit to the Russian Church, 416 note.
Pantheism, 43; of the 12th century, 216 note; of the 18th, 427 note.
Papacy, not a usurpation, 4 *f*, 100 *ff*, 185 *f*; its decline, 242 *f*; its work, 245, 409.
Pascal pessimistic, agnostic, 312 *ff.*
Pelagianism, 153 *ff.*
Personality, 139 note, 399.
Pessimism, 110, 351.
Philosophy, foreign to Latin church, 114 *ff.* See *Greek philosophy.*
Plato, 25, 31, 43, 51. See *Aristotle.*
Plotinus quoted, 73.
Plutarch, 35, 45, 69.
Polytheism revived at Rome, 100.
Prayer, 352, 378.
Prayer for the dead, 126, 168.
Prayer-Book, 324 *f*, 327.
Preaching, revival of, 251 *f.*
Predestination, 159. See *Election.*
Presbyterianism, 297 *f*, 327 *f.*
Priestly character of clergy, not taught by Clement, 62; in Latin church,

104; Luther, 283; Calvinism, 320 *f*; Church of England, 324 *ff*, 412.
"Private judgment," 275 *f*.
Probation theory of life, Cyprian, 125; Luther, 277 *f*; revived in 17th century, 308. See *Education*.
Progress, its method, 373 *f*, 423 *ff*.
Prophecy, 39 *f*, 354.
Protestantism, foreshadowed by Montanism, 105 *ff*, 127; 12th century, 207. See *Reformation*.
Pseudo-Dionysius, 182, 191; mistaken identity, 257; teaching, 258 *ff*.
Punishment, remedial, 53 *f*.
Purgatory, Augustine, 166 *f*.
Puritanism, 327-333.
Pusey, 413 *f*.

Quakers, 332, 437 note.
Quinet, quoted, 345 note.
Quod ubique, etc., 161 note.

Ranke, quoted, 245 note.
Rationalism, a desire for an ideal, 217 *f*; effort to reconstruct religion, 348 note, 358 *f*.
Raymond of Sabunde, 344 and note.
Reaction, its necessity, 409, 424.
Realism, 215, 246 *f*.
Reason, Augustine, 147; and authority, 211 *ff*; and revelation, 226, 340 *f*, 348 *f*; its exercise necessary, 428 note.
Redemption=education, Clement, 51 *f*, 57; actually accomplished, Athanasius, 82 *f*; Augustine, 158; Greek and Latin conceptions contrasted, 178. See *Salvation*.
Reformation, revolt from church authority, 268 *f*; not a break in history, 270 *f*; its main object not the correction of abuses, but the principle from which they flowed, *i. e.*, the Latin idea of the church, 272 *f*; its principles, 276 note; attendant evils, 294 *ff*.
Relic worship, significance, 244.
Religion, definition of, 381.
Remusat, 210 note, 217 note.
Resurrection, not fleshly, Clement, 67; of Christ attested by the church's life, 84; Greek and Latin doctrines contrasted, 166 *f*, 179 *f*.
Revelation, in Greek thought, an internal process, 25 *f*, 47 *f*, 50, 80 *f*, 90, 176 *f*, 279, 288, 318, 394; in Latin thought, a "deposit," 150, 177, 227, 254, 273, 410, 413 *f*; deism, 348 *f*; Mansel and Maurice, 421 *ff*.
Ritschl criticised, 9 *f*.
Ritual, origin, 132; in Church of England, 321 *ff*, 330, 418.
Roman Catholic Church, its catholicity limited by the epithet Roman, 387; Jesuits and Catholic reaction, 316, 336, 409; controversy with Protestantism, 337 *f*; variations of Romanism, 140 note, 230 *ff*, 291. See *Latin church*.
Roman law, influence on Christianity, 34, 117, 152, 202.
Ruskin, quoted, 405 note.

Sabellianism, its danger, 75 *f*, 430.
Sacramentarianism, 163 note, 412, 415, 419 *f*.
Sacraments, as symbols, 62 *f*, 420; and grace, 163 *f*, 193, 412, 419 *f*; Luther and Zwingle, 291 *f*.
Sacrifice, Clement, 56, 63 *f*.
Saints, worship of, 244 *f*.
Salvation, an ethical growth, Clement, 56; an escape from wrath, Cyprian, 125; Luther, 278 *ff*; Calvin, 300, 308 *ff*. See *Redemption*.
Satan, outwitted by Christ, 200 *f*; Luther, 286; Calvin, 299.
Schelling, 383, 432 note.
Schism of Greek and Latin churches due, not to a question of words, but of theology, 3, 98, 175 *ff*, 436.
Schleiermacher, his training, 382 *f*; Plato, illuminism, 383 *f*; immanence of God, 385 *f*; Christ, 386; anti-Calvinistic, 386, 399; election, 387 *f*; probation and education, 389 *ff*; the supernatural, 390 *f*; Bible, 392 *f*; biblical criticism, 393; Christian consciousness, 394 *f*; the church, 395; salvation, 396; his influence, 397 *ff*; defect of his idea of God, 427 *f*.
Scholasticism, its endeavor, 205 *ff*; turns from Plato to Aristotle, 215; its work, 246 *f*; bibliography, 237 note.
Science, rise of modern, 346; unhappy breach between religion and science, 411 note.
Scotus, Duns. See *Duns Scotus*.
Scotus, John (Erigena), 190.
Scripture. See *Bible*.
Second coming of Christ a present process (Clement), 66 *f*.
Sectarianism in England, 331 *ff*.
Seneca, 30, 44.
Shelley, 405.
Sin, in Greek theology, 13 *f*, 41 *f*, 50, 81 *f*; in Latin theology, 157, 159, 199, 202 *f*, 210; Stoicism, 31; Luther, 277 *ff*; Zwingle, 289 *f*. See *Original sin*.
Sisinnius and Nectarius, 136 note.
Skepticism in the Latin church, 242; latent in Calvinism, 304; in Pascal, 312 *ff*; in deism, 354 *ff*; in Tractarianism, 421.
Smith, John, 341.
Socrates a Christian, 30, 291, 435.
Solidarity of the race, 82, 178, 204.
Spinoza, 383, 401, 403.
Stephen, Leslie, criticised, 356 note.
Stoic philosophy, 2, 30; its defects, 31, 45; the immanence of God, 44, 80, 99 *f*.

Strauss attacks the historicity of Christianity, 434 *ff*.
Subordinationism, 75.
Supererogation, works of, 204.
Superstition, its growth in the 3d century, 126; in the Middle Ages, 244 *f*.
Swedenborg, 369 note.

Talbot, E. F., quoted, 413, 414 note.
Tauler, 249 note, 262.
"Teaching of the Twelve Apostles," 24 note.
Tertullian, argument against heresy, 117 *ff*; becomes a Montanist, 106, 120.
Theodore of Mopsuestia, 161.
Theosophy, oriental, 35 *f*.
Tillotson, 341, 365.
Tindal identifies Christianity with the religion of nature, 350 *f*, 365.
Toland, 348 *f*.
Tractarianism, opposes liberalism, 410; revives Latin theology, 410 *ff*, 163 note; its leaders, 410, 413; its merits, 414, 417; its mistakes, 412, 415, 417 *ff*, 421 note.
Tradition, Irenæus, 116 *f*; Sisinnius, 136 note; Newman, 411; Pusey, 413.
Transcendence of God, 1, 3; Arius, 86; Latin Christianity, 156, 176, 217 *f*; Calvin, 302; Pascal, 312 *ff*; in modern thought, 362 *f*, 430. See *Immanence*.
Transubstantiation, 193, 213.
Trinity, Origen's progress toward the doctrine, 74 *ff*; Athanasius, 89 *ff*; 'ομοούσιος, 91 *ff*; Latin church, 130 *f*; the doctrine the fulfillment of Greek philosophy, 92; its interpretation, 428 note, 430; Hegel, 431 *f*.
Tulloch on Tractarianism, 421 note.

Unity, need of a principle of, 34 *f*, 435-438.
Universality of Christianity, 27, 51 *f*, 67.

Vacherot, quoted, 190 note, 259 note.
Vincens of Lerins, the Vincentian rule, 161.

Wesley, 366 *f*, 374 *f*, 378 *f*.
Whichcote, 340 *f*.
Whitefield, 366 *f*, 374 *f*, 378.
Will, arbitrary will of God, Augustine, 158; Aquinas *vs.* Scotus, 232 *ff*; Loyola and Calvin, 235; Mohammedanism, 234, 302.
Will, freedom of, Greek theology, 49 *f*, 82; denied by Augustine, 50 note; denied by Luther, 286; asserted by Wesley, 378.
Wilson's Bampton Lectures, 16 note, 292 note.
Woman, her prominence with the Montanists, 106.
Woolston on miracles, 354.
Wordsworth, 404.
World, not evil because the dwelling-place of God, 65 *f*.
Worship of Jewish church not to be perpetuated in Christianity, 26 *f*, 33; superstition in Christian worship, 126 *f*, 244 *f*.
Wycliffe, and preaching, 252; the church, 253; the Bible, 254 *f*.

Zwingle, the divine immanence, 288; revelation, 288; Bible, 289; sin, 289; salvation, 290; sacraments, 291 *f*; controversy with Luther, 291 *f*; Zwingle misunderstood, 293.

www.ingramcontent.com/pod-product-compliance
Lightning Source LLC
Chambersburg PA
CBHW022057300426
44117CB00007B/488